ECONOMIC WOMAN:
DEMAND, GENDER, AND NARRATIVE CLOSURE IN
ELIOT AND HARDY

DEANNA K. KREISEL

Economic Woman

Demand, Gender, and Narrative Closure in Eliot and Hardy

UNIVERSITY OF TORONTO PRESS
Toronto Buffalo London

ISBN 978-1-4426-4249-2 (cloth)

Library and Archives Canada Cataloguing in Publication

Kreisel, Deanna K.
Economic woman : demand, gender, and narrative closure in Eliot and
Hardy / Deanna K. Kreisel.

Includes bibliographical references and index.
ISBN 978-1-4426-4249-2

1. English fiction – 19th century – History and criticism.
2. Economics and literature – Great Britain – History – 19th century.
3. Eliot, George, 1819–1880 – Knowledge – Economics.   4. Hardy,
Thomas, 1840–1928 – Knowledge – Economics.   5. Women in literature.
6. Economics in literature.   I. Title.

PR878.E37K74 2011   823'.8093553   C2011-903217-1

University of Toronto Press acknowledges the financial assistance to its
publishing program of the Canada Council for the Arts and the Ontario
Arts Council.

  Canada Council   Conseil des Arts  ONTARIO ARTS COUNCIL
       for the Arts   du Canada   CONSEIL DES ARTS DE L'ONTARIO

University of Toronto Press acknowledges the financial support of the
Government of Canada through the Canada Book Fund for its publishing
activities.

For Emma and Gwendolen

Contents

Acknowledgments

While the following readings focus on ways in which authors seem to have trouble ending their books, I am confronted instead with the problem of beginning: how to honour, thank – and even remember – all the people who have helped me with this project over the course of many years. To begin, then, with the beginning: my teachers at Northwestern, who oversaw the project which was the germ of the present study. If the mark of proper psychoanalytic transference is feeling slightly sorry for anyone who has a different analyst, then I can testify that there is such a thing as thesis-writing transference. My mentors Jules Law, Christopher Herbert, and Michal Ginsburg were simultaneously the most rigorous and stringent, yet supportive and helpful, committee members anyone could hope for, and I feel slightly sorry for anyone who had to go through this process without them.

I would also like to thank, for their numberless constructive insights and general intellectual and emotional support, the reading-group members who have commented on drafts of these chapters over the course of many years: John Anderson, Traci Carroll, and Matt Roberts; Nina Barrett and Roshanna Sylvester; Trish Tilburg and Vivien Dietz; and Greg Mackie, Vin Nardizzi, and Rob Rouse. Thanks also to the scholars and friends who read parts of the manuscript *ex parte* and provided helpful commentary and suggestions: Nancy Armstrong, Bonnie Blackwell, Helen Deutsch, and Elizabeth Meese. I would also like to thank the anonymous readers of the manuscript at the University of Toronto Press for their extraordinarily detailed, insightful, and generous commentary on various versions of these chapters. Thanks also to Richard Ratzlaff, my editor at the Press, for his kindness and support (and for always providing detailed subject lines on his emails, so I wouldn't have to psych myself up for an hour before opening them).

I have had the good luck to be able to think about this project in a variety of intellectually stimulating environments, and much of that thinking was supported by grants and fellowships. I would particularly like to thank the Hampton Fund at the University of British Columbia for a generous research travel grant, the Newberry Library for a short-term fellowship, and Mississippi State University for a research travel award. Thanks also to Reg Gibbons and the staff of *Tri-Quarterly*, who employed and sheltered grad-student me above and beyond the call of duty, and gave me all those good stories to read. I would also like to acknowledge the help of the librarians at the Newberry Library, the Widener and Houghton Libraries at Harvard, and the British Library. Thanks also to colleagues at Keene State College, Mississippi State, Duke University, and Warren Wilson College who welcomed and housed me during my peripatetic academic career; particular thanks to Carol Howard and Michael Matin at Wilson for keeping me going in this profession.

Portions of this book appeared in articles published in *Novel: A Forum on Fiction* and *ELH (English Literary History)*, and I would like to thank the editors of those journals for permission to reprint that material here.

I am deeply indebted to those colleagues and friends who patiently listened to me natter on about various obsessions during the final stages of this project, and provided sustaining conversation and intellectual friendship: Suzy Anger, Dan Brayton, Alex Dick, Bo Earle, Jen Hill, Antonia Losano, Tina Lupton, Greg Mackie, Vin Nardizzi, Bryan Rasmussen, Bethany Schneider, Jeff Severs, and Katie-Louise Thomas. Thanks in particular to Vin and Greg for all the fabulous cocktails and movie dates, and to Jeff Toward and Louise Mâsse for multiple Thanksgiving dinners and poker games. My sincere gratitude also to those senior colleagues at UBC who mentored me and talked me down from many a ledge: Patsy Badir, Miranda Burgess, Mary Chapman, Siân Echard, Stephen Guy-Bray, Liz Hodgson, Laura Moss, Sandy Tomc, and Mike Zeitlin. My research assistant and co-teacher Tyson Stolte was a bottomless font of good sense, mad library skillz, and baseball statistics.

I extend special thanks and affection to those friends and comrades-in-arms who were there at the very beginning of this venture: Paul Jaskot, *postcardiste* extraordinaire; Kirsten Elling, fellow *connoisseuse* of the post-camping shower; Helen Deutsch, intrepid companion of the open highway; and Gwenan Wilbur, poetess and hostess without peer.

Love, gratitude, and another round of margaritas to my Keene Girls: Maura Glennon, Corinn Columpar, Rosi Bernardi, and Renate Gebauer – remember, it's just a conifer.

My boundless thanks and love to buddies, travel companions, and cherished friends Trish Tilburg and Thomas Ricard (Oui Four!); to intrepid voyagers, grammar checkers, and poetic inspirations Wendy Rawlings and Joel Brouwer; to my favourite epicures and adventurers Harold Weber and Petra Schuler; and to my dearest 'intentional family' Sandy Huss and Elizabeth Meese.

For their support throughout the years, thanks and love to my parents; love and gratitude also to my adopted family in New Zealand: Lyn, Meredith, Hamish, and Callum MacKenzie, and Ra McBeth and kids. Finally, and most importantly, to Scott MacKenzie, abettor, accessory, accomplice, affiliate, aide, ally, associate, backer, buddy, chaperon, chum, coworker, coadjutant, cohort, collaborator, colleague, complement, comrade, confederate, consort, convoy, counterpart, crony, friend, guide, helpmeet, lover, mate, nurse, pal, partner, patron, playmate, protector, roomie, and supporter: there aren't enough words in the thesaurus to express how much I thank you and love you.

ECONOMIC WOMAN

Introduction: Demand; or, the Cephalopod

In an 1853 essay entitled 'The Circulation of Matter,' chemist James F.W. Johnston explains to a popular readership the unceasing processes by which the raw materials of the planet are combined into new forms, broken down, and combined again:

> The same material – the same carbon, for example – circulates over and over again … It forms part of a vegetable to-day – it may be built into the body of a man to-morrow; and, a week hence, it may have passed through another plant into another animal. What is mine this week is yours the next. There is, in truth, *no private property* in ever-moving matter. (552, emphasis added)

This salutary affirmation of the homology between self-regulating processes in nature and the self-adjusting operations of the economy is a Victorian commonplace; Johnston's rhetoric fits in a long tradition of such analogies from the eighteenth-century physiocrats through to Adam Smith and David Ricardo and the nineteenth-century labour-theory economists writing in their wake. Johnston's claim is curious only in that he seems to disparage, through his choice of simile, one of the other lynchpins of laissez-faire capitalism: private ownership of property. The seeming contradiction may be explained by considering another mid-Victorian precept, one no less dearly held for being largely unexamined: the unconscious fear of a catastrophic failure of economic circulation in the form of diminished demand, general gluts, and ultimate stagnation. Johnston's implicit denial of the fiscal benefits of private property is of a piece with a deeply held mid-Victorian fear of economic enervation.

The aim of this study is to recover the traces of this anxiety – or, more properly speaking, to recover the cultural effects, particularly in the domain of the novel, of the demand theory of value, which had as its corollary (and its impetus) a mistrust of the self-adjusting properties of the young capitalist economy. There has been a recent intensification of interest in the connections between Victorian literature and political economy, and my goal here is both to contribute to this lively discussion and to inflect the way that nineteenth-century economic models have been treated by literary critics, who have tended to focus on the labour theory of value enshrined by Ricardo – and familiar to us from Karl Marx – that was dominant in England before 1870. Although recent studies by Regenia Gagnier, Catherine Gallagher, and Mary Poovey have been attentive to the diachronic shift from Ricardo's labour theory of value to the rise of the marginal utility school, there has been little attention paid on the part of literary scholars to the tensions within the Ricardian school, and between the adherents of this model and their heterodox critics.[1] This study will chart the contours of these dialectically produced tensions present in – and due to – the realist novel. It is my contention that certain literary and narratological effects become legible only when one is attentive to the important psychological consequences of an ever-present fear of economic stagnation – a fear that was part of a larger critique of the sanguine promises of self-regulation that characterized the dominant economic model.

This anxiety takes on a particular urgency in the work of counter-Ricardian demand-theory writers such as Thomas Malthus and John Ruskin; an example from the latter's work will help to elucidate this concern a bit more. In the 1863 work *Munera Pulveris*, Ruskin, taking a fairly radical stance for the time, exhorts his fellow citizens to refrain from unnecessary accumulations of currency:

> The holder of wealth ... may be regarded simply as a mechanical means of collection; or as a money-chest with a slit in it, not only receptant but suctional, set in the public thoroughfare – chest of which only Death has the key, and evil Chance the distribution of the contents. (*Works* 17:169)

Ruskin's analogy is emblematic of mid-Victorian anxieties about the stagnation of economic demand; money that is taken out of circulation through hoarding is money that is not being used to sustain economic growth through exchange. The problem with private wealth in this schema is precisely its privacy: its vulnerability to the whims and fancies of individual owners and investors who are not acting with the best interests of the system in mind. Unlike Johnston's carbon, which belongs to no one, money and monetary instruments are subject to the depredations of ownership and thus expose the fragility of the circulatory system they are meant to embody and sustain. Johnston's analogy signifies because of the implication that private property is, by definition, that which is outside circulation: the molecular building blocks of all matter – ever-moving and thus unownable – are the exact opposite of privately held wealth – by definition stationary, non-circulating, and thus an implicit threat to the operations of an economic system dependent on ceaseless exchange.[2]

This is an idea to which many Victorian authors and commentators repeatedly return. It takes on a comic twist, for example, throughout the novels of Dickens: think of Wemmick's 'portable property' in *Great Expectations*, or the pathetic scene in *Dombey and Son* in which Captain Cuttle and Uncle Sol try to figure out how to pay off a bond that has come due:

> 'You've got some money, haven't you?' whispered the Captain.
>
> 'Yes, yes – oh – yes – I've got some,' returned old Sol, first putting his hands into his empty pockets, and then squeezing his Welsh wig between them, as if he thought he might wring some gold out of it; 'but I – the little I have got, isn't convertible, Ned; it can't be got at ... It's here and there, and – and, in short, it's as good as nowhere,' said the old man, looking in bewilderment about him. (142)[3]

To have possessions is not necessarily to have purchasing power; only 'convertible' or liquid assets are circulable (by definition) and therefore can function as repositories of true value. For Ruskin, the problem of circulation is one that pertains specifically to currency: when one is not spending, one is not expressing demand (and vice versa).[4] Hoarded money might as well be a pair of withered teaspoons and some knock-kneed sugar-tongs.

In his denial of the universal benefit of saving, Ruskin rhetorically equates images of transgressive female sexuality with the horrors attendant upon unwise economic management. In his schema, the hoarding capitalist is little more than a prostitute, a 'slit' for the collection of money set in the 'public thoroughfare' of the street. This degraded hoarder is a figure of danger, whose figurative female genitalia evoke the image of vagina dentata ('not only receptant but suctional') and thus suggest the possibility of symbolic castration for the hapless debtor whose money disappears into the coffers of the miser. Death is the only effectual abrogation of this disturbing situation; the decease of the threatening figure releases the purloined stores of value in a discharge of economic energy, potentially restabilizing the financial balance that had been threatened by the 'sexual' transgressions of the hoarder.

In Ruskin's metaphor, perverse feminine sexuality, stores of value, and economic stagnation are interconnected. This is a series of associations that was perhaps most legible in Victorian discussions of prostitution. In 'Harlotry and Concubinage,' commentator John Wade blames rampant economic competition for the social evils of the sex trade:

> The permanent cause is doubtless the general competition. This however is a question with two sides. Competition is favourable to consumers; it cheapens commodities, while it tends to lower wages and profits. But consumers are more numerous than the producers, and the greater good cannot be sacrificed to a lesser evil ... Better remedies than interference with these natural laws are those in course of adoption – namely, emigration, and shortening the hours of labour, by which, *and the greater consumption they would induce*, work would be made more abundant. (377, emphasis added)

While Wade does not explicitly link degraded sexuality and moribund consumption as does Ruskin, the implication is obvious – and the remedy is sought in economic measures that would, among other things, stimulate consumer activity.

While the association of monstrous femininity and social disorder generally (and economic malfeasance specifically) is certainly not new to the Victorians, it took on a particular urgency during this period: the association between moribund demand, resultant gluts, and female economic management articulates anxieties about the possible stagnation of the capitalist economy and its inability to sustain growth without intervention. It is during the nineteenth century that concerns about the function of economic demand and monetary circulation became markedly more importunate, an intensification we can trace in the insistent repetition of images of hoarding, self-denial, and undue thrift in the Victorian novel – particularly on the part of female or feminized characters.

The relationship between perverse economic management and femininity is complex and multifaceted, particularly in Ruskin. The most striking phrase of his analogy quoted above, 'not only receptant but suctional,' was added in a later version of the essay; in his *Works*, the following editorial footnote appears after the phrase 'money-chest with a slit in it':

> [In the original essay the following note was here subjoined, the words in the present text – 'not only receptant but suctional' – being omitted: –
> 'The orifice being not merely of a recipient but of a suctional character. Among the types of human virtue and vice presented grotesquely by the lower animals, perhaps none is more curiously definite than that of avarice in the cephalopod, a creature which has a purse for a body; a hawk's beak for a mouth; suckers for feet and hands; and whose house is its own skeleton.'
> The cuttle-fish is the most familiar member of the class of *Cephalopoda*.]
> (17:169)

The municipal menace of the prostitute, the 'money-chest with a slit in it' set in the 'public thoroughfare of the street,' was originally joined by her domesticated cousin, the thrifty household manageress who 'has a purse for a body.'[5] Elsewhere in his writings, in a disconcerting screed against the grasping natures of women, Ruskin returns to the image of a primitive aquatic life form:

> Not only do you declare yourselves too indolent to labour for daughters and wives, and too poor to support them; but you have made the neglected and distracted creatures hold it for an honour to be independent of you, and shriek for some hold of the mattock for themselves. Believe it or not, as you may, there has not been so low a level of thought reached by any race, since they grew to be male and female out of star-fish, or chickweed, or whatever else they have been made from, by natural selection – according to modern science.[6]

Ruskin was not the only writer to associate avarice and female monstrosity in this way; indeed, his use of invertebrates as metaphors for human, particularly feminine, greed has several later echoes in a central work of the Victorian canon, George Eliot's *Middlemarch*. In the famous passage analysing Mrs Cadwallader's matchmaking activities under different levels of 'magnification,' the narrator describes the rector's wife as an invertebrate 'creature exhibiting an active voracity into which other smaller creatures actively play' (55). Later in the novel,

Eliot implies that Rosamond Vincy is a 'lovely anencephalous monster' (161) that Lydgate means to add to his collection.[7] The names of both classes of creatures imply problems with their brains: one has its brains in its feet, and the other is without brains at all. (It is, of course, Rosamond's greed and desire for excess – her poor economic management skills – that later contribute directly to Lydgate's professional disappointments.)

While it would be an overstatement to claim that Victorian political economy is rife with images of vagina dentata, parsimonious prostitutes, and shrieking domestic harpies, such associations between womanhood and economic management (particularly the dangers of unwise economic management) were commonplace. As many contemporary scholars have discussed, mainstream Victorian ideology constituted women as caretakers of domestic wealth superintending household resources to maximize the moral and spiritual health of their families.[8] One Victorian woman writer states this ideal quite explicitly: 'The position of many women absolutely forbids their aiding their husbands in gaining a livelihood, but every wife is a steward of her husband's wealth, and should consider herself in that light. Every little act of carefulness, every piece of forethought, every prevention of accident, illness, or waste, becomes a sacred duty' ('Our Households' 76).

This is an ideal that is not restricted to middle- and upper-class women who have more significant resources to 'steward.' As Frances Power Cobbe claims in an article decrying domestic abuse, it is equally the responsibility of poor women (in a rather superhuman fashion) to be admirable, 'industrious' caretakers of domestic resources:

> Poor, stupid, ignorant women as most of them are, worn out with life-long drudgery, burdened with all the pangs and cares of many children, poorly fed and poorly clothed, with no pleasures and many pains, there is an enormous excuse to be made for them even if they do sometimes seek in drink the oblivion of their misery … But for those who rise above these temptations, who are sober where intoxication holds out their only chance of pleasure; chaste in the midst of foulness; tender mothers when their devotion calls for toilsome days and sleepless nights, – for these good, industrious, struggling women who, I have shown, are the chief victims of all this cruelty, – is it to be borne that we should sit patiently by and allow their lives to be trampled out in agony? (76)

The rhetoric of this lament, while at least superficially exonerating poor women for giving in to the 'temptations' of drink and slovenliness, also holds out the promise of help and the claims of Christian charity particularly to those women who are 'sober,' 'chaste,' 'tender,' and 'industrious.'[9] Victorian women, consistently figured as the proper caretakers of familial wealth, were potentially open to both praise and abuse for their handling of economic resources. Their consumption decisions could supposedly make or break the fortunes of their relatively passive husbands.[10] As Ruskin admonishes his young schoolgirl interlocutors in the lengthy dialogue-essay 'The Ethics of the Dust': 'You must either be house-Wives, or house-Moths; remember that. In the deep sense, you must either weave men's fortunes, and embroider them; or feed upon, and bring them to decay' (*Works* 18:337).

Yet as Ruskin's exhortation suggests, the dangerous, grasping female figures discussed above are only one side of the representation of household economics. Later in *Munera Pulveris*, in a section aptly entitled 'Coin-Keeping,' Ruskin opines that 'the circulation of wealth, which ought to be soft, steady, strong, far-sweeping, and full of warmth, like the Gulf stream, being narrowed into an eddy, and concentrated on a point, changes into the alternate suction and surrender of Charybdis' (*Works* 17:208). The reappearance of the word 'suction' here draws our attention to the persistent metaphorics of the female body. The phrase 'alternate suction and surrender,' with its ambivalence between castrating and submissive genitalia, aligns the image of the hoarded money supply even more insistently with the trope of monstrous female sexuality (even as the invocation of Charybdis gestures toward an intertextual awareness of other female monsters). Once again, the possibility of excessive accumulation is linked to an image of excessive, transgressive female sexuality.

But Ruskin extends his analysis of hoarding even further by imagining its opposite: a flow of money 'soft, steady, strong, far-sweeping, and full of warmth.' This is the positive alternative to the degraded and dangerous body of the prostitute: the nurturant maternal body that is woman in her 'natural' state, before the distortion of accumulation renders her a menace. (Prostitution commentator John Wade provides an interesting twist on the prostitute-Charybdis association: 'It is impossible to consider public women an unmixed evil. They are the breakwaters of an artificial state of society, upon which the unruly passions of its members dash and lose themselves' [382].) What is implied in Ruskin's Gulf Stream image is the existence of a 'natural' state of circulation, a pure economy of free exchange that is metaphorically aligned with the putatively innate role and properties of the womanly body[11] – and not just any womanly body, but the fertile, maternal, lactating body, with its free-flowing supply of fluid sustenance.

This conflation of maternity, fluidity, and household management was a convention in the Victorian discourse of proper womanhood: 'What higher aim or hope can be held out to any living creature than to be a mother?... Calm and quiet, refreshing as a fountain in the desert, as the charm of a rock in a weary land, is the true mother ... But with all these essentially womanly qualities she is an excellent manager, and displays business-like abilities' ('Our Households' 75–6). These passages present another possibility of closure from the first: if the money-chest image suggests that death is the proper fate of the degraded or transgressive woman, then the fluid, Gulf Stream images suggest that nurture, maternity (and, by extension, marriage) form an alternative type of (en)closure for the pure woman. In these two images we can thus see inscribed the two possible endings for Victorian plots: death and marriage. In both cases, the descriptive recourse for the economic metaphor is the womanly body, in both its 'natural' and 'degraded' states, a trope that persistently links issues of economic surplus and accumulation with feminine sexuality.[12]

1 Political Economy and the Novel

'In economics, hope and faith coexist with great scientific pretension and also a deep desire for respectability,' wrote John Kenneth Galbraith (104). He could just as easily have been describing the nineteenth-century novel. While the scientific predilections – and concern with respectability – of canonical Victorian novelists have been analysed extensively by numerous critics in recent years, discussion of the economic preoccupations of these same authors has been rather more fitful.[13] The omission seems understandable: while authors such as George Eliot, Thomas Hardy, and H.G. Wells left behind rich and extensive records of their intellectual engagement with contemporary scientific researches and discoveries, they were not so forthcoming about their opinions on the vital economic questions of the day.

Yet there are two important reasons to consider the relationship between the themes and techniques of the novel and the rhetoric of Victorian political economy. First, there is the fact that – just as with scientific research – 'lay people' such as novelists and public intellectuals were much more actively engaged with the work of economic writers than they are today. (Indeed, as Gagnier claims, imaginative writers' 'view of socioeconomic relations extended considerably beyond that of the political economists' themselves [*Insatiability* 37].) As we shall see, the discourse of political economy took on a particular importance for the reading public given the volatile, unsettling, and seemingly mysterious economic climate throughout much of Victoria's reign.

Second, the novels themselves are testament to the psychological and intellectual impact of this volatility. The nineteenth-century novel is obsessed with the images and accoutrements of the burgeoning capitalist economy: gold-hoarding misers, iron chests, and precipitous bankruptcies. Victorian realist authors were responding to, as well as shaping, the broader public perception of the 'dismal science.' Indeed, in the work of Harriet Martineau and Millicent Fawcett, celebrated authors of allegorical economic 'fables' with explicitly ethical morals to impart, the line between political economy and literature is even more blurred. (Given the prevalent Victorian image of women as prudent economic overseers, it seems fitting that the two greatest popularizers of classical political economy are female authors.)

As Gallagher notes in her recent study of nineteenth-century political economy and the novel, 'Before novelists like Charles Dickens and George Eliot incorporated them into extended narrative forms ... political economy's organic processes were already structured as plots, as highly consequentialist, if extremely schematic, stories' (*Body* 35). As this book will demonstrate, these 'plots' tended toward the apocalyptic: nineteenth-century economists were particularly concerned with the question of how long the young capitalist economy could continue to grow before reaching stagnation. Unlike the physiocrats of the previous century, most nineteenth-century theorists feared that the economy was not an organic, closed, or self-regulating system, but instead an unstable one which was doomed to reach some kind of natural stagnation state – an end to profit and the accumulation of capital.[14] This anxiety stood in a complicated relationship to the school of classical political economy – peopled by followers of Adam Smith and David Ricardo – that was dominant through much of the nineteenth century. In her study *A/Moral Economics*, Claudia Klaver discusses a different counterstrain to this economic doxa, the 'discourse of morality, ethics and virtue' that she argues functioned 'as discarded remainder, as supplemental effect, as disturbing factor, or as ground for a radical revisioning of economic knowledge' (xii). Klaver's formulation, while used here to describe a different area of economic critique, also captures perfectly the relationship between the party line of classical laissez-faire economics and the discarded, supplemental, disturbing, and radical discourse of consumer demand. While I do not take the discourse of ethics as my central topic, later chapters will examine in some detail how ethical concerns overlapped with and informed the other critical strains that are the focus of my analysis: the demand theory of value, arguments against laissez-faire, and concerns about the gold standard.

Since much of the ensuing analysis will depend upon an understanding of the precepts of the second of these strains, laissez-faire, I will briefly explain here the sense in which I use the term. The phrase can be traced back to the late seventeenth or early eighteenth century, and became associated first with Adam Smith and then with Ricardo and other adherents of the labour theory of value following in the classical tradition.[15] (It is important to note, however, that the term 'laissez-faire' itself was not used by Smith or the other classicals.) The appellation basically refers to an economic and political philosophy that advocates minimal state intervention in the economy. The definition of 'minimal,' the conditions under which the state should or could intervene, and the philosophical sources of the position vary widely. (Rationalizations for laissez-faire varied from Smith's belief that state intervention usually serves the interests of the wealthy land-owning classes, to arguments for optimal resource allocation.)[16] Throughout this study, I use the term in the sense traditionally and commonly employed: as characterizing a loose 'school' of classical economists, from Smith through to the Ricardians (and beyond), who advocated free trade, free markets, minimal government interference in the economy, and the gold standard. Most important for my purposes, the Victorian writers I discuss characterized Smith and Ricardo as the 'fathers' of laissez-faire, and applauded the rise of the new schools of economics at the end of the century as the death of the principle.[17]

The sanguine assurances of laissez-faire capitalism rested on two fundamental principles, which I will mention briefly here and discuss at greater length in the next chapter and in the readings of novels that follow. The first is the belief in Say's Law or the 'law of markets': first formulated by Jean-Baptiste Say in the early nineteenth century, this principle essentially stated that there can be no general glut of commodities because the production of any good for market implies a concomitant demand by its producer for another good – in other words, 'products are paid for with products.' Say's Law is a bedrock of laissez-faire; the belief that state intervention in the economy is unnecessary or harmful necessitates a belief that the relationship between demand and supply is self-adjusting – and vice versa. The second is the classicals' insistence on a metallic monetary standard, a system of 'specie convertibility' in which every bank note is redeemable by the Bank of England for its stated value in gold. The concept of a free-floating currency provoked a great deal of anxiety among nineteenth-century commentators, particularly with regard to the seemingly magical creation of value through the issuance of paper notes and promises-to-pay. The gold standard was a panacea particularly for laissez-faire advocates; as historian Joseph Schumpeter notes, it was *'laissez-faire* men' who 'wished to regulate the note issue precisely in order to make the currency "automatic" and to leave banking business ... entirely free' (*History* 696).[18] The structural irony of a free market depending upon regulation of currency is one of the many tensions and contradictions within the laissez-faire ethos.

The nineteenth-century wranglings over the gold standard and Say's Law were in effect a debate over the economic effects of surplus: surplus capital and goods on the one hand (the bane of the demand theorists), and surplus 'value' on the other (the bane of the Ricardians). While classical political economists argued that accumulation was absolutely necessary in order to fuel the engine of capitalism (which threatened to burn out eventually anyway), their heterodox critics warned that excessive surpluses would lead to stagnation if consumer demand could not keep up with the supply of goods; as historian Mark Blaug pithily puts it, 'The process of capital accumulation leads inherently to secular stagnation; this is Malthus's basic argument' (*Economic* 161). As the first chapter of this book will argue in more detail, this anxiety over failures of demand was present throughout the century – both as a heterodox counterargument and as a subterranean anxiety within the work of the classical economists themselves – and did not spring into existence, wholly formed, with the rise of the marginal utility school in the 1870s.[19]

This pervasive worry among nineteenth-century intellectuals that capitalism must, by its very nature, self-destruct or reach a stagnant end presents a cogent argument for linking the concerns of closure and political economy found in so many Victorian novels. Indeed, this discovery forms the departure point for my analysis. Yet there is an even more compelling reason to examine these two thematic preoccupations in light of each other. The novels themselves, insofar as they are concerned with both closure and economics, often metaphorically appose these two concerns to images of women and 'feminine' sexuality – particularly to excessive or degraded female sexuality.[20] Victorian anxieties about the growing capitalist economy are rhetorically linked, in the novels of George Eliot and Thomas Hardy, to images of feminized sexuality: the novels I examine – *Adam Bede, The Mill on the Floss, The Mayor of Casterbridge,* and *Tess of the d'Urbervilles* – share a concern with symbolic economies and also with wayward femininity. What follows is an analysis of the relationship between key metaphors common to nineteenth-century economics – surplus, excess, and circulation – and the narrative modes of these four novels. In particular, I argue that the phantasmagorical figure I term 'economic woman,' the idealized model of feminine sexual restraint and wise domestic management, mobilizes a set of metaphors that are utilized by the discourses of political economy and the realist novel alike. The figure of economic woman, like a trompe l'œil drawing, is shadowed by her opposite: the degraded prostitute whose sexual excesses and economic mismanagement seem to threaten the very stability of the young capitalist economy.

I have chosen to study novels by George Eliot and Thomas Hardy exclusively for a number of reasons. First, both authors were explicitly interested in economic questions, and generously larded their narratives with metaphors and concepts drawn from contemporary political economy and philosophy. Furthermore, both authors were specifically concerned with the impact of economic changes on women, and how women acted as agents – and victims – of those changes. Finally, the novels of Eliot and Hardy form a neat heuristic framework within which to examine popular versions of political economy. While any number of Victorian authors, such as Elizabeth Gaskell, William Makepeace Thackeray, and of course Charles Dickens, were preoccupied with economic themes, the novels of Eliot and Hardy simultaneously bracket the period of high realism and span a number of important economic developments throughout the century. For this reason, I have chosen to study Eliot's first two novels, published in 1859 and 1860, and two novels published by Hardy after the rise of the marginal utility school in 1870. Of course, the two authors are kindred enough in other ways that the combination has appealed to a number of scholars before me, most notably Gillian Beer in her brilliant study *Darwin's Plots.* The propensities that Eliot and Hardy share – a commitment to psychological realism, a privileging of character development, a weakness for long passages of narratorial commentary – form a backdrop against which their economic predilections are thrown into sharp relief.

Any study of this kind, which attempts to trace the connections between artistic productions and their cultural context, is built upon an armature of methodological and evidentiary assumptions – some clearly stated, some largely assumed, and others more or less unconscious. While my analyses of the novels will inevitably betray more fully my theoretical investments, following is a description of the basic premises with which I proceed, and an attempt to describe the scope and limits of those premises.

The readings of individual novels that comprise the rest of this study are largely rhetorical, and are deeply indebted to the considerable body of critical work on metaphor undertaken in the past few decades. While my analyses of Eliot and Hardy are not explicitly psychoanalytic in the traditional sense, they are steeped in the assumptions of Freudian and Lacanian theory, particularly with regard to the legibility of metaphors and other textual 'symptoms.' I am most interested in metaphorical usages that resonate across disciplinary boundaries. I take it as given that we cannot import a metaphor from one domain of culture to another without also importing, often wholly unintentionally, the synchronic resonances that accompany it. In the introduction to her recent study *Genres of the Credit Economy*, Poovey comments on a similar phenomenon operating across the domains of literature and economics, namely the existence of 'specific words – like *credit* and *value* – that retained a place in the lexicons of both sets of genres and that remained as switchpoints or sites of overlap between them' (7). While of course these importations of resonances and meanings across disciplines are often fortuitous, I contend that this qualification does not make them any less real or any less readable. That legibility is, of course, partial and contestable, although the signifying echoes of metaphor are rendered more audible through repetition.

The readings of novels that follow are, in addition to being rhetorical, also narratological. They proceed on the assumption that plots become vehicles for meaning mostly in their failure. By 'failure' I do not necessarily mean aesthetic inadequacy, but rather a betrayal of certain kinds of readerly expectation. My analyses of these novels focus on moments of tension between what actually happens in their plots and what an informed reader anticipates will happen. (I elaborate on the construction of the 'informed reader' more fully below.) These gaps between expectation and fulfilment can occur either because the language and claims of the narratorial voice are at odds with the events of the story, or because the broader cultural and generic expectations of story are somehow thwarted. My model for the first kind of reading is the work of structuralist critics, particularly Roland Barthes, and for the second, psychoanalytically oriented critics like Peter Brooks and D.A. Miller. It is around the strictures of narrative closure that we most often see a tension between these expectations and the exigencies of plot. Both Brooks and Miller have attempted to chart the culturally specific ways in which these expectations are both generated and thwarted. In the service of this same kind of exploration, I also analyse the contemporary reviews of the novels I examine, since they often furnish clues about the ways in which readerly desires were – and were not – fulfilled by certain plots. I see no inherent contradiction between formalism, including narratological reading, and the historically inflected investigation that goes by the name 'cultural studies.' As Martha Woodmansee and Mark Osteen remark in the introduction to their influential volume *The New Economic Criticism*, 'The most successful economic criticism must combine several angles of attack' (36), as 'sensitive close reading of a text's intratextual economies of meaning can supply the microscopic lenses needed to supplement the telescopic vision of historicist criticism' (37).

This general reading strategy, which is often termed 'new historicism,' 'discourse analysis,' or 'cultural studies,' has come under attack of late, most recently by Poovey in her study *Genres of the Credit Economy*. Because one aspect of her critique touches particularly on the question of narratological 'tensions' and readerly expectation, this seems an opportune moment to address that objection. During her discussion of two treatments of Martineau's *Illustrations of Political Economy*, one by Gallagher in *The Industrial Reformation of English Fiction* and one by Poovey's own former student, Klaver, in *A/Moral Economics*, Poovey objects to the very methodology I have been proposing:

> The failure of Martineau's own text to fit perfectly into what should be the organic unity of 'discourse' leads to these critics' judgments about the text's relative 'success' ... [E]ach critic presents the interpretation she generates ... as an emanation from or a product of Martineau's own text. By implication, that is, Gallagher and Klaver present their interpretations *as dictated by form* and, thus, by implication again, as identical to the interpretation any reader – even a nineteenth-century reader – would produce if she had read Martineau's text ... This assumption about the ability of form to dictate response belongs to the *ahistorical* bias of all variants of Literary

formalism and, thus, to the incompatibility between this theoretical position and the desire to construct a historical narrative. (342, emphases in
original)

My objections to this line of reasoning are twofold. First of all, Poovey
makes a fairly large assumption of her own: all 'variants of Literary
formalism' have an 'ahistorical bias.' I see absolutely no necessary contradiction between an interpretation of a text that attends to the creation and thwarting of readerly expectation, for example, and a larger
'historical narrative' that contextualizes both those expectations and
their failure within a broader political, cultural, and social context. Indeed, this is precisely what the following analyses will attempt to do.
But this is the weak form of this particular objection. I would endorse
even a stronger form, and attest that there is also no necessary contradiction between particular formalist and historicist reading methods
in general: between, for example, psychoanalysis and new historicism.
Again, the readings that follow will attempt to demonstrate this point.
While, as I explained above, I do not perform classic psychoanalytic interpretations of literary texts, I take psychoanalysis to be the grounding
energy behind my way of reading literature, in the sense that I believe
in the historical recoverability of a 'cultural unconscious' whose traces
and symptoms are more or less legible, particularly in the popular texts
of the culture in question. The purpose of excavating historical context
should be to generate or support our understanding of the production
and reception of those texts, and that production and reception history in turn should help us present-day critics to interpret these texts in
a way that is satisfying to contemporaries within our own discourse
community.

The irony of Poovey's vehemently asserting her own (and others')
relativistic bias is that these assertions seem to be part of a thinly dis-
guised attempt to construct a new sort of transcendent critical position
based on the disavowal of interpretation. This is a mistake we were
supposed to have stopped making after Stanley Fish critiqued 'anti-
foundationalist theory hope' (27) in his own discussion of literature and
economics. Poovey has taken her cue here – and the term 'historical
description' – from Ian Hunter, but her own application of the principle seems unnecessarily reductive: we should not be aiming to create
interpretations because interpretations are inherently ahistorical and
formalist; ahistorical and formalist interpretations do not enable us to
'construct historical narrative.' Leaving aside for the moment the real
possibility that one might want to perform literary interpretations that

do not construct historical narratives, we still must ask: Why is 'interpretation' inherently ahistorical? If we do not grant Poovey this rather sweeping premise, the rest of her argument crumbles away. But even more disturbingly, I find it very difficult to read Poovey's new methodology as doing anything other than supplanting one heuristic frame for critical readings with another: the approval or disapproval of one's fellow critics by the fantasized 'recognition' of the original text's author. While there are certainly philosophical pitfalls attendant upon the former, the latter strikes me, in its complete unverifiability, as far more problematic.

My second critique is rather more methodological, although certainly not any narrower for that. Poovey's objection to the 'extrapolation of a universal subject position' (342) from which to adjudge the success or failure of a text's 'fit' with its discursive context appears to be based entirely on her own former reading practice: 'Having spent weeks devising what I considered a theoretically sophisticated account of the narrative dynamics of Dickens's novel, I suddenly realized that I could not claim that my interpretation had any validity at all *as historical evidence* or as evidence for a historical argument' (343, emphasis in original). And this because, in the case of Martineau for example, 'It is not that our contemporaries' (or my past) evaluations are wrong ... It is just that we made our evaluations for reasons that Martineau's first readers did not share, from professional contexts they did not occupy, and in terms that few of them would have recognized' (351). Now as to this last objection, I can only respond: So what? The ability or inability of a fellow toiler of two hundred years ago to recognize, fully understand, and implicitly endorse modern-day critical conclusions seems quite an odd criterion to apply to current knowledge production. Again, this seems an attempt to construct, through the back door as it were, an objective or transcendental critical position by aiming to produce only readings that would have been 'recognizable' (according to whom?) to the Victorians themselves. But the first two clauses seem to me even more problematic. Much, if not most, 'new historical' criticism is keenly alive to the reactions, judgments, critiques, and responses of the readers and authors of the texts it interprets. While of course it would be foolhardy to posit the perfect transparency of those authors' intentions and those readers' reactions, there is still a rich and fertile middle ground between brutally imposing one's own critical categories on a nineteenth-century text and giving up the entire notion of interpretation as untenable.

In the textual readings that follow, I will pay a great deal of attention to the conundrums, textual infelicities, and even failures that George Eliot and Thomas Hardy, along with their readers and reviewers, felt to bedevil the novels I interpret. The records of these puzzlements are, of course, available in journals, letters, and reviews, sources that Poovey for some reason feels to be no longer of any interest to her own literary enterprise: 'nor do I deal with nineteenth-century reviews of these novels' (356).[21] Even though attending to these sources would seem to be the most efficacious way out of the epistemological double bind she has set for herself, Poovey prefers to reify this intellectual challenge as a kind of critical *trou-de-loup*:

> Inevitably, I view these novels through the classificatory terms and analytic procedures associated with my own discipline, but I try not simply to repeat the formalism residual in so many Literary critical methods. By emphasizing description, function, and classification – the elements of genre – instead of meaning and representation – the elements of interpretation – I try to reflect on the process by which novels became aesthetic objects and representation became problematic as part of that history of reading and schools that transformed (some) readers into Literary critics and left others simply loving to read. (356)

I will let this last clause simply pass in shocked silence. However, what I cannot silently let pass is Poovey's rather disingenuous tendency to forgive her own 'inevitable' importation of modern critical categories while so ruthlessly taking others to task for bending to the same necessity:

> Even though I have abandoned the terms Trollope and his contemporaries used, then, insofar as I have respected the difference he created, I think that I have produced a description of Trollope's writing that he would have recognized. Insofar as I have invoked another distinction, however – one that opposes identification with characters to an engagement that focuses on a novel's form (artistry) – I have clearly moved further from Trollope's accounts of the novel's craft. While it is inevitable that my analytic categories differ from the ones Trollope used, I suggest that his own novel contains passages that support this emphasis on art. (411)

The belief that one is producing descriptions, and even interpretations, that are supported by passages in the text under consideration is assuredly one that all responsible literary critics share, presumably (perhaps especially) even those practicing so-called new historicism.

2 Plan of the Study

In the opening chapter, 'Popular Demand: Surplus and Stagnation in Nineteenth-Century Political Economy,' I first discuss nineteenth-century debates over the progress of capitalism, analysing how apparently incommensurable accounts of capitalist development are given by adherents of the Ricardian progressive-growth model and Malthusian heralders of stagnation or the stationary state. This anxiety about the end of capitalist growth takes the form of a sustained questioning of the economic effects of excessive accumulation, the efficacy of laissez-faire, and the operations of the gold standard. Turning to the work of mid-century economists, I then discuss the challenge posed to Ricardian economics by John Ruskin, who both denied the supremacy of the 'law of supply and demand' and advocated an ethical, prescriptive political economy. I then examine the work of one pro-Ricardian economist, Herbert Spencer, and demonstrate that the contradictions and tensions in his account of laissez-faire economic policy are papered over by a fixation on gold as a standard of value. The chapter ends with a discussion of the rise of the marginal utility school, the first new sustained theory and system of value since the Ricardian labour theory, and an examination of the continuities between political economy after 1870 – both marginal utility and the new 'historical school' – and the demand theory from the earlier decades of the century. It is this marginalized or repressed strain of thinking that will be the subject of the literary readings that follow.

In the second chapter, '"Fine Clothes an' Waste": Utopian Economy and the Problem of Femininity in *Adam Bede*,' I argue that Eliot's first novel attempts to portray a contained, stable economic system – a nostalgic and pastoral reverie of a prelapsarian, precredit world – and at the same time to condemn the seducer Arthur Donnithorne's reductive moral calculus, which envisions the consequences of human actions as finite and reparable. Yet as the novel takes issue with Donnithorne's ethical naivety, demonstrating the ways in which the repercussions of his actions extend beyond his narrow vision of them, it simultaneously problematizes the stability and containment of the utopian physiocratic economy it wants to portray. Problematic demand and consumption are on display in the form of aristocratic luxurious expenditure, which is linked, in the logic of the novel, to a compensatory ethics that attempts to 'liquidate' moral debt with an incommensurate 'currency.' Eliot is able to resolve these contradictions, and restabilize the economic balance of the novel, by the abrupt and yet oddly understated elimination of Hetty, the figure who is linked to excesses of appetite and desire. Her inadvertent recalcitrance, her bodily refusal to be transferred from Arthur to Adam and thus act as a stable currency in the economic logic of the novel, sharply calls into question the utopian barter system that *Adam Bede* attempts to invoke: it is only when the 'hidden dread' of her pregnancy makes itself manifest that the extent of Hetty's transgression and Arthur's treachery becomes clear. Hetty's body does violence to the orderly alternative plot that the men work out together, and through her banishment and death the novel comes to an end.

The third chapter, 'Superfluity and Suction: The Problem with Saving in *The Mill on the Floss*,' extends my argument about demand and consumption by claiming that in her study of the encroachment of industrialized capitalism onto the pastoral landscape, Eliot rehearses concerns about the effects of excessive accumulation both on the moral lives of her characters and on the form of the novel. The sexual transgressions and inappropriate desire of Maggie Tulliver are ultimately more troubling than those of Hetty, because they rehearse questions about the operations of demand that have been repressed by mainstream Victorian economics. By dividing the novel into separate plots – the 'Tom' story of economic striving and the 'Maggie' story of romantic struggle – Eliot is able to examine the tensions between the competing nineteenth-century economic narratives of unbridled accumulation and ultimate stagnation. Maggie's story, inextricably bound up with questions of appetite and desire, presents an uncomfortable alternative to the prevailing economic theory from which questions of effective demand have been banished. Furthermore, the 'Maggie' plot, which invokes sudden, dangerous, and chaotic endings of all kinds, links questions of appetite and desire to questions of closure and metaphorical death, underscoring the threatening and problematic role of economic demand in the broader optimistic view of Victorian political economy. It is because of the profound and disturbing challenge she presents that Maggie is eventually 'eliminated' – thus resolving the tensions between alternative narratives of capitalism, but at the price of novelistic plausibility.

The fourth chapter, '"All Was Over at Last": Epistemological and Domestic Economies in *The Mayor of Casterbridge*,' argues that the novelistic concern with economic transgression is extended to include the ultimately feminized and degraded figure of Michael Henchard, who is banished from the novel's (ironically) idealized vision of bourgeois domesticity. In a process of displacement and substitution governed by symbolic rules of kinship and exchange, Elizabeth-Jane, the novel's original repository of feminine weakness and excluded knowledge, comes to embody the masculine principles of narrative omniscience and governance of economic processes. While the putative main plot of the novel concerns the eclipse of Henchard's traditional economic methods by the dynamic and new-fangled Farfrae, a quiet coup takes place in the domestic plot overseen by Elizabeth-Jane: at the end of the novel the feminized and enfeebled Henchard is utterly dependent upon his 'daughter's' patronage and recognition, while her word has become 'law in buying and selling.' By ascending to the patriarchal role at the end of the novel, Elizabeth-Jane effects a reparation for Henchard's traffic in women; while his transgressive desire proves his undoing, her economic discipline affords her an ambivalent triumph at the novel's close – in a sense, Hardy 'over-corrects' the economic transgressions of Henchard and leaves us with an insipid and anhedonic heroine with whom it is difficult to identify.

The final chapter, 'Self-Sacrifice, Skillentons, and Mother's Milk: The Internalization of Demand in *Tess*,' argues that in Hardy's later novel, concerns with symbolic economies extend to include a more general and far-reaching examination of the relationship between individual desire and social determination. As the classical economists' labour theory of value is being challenged by a new emphasis on demand from the marginal utility school, the rhetorical emphasis – both in political economy and in the novel – begins to shift from questions of accumulation to questions of consumption. Tess, as heroine, is a locus of these new concerns and rhetorical shifts; she demonstrates Hardy's growing emphasis on the sphere of individual action by engaging in a process of 'internalization' throughout the novel, taking on a compulsion to self-sacrifice. In this way she herself effects the fatal closure that has seemed to come 'from without' in the previous novels I have examined. This internalized impulse is the direct result of a novelistic project that seeks the effects of the social and collective upon the individual character: *Tess of the d'Urbervilles* consistently effects a process of internalization wherein natural, social, and even rhetorical operations are envisioned as taking place within the individual, and are in turn relocated physically within the human body. This movement of internalization within the individual – and specifically within the individual body – crystallizes around the portrayal of economic forces and compulsions originating outside the individual, at the level of the social and collective. In her role of individual, desiring actor caught in the determining web of economic relations, Tess straddles the shifting tectonic plates of early and late nineteenth-century economic theory: she is the true avatar of the new accumulating/consuming economic agent.

Having outlined my theoretical predilections above, I would now like to delineate the boundaries of the following analysis. I am primarily concerned with the popular metaphors of political economy publicly discussed during the Victorian period, and in how these metaphors are reflected in and developed by the novels of Eliot and Hardy. To borrow a distinction from the great modern economist Joseph Schumpeter, I am not so much interested in a history of economic analysis as I am in a history of economic thought, 'the sum total of all the opinions and desires concerning economic subjects, especially concerning public policy bearing upon these subjects, that, at any given time and place, float in the public mind' (Schumpeter, *History* 38).[22] The idea of an economic 'public mind' was one shared by the Victorian critics I write about; in a mocking dismissal of a sudden fashion for praying for rain, Ruskin comments: 'It had suddenly, it seems, occurred to the public mind ... that it must be unreasonable to expect God to supply on our immediate demand what could not be provided by previous evaporation' (*Works* 34:115).

This is not to claim that the 'economic thought' I refer to was by any means homogeneous or uncontested. I am interested in one particular segment of that thought: in received middle-class notions of economic theory, what we might crudely call the dominant ideology regarding the important economic questions of the day. The reason for the narrowness of my analysis is simple: the writers and readers of the novels I study were members of this dominant class. I turn to the rhetoric of political economy solely in the interest of explicating literary texts, and in an attempt to understand certain puzzling aspects of novels and the construction (in all senses of that word) of novels.

In attempting to reconstruct and understand the influences on Eliot's and Hardy's economic thought, I have used a variety of sources. First, I read the writers they read: Herbert Spencer, Ruskin, and J.S. Mill, in addition to the earlier thinkers who contributed directly to these writers' intellectual development. Second, I read and analyse the public debates over economic questions found in popular Victorian journals. It is particularly important to read later-century popular journal articles on political economy in order to trace the discipline's cultural effects, as the professional treatises become increasingly mathematical and inaccessible to the educated layperson over the course of the century. While only in a few instances do I have direct evidence that Eliot or Hardy read any one specific article or essay, I rely on the fact that they were both clearly engaged with the economic ideas I discuss, as well as the fact that those ideas were so pervasive and influential. As Gallagher notes, novelists at times 'engaged political economy explicitly; at other times, they unconsciously shared the imaginative universe of that discipline simply by cohabiting with it in a larger realm of conjecture about the circulation of life, value, death, pain, and pleasure' (*Body* 61).[23]

I also depend upon the work of historians of economic thought who have done the painstaking ground work that enables and informs my readings of these novels. I am particularly indebted to the work of Boyd Hilton, whose description of popular middle-class economic thought forms the real departure point for my analysis. I summarize the work of these historians throughout the rest of this study, and comment specifically on the ways in which it illuminates and informs my readings of novels. It is the evidence that follows – the quotations from and summaries of Victorian economic texts – that constitutes, I hope, the most eloquent testimony to the anxiety and uncertainty attendant upon the growth of the new capitalist economy. My aim in the readings that follow is to demonstrate how four novels that are not overtly about political economy (or, in the case of *The Mill on the Floss*, only partially so), become fully legible only when we consider their engagement with contemporaneous economic debates and their pervasive deployment of metaphors drawn from political economy.

1 Popular Demand: Surplus and Stagnation in Nineteenth-Century Political Economy

The natural tendency of profits then is to fall ... As soon as wages should be equal [to] ... the whole receipts of the farmer, there must be an end of accumulation; for no capital can then yield any profit whatever, and no additional labour can be demanded, and consequently population will have reached its highest point.

> Ricardo, *Principles* 71

Her writing can only keep going, without ever inscribing or discerning contours ... [Her language] knows neither enclosure nor death.

> Cixous 259–60

'Why, the Scotch tunes are just like a scolding, nagging woman,' Bartle went on ... 'They go on with the same thing over and over again, and never come to a reasonable end.'

> Eliot, *Adam Bede* 307

1 Narratives of Capitalism

The rhetoric of classical economics, and its elaboration in the popular journals, pamphlets, and tracts of the early and mid-nineteenth century, was the site of a fierce contest between seemingly optimistic and pessimistic prophets of the future of capitalism. As Boyd Hilton states in his study of evangelical thought in the first half of the century, the period was characterized by 'a persistent oscillation between optimism and pessimism, a constant uncertainty as to whether happiness or misery best testified to God's efficient governance of the mortal world' (*Age* 35).

While Hilton's analysis specifically locates this oscillation in amateur religious economic writings, it is also true that in the broader context of political economy as a whole, apparently contradictory accounts of capitalist development are given variously by adherents of the Ricardian progressive growth model and heralders of stagnation or the stationary state. Some popular accounts of the workings of capitalism paint a picture of self-contained, self-regulating circulation, something like the workings of a natural organism or a perpetual machine, needing no outside intervention. Thomas DeQuincey, for example, characterized the economy as made up of parts '(like so many organs of a complex machine) [that] must eternally operate by aiding or by thwarting each other' (100). Other predictions, however, are more pointedly dire: the 'dismal science' of political economy is an apocalyptic vision wherein no degree of intervention can stave off the inevitable stagnation of capitalist growth. Indeed, a marker of the intractability of this battle is the persistent attempts of modern historians to claim that classical political economy is 'really' either one or the other – blithely nonchalant about the unlimited future of economic growth, or dour in its predictions of inevitable stagnation. In fact, it is both – it is a contested field, full of opposition, disagreement, and ideological struggle.

Both accounts are pre-eminently concerned with the question of the end of capitalism: one with rehearsing the possibility only to vehemently deny it, the other with asserting its practical inevitability. This anxiety about the death of capitalism is particularly striking because in both cases, for the growth theorists and their critics, the question is inextricably bound up with both the descriptive concepts of accumulation, surplus, and demand, and the prescriptive question of optimal government intervention in the economy. The disagreement between the optimistic and pessimistic writers on political economy can be described as a dispute between those who feel the demand function is largely inconsequential – and thus that the economy is self-regulating – and those who think it is of central concern – and thus that action must be taken to attempt to stave off stagnation. A shared anxiety about an end to the capitalist economy engendered two differing prescriptions for avoiding it: on the part of the laissez-faire economists such as David Ricardo and Herbert Spencer, the call for unlimited and expanding capital accumulation underpinned by a gold standard, and a concomitant insistence on the self-regulating capacity of the capitalist economy; on the part of the early demand function theorists such as Thomas Malthus and John Ruskin, an insistence on the importance of consumption and a warning against overaccumulation and hoarding. In both cases, there are dire warnings against what will happen if the prescription is not followed: what is seen to be at stake is the very continuation of English capitalism. In both cases, regardless of the Ricardians' superficial protestations of unlimited growth, an intractable pessimism seems ultimately to win the day.[1] And in both cases, the anxiety about the continued functioning of the economy comes to rest on the vexed and ubiquitous question of surplus.

By 'surplus' I mean that amount of goods produced, in any economy operating above subsistence level, that is greater than the basic needs of the society's consumers (plus the replenishment of the means to continue producing those goods). In feudal economies, according to the simple classical economic model inherited from the eighteenth-century physiocrats, economic surplus was extracted from the land by peasant farmers, who paid it to landlords in the form of rent, who consumed it in various luxurious and sumptuary expenditures. 'Capitalism' thus denotes those economies in which part of this economic surplus is not consumed by the owners of the means of production (either landowners or capitalists), but is reinvested in the means of producing more goods – not merely in replacing worn equipment or seed stock in order to maintain a consistent return, but in accumulating greater and greater stores of the means of production in order to secure continuing growth.

The great question of how to dispose of economic surplus is what divides the classical theorists and their critics. At first glance, the debate seems irresolvable. Ricardo and his followers insist on the unalloyed benefits of capital accumulation for the growth of the economy. They defend this position with an appeal to the 'law of markets' first described by French economist Jean-Baptiste Say and popularized by James Mill. Ricardo himself provides us with the best summary of the law:

> There is no amount of capital which may not be employed in a country, because a demand is only limited by production. No man produces but with a view to consume or sell, and he never sells but with an intention to purchase some other commodity ... By producing, then, he necessarily becomes either the consumer of his own goods, or the purchaser and consumer of the goods of some other person. (*Principles* 192–3)

Therefore, in the long run, it is impossible for there to be overproduction or overaccumulation of capital; stagnation, through a failure of

demand to keep pace with supply, need not be a concern.[2] This principle is both the bedrock and the enabling condition of laissez-faire economic policy; the belief that intervention in the economy is unnecessary
springs directly from (or leads directly to) a faith in the self-adjusting
nature of the demand-supply balance. This confidence in the salutary
effects of capital accumulation and the impossibility of general gluts
reaches its apotheosis in the work of the most staunch believer in
laissez-faire the Victorian era produced, Herbert Spencer, whose belief
was so unshakable that he could blithely characterize capitalism, *ante
hoc*, as an economic organization in which the 'accumulation of surplus
capital [is] ever going on' ('State-Tamperings' 331).

However, there were significant challenges to the supply-side model
and Victorian laissez-faire public policy. There were significant tensions within the approach itself and among its adherents, as well as
serious attacks mounted by those outside the mainstream school. One
of the most impassioned critiques came from Ricardo's contemporary,
friend, and correspondent Thomas Malthus, who could be considered
nominally an insider – he is often grouped among the classicals, and
his friendship with Ricardo invites this categorization – but whose disagreements with the central postulates of that school position him more
compellingly as a heterodox critic.[3] Later in the century, Malthus's
warnings about both stagnation and the social costs of laissez-faire
were developed and expanded by Ruskin. And finally, by the 1870s and
1880s, the marginal utility school, with its emphasis on consumer demand as the most important determinant of value, had all but eclipsed
the Ricardian economics of the earlier decades of the century.

Other modern critics, most recently Catherine Gallagher in her study
The Body Economic, have attempted to uncover 'lost' or marginalized
critiques of Ricardian economics. Gallagher isolates two complementary strains of thought in early nineteenth-century political economy and
traces their resonances in the novels of Charles Dickens and George
Eliot. She uses the terms 'bioeconomics' to refer to 'political economy's
concentration on the interconnections among populations, the food
supply, modes of production and exchange, and their impact on life
forms generally,' and 'somaeconomics' to refer to 'the theorization of
economic behavior in terms of the emotional and sensual feelings that
are both causes and consequences of economic exertions' (*Body* 3).

While I find her parsing of political economy instructive and in-
triguing, my own core samples of the discipline are bored at a different angle: I am primarily interested in excavating the latent demand

strain in classical political economy, from Malthus through to Ruskin and beyond. While Gallagher's 'somaeconomics' is roughly covalent with what I term the Malthusian strain in political economy, she in fact characterizes Malthus as a 'bioeconomist' par excellence; she does not discuss the aspects of his work, developed in his *Principles of Political Economy*, that I find the most relevant for my own purposes: his critique of Say's Law, his anxiety about general gluts, and his concern with consumption and expenditure. Indeed, while Gallagher helpfully reminds us of the importance of consumer demand and desire in De-Quincey (30–1) and McCulloch (55–6), she does not attend to this aspect of Malthus's own work, although his contemporaries thought of his contribution to pure political economy as much in terms of his great debates with his friend Ricardo over consumption and demand as in terms of his theory of population.[4] While Gallagher's characterization of capital as appearing to 'place sensate life in abeyance, to abstract it from biotic form while preserving its potential force,' and her claim that this power 'seized the literary as well as the economic imagination of nineteenth-century Britain' (61) are cogent and apt, I would add that this very power, in its potential to overwhelm and flood the delicate balance of the marketplace, had every bit as profound an effect on the Victorian literary and economic imagination.

The rest of this chapter is devoted to an analysis of these counter-strains within Victorian economic doxa. First I discuss the Malthusian and Ruskinian challenges to the supply-side theory, and then I examine a laissez-faire 'case history,' an article by Spencer, in order to draw out the tensions and contradictions within the Ricardian model itself, particularly its treatment of the gold standard. Finally I turn to the 'new economics' at the end of the century: the historical school as well as marginal utility theory, which ultimately enthroned the demand function as the key determinant of value at the end of the century. The subsequent chapters will be dedicated to an analysis of the homologies between the rhetoric of political economy and images and descriptions of Victorian womanhood, and how these related tensions, metaphors, and themes are developed in and by the narrative structures of the novel.

2 Malthus, Ruskin, and the Anti-Ricardians

One of the most sustained considerations of demand in the early part of the century comes from a writer who is not particularly confident about its inalienable operation: Thomas Malthus. The work of Malthus – particularly in his *Principles of Political Economy* and his correspondence and debates with other political economists – is crucial in this regard because he codifies and popularizes many earlier economists' insights about demand, which were becoming lost in the superficially optimistic fervour of the early part of the nineteenth century. For the eighteenth-century French school of economics known as Physiocracy, as exemplified by the writings of its founder François Quesnay, the only source of economic surplus was agriculture – produce extracted from the land that is greater than the amount needed for subsistence.[5] Quesnay's famous Tableau Économique describes an ideal economy that is a self-regulating, enclosed circle: all available surplus (the value remaining after the payment of subsistence wages and the maintenance of the means of production) will be consumed by the landowning class, without remainder. What is crucial about this model is that it assumes no capital growth: no surplus is accumulated and therefore there is no change in the balanced cycle of inputs and expenditures from year to year. While there is a surplus being generated, it is in the form of rents and, in theory, is wholly consumed in luxury expenditure by the landowning class. While this system seems, on first blush, to be perfectly consonant with the later assurances of Say and other adherents to his 'law of markets,' according to historian Mark Blaug precisely the opposite is true: 'Say directed the Law of Markets *against* his physiocratic predecessors because they had argued that income received is not automatically restored to the income stream' (*Economic* 29, emphasis added). According to the physiocrats' model, landlords can withhold their income from the system (Ruskin's feared hoarding), thus leading to overproduction in relation to consumption and disrupting the balance of demand and supply. Say rejected this possibility and in response formulated the principle that 'supply creates its own demand.'[6] According to Blaug, the physiocrats' insights about possible disruptions in the demand-supply balance are later enshrined in Malthus's work on underconsumption-ism and his advocacy of luxurious expenditure in maintaining the circular flow of the economic system. (I will return to these crucial ideas later in this chapter.) In this sense, Malthus is the father of the demand strain in classical political economy, just as Ricardo is the father of the supply side and the labour theory of value which, depending on one's perspective, were ultimately triumphant from mid-century through to the rise of the marginal utility school after 1870.

Malthus first directly addresses the question of demand in the section of his *Principles of Political Economy* where he considers the question of value. Having decided to reject the notion of 'value in use' as a strictly metaphorical term, he turns his attention entirely to exchange value, which he claims 'does not depend merely upon the scarcity in which commodities exist, nor upon the inequality of their distribution; but upon the circumstance of their not being distributed according to the wills and powers of individuals' (52).[7] 'Reciprocal demand' as Malthus terms it, or the simultaneous desire of 'individuals' for particular commodities that can be exchanged for one another, alone determines the respective values of those commodities. It is Malthus's elaboration of this central concept throughout his career, his insistence on the importance of demand in the determination of value, that separates him from the mainstream of Ricardian thought and its labour theory of value. Malthus, *contra* Ricardo, insists that it is not production costs that 'create' value, but rather the desire of consumers to acquire and exchange commodities.[8]

The claim that value inheres in demand has several corollaries in Malthus's work. First, the invocation of demand as a crucial component in the determination of value means that demand is no longer taken for granted – it is no longer presumed to be a negligible variable that mechanically determines supply and can thus be discounted. Malthus is particularly concerned with the functioning of the 'demand side' of the economic equation. This leads him to consider the question of who, exactly, can be depended upon to consume the products of capitalism in sufficient amounts to ensure the continued growth of the economy. At first, he considers the optimal proportion of 'productive' consumers (those whose labours produce the material objects that alone constitute wealth) to unproductive consumers in a society. His great fear is, in fact, that capitalists do not possess a desire to consume sufficient to ensure the increase of national wealth: the 'great object of their lives is to save a fortune' (456), not to enjoy the fruits of their labour. More important, they have little leisure time in which to consume, being obliged to work long hours in order to make said fortunes. Therefore, there must be 'a considerable class of other consumers, or the mercantile classes could not continue extending their concerns, and realizing their profits' (466).

Yet who are these consumers to be? It cannot be the labourers themselves, for two reasons. First, whether or not they have the desire, they simply lack the means to consume enough to take up the slack. Second, even if they were suddenly able to greatly increase their consumption of material goods, this intensified demand would so enlarge the costs of production, and thus diminish profits, that these hyperconsuming labourers would 'impede the growth of wealth more by diminishing the power of production, than they could encourage it by increasing the demand for produce' (477). The remaining class, the landowners, also cannot be relied upon, since their level of demand is frequently insufficient to ensure the full employment of capital (475). The only hope rests with the 'unproductive labourers' – the professionals and clergymen and soldiers and politicians whose labour does not add to the stock of material items clamouring to be consumed. A society cannot function without this crucial class of consumers; they appear, according to Malthus, 'to be absolutely necessary' (477).

Yet even given this qualified assurance, Malthus is far from sanguine about the ability of the three classes together to accomplish the 'consumption required.' He returns throughout his work to the question of how new demands are to be created and sustained, new tastes and desires implanted, new cravings for expenditure encouraged. This multiplication of desires is absolutely necessary in order to stave off the threat of overproduction, overaccumulation, and general gluts. One of the ways these new tastes can be cultivated, for example, is through foreign trade:

> No country with a very confined market, internal as well as external, has ever been able to accumulate a large capital, because such a market prevents the formation of those wants and tastes, and that desire to consume, which are absolutely necessary to keep up the market prices of commodities, and to occasion an increasing demand for them, and for the capital which is to produce them. (448)

This is a rare moment of qualified hopefulness for Malthus; generally, his invocations of the necessity of inculcating new tastes in the populace end with his despair at the great difficulty of doing so. While this cultivation of 'wants and tastes' is crucial, unfortunately, it is also a quite Herculean endeavour. Malthus claims that the desire to consume is a feeble thing when left to its own devices: 'Instead of being always ready to second the physical powers of man, [wants] require for their developement, "all appliances and means to boot"' (470). For Malthus the desire to consume must somehow be propped up by society, consciously encouraged, and not allowed to fall back into a state of ineffectual weakness.

Malthus never clearly states exactly how these societal incentives are to work;[9] however, he does give us a tantalizing hint earlier in his analysis, when he defends the supposed indolence of the Irish peasant by noting that 'in the state of society in which he has been placed, he has not had a fair trial; he has not been subjected to the ordinary stimulants which produce industrious habits' (396). Apparently one's 'state of society' plays a crucial role in stimulating one's habits and, presumably, one's appetites as well – yet Malthus remains disappointingly silent about how this process works. What is more important for Malthus is the conviction that, far from being a natural quality of humankind, the desire for material objects is a product of capitalist economic organization. This conviction of the very real problem of creating and sustaining consumer demand leads Malthus to a direct attack on Say's Law and on the staunch faith in the operation of demand that underpins Ricardian economics: 'This doctrine [of M. Say] ... appears to me to be utterly unfounded, and completely to contradict the great principles which regulate supply and demand' (353).

Malthus's rejection of Say's Law and warnings against underconsumption and general gluts were the fodder for his fabled disagreement with Ricardo. Conveniently enough for historians of economic thought, the two men were close friends who debated many of the crucial questions of political economy in a correspondence lasting several decades. Their overt, and marked, disagreements form a neat heuristic framework from which to consider the tension between the optimistic and pessimistic strains of economic thought throughout the rest of the century. There is a voluminous critical literature on this debate; modern historians of economic thought have continued the battle on the plane of exegesis – which version of Say's Law was each writer advocating, which one holds true for the long term, which is only applicable to barter economies? While analyses still differ to this day (see note 2 to this chapter for a brief discussion of the recent literature), what is important for my purposes are the interpretations that Ricardo and Malthus themselves favoured – and their logical implications. The crucial point for Malthus is that general gluts and stagnation are a real danger, given the fact that landowners and other holders of wealth can withdraw their income from the economic system and thus reduce the aggregate consumption capacity. While a debate still continues among historians over whether or not Malthus believed that savings always equals investment,[10] my contention is that this exegetical question does not affect the larger conclusion that Malthus reached regarding the inevitability of gluts. If savings does not equal investment – that is, if landowners can withdraw their income from the stream and simply hold onto it – then a diminishment of aggregate demand will obviously ensue. However, even if all income were invested rather than saved or hoarded, then according to Malthus the increased productive capacity due to this investment would lead to an overproduction of goods. Given these two possibilities, unless consumption increases exogenously (either through stimulated desires for luxurious expenditure or increased foreign trade), then general gluts are not only possible but inevitable.[11]

Malthus's conviction of the improbability of creating new desires for consumption leads to the second corollary of his demand theory of value, one that Christopher Herbert has discussed at some length in his analysis of the concept of 'culture' in Victorian political economy: the persistent anxiety that there may be a cataclysmic failure of consumer demand (Herbert 105–28). It is not only the capitalists who lack a sufficiently robust consumptive desire to ensure the growth of the economy; it is not only the desire to save that leads one to forego the consumption of luxuries. There are, according to Malthus, two fundamental and irreconcilable desires at work in the human breast: the desire to consume and the love of indolence.[12] One of the cardinal errors to which Say, Ricardo, and James Mill are subject, he argues, is 'the not taking into consideration the influence of so general and important a principle in human nature, as indolence or the love of ease'; political economy must not assume that 'luxuries are always preferred to indolence' (358). What is so striking about this warning, as Herbert points out, is the fact that it proposes that the insipidity of consumer demand, its lack of intensity in the face of a greater inertia, is every bit as fundamental a principle as the desire for luxuries – if not more so.[13]

For Malthus, one is either working too hard to consume the products of one's labour, or too fundamentally lazy to procure objects to consume. In defining his position against that of Adam Smith, who had claimed that the desire of consumers for luxury and ornament 'seems to have no limit or certain boundary,'[14] Malthus demurs: 'That it had no limit must be allowed to be too strong an expression, when we consider how it will be practically limited by the countervailing luxury of indolence, or by the general desire of mankind to better their condition, and make a provision for a family' (468). The two possible causes of a catastrophic failure of demand, a propensity to save and a tendency toward laziness (i.e., a too-feeble desire to consume), are inextricably intertwined in Malthus's analysis.

Malthus marks the effective interchangeability of these two tendencies in an example illustrating the possible causes of a decline in demand for decorative trimmings. In the first case, a farmer who has discovered that he can obtain the necessaries of life without undue toil, and his 'tastes for ribands, lace and velvet not being fully formed' (note the naturalizing language here), will tend to 'indulge himself in indolence,' causing the manufacturer of these items likewise to slack off on production (358–9). In the second scenario, where a love of parsimony is the problem being considered, the farmer, 'disposed to save with a view of bettering [his] condition, and providing for [his] families in the future' (363), will decide to wear simpler clothing and thus cause a chain reaction throughout the economy – which will, presumably, eventually lead to stagnation. It makes no difference that one of these causes of underconsumption is ostensibly noble while one is a cardinal sin: for Malthus, the operation of the capitalist economy depends on a great desire to consume, and anything that interferes with that desire is inherently problematic.

For Malthus, these potential causes of underconsumption haunt his account of the 'progress of wealth' like fraternal twin ghosts. At the same time, the failure of other economists to recognize their danger leads to a fatal misunderstanding of the way both the economy and economic models work. The misrecognition of both the feebleness of human demand and the dangers of parsimony generates the fundamental error upon which classical political economy has rested: it is 'to found a doctrine upon the unlimited desire of mankind to consume; then to suppose this desire limited in order to save capital, and thus completely alter the premises; and yet still to maintain that the doctrine is true' (468–9). Malthus himself makes no such mistake; he dispassionately declares both that 'great powers of production' cannot be possible without 'great powers of consumption' (481) and, simultaneously, that the consumer taste necessary to ensure such great consumption is 'a plant of slow growth' (359) which is perpetually in danger of dying.

The strong streak of pessimism in Malthus's work can thus be attributed to his conviction of human beings' innate laziness, insipid desires, and perverse desire to hoard. In fact, it is a striking feature of Victorian criticisms of Say's Law generally, from Malthus and his evangelical popularizer Thomas Chalmers,[15] through to Ruskin at mid-century, that they are so pessimistic: it seems that to invoke the notion of demand is to imagine its failure. As James Clark Sherburne notes, 'In the history of economics, there is a close connection between a tendency to think in physiocratic or organic modes and a willingness to recognize the danger of crises due to a disproportion between production and consumption' (130). On one level, this has a certain contrapuntal logic. Because the supply-side theorists, from Adam Smith through John Stuart Mill, who adhered to the labour theory of value and the promise of Say's Law, are necessarily sanguine about the operations of consumer demand (it is only by essentially dismissing the possibility of underconsumption that one can ignore the role of demand in the determination of value) the critics of the labour theory are left to sound the warning about the possibility of a failure of demand. Thus, a pessimistic view of the demand function, the consequent possibility of economic failure from overaccumulation and general gluts, and a mistrust of laissez-faire are the legacy of critics of the labour theory of value throughout the first half of the century.

Writing at mid-century, Ruskin followed Malthus in worrying that excess accumulation would lead to dire economic consequences. As Gallagher notes, 'Ruskin's critique of political economy resembles that of the early Malthus in provisionally accepting the premise of the labor theory of value while rejecting its normal implications' (*Body* 89).[16] While I would argue that even the phrase 'provisionally accepting' is too strong a description for Ruskin's attitude toward the labour theory of value, I certainly agree that Ruskin follows Malthus in his critique of the usual concomitants of that theory – most notably, laissez-faire economic policy. Of course, Malthus's criticisms of laissez-faire were muted and limited, while – as is widely acknowledged in modern criticism and is obvious from even a cursory examination of his economic writings – Ruskin is a sharp critic of laissez-faire.[17] Ruskin's critiques focus particularly on the doctrine of self-regulating supply and demand that underpinned the classicals' advocacy of minimal intervention. As he himself declares in *Munera Pulveris*, the law of supply and demand is 'false always, and everywhere'; and furthermore, 'wise economy, political or domestic, consists in the resolved maintenance of a given relation between supply and demand, other than the instinctive, or (directly) natural one' (*Works* 17:136–7). One can hardly be more directly or outspokenly opposed to laissez-faire than this.[18] As modern historian Willie Henderson notes, 'If Mill thought that "every departure from laissez-faire, unless required by some great good, is a certain evil" (Mill, *Principles*, p. 950), Ruskin effectively started from the opposite understanding' (Henderson 40).

Ruskin's scepticism about the self-regulating capacity of the capital-

ist economy extends to include the 'natural' process of capital accumulation as well. He is much more concerned to delineate the proper
ends of economic growth than the means of achieving it. For Ruskin,
the concept of value is more than just a matter of ascertaining the de-
terminants of market price. An object has intrinsic value insofar as it
is capable of sustaining and enriching life (absolutely regardless of its
owner's appreciation of that capability), whereas effectual value describes the combination of an object's intrinsic value and the 'accept-
ant capacity' of its owner – his or her ability to appreciate the object's
worth (*Works* 17:154). (A flute has great effectual value for a flautist, but
almost none for someone who does not know how to play.) His system
of economics, as outlined in *Munera Pulveris*, is much more a prescriptive than a traditionally descriptive one, as he himself acknowledges:
'Political economy is neither an art nor a science; but a system of conduct and legislature ... The study which lately in England has been
called Political Economy is in reality nothing more than the investigation of some accidental phenomena of modern commercial operations'
(*Works* 17:147).

This is a sentiment Ruskin returns to over and over again throughout
his writings: 'That wages *are* determined by supply and demand is no
proof that under any circumstances they must be – still less that under
all circumstances they ought to be' (*Works* 17:516); 'the economy I have
taught, in opposition to the popular view, is the science which not merely
ascertains the relations of existing demand and supply, but determines
what *ought* to be demanded and what can be supplied' (*Works* 17:522);
and in a letter to the editor of the *Scotsman*: '[Professor Hodgson] ven-
tures (he says) to suggest that possibly I with others "believe that economists confused existing demand with wise and beneficial demand,
and existing supply with wise and beneficial supply." I do believe this.
I have written all my books on political economy in such belief' (*Works*
17:504). This is not only a moral question for Ruskin (although it is, of
course, first and foremost exactly that); it is also a disciplinary question,
a bold and iconoclastic claim about what the new science of political
economy ought to take as its premier task: 'There may be all manner of
demands, all manner of supplies. The true political economist regulates
these; the false political economist leaves them to be regulated by (not
Divine) Providence' (*Works* 17:522–3). For Ruskin – as indeed for his
contemporaries on both sides of the debate – the question of supply
and demand (Say's Law) is inextricably intertwined with the question
of economic intervention (laissez-faire policy).

Ruskin has little interest in describing, or even investigating, the commercial operations of the capitalist economy. He is so far from interested in discussing the process of capital accumulation that he even asserts, in *Unto This Last*, that 'capital which produces nothing but capital is only root producing root; bulb issuing in bulb, never in tulip; seed issuing in seed, never in bread' (*Works* 17:98). Yet this aversion manifests itself not merely in an avoidance of the topic of surplus capital; Ruskin actively attacks the very heart of Say's Law when he warns against the possibility of excessive accumulation (for laissez-faire advocates, savings are by definition equal to investment). In the image of the hoarding miser I examined in the introduction, Ruskin likens the capitalist who accumulates wealth to a prostitute, a dangerously transgressive figure and subverter of public mores. For Ruskin, the real danger is not that capital will not accumulate quickly enough, or in large enough quantities, as is the concern for many of his contemporaries, but rather that it will accumulate to the point of stagnation – and ethical iniquity. In The Guild of St George Master's Report of 1879, for example, Ruskin worries that 'in the practical world this restoring the equilibrium [between capital accumulation and demand for labour] is not so easy; for instance, the iron manufacturers of the United States, deceived by the demand for iron six years ago, built new furnaces, and hired thousands of men, and invested thousands of dollars, but the expectations have not been realised, the demand has fallen off, the works are shut up – and what of the poor workmen?' (*Works* 30:25). One of his recent critics comments that Ruskin is so far 'from stressing growth and accumulation that he considers the value of capital to be realized in its "destruction" or "diminution"' (Sherburne 147). Wealth, capital, surplus – all are only good in their proper realization, not in their mere growth: 'all essential production is for the Mouth; and is finally measured by the mouth ... Consumption is the crown of production; and the wealth of a nation is only to be estimated by what it consumes' (*Works* 17:101).

However, proper consumption is not merely a matter of quantity for Ruskin; the questions of production, consumption, and supply were deeply ethical ones for him, as opposed to most of his contemporaries. On the one hand, it was the moral responsibility of manufacturers to inculcate the right kind of demands in their consumers: 'Remember always that your business, as manufacturers, is to form the market, as much as to supply it ... Every preference you have won by gaudiness must have been based on the purchaser's vanity; every demand you have created by novelty has fostered in the consumer a habit of discontent' (*Works* 16:344). On the other hand, Ruskin placed even more responsibility on consumers, requiring them to be attentive to the social effects of their tastes and desires: 'Wise consumption is a far more difficult art than wise production' (*Works* 17:98). According to Ruskin, 'In good English, a person's "demand" signifies, not what he gets, but what he asks for' (*Works* 17:84n). He is at great pains to emphasize that the consumption function is the driving engine of an ethical economic system, and that consumers thus bear responsibility for making good decisions: 'Demand what you deserve, and you shall be supplied with it, for your good. Demand what you do not deserve, and you shall be supplied with something which you have not demanded, and which Nature perceives that you deserve, quite to the contrary of your good' (*Works* 17:424–5). More specifically, the consumer is to avoid demanding products whose manufacture is degrading or harmful to workmen, both morally and aesthetically; as he declaims in *The Stones of Venice*, '[Evil] can be met only by a right understanding, on the part of all classes, of what kinds of labour are good for men, raising them, and making them happy; by a determined sacrifice of such convenience, or beauty, of cheapness as is to be got only by the degradation of the workman; and by equally determined demand for the products and results of healthy and ennobling labour' (*Works* 10:196). As David M. Craig notes in his capacious and rich recent study *John Ruskin and the Ethics of Consumption*, in 'Ruskin's ideal economy consumers would strive to imagine what good things should be made, to what use they should be put, to whom they should be distributed, and what excellences must be developed for individuals to achieve social abundance and individual flourishing ... Ruskin aims to provoke individual consumers to reflect on their choices and to intervene in market exchanges aware of the moral operations of money and their responsibilities to other people and the world around them' (Craig 328, 333).[19]

For Ruskin, the consumption and manufacture of art (including literature) were not exempt from the ethical strictures that would regulate supply and demand in his ideal economy; speaking of an inferior work of art, he observes: 'Why, then, is it *not* immortal? You yourselves, in compliance with whose demand it was done, forgot it the next week ... The reason is that this is base coin – alloyed gold. There *is* gold in it, but also a quantity of brass and lead – wilfully added – to make it fit for the public' (Works 22:357).[20] The public and the artist, the consumer and the manufacturer, collude in the production of inferior and even deleterious goods: both parties are responsible for managing the consumption relation in a way that is healthful for consumer, producer, and workman alike. It is important to remember, however, that for Ruskin this is ultimately a question of consumption: he is, as I noted above, far less interested in parsing practical questions of production-supply balances than he is in imagining the proper (and ethical) role of the consumer. Thus, his rhetoric is always aimed at the demand side of the equation: 'Whatever a class of consumers, entirely unacquainted with the different qualities of the article they are buying, choose to ask for, will be duly supplied to them by the trade. I observe that this beautiful system is gradually extending lower and lower in education; and that children, like grown-up persons, are more and more able to obtain their toys without any reference to what is useful or useless, or right and wrong; but on the great horse-leech's law of "demand and supply"' (*Works* 19:147). While the consumer (or the consumer's parents?) is responsible for managing his own desires and tastes, the manufacturer is implored to inculcate proper desires and tastes, not merely to stop producing inferior products;[21] in other words, the final recourse is to change demands, tastes, and desires. As he insists in *Unto This Last*, the 'final object of political economy ... is to get good method of consumption, and great quantity of consumption: in other words, to use everything, and to use it nobly' (*Works* 17:102).[22]

Ruskin's economic writings, for the most part, puzzled and outraged his contemporary critics. One Victorian review of *Unto This Last* characterized the work as a 'glittering fog' of 'political economy in the clouds,' 'meddl[ing],' and 'nonsense' ('Political Economy in the Clouds' 651, 655, 654). This reviewer sums up by dismissing Ruskin's work thus: 'But more unpardonable still is the ignorance of which we have convicted Mr. Ruskin, ignorance of the very nature and objects of the science, aggravated by the grossest misrepresentations of its most distinguished cultivators' (659). Another anonymous journalist, reviewing the same work, reflects: 'The attack made by Mr. Ruskin on the principles of political economy at once displays not only the weaknesses of his intellect and the utterly unscientific turn of his mind, but also a want of power in seizing upon the real questions at issue between him and his opponents, that is something marvellous in itself' ('Politics, Sociology, and Travels' 530).[23]

Ruskin was deeply pained by the harsh reception of his work. Initially he attempted to counter his critics head-on, entering into a spirited debate with W.R. Greg about the question of luxurious expenditure in the pages of *The Contemporary Review*, for example. In this exchange

Ruskin argued, *contra* Greg – and predictably enough – that the luxurious spending of the rich is not simply beneficial to the economy, but must be considered in light of equitable distribution and exploitation ('Home and Its Economies'). Finally, it seems, the *ad hominem* nature of many of the critiques of Ruskin's work became too much for him to bear; the popular perception of the later Victorians was that he had literally gone mad because of the general rejection of his ideas: 'We are likely to see … from the irritability and exaggeration that may accompany his closing years, and from his mental infirmities, an argument drawn by the dull against the sanity and truth of the teaching of his health and youth' (Stimson 442–3).

Only later in the century did Ruskin's ideas start to gain wider acceptance and credibility, as popular later-century critiques of laissez-faire 'caught up' with his progressive socialism, his insistence on the inseparability of governmental economic policy and ethical humanism, and his writings on effective demand and value. Two American commentators writing in the 1880s, for example, lauded his Christian sympathy, his crusade to make 'a safer and lovelier life for man' (Wilson 243), and his prescient anticipation of the historical school of the 1880s (Stimson 445). In particular, his avant-garde understanding of the possibility of general gluts is singled out – with an aquatic metaphor very similar to those Ruskin employs in *Munera Pulveris*: 'England and America, the great rivals in manufactures, pour cottons and woolens into the world's markets till they are flooded; and between the two sources there is slack water which no amount of push or enterprise can lift in heaps or make active' (Wilson 251–2). In a laudatory book-length study of Ruskin's work, the heterodox economic writer J.A. Hobson admires the heterodox writings of his forbear, claiming that the 'doctrine of the social utility of unlimited saving, the assumptions that industry is limited by capital, and that the demand for commodities is not demand for labour, are successfully exploded by Mr. Ruskin' (*John* 135–6).[24]

This same attempt to trace precursors to late-century heterodox economics occurs with the work of Malthus. As one commentator notes in 1885: 'Malthus and Ricardo were the rival successors of Adam Smith. Ricardo, with his arithmetical methods and his systematic treatment, exercised the more shaping influence upon the course of English political economy, although Malthus was the better economist, the broader thinker, and the more original investigator … Mr. Bonar finds in [historical-school economists] Thornton, Cliffe Leslie, and Walker – and doubtless he would include Sidgwick – the lineal inheritors of Malthus'

(Shaw 211). And as W.S. Jevons wrote in 1879, Malthus had a 'far better comprehension of the true doctrines' represented by then-current economic theory than adherents of the Ricardo-Mill school, by whom he was 'driven out of the field' (*Theory* lvii). The argument against laissez-faire and the reign of Say's Law formed a line of continuity between Malthus, Ruskin, and late-century economics which was clearly visible to later Victorian commentators.

The relationship between the Ricardian and Malthusian strains in political economy has often been characterized, in diachronic terms, as a struggle for ideological dominance throughout the nineteenth century. John Maynard Keynes, writing several decades after the ultimate 'victory' of the demand theorists in the 1870s, characterizes the debate over value in precisely these bellicose terms: 'Ricardo conquered England as completely as the Holy Inquisition conquered Spain' (32). While Keynes does see the debates over value and demand explicitly in terms of a battle for ideological supremacy, he greatly overstates the case for Ricardo's victory: 'Not only was his [Ricardo's] theory accepted by the city, by statesmen and by the academic world. But controversy ceased; the other point of view completely disappeared; it ceased to be discussed. The great puzzle of Effective Demand with which Malthus had wrestled disappeared from the economic literature' (32). In fact, while I am sympathetic in general to Keynes's reading of the ascendency of the Ricardian school (see note 31 to this chapter), the history of Victorian economic thought is far more complicated than this particular quotation allows.

In addition to the more academic writings of Malthus and Ruskin, there were also many anti-Ricardian voices raised in the journal and pamphlet literature that were the popular fora for such debates.[25] As historian Barry Gordon has pointed out, there is a lively opposition to Say's Law and the rule of Ricardianism in the economic press throughout the first half of the century.[26] Contributors to this debate in the periodicals included, in addition to Malthus himself, such writers as David Robinson in *Blackwood's Magazine* and, by the late 1830s, Herman Merivale in the *Edinburgh Review* – that former bulwark of Ricardianism. George Poulett Scrope launched a series of sustained and cogent attacks on Say's Law in the pages of the *Quarterly Review*, and even Thomas DeQuincey, a former staunch Ricardian, began to sound the alarm against hoarding and overaccumulation by the 1840s. DeQuincey is an interesting case, since he most often is described by historians as a devout supporter and close friend of Ricardo and strong advocate for classical political economy and laissez-faire; however, as Josephine McDonagh demonstrates in her study of the author, later in his career he began to turn away from the Ricardian theory of value and to embrace a proto-demand theory based on the effective desire of consumers for goods (McDonagh, *DeQuincey's* 52–4, 60–5).[27] Gallagher also remarks upon the 'impulse' in his economic writings of the 1840s to 'draw out and examine the issue of subjective desire in political economy' (*Body* 30), as does Gordon Bigelow (100–3), while historian Peter Groenewegen is even more adamant about this change of heart, characterizing it as DeQuincey's '*volte face*' ('Thomas' 52).[28] In fact, this shift in DeQuincey's emphasis is part of a larger trend: according to Gordon, the reputation of Ricardo in the periodicals was largely in abeyance by the end of the 1840s ('Criticism' 385). A more precise (and dramatic) date for the end of 'technical' Ricardianism could be given as 1831, the year that Torrens posed to the Political Economy Club the ingenuous question: 'Are any of the principles first advanced [by Ricardo] now acknowledged to be correct?'[29]

An even more important place to look for heirs to Malthus's critique of Ricardo – particularly his adherence to Say's Law – is in the amateur economic writers of the period. While the literary popularizer Harriet Martineau was a staunch and vociferous cheerleader for Ricardian economics,[30] there was another group of non-professional writers who were just as influential in their critiques of Ricardo: the evangelical economists discussed by Hilton in his study *The Age of Atonement*. As Hilton points out, these critiques signal the continuing influence and importance of Ricardian economics; while the posing of Torrens's question in 1831 marks the end of the sway of Ricardianism in such technical economic questions as value, rent, and wages, the far more important question for non-professionals, he maintains, is the question of Say's Law and effective demand.[31] The evangelical writers he analyses keenly felt the need to keep their anti-Ricardian criticism at a high boil.

While there is no need for me to exhaustively retrace an argument so brilliantly elaborated elsewhere, I would like to touch on several points in Hilton's work that are particularly apposite to my analysis. First, he discusses the tension between optimistic and pessimistic strains in political economy, reinscribing them as tensions between different religious ideologies (or, more accurately, between Christian or evangelical economists and their professional, largely secular, counterparts).

Interestingly, however, Hilton uses these terms somewhat differently than I have presented them; he tends to characterize his evangelicals as 'optimistic' even when they are exhibiting attitudes that I have labelled 'pessimistic,' particularly the acknowledgment that underconsumption and gluts are a very real threat to the economy.[32] The reason for this seeming paradox, and one of the central insights of Hilton's book, is that the evangelical writers are never more optimistic than when they are sounding dire warnings about the economy: periodic economic crises had come to seem 'beneficial, timely reminders of the existence of providential government' (125). Furthermore, an essentially liberal-Tory attitude toward failure – that periodic bouts of bankruptcies are beneficial in weeding out the 'false' fortunes amassed during times of bubble credit – was also part of the evangelical ethos, with the added twist that commercial crises were largely seen as instances of special providence, and the repentant bankrupt as 'atoning' for collective commercial sins (131–47).[33]

What is most significant about Hilton's study, for my purposes, is his insistence that the critique of Ricardianism to be found in evangelical writings represents the 'underlying attitudes and assumptions of the period' (6) – a supplement to the 'official mind' that I would characterize as the economic unconscious of mid-century England: a substratum of anxiety about economic operations – especially saving, credit, and the gold standard – that we so often see developed in the themes and plots of Victorian novels. As one Victorian commentator writing at the end of the century characterizes the operations of economic 'oppression,' 'The new economy is not a system evolved from the brains of a few men intoxicated with impossible ideals. It is rather the outcome of thoughts which business men themselves have barely suppressed, and which the economist now insists on dragging to expression' (Smart 289).

For Hilton, the genesis of these underlying attitudes is squarely located in the writings of Malthus, whose *Essay on Population* he characterizes, following G.M. Young, as one of the two 'classic texts' of his Age of Atonement.[34] For Hilton, Malthus embodies that strain of clerical writing that evinced a belief in a '*natural* (and therefore limited) rate of economic growth, based on a *natural* or effective level of consumer demand'; economic change was 'seen as cyclical rather than linear-progressive' (67, emphases Hilton's). It was the Reverend Thomas Chalmers, Malthus's great popularizer, who 'transform[ed] Malthus's long-run stagnation thesis into an explanation of business cycles' (119)

by conceiving of these cycles as 'fluctuations' caused by sin, which fluctuations encouraged further sin – the only relief from which is through
Christian faith (119–20). One of Hilton's most helpful insights is his
claim that Victorian analysts' attempts to understand periodic commercial crises focused on 'two quite different types of explanation ...
monetary mismanagement by government or Bank of England, and
human avarice and ambition' (125), in other words, the problem of the
gold standard and the great 'sin' of speculation, themes which were
of grave importance not only to Victorian economists, but to Victorian
novelists as well.

3   Herbert Spencer's Laissez-Faire Case Study; or, Gold as a Standard of Value

As we have just seen, the simple formulation of the economic-growth
question is that Victorian economists were divided neatly into two
camps: the Ricardian supply-side theorists, who advocated unlimited
capital accumulation, and those, like Malthus, Ruskin, and the evangelical economists, who warned against the dangers of excess accumulation and hoarding. Yet even among those laissez-faire theorists who
advocate strong capital growth, there is still a real and marked anxiety
about the possible effects of unlimited accumulation. This undercur-
rent of uncertainty is perfectly summarized by Ricardo's account of
stagnation illustrated by the notorious 'corn model.' It is his paradoxical adherence to this model of ultimate stagnation that undermines the
optimism of laissez-faire; this paradox was – and is – widely remarked
upon in political economy. As one recent critic has pointed out, 'For
most nineteenth-century commentators, and the great majority of later
ones, it has been common knowledge that Ricardo ... envisaged a de-
clining general rate of profit' due to capital accumulation and diminishing returns in agriculture (Peach, *Interpreting* 6).

According to the trajectory of this theory – whose beginning-middle-
and-end structure inspired my appellation 'narrative' of capitalism – a
young economy enjoys, at the outset, a high profit rate and thus a high
rate of capital accumulation; then, as wage rates rise, population increases, thereby increasing the need for corn and bringing more land
under cultivation.[35] The margin on corn is thus pushed down (due to
diminishing returns), leading to rising rents and falling profits; this
process continues until profits are close to zero and capital accumulation ceases. As profits approach zero in agriculture, capital is shifted to

manufacturing; in long-run equilibrium, however, profits must be the same throughout the economy (or resources would shift to the higher-profit sectors), so eventually, profits approach zero throughout the economy.[36] This result is also, perhaps somewhat confusingly, referred to as the 'stationary state' – thus both the laissez-faire classicals and their demand theory critics ultimately arrive at the same pessimistic conclusion, albeit by different routes.

As should be fairly obvious, Ricardo's theory is irreconcilable with the unbridled optimism of Say's Law.[37] It is not my concern here to trace the prodigious amount of recent critical commentary devoted to the contradictions of Ricardo's theory;[38] I am more interested in understanding how this contradiction was elaborated in the work of his Victorian heirs – economists and novelists alike. Having established that the concern with excess accumulation was one shared by Ricardians as well as their critics, I would like to suggest that this anxiety about economic surplus is inextricably intertwined, for these theorists, with an anxiety about the monetary surplus created by the operations of the credit economy. This particular type of surplus is a characteristic of economies which engage in anything beyond one-to-one barter trade: when objects are traded for a medium of value, or 'promises-to-pay,' instead of directly for each other, and money is used as a store of value, a pool of surplus value or float is created which represents the value of all outstanding debts which have not yet been collected.[39] This pool is 'surplus' because it is in a sense created value: in a complex credit economy, it is impossible for all outstanding memoranda of debt to be liquidated simultaneously, since some memoranda of debt are dependent upon others being collected, and so on, in a complex and interdependent chain. (This interdependence explains how collapses of banking economies are possible, when a large number of depositors make a 'run' on a bank simultaneously, demanding the cashing of certificates of promise.) The understanding of the operations of this kind of credit economy is simultaneous with the rise of the classical school. The eighteenth-century physiocrats had emphasized the circularity of economic operations, their organic and self-contained nature; only with the classical economists do we see an economic model which describes the ballooning of the economy through surplus, accumulations of capital, and credit.

Because of this new realization of the instability and delicacy of the credit economy, there is a new, concomitant obsession with the gold standard. The fascination of the Victorians with the gold standard cannot be overstated. Heated debates over the issue raged in the popular periodicals of the day; Parliament spent untoward amounts of time arguing the merits of various monetary-standard policies; and, of course, the spectre of gold haunted the pages of the Victorian novel. A proper understanding of the representational function of the gold standard could even stand in, at times, for other kinds of knowledge, comprehension, and moral rectitude. George Eliot thus describes Tertius Lydgate toward the beginning of *Middlemarch*:

> A liberal education had of course left him free to read the indecent passages in the school classics, but beyond a general sense of secrecy and obscenity in connection with his internal structure, had left his imagination quite unbiassed, so that for anything he knew his brains lay in small bags at his temples, and he had no more thought of representing to himself how his blood circulated than how paper served instead of gold. (135)

Both circulatory processes are opaque to the ignorant and uncaring young man; the inability to understand monetary representation (apparently a fault that Lydgate never remedies, even as he redresses the former) is part and parcel of a more general characterological flaw.

As the rest of this chapter argues, the intensive Victorian debates over the gold standard functioned as a sort of public reaction-formation, an attempt to resolve both the epistemological uncertainties of the credit economy and the tension between the self-regulating and stagnation models of nineteenth-century economics. The gold standard became a bedrock principle for proponents of laissez-faire economic policy; as one modern commentator has noted, the vast majority of Victorian economists tended to 'defer to [the gold] standard as the major linchpin of a self-adjusting competitive economy' (Sherburne 142).

Many advocates of the gold standard, of course, believed that gold had inherent, 'natural' value; if promises-to-pay could be matched up, one-to-one, with a particular amount of gold, then the uncertainties of the credit economy would be resolved.[40] The credit economy, in effect, would be operating much like a complex barter economy, with traders exchanging items of real worth instead of mere certificates or memoranda of debt.[41] (In fact, J.S. Mill insists on this very equivalence when he claims that 'the relations of commodities to one another remain unaltered by money' [3:507] – money meaning gold, of course.) In order to demonstrate the real force of this argument, and the full extent of laissez-faire theorists' obsession with the gold standard, I will examine more closely one Victorian writer's polemical distinction between credit and barter economies.

> Given a nation made up of liars and thieves, and all trade among its members must be carried on either by barter or by a currency of intrinsic value: nothing in the shape of promises-to-pay can pass in place of actual payments; for, by the hypothesis, such promises being never fulfilled, will not be taken. On the other hand, given a nation of perfectly honest men ... and nearly all trade among its members may be carried on by memoranda of debts and claims, eventually written off against one another in the books of bankers.[42]

In his 1858 article on the monetary system and paper currency, 'State-Tamperings with Money and Banks,' Spencer begins an analysis of the current state of affairs with an appeal to the two ideal, yet radically opposed, economic systems of barter and credit. In the first example, a nation made up entirely of liars and thieves, all exchange must take place either by barter or through a currency with 'intrinsic value' (e.g., gold or gold coin), for naturally no rational person would accept promises-to-pay from his or her neighbour under such circumstances. In a nation of people of absolute integrity, on the other hand, trade may be carried out almost entirely through 'memoranda of debts and claims, eventually written off against one another in the books of bankers,' in other words, entirely through a currency of promise and credit. These two ideal systems are introduced in the interest of contrasting them with, and thus contextualizing, the present, actual system of economic exchange, a mixed system with a currency partly of credit (bank notes and promises-to-pay) and partly of intrinsic value (gold itself).

These two opposed limit cases are 'ideal' for two reasons: first, in the narrowest sense of the word, because they do not and cannot exist in their pure forms in the real world; second, because they are both in some sense preferable to the contingencies and difficulties of the actual mixed system. While they are presented as utopian and dystopian extremes, the terms in which Spencer describes them in fact delineate them as two alternative utopias: their very simplicity in explanation, the tiny amount of space they occupy in his explanatory framework (one paragraph in twenty-one pages), bespeak their self-sufficiency, their self-regulating capability – the highest good, of course, in Spencer's laissez-faire universe. What makes them ideal in this sense, Spencer implies, is their epistemological transparency: in each instance, individual economic actors know with absolute certainty the terms of potential transactions in which they may engage. Responses are always perfectly appropriate; there is no element of doubt and, hence, no risk. (This is opposed to the uncertainties and dangers of the mixed system, where 'daily experience,' 'personal experiment,' and 'current opinion' must substitute for the a priori understanding of the pure economies.)

Spencer's descriptive language underscores the simplicity of these ideal states; the two systems are sketched out quickly, in absolute terms, in order to provide contrast to the problems of the mixed economy Spencer wishes to discuss later: in the first system, we learn, 'promises being *never* fulfilled, will not be taken'; in the second, that 'paper will pass current for *whatever* it represents' (emphases added). Spencer frames his description of the two systems with markers of their naturalness, their purity, their absolute transparency: 'These are truisms' he claims at the beginning; at the end, they are 'self-evident truths.' The nation of rogues and scoundrels, far from yielding an impossible, undesirable, or even unmanageable economic system, in fact generates an economy of the greatest simplicity and ease.

Yet this reading misses an even stronger sense in which the all-barter economy is marked as the ideal in Spencer's analysis. His descriptions of the two opposed economies are not parallel; they are not both absolutely pure and self-regulating. In fact, the seemingly utopian system of pure credit, Spencer implies, must depend upon the ability of creditors to liquidate claims if called upon to do so. The full description is worth repeating here:

> Given a nation of perfectly honest men ... nearly all trade among its members may be carried on by memoranda of debts and claims, eventually written off against one another in the books of bankers; seeing that as, by the hypothesis, no man will ever issue more memoranda of debts than his goods and his claims will liquidate, his paper will pass current for whatever it represents. *Coin will be needed only as a measure of value* ... (emphasis added)

This description breaks down fairly neatly around the semicolon in the first sentence. While the first half of this statement preserves the sense of a pure credit economy in which all debts and claims eventually will be balanced against one another without the necessity of translating them into tangible goods or an intervening currency of intrinsic value, the second part of the description betrays the fact that Spencer cannot imagine a pure credit economy without the mediation of a standard of value in the form of precious-metal money. The balance of claims in the books of bankers is initially imagined as completely self-contained and without necessary reference to an outside standard, yet Spencer's almost off-hand appeal to coin as a 'measure of value' betrays the fact that he, along with most of his contemporaries, cannot envision a system where monetary value is purely conventional.[43] The very casualness with which Spencer troubles the purity of his description of the ideal credit economy indicates the depth and tenacity of Victorian assumptions about monetary standards. Just as his 'self-evident truths' and 'truisms' marked those claims that he felt would go unquestioned by his readers, so this unapologetic undermining of his own ideal limit case through an invocation of coin indicates the extent to which such an appeal would appeal.

This reference to a 'measure of value' is a safeguard against the threat of infinite regress that a pure credit economy would represent: Spencer and his contemporaries feared that where claim is balanced only against claim, value would become radically unstable; there would be no way to know the worth of a memorandum of debt or promise-to-pay without imagining its value in gold or some other intrinsically valuable medium of exchange.[44] Since paper currency and memoranda of debts are, in common parlance, mere promises-to-pay, the economic transaction is complete only upon exchange of items of 'real' value: 'All bank-notes, cheques, bills of exchange, etc., are so many *memoranda of claims*. No matter what may be the technical distinctions among them, on which upholders of the "currency principle" seek to establish their dogma, they all come within this definition' (329, emphasis in original). The tendency, therefore, in Spencer's analysis and elsewhere, is always toward 'liquidation,' the stabilization and naturalization of debt through translation into goods or gold: 'Under the ordinary state of things, the amount of available wealth in the hands, or at the command, of those concerned, suffices to meet these claims as they are severally presented for payment; and they are paid either by equivalents of intrinsic value, as coin, or by giving in place of them other memoranda of claims on some body of undoubted solvency' (329). While Spencer attempts to envision a radical limit case, an economy of pure credit, he cannot entirely escape the notion that a standard must be in place in order to guard against the instability of claims translating merely into other claims.

In other words, the concept of credit is inextricable from the concept of an intrinsically valuable medium of exchange; the introduction of the promise-to-pay, with its threat of indeterminate and unstable value, necessitates the introduction of a fixed standard. The value of paper money (the most important form of promises-to-pay) is thus imagined as entirely dependent upon its ultimate (or rather perceived) translatability into goods or gold, even in an ideal and seemingly pure economy of credit. While Spencer's two ideal economies are presented as pure and radically opposed limit cases, it is in fact impossible for Spencer to imagine a credit economy that is not bolstered by a standard of value such as coin would represent. The pure economy of credit is everywhere invaded and adulterated by its opposite.[45]

Spencer's analysis moves directly from this initial opposition, that of pure barter and pure credit economies, to a description of the actual mixed system currently in place. Yet the utopian impulse does not die here, but continues in an altered form: for Spencer's purpose in this analysis is to argue for a 'natural,' balanced state in which the government does not tamper with economic forces but allows them to regulate themselves. Given this state of non-interference, Spencer argues, the proportion of paper money to coin will maintain a 'natural balance' based on 'moral causes,' both relatively permanent (the level of honesty of one's fellow citizens) and temporary (variations in the quantity of available capital) (327–8). The ostensible purpose of Spencer's article being to refute the popular prejudice against promises-to-pay, he is at great pains to demonstrate that such promises are beneficial and natural, and will eventually be liquidated without government interference:

These expansions of paper-circulation which naturally take place in times of impoverishment or commercial difficulty, are highly salutary. This issuing of securities for future payment when there does not exist the wherewith for immediate payment, is a means of mitigating national disasters. The process amounts to a postponement of trading-engagements which cannot at once be met. (331)

In other words, as Spencer goes on to claim, the free circulation of promises-to-pay prevents unnecessary bankruptcies by allowing those in temporary financial difficulty enough time to liquidate the claims against them (i.e., the creation of a monetary value or float is beneficial to the operations of the growing economy).[46] He addresses the seeming contradiction between free circulation of promises-to-pay and an insistence upon specie convertibility elsewhere: 'That the state should compel every one who has given promises-to-pay, be he merchant, private banker, or shareholder in a joint-stock bank, duly to discharge the responsibilities he has incurred, is very true. To do this, however, is merely to maintain men's rights – to administer justice; and therefore comes within the state's normal function' (*Social Statics* 434).

Yet it is not the mere passage of time that is to perform this 'natural' liquidation of debts, as Spencer argues. Instead, it is the magical process of capital accumulation:

> If [those who cannot meet their claims] are permitted to avail themselves of that credit which their fellow-citizens willingly give them on the strength of their proffered securities, most of them will tide over their difficulties; and in virtue of *that accumulation of surplus capital ever going on*, they will be able, by-and-by, to liquidate their debts in full. ('State-Tamperings' 331–2, emphasis added)

The two types of surplus I have already delineated – economic and monetary – are thus seen as entirely dependent upon each other and as inseparable components of the burgeoning capitalist economy. Monetary surplus through float is created and enabled by economic surplus or capital accumulation, and vice versa. The supposedly natural process of capital accumulation and the supposedly natural operations of specie convertibility are thus mutually dependent and constitutive.

Given the fact that the entire burden of Spencer's argument rests on his ability to convince the reader that the extension of promises-to-pay to those in financial straits will not do irreparable harm to the country's economy, that it will in fact balance itself out through 'natural' processes not requiring state intervention, his description of these processes – 'that accumulation of surplus capital ever going on,' 'they will be able, by-and-by, to liquidate their debts' – is rather stunningly glib. Just as we saw with the gold standard above, only the fact that Spencer is making an appeal to a background assumption, a cultural belief so widely shared as that of the inexorable and ubiquitous process of capital formation, could justify such an off-hand comment at the crux of his analysis. For it is, it bears repeating, the crux: in order for Spencer to convince his audience that the circulation of promises-to-pay is, in his favourite term, 'self-adjusting,' he must explain how these promises are to be liquidated. The very heart of his argument is this curious assertion that surplus capital is continuously and unproblematically accumulating, when this assumption should be one of the most closely examined and argued in his analysis.

Thus, Spencer's argument about the current economic system being able to function in a 'natural' condition without state tampering is founded upon two crucial, widely held, and therefore invisible, assumptions: that there be a standard of value in the form of a precious-metal currency, and that the accumulation of surplus be 'ever going on.' Both of these assumptions, in the logic of Spencer's argument, are the necessary by-products of a radical epistemological uncertainty about the intentions of one's fellow-citizens, and thus can be traced back to the rhetorical moment when Spencer abandons his utopian economies to deal with the contingencies of the mixed system. It is the very necessity of these two facts that marks the present economy as post-lapsarian, and it is the same impulse to render them invisible that attempts to forge a new kind of utopia out of the present system: the impulse to argue for the self-regulatory capability of industrial capitalism in a 'natural' state.

Yet as we have already seen, this rhetorical break does not in fact occur between the two ideal economies and the actual mixed system, but rather between the pure barter economy and any economy in which credit is a part. While Spencer distinguishes sharply between pure barter and credit economies on the one hand and mixed economies on the other, the epistemological transparency of the utopian ideal is lost, not at the point of uncertainty about others' intentions, but at the point where one type of currency (paper money, promises-to-pay) comes to stand in a relation of value to another (precious metal, goods). Even the seemingly ideal economy – a nation of complete honesty – is dependent, in Spencer's analysis, upon a standard of value into which other kinds of currency can be translated, and it is this representative relation that renders economic exchange opaque. It is the act of representation, of translation from one medium to another, which necessitates those mechanisms – constantly accumulating surplus capital, a fixed standard of value – that trouble the self-regulating purity of Spencer's 'natural' economy.

Thus the foundational opposition in Spencer's argument is not that between the pure economies and the mixed economy, but that between barter economies and credit economies. It is the extension of credit, the deferral of payment, the suspension of stable one-to-one exchange, which is both enabled by and necessitates a standard of value, and which is both enabled by and necessitates the accumulation of surplus capital.[47] The anxiety about surpluses of value, created through the overzealous issue of promises-to-pay (either by banks or by private citizens), haunts the account of laissez-faire capitalism just as anxiety about surpluses of capital and goods haunts their heterodox critics.

That said, it must be acknowledged that a general preoccupation with the gold standard is not the legacy of laissez-faire theorists alone. Speculation and the question of the monetary standard – and more largely, the question of credit – are inextricably connected in the Victorian economic mind. Many contemporary writers noticed that the period when England was off the gold standard (1797–1821) was a time of unprecedented growth, investment, and fortune-making.[48] Even after the legislation of the gold standard in 1816 and its implementation in 1821, the cycles of quiescence – investment – mania – crash which seemed to be happening every ten years (with crashes in 1825–6, 1837, 1847, 1857, and 1866) kept the question of credit, value, and 'real money' constantly in the forefront of public consciousness. It was, as several modern commentators have noted, the unstable and vulnerable nature of the credit system which precipitated these periodic crises.[49] In turn, speculation, credit, and the monetary standard were also seen as intimately connected to the ubiquitous question of surplus. Not only does speculation (when successful) create great economic surpluses, but great monetary surpluses, often in the form of extended credit, are necessary for mass speculation. Furthermore, investment manias provide an outlet for surplus capital; for example, as E.J. Hobsbawm points out, the Great Railway Mania of 1844–7 provided opportunities for the investment of surplus capital that could not be disposed of previously.[50]

One of the reasons that paper money – along with the promises-to-pay such as memoranda of debt and cheques that the Victorians did not consider 'money' – was so anxiety-provoking was, of course, the fact that the economy of nineteenth-century England was locked into this cyclical mania-crash pattern that periodically wiped out fortunes based on credit and (what we would term) leveraged investment. Because of these periodic collapses of credit, there was a real crisis of representation regarding the gold standard and paper issues.[51] The 1819 decision to legally implement the gold standard in 1816 by no means ended the debates; there were periodic challenges to the gold standard – the first of which, in the 1840s, Sir Robert Peel made it his personal crusade to fend off[52] – and the debates between the Banking School and the Currency School continued throughout the decades following the resumption of convertibility.[53] As one recent commentator points out, there was 'considerable continuity between these later debates and the bullionist controversy' of 1797–1819 (Laidler 70). Of course it was Ricardo himself who had been one of the main proponents of the Bullionist position.[54]

The Victorians thus grappled with the question of what was 'real' money or value in a complex credit economy where it is impossible for all outstanding memoranda of debt to be liquidated simultaneously. The understanding that this kind of economic organization is ultimately founded on the credulity, trust, and patience of its members is one of the many factors which, ironically, led to these periodic crises: 'ironically' because without a widespread belief that the delicate infrastructure of the economy will sustain itself, that a promise-to-pay will remain good into the future, the infrastructure is doomed to fail. One of the most poignant examples of this psychological dimension is the famous incident in 1825 wherein a run on the Bank of England was stopped by the miraculous discovery of a box of 700,000 one-pound notes in the bank's cellar – notes in which the public still reposed confidence, presumably, because of the recent return to specie convertibility.[55]

The Victorian difficulty with the monetary standard extends beyond the circle of strict laissez-faire economists to include not only the investing public, but even such heterodox iconoclasts as Ruskin. Ruskin, for all his vehement protest against laissez-faire, is far from free of an obsession with monetary standards. On the surface, he does differ significantly from mainstream theorists in that he ostensibly has a 'nonchalant attitude' toward the gold standard (Sherburne 140). According to Ruskin's own protestations in *Munera Pulveris*,

> The use of substances of intrinsic value as the materials of a currency, is a barbarism – a remnant of the conditions of barter, which alone render commerce possible among savage nations. It is, however, still necessary, partly as a mechanical check on arbitrary issues. (*Works* 17:159)

This sentiment is a nearly word-for-word repetition of a passage in *Unto This Last*:

> The use of objects of real or supposed value for currency, as gold, jewellery, etc., is barbarous; and it always expresses either the measure of the distrust in the society of its own government, or the proportion of distrustful or barbarous nations with whom it has to deal ... Intercourse with foreign nations must, indeed, for ages yet to come, at the world's present rate of progress, be carried on by valuable currencies; but such transactions are

nothing more than forms of barter. The gold used at present as a currency is not, in point of fact, currency at all, but the real property which the currency gives claim to, stamped to measure its quantity, and mingling with the real currency occasionally by barter. (*Works* 16:186–7)

In a footnote appended to the term 'real property' above, he clarifies: 'Or rather, equivalent to such real property, because everybody has been accustomed to look upon it as valuable; and therefore everybody is willing to give labour or goods for it' (*Works* 16:187).

Ruskin, then, along with Spencer, aligns the use of materials of so-called intrinsic value with the 'barbarous' conditions of barter. At first he seems to posit that the relatively sophisticated modern capitalist economy requires no such primitive parameters of exchange: it is enough for traders to give promises-to-pay (paper currency) in place of real goods. However, with the off-hand qualifications at the end of both statements ('check on arbitrary issues' in *Munera Pulveris* and 'intercourse with foreign nations' in *Unto This Last*), Ruskin undoes all the work he had done in the preceding bold declarations. The qualification in *Munera Pulveris* is particularly ambivalent: it is, of course, precisely as 'check' that Victorian economists and politicians advocate the gold standard in the first place: the intense anxiety over the one-to-one correspondence of gold to paper was largely due to the fear of such inflationary issues of currency.[56]

Ruskin's curiously conflicted attitude toward the gold standard is exemplified by his – quite bold and progressive – statement in *Munera Pulveris*: 'If all the money in the world, notes and gold, were destroyed in an instant, it would leave the world neither richer nor poorer than it was. But it would leave the individual inhabitants of it in different relations' (*Works* 17:158). This is a relatively unusual view, for a Victorian writer, of the role of currency, and is a direct result of his insistence, throughout his work on both political economy and art, that 'value' denotes 'the strength, or "availing" of anything towards the sustaining of life' (*Works* 17:153). For Ruskin, the question of value is separate from the question of price or cost; an object is valuable insofar as it contributes to 'Life,' meaning 'the happiness and power of the entire human nature, body and soul' (*Works* 17:149). Thus, a painting or book that contributes to human happiness and moral and intellectual growth is more valuable than accumulated riches that cramp and corrupt the nature of their owner. To return to the quotation above, then, what Ruskin is arguing is that value is quite separate from money – currency or gold.

The wealth of the world consists in its store of objects (of this particular kind) of inherent value, while currency is merely a documentary claim on some of those objects. Therefore, were all currency to be destroyed, the world would have neither greater nor less wealth, but the distribution of that wealth would be changed.

What is interesting about this claim, for the purposes of my argument, is the conflicted attitude toward the value of currency that it betrays. On the one hand, it seems to indicate Ruskin's complete freedom from the fetishism of gold that tends to beset his contemporaries: he freely acknowledges that gold has no 'inherent' value – even as universal object of desire – and thus its disappearance would not affect the amount of real wealth in the world. But this statement also, in a Janus-like reversal, indicates Ruskin's denial of the operations of credit in the creation of wealth. It is not the case that the amount of wealth would remain the same were all currency to be destroyed, for a credit economy also creates value through the operations of float (which Mill isolates, against his own protestations, as the property of currency to act as a store of value). Ruskin himself even addresses this issue at one point:

> A sound currency, insofar as it by its increase represents enlarging debt, also represents enlarging means – but in this curious way, that a certain quantity of it marks the deficiency of the wealth of the country from what it would have been if that currency had not existed. (*Works* 17:204–5)

For Ruskin, every promissory note represents wealth that has not yet been created; it stands in for future valuable goods and will cease to exist or be necessary once the object of real value has been transferred in its stead.[57] But in another sense the amount of value 'in the world' has thus been increased by the amount of currency, for while a promissory note may be destroyed after the transaction is completed, currency instead circulates and continues to represent objects of value in other transactions: as long as all holders of memoranda of debt do not attempt to liquidate them simultaneously, a surplus of value continues to operate in the credit economy. (Indeed, it is the very impossibility of that simultaneous liquidation that illustrates the operations of this type of credit.) What Ruskin characterizes as currency's signification of 'deficiency of wealth' is in fact its signification of increase in value.

This failure to account for value creation through credit betrays Ruskin's closeness to the monetary preoccupations of his contemporaries. The same concern with liquidation is present in both Spencer's and Ruskin's accounts; it is the epistemological uncertainty attendant upon credit transactions that demands the translation of currency into objects of real value, and it is the fear of the impossibility of this translation that inaugurates a fixation on gold.[58] This fixation, in Ruskin's case, is betrayed by his inability to imagine a currency system without a check on 'arbitrary issues'; in other words, a currency system that would allow for the creation of surplus value without concern for a perfectly stable one-to-one translation of currency into inherently valuable goods.[59] It is this translation, this correspondence, that is the primary concern of all Victorian writings on the monetary standard. It is an unconscious aversion to creations of surplus.

4 The Reign of Demand: Late-Century Victorian Political Economy

> The new economy is not a system evolved from the brains of a few men intoxicated with impossible ideals. It is rather the outcome of thoughts which business men themselves have barely suppressed, and which the economist now insists on dragging to expression.
>
> (Smart 289)

The problem of surplus, and fears about the possibility of underconsumption, did not simply go away with the rise of the marginal utility school in the 1870s. On the contrary: the corollary to a new insistence on demand as a determinant of value was a greatly increased concern to inculcate and develop new consumer desires. In her recent study of the relationship between the marginal utility school and aesthetics in the late nineteenth century, Regenia Gagnier writes: 'Under marginal utility theory, scarcity was relocated in the human mind itself, as a consequence of the insatiability of human desires ... Thus the idea of needs, which were finite and the focus of political economy, was displaced by the idea of tastes, which were theoretically infinite' (*Insatiability* 4). Theoretically infinite, yes – but as Gagnier herself acknowledges and I will argue further in the final chapter of this book, by no means unproblematic or guaranteed. Gallagher discusses the difficulty that the marginalists had in reconciling their new theory with the idea of continued consumption: 'When one gets used to riches they become merely the neutral ground of existence, and hence it might be expected that the desire to amass more of the same would abate' (*Body* 127). As numerous other critics – including Thomas Richards, Andrew Miller, Jeff

Nunokawa, Rachel Bowlby, Lawrence Birken, and Gordon Bigelow –
have argued, the concern with instilling new tastes and desires and with
catering to the newly crowned consumer became paramount in the
final decades of the Victorian era.[60] As we shall see, there were strong
continuities between Malthusian exhortations to stimulate consumer
desire and late-century concerns about the inculcation of new tastes.

The 1870s and 1880s saw an efflorescence of journal and magazine
articles purporting to explain the new style of economics to the general
reader. As one such popularizer noted in 1870, 'Not for two decades has
there been in England such an awakening in regard to the questions of
industry, trade, pauperism, emigration, and all kindred subjects ... as
within the past year' (Baird 330). As H.S. Foxwell, professor of political
economy at Cambridge (and successor to Jevons's Chair of Economics at University College, London), claimed in 1887, 'The standard of
economic instruction has been raised in a remarkable degree, and the
amount of interest and activity in economic study is greater than at any
previous time in our history' ('Economic' 91–2).

The amateur readers of these popular treatises were learning two separate things. First, that there were actually two revolutions in economic
thought occurring simultaneously. While the marginal utility theorists
were unseating the labour theory of value (which I discuss more fully
below), the 'historical' school of economists was attacking the methodology of classical political economy and claiming that more sociological
and anthropological data-gathering – on the habits and behaviours of
real people – must be done. Heterodox writers like Foxwell and T.E.C.
Leslie, influenced to a certain degree by intellectual developments in
Germany, challenged what they saw as the cold, selfish assumptions of
laissez-faire and the deductive method of Ricardianism and argued for
a radical rethinking of economic method and policy.

This debate was framed as a distinction between inductive and deductive reasoning.[61] Maurice Block, a defender of the tenets of classical
political economy, claimed in 1877 that the schism had become so great
that the discipline could be characterized as two distinct schools (96).
While nearly all writers agreed that the great practitioner of the deductive school was David Ricardo,[62] they argued over who could claim
Adam Smith as their own. Leslie, one of the leading lights of the historical school, characterized Adam Smith as an inductive reasoner par
excellence: 'Adam Smith's historical and inductive mind ... preserved
him from the realistic error' (416). Robert Lowe, however, writing in the
journal *The Nineteenth Century* in 1877, critiqued a recent address to the

British Association by the president of the section of Economic Science and Statistics, which had attacked the assumptions of classical political economy. According to Lowe, the speaker claimed that Adam Smith himself had used the inductive method, which Lowe sees as an unfair appropriation by the new iconoclasts of the grandfather of economics: 'I challenge those who are seeking to make out their case by loading him with praise to which he is not entitled to produce a single instance from the *Wealth of Nations* where Smith has had recourse to the method of induction' (Lowe 865). It is not clear, however, that the imprimatur of Smith was an entirely desirable thing for the followers of the new economics: writers of the German historical school designated – somewhat disparagingly – the deductive method of Ricardo and his followers *Smithianismus.*[63]

Whether tracing the deductive method to Smith or Ricardo, however, the proponents of inductive methodology claimed that the entire history of nineteenth-century economic thought had been founded on an erroneous assumption. Classical political economy had assumed a set of premises predicated on the heuristic ideal of a rational 'economic man,' and then proceeded to generate a model based on these premises:

> A candid reading of the leading works on this subject will produce the conviction that the writers have troubled themselves very little with anthropological investigation ... They have assumed, as the basis of their science, a certain conception of man, and have employed their acuteness in determining what results will follow from the social labors of this assumed being. The premises have not been adequately verified; the system is, in so far, an ideal one, and it is, therefore, a matter of some chance whether its results are correct or not. Economic science has never been based on an adequate anthropological study. ('Unrecognized Forces' 710–11)

As another defender of the historical school pronounced, in somewhat stronger language: 'The disciples of Ricardo may say, These quacks abuse a good method ... To this we reply: the method [deduction] is a vicious one, even when employed by Ricardo himself' ('New Political Economy' 783). Real-world data about the behaviours of real consumers is what is wanted: 'Earnest has been the opposition to the inductive method, its superiority is proved by its fruitfulness, which is too great for any one to dispute' (787). Proponents of the inductive school thought that the success of the method resulted from its uncovering truths of nature: 'We are more hopeful of results from the second line of [economic] development, that which continually aims at the closer approximation to the actual condition of things, by admitting among the data more and more of the causes which co-operate in nature' (Solly 476). The unverified 'truths' of Ricardian premises, and the deductions based on them, must yield to the data found in the real world.

Writers on economics in popular journals were fully aware of the widespread and devastating nature of these attacks on economic orthodoxy. J.E. Cairnes admitted that he was 'unable to recall a single work published within the last twenty years in which principles, more or less fundamental in … the accepted system of political economy, have not been freely brought in question' ('New' 71). But perhaps the most telling indication of the strength of interest in the new inductive methodology in England is the vociferousness of its critics and detractors, most of whom seemed to be American. The debate was lively and heated on both sides of the ocean, and the American defenders of *Smithianismus* fought hard for the golden idols of deduction and 'economic man.' As one observer of the English scene expostulated in defence of 'The English Political Economy,' 'The imperfections alluded to are inseparable from all exact knowledge … The introduction of ideal conditions instead of the real conditions is a necessary first step in any rational system' (Newcomb 295). Edward Caird, writing in the new American periodical *The Quarterly Journal of Economics*, and E.L. Godkin, in *The North American Review*, also wrote strong defences of the classical English school of deduction against the new historical methodology. The former warned quite sternly against the dangers of being swept up in the new economic vogue:

> Those who permit themselves to be carried away by the prevailing tendencies of the present time, and do not thoroughly study the old economical work, as well as the best modern interpreters of it, will never do much good in building up the economy of the future. They will simply be parts of that mob which is always carried away, at every time, by the popular abstraction. (214)

Whether they were in favour of the new inductive, 'historical' school or not, it is clear that commentators in the popular and economic journals of the time could not fail to recognize the intensity and significance of the attacks on the old methodology.

Many of the new historical-school writers saw themselves as explicit heirs to the economic theories of Ruskin, particularly their moral and humanizing character. As historian Willie Henderson notes, William Smart, T.E.C. Leslie, and John Kells Ingram all 'championed the historical approach to economics, with a Ruskinian flavour in the late 1870s' (Henderson 27). Writing in *The Fortnightly Review*, Smart lauded the ethical, 'Ruskinian' turn in economic thought: 'The new economy refuses to consider the labourer as a machine for making wealth. It treats him as a spirit for whom all wealth exists' (288–9). Another economic writer praised Ruskin for 'denounc[ing] the waste and mischief of ill-directed, foolish or depraved consumption' (Devas 30), and demanded an even more stringent application of Ruskinian ideology: 'As a primary consequence of Ruskin's principles on value and wealth, economics must be essentially ethical, the application of the moral law in particular departments of human life' (34).[64]

The second important lesson being communicated to the journal-reading public of the 1870s and 1880s was the theory of marginal utility – or more precisely, the kernel of that theory, that demand determines value. The theory of marginal utility basically states that the satisfaction or benefit (utility) to a consumer of an additional unit of any good is inversely related to the number of units of that good she already has. The value of commodities is no longer seen to be determined by their cost of production, or the cost of labour required to produce them, but instead in terms of consumer desire. The principle was simultaneously 'discovered' by three theorists working independently, W. Stanley Jevons in England, Léon Walras in France, and Carl Menger in Austria.[65] The rise of the marginal utility school was a marked shift both in content (the demand theory of value) and in methodology (the mathematical model).[66] Suddenly, 'economics,' as the study was starting to be called (between the first and second editions of his *Theory of Political Economy*, Jevons changed multiple usages of 'political economy' to 'economics'), became a professional discipline requiring highly specialized knowledge and advanced mathematical skills – no more art critics and housewives penning economic treatises in between other pet projects. As one Victorian commentator complained, when Jevons 'went so far as to demand that his disciples should all be familiar with the differential calculus as an antecedent condition to the comprehension of his transcendentalism, some of us – fairly aghast – gave it up in despair' (Jessopp 619).

The content of the theory, however – the new focus on consumption and consumer enjoyment – was arguably of more immediate, personal interest to amateur followers of economics. As Jevons himself was to write in the second edition of his treatise,

It is surely obvious that Economics does rest upon the laws of human enjoyment ... We labour to produce with the sole object of consuming, and the kinds and amounts of goods produced must be determined with regard to what we want to consume. Every manufacturer knows and feels how closely he must anticipate the tastes and needs of his customers: his whole success depends upon it; and, in like manner, the theory of Economics must begin with a correct theory of consumption. (*Theory* 43)

One of his popular exegetes explains that Jevons extends this insight even further, extrapolating from the concept of consumer enjoyment a new set of economic definitions: 'A *commodity* is defined as any object, action, or service which can afford pleasure or ward off pain; and the word *utility* is used to denote the abstract quality whereby an object becomes entitled to rank as a commodity' (Darwin 244).

The corollary of this new focus on the pleasure of the consumer and the utility of the commodity is the problem of demand. The pressing question of how to chart and quantify consumer demand only intensified as the new economic theory developed. One writer acknowledges the usefulness of Cairnes's discussion of two case studies of change in demand – in the first where demand changes direction and in the second where it increases – and claims that 'had he lived a few years longer, he would doubtless have expounded, with equal lucidity, the third case of the aggregate demand for commodities undergoing decrease' (Solly 480). To invoke demand as a determinant of value is eventually to worry about its demise. As Leslie acknowledges, 'it must surely be evident that we need an investigation, not merely of the motives and impulses which prompt to the acquisition of wealth, but also of those which withdraw men from its pursuit, or give other directions to their energies' (419–20). Part of the new science of economics must be an analysis of what causes – and what undermines – the consumer's demand for commodities.

We are, of course, in Malthusian territory here: one of the most striking characteristics of the rhetoric of marginal utility is the extent to which it replicates and codifies the insights of the earlier economist. Indeed, many of the writers of the new school explicitly recognized this debt. James Bonar, in his 1885 study *Malthus and His Work*, emphasizes the continuity of Malthus's insights with the new economics. One reviewer of his study notes, 'Mr. Bonar shows that Malthus was the veritable precursor of the "new school," which studies human society as it actually exists' (Shaw 211). As William Smart claims in an 1891 essay, 'I think I am justified in saying that a New Economy is being written, and in trying to interpret its general drift. Its first principle is that Political Economy is not the science of Wealth, but the science of Man in relation to Wealth – a proposition originally given by Malthus' (287).[67]

Just as in Malthus we saw the translation of the problem of demand into the question of how to inculcate wants and desires in consumers, so in the 'new economics' we see a similar anxiety about how to induce the public to consume. As Leslie notes, 'Unproductive expenditure and consumption … do not necessarily tend to diminish wealth. They are the ultimate incentives to all production, and without habits of considerable superfluous expenditure … a nation would be reduced to destitution' (418). This is a far cry from the common wisdom even a few years before the rise of the marginal utility school. In an 1868 essay entitled 'The Verdict of Political Economy upon Luxury,' E.S. Talbot had claimed that the tenet of then-recent (classical) political economy denouncing luxurious expenditure had been readily accepted by the public because it was consonant with Christianity (201–2).[68]

Concomitant with the danger of slack spending, of course, is the danger of overproduction and thus stagnation. One commentator – interestingly enough, in the course of an 1885 summation of Ruskin's career – rather histrionically declares:

> One of the greater evils of competition is over-production. No individual or corporation is content with what has been gained or is being gained. Thousands and millions must be added to thousands and millions; and, to this end, loom and hammer are set in motion with multiplied and endless clatter, to produce utilities or futilities out of whatever can be woven or welded. The grand result is that in a short time an amount of goods, or bads, are thrown off, which all the world, including the Congo negroes, cannot consume. (Wilson 251–2)

'Superfluous expenditure' (Leslie 418) is the antidote to superfluous goods. Without significant consumer demand, without a strong public taste for luxurious consumption, the threat of gluts looms large. Yet the producers of goods must simultaneously show restraint, to avoid flooding the world with 'futilities.' In this sense, the Ruskinian emphasis on consumer restraint and self-discipline at mid-century has been recast, by his self-described admirers and heirs, as a call for producers' restraint: 'Consumption is the sole object of production, and the kinds and amounts of the commodities produced must be governed

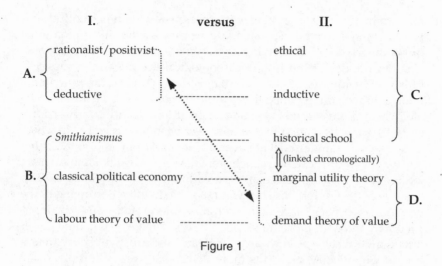

Figure 1

by man's requirements' (Darwin 245). The new economics thus bears a striking similarity to the earlier heterodox writings of both Malthus and Ruskin. In fact, there is a sense in which each of the two new strains develops elements in one of these iconoclastic forbears: the historical school augments and extends Ruskin's emphasis on ethics, sympathy, and charity,[69] while we can trace the marginal utility school's concern with demand (and failures of demand) straight back to Malthus.

So far I have emphasized the radical discontinuity of the 'new economics' and its Ricardian forbears; in fact, the question of whether or not marginal utility represented a decisive break either (diachronically) from classical political economy or (synchronically) from the historical school was a matter of some debate for the Victorian authors themselves – as well as for modern historians of economic thought. In order to simplify my discussion of these various later-century strains and counterstrains, I have included a schematic which places these various philosophical emphases in relation to each other graphically (see figure 1). While the chart itself is necessarily simplistic and reductionist, I hope it will enable the discussion that follows to be clearer and also more nuanced.

In each case the term on the left-hand side of the chart is in opposition to its partner on the right: these oppositions (with the exception of the second from the bottom, which I discuss shortly) are fairly uncontroversial and represent the way both the Victorians and orthodox modern historians conceptualize the tensions within nineteenth-century economic discourse. The standard reading of the shift to marginal utility theory is that, conceiving for a moment the relationship between Column I and Column II as a chronological progression, complex D broke decisively from complex B (the reading of the Victorian writers I quoted above), but retained the qualities in complex A. Historian Donald Winch discusses this question at great length in his very helpful essay 'Marginalism and the Boundaries of Economic Science,' in which he surveys the modern debate over the novelty of the marginal school and reaches the 'unexciting conclusion' that 'the advent of marginalism led to a pervasive shift of emphasis within economics [Complex B → Complex D], and that this shift was associated with a narrowing of the boundaries of the science which could be interpreted – and was interpreted by many of those most directly concerned – as entailing closer attention to what was knowable by means of deductive theory [retention of Complex A] and thus more defensible from a "professional" point of view' (342). Another fairly standard reading, which for obvious reasons tends to go hand-in-hand with the first, is that the connection between complexes C and D is purely chronological: the marginal utility school and historical/inductive method happened to spring up as challenges to Ricardian orthodoxy at the same time, but beyond that temporal coincidence, have little of significance in common. This is also the view of many of the Victorian writers I have quoted so far.

My aim here is to complicate this picture substantially: these standard readings flatten out the extent to which the influence, consonance, and sympathy among these various strains (or 'complexes') were the subject of intense debate in the last decades of the nineteenth century. First is the question of the radicalness of the break between marginal utility and Ricardian economics. Several late-Victorian commentators noted that Jevons's methodology, in its use of mathematical models, deductive reasoning, and the abstraction 'economic man,' was in fact an heir to the deductive or Ricardian school. As Henry Solly asserted in 1879, political economy 'admits of indefinite development ... as regards the accuracy of calculation in the required deductive reasoning,' and credited Jevons with furthering the science in this direction (473) – a development he was not entirely happy with: 'People are getting more and more impatient with the artificial limitations required for the adoption of the deductive method in any form' (475). Historian Mark Blaug painstakingly traces the roots of the marginal revolution in earlier nineteenth-century writers, essentially arguing that it was not nec-

essarily a 'revolution' at all (*Economic* 287–9).[70] Catherine Gallagher and
Claudia Klaver also choose to emphasize the continuity between classical political economy and marginalism – for different reasons. Klaver
claims that 'the difference between Ricardo and Jevons is ... primarily
one of degree' (181–2), and emphasizes the (continuing) amoral nature
of professional economic theory as opposed the more humane, ethical
strain found in the heterodox and popularizing writers like Ruskin and
Martineau. Gallagher notes that 'because historians have been so intent
on describing the marginalists' break with previous British economic
thought ... they have obscured the underlying continuities' (*Body* 123),
yet does not agree with Klaver and Gagnier that Jevons's work represents a move away from a former world of kinder, gentler (more ethical) economic theory (Gallagher, *Body* 123–4n).

Whichever conclusion one reaches, it is important to note the funda-
ments of the two interpretations: the orientation that emphasizes the
Ricardian-marginalism continuity does so by focusing on the two approaches' shared deductive methodology, use of abstraction, reification
of 'economic man,' and – with the exception of Gallagher – insistence
on the selfishness (or at least self-interestedness) of the individual economic actor as the driving force behind economic change.[71] Writers in
this camp also tend to claim that marginal utility theory represents an
intensification of these features of classical political economy – including laissez-faire.[72] The orientation that emphasizes the radical break between classical political economy and the marginal utility school does
so by focusing on the novelty of the demand theory of value. Given
that my central aim in this study has been to uncover the traces of the
demand function in earlier nineteenth-century economic thought (and
thus not its novelty), I am on the one hand inclined to notice the continuities between the two approaches – at least as far as this central concept is concerned. However, I remain agnostic on the verdict of modern
exegetes, partly because I am more interested in the attitudes of the
Victorians themselves and recognize that a great many of those commentators, for very different reasons, emphasized the radical discontinuity between classical political economy and marginal utility theory.

Second is the question of the relationship between the marginal
utility school and the historical/inductive practitioners (or between
Complexes D and C). Klaver emphasizes their antagonism: 'The differences between their [Ruskin's and Jevons's] economic writings are
fundamental and extensive, including differences in definitions, scope,
discursive form, and methodology as well as readership, reception,

and institutional location' (161). In other words, Klaver insists on the continuity between D and A/B (in a somewhat heterodox fashion) and the discontinuity between D and C (in a thoroughly orthodox one).[73] I agree with Klaver's larger point about the important differences between the Ruskinian and deductive strains of political economy (the central argument, after all, of this entire study), and concur that the use of calculus and the claims to exactitude (and to a 'masculine' cultural authority) do link marginal utility theory methodologically to classical economics as well as to the 'scientific and amoral' (Klaver 162) domains of human knowledge. However, as Klaver acknowledges, there are very real and important similarities between Ruskin's and Jevons's approaches: 'Like Ruskin, Jevons criticizes both classical economic value theory and the method of classical political economy. Also like Ruskin, Jevons argues for the importance of consumption and the consumer in any economic model, against classical theory's sole focus on production. But beyond these two general points, the similarities between the two economic projects cease' (173). Yet it was precisely these 'two general points' that were the central aims of a radical revision of economic thought in the latter part of the nineteenth century; certainly this is the way the Victorians themselves envisioned what was happening in the 1870s and 1880s.

Furthermore, in focusing exclusively on Ruskin himself and not including in her analysis the writings of the British historical school economists who were (only partly) influenced by Ruskin, Klaver overemphasizes the differences between the two 'strains' of political economy at the end of the century; as she herself acknowledges, her emphasis on these discontinuities is somewhat idiosyncratic (162–3). Her decision not to include in her analysis the work of Leslie or other historical school economists – in whose work the most vehement call for a new moral and ethical economic science was to be found – is perhaps understandable given that she chooses to focus on how the new economics, represented by Jevons, 'dramatically refocuses economic inquiry away from the complex moral, ethical, and social concerns taken up, however differently, by Mill and Ruskin' (174). (This is a strain of argument she shares with Gagnier, who argues that under marginal utility theory 'choice ceased to be a moral category' [*Insatiability* 4].)[74] However, this emphasis ignores the large body of historical school writing at the end of the century, which, as several Victorian and modern commentators have noted, was more consonant with the thinking and temperament of the British public than the marginal utility school.[75] Although neoclassical economics ultimately won the day in the early decades of the twentieth century and marginal utility theory had more institutional power, the historical approach was more culturally influential than the marginal utility school during the late Victorian period (see, for example, Blaug, *Economic* 291–2).[76] Even more crucially, the ethical impulse of pre-1870 political economy remains every bit as vital in post-1870 'economics' – we simply must look for it in a different place. As the following chapters will demonstrate, economic metaphors and modes of thought continue to be imbricated with those of morality: questions of right consumption, demand, and value cover both domains, and are intimately connected in the imaginative universes of the novels I will analyse.

Many Victorian commentators, in fact, insisted upon the similarities between the two challengers to Ricardian doxa. Leslie, commonly characterized as the father of the British historical school, furnishes a good example of an economic writer who saw no significant philosophical difference between that approach and marginal utility theory. In the foundational essay 'The Philosophical Method of Political Economy,' Leslie lays out the tenets of the historical, inductive school – but in the course of doing so, he also strongly asseverates that consumer demand is the true determinant of value, applauds luxurious expenditure and the inculcation of new tastes and desires, and even quotes Jevons admiringly. As he insists, 'The real motives [for production] are the wants and desires of consumers; the demands of consumers determining the commodities supplied by producers' (415–16), and repeats shortly thereafter, even more directly, 'The value of commodities rises and falls with changes in the degree and direction of these desires' (416). However, as I mentioned above, he also expresses a distinctly Malthusian concern that such desires are not infinite or even guaranteed: 'The desire for [wealth] is by no means necessarily an incentive to industry, and still less to abstinence' (417).

Just as with Malthus, however, the anxiety over consumer demand is simply part and parcel of an insistence on its centrality to economic theory. Leslie's quotation of Jevons, a 'distinguished English economist and a man of science,' points out the fact that Jevons had recently acknowledged the need for a 'true theory of consumption' (419). Leslie then goes on to make the most straightforward possible plea for a new discipline that combines the insights of marginal utility theory with historical, inductive methodology, two approaches which he sees not just as compatible, but complementary: 'No such theory, however, respecting the effect of consumption on either the nature or the amount of wealth can be forthcoming without a study of the history and the entire structure of society, and the laws which they disclose' (419).

Many Victorian popularizers writing in the last decades of the century were much more concerned with the significant conceptual similarities between the two strains of 'new economics,' and the challenges they both posed to a century of economic doxa. Foxwell, from the vantage point of the late 1880s, not only insists most strenuously on the continuity between the two schools, but also notes that the perception that practitioners of mathematical and historical methodologies themselves emphasized their differences is mistaken: the historical school adherents, he writes,

> are not in any necessary antagonism to economists of the mathematical type ... If there is a real difference between the two groups, it is rather in regard to the relative value they would assign to theory in the solution of practical difficulties. But this difference exists almost as strongly between the individuals in either group as between the groups themselves taken as a whole; and, in any case, it is a difference of degree rather than of antagonism, and should not seriously disturb the harmony of the economic world. ('Economic' 90)

He further insists that the current climate is 'as much marked by the convergence of the ... lines of inquiry as we have noticed as it has been by their separate appearance and individuation' (91), and groups together Marshall, Jevons, Leslie, Ruskin, and the German socialists, claiming that 'whatever apparent discordance there may be between the various members of this group, the new school of economy can and does assimilate the best part of the teaching of them all, without any sense of inconsistency or contradiction' (100). He dismisses the clearest and most direct case that can be made for dividing the new economics into two separate schools, the widely felt methodological distinction between induction and deduction:

> Professor Dunbar ... regards the movement as a conflict between the supporters of the inductive and deductive methods. No doubt, this has been stated in so many words by some of the new school; but it does not represent their practice and their real meaning ... It is speculative and not theoretical economy which is to be condemned ... Of pure theory proper, Jevons is almost the only English representative. There is no quarrel with such theory, *nor with its inductive basis.* (101, emphasis added)

For Foxwell, the true break between the deductive and inductive schools was a diachronic shift between pre-1870 political economy and the 'new school' which comprised both the historical and the marginal utility theorists, not a synchronic one between the two current approaches. Foxwell even goes so far as to claim that in the case of Jevons and Alfred Marshall, the mathematical-marginal theorist par excellence and his most indefatigable popularizer, 'It would be difficult to refer [them] specially to either school' (91), and admires in passing Jevons's 'remarkable' historical study of Cantillon (92).

For many Victorian economic popularizers, in short, the truly important and radical changes going on in the last thirty years of the nineteenth century constituted nothing less than a complete unseating of classical political economy – the fact that the attacks came from two somewhat different directions was not nearly as significant as the fact that an exciting new challenge to economic doxa was underway. Many of these writers (usually from the historical-school perspective)[77] saw the theory of marginal utility as perfectly compatible with the inductive approach – or at least could be, and should be, in practice. In other words, for them there is no radical or necessary break between Complex D and Complex C.

Just as we saw with the question of Ricardian-marginalism continuity, there was – and is – a range of opinions on the matter, which depended on the elements of the two schools one chooses to emphasize. For those who insist on the differences between historicism and marginalism, the important question is methodological: marginal utility theory is scientific, mathematical, and deductive, while historicism is impressionistic, 'literary,' and inductive. For the writers who insist on the continuity between the two approaches, these methodological disagreements seem unimportant compared to what generally characterizes the 'new economics': a concerted attack on classical political economy and an emphasis (or intensification of emphasis) on the individual actor as opposed to economic classes. As one explicator of marginal utility noted: 'Curves of this sort [graphing consumer utility] are clearly of only individual application, for we cannot compare A's pleasure with B's; and the curves further depend on the peculiar idiosyncrasy of the individual' (Darwin 244). While the methodology may be mathematical, proponents – as well as detractors – of Jevons's economics noted that graphs and calculus were useless without a clear definition of utility, as well as data about how individual consumption choices are made. As Joseph Schumpeter decisively stated in 1909, 'Almost every modern writer starts with wants and their satisfaction, and takes utility more or less exclusively as the basis of his analysis ... I wish to point out that, as far as [this *modus procendi*] is used, it unavoidably implies considering individuals as independent units or agencies. For only individuals can feel wants' ('On the Concept' 214). Modern commentators also note the importance of this conceptual shift; according to Klaver, marginal utility theory went even farther than Ricardian economics 'in constructing economic agency in terms of self-interested, autonomous, even isolated individuals ... Jevons's creation and reification of "economic man" is also more effective than Ricardo's because it is able to fold into itself certain of the irrational as well as rational aspects of human subjectivity' (182). For Gagnier, 'the marginalists shifted the analysis of economic phenomena from a methodology based on factors of production and class to one based on the individual' (*Insatiability* 51), which 'actually privileged subjective psychological factors on the part of the consumer' (*Insatiability* 11).

The fact that this particular strain of thought can be read as a continuation of the heterodox work of early demand-side theorists such as Malthus only strengthens the intuitive sense that individualism and marginal utility (*qua* demand theory of value) go hand-in-hand: in his critique of Say's Law, Malthus accuses his opponents of treating 'commodities as if they were so many mathematical figures, or arithmetical characters, the relations of which were to be compared, instead of articles of consumption, which must of course be referred to the numbers and wants of the consumers' (*Principles* 1:355). As historian F. Cameron Maclachlan notes, 'Malthus recognizes that his mode of reasoning, unlike that of his opponents, makes ultimate reference to individual wants and behavior' (568).[78]

However, while both Victorian and modern commentators thus emphasize the importance of individualism in marginal utility theory, my claim that an intensified individualism was the crucial concept uniting both strains of the new economics might seem, at first blush, counterintuitive. Many historical-school writers decried the emphasis on the individual in both classical political economy and marginalism (in fact, this is the most important perceived difference between complexes D and C for contemporary economic theorists on both sides of the putative divide). As Foxwell noted in his critique of Ricardian economic theory, 'We have been suffering for a century from an acute outbreak of individualism, unchecked by the old restraints, and invested with almost a religious sanction by a certain soul-less school of writers. The narrowest selfishness has been recommended as a public virtue' ('Irregularity' 249–50). Hobson, whom I quoted earlier as a late-century cheerleader for Ruskin's political economy, also denounces what he terms the 'protean fallacy of individualism, which feigns the existence of separate individuals by abstracting and neglecting the social relations which belong to them and make them what they are' (*Social* 69). Another of Ruskin's later-century champions discusses this same tendency toward individualism, in somewhat less disparaging terms, characterizing it as the central difference between the ethical economics of Ruskin and the laissez-faire policy recommendations of Spencer: 'Spencer rests his faith in the slow, impersonal processes of evolution ... Every individual is to be left free to do what he pleases, providing what he pleases does not limit the like freedom of every other individual' (Wilson 250).[79]

Whereas the label 'individualism' became something of a lightning rod for contemporary writers anxious to promote the merits of their own approaches (and indeed, the term remains a vexed one for modern exegetes), I would like to suggest that a deeper ideal of individualism did in fact unite the two strains of the new economics. As I contend, the calls of the inductive school proponents for real-world data on the economic behaviour of individuals, and their demand for more anthropological studies exploring cultural as well as individual differences among economic agents, were perfectly consonant with marginal utility theory's emphasis on the importance of pleasure and utility to individual consumers. As we have already seen, many Victorian commentators called for a synthesis of the two methodologies: Leslie, Schmoller in his *Grundriss*, and even (in a slightly qualified form), Jevons himself ('Future' 194–7).

Many commentators acknowledged not only the ideal of an integrated economics united by attention to individual consumer decisions and historical, inductive research, but also the fact that in many ways, the historical school already was marked by an individualist bent. According to historian Joseph A. Schumpeter, six key perspectives characterized the historical school of economics: relativity, the unity of social life, an anti-rationalist point of view, evolution, interest in individuality rather than generality, and organicism (*Economic* 176–80). As he later elaborated in his magnum opus, *History of Economic Analysis*, not only are the 'ethical' approach and the 'individualist' approach not mutually exclusive or contradictory, but they are often facets of the same general methodology. According to him, the historical school 'professed to study *all* the facets of an economic phenomenon; hence *all* the facets of economic behavior and not merely the economic logic of it; hence the *whole* of human motivations as historically displayed, the specifically economic ones not more than the rest for which the term "ethical" was made to serve, presumably because it seems to stress hyperindividual components' (812, emphases in original). Schumpeter's characterization here, while not exactly flattering to the historical school in context, does make the important point that beneath its drive toward totalization of description lay a fundamental concern with the actions of individual economic agents. While the 'individuals' of classical political economy were not 'living and fighting beings' but 'continued to be mere clothes-lines on which to hang propositions of economic logic' (*History* 886–7), both marginal utility theory and the 'historico-ethical school' at least attempted to psychologize individual economic actors through continued attention to the subjective factors affecting decision making rather than to the aggregate behaviour of large classes such as landlords, workers, and capitalists.[80]

One striking feature of these tensions in economic discourse in the latter decades of the century is their markedly gendered character. We have seen how for Ruskin, the improvident (or more accurately, overly provident) saver is likened to a castrating prostitute, and the free circulation of currency to maternal sustenance. Gordon Bigelow, in his study *Fiction, Famine, and the Rise of Economics in Victorian Britain and Ireland*, also discusses the gendering of economic terminology from Smith and Rousseau to Dickens and beyond. Bigelow notes how eighteenth-century economic writers, including Adam Smith, 'argued that the prudent codes of the business man, conceived in terms of masculine virtue and restraint, would tame the excessive desire of the effeminate speculator'; this is in marked contrast to Rousseau's conceptualization, in which 'the development of complex forms of social interaction are figured as castration, the effeminate absence of physicality' (39). However, as Bigelow later points out, this general characterization is marked by inconsistencies in Smith's work. Elsewhere Smith, in a sort of Rousseauian throwback, laments the loss of general martial prowess that accompanies the division of labour, and likens specialized workers to 'cowards' who are emasculated by their narrow round of work:

A coward, a man incapable either of defending or of revenging himself, evidently wants one of the most essential parts of the character of a man.

He is as much mutilated and deformed in his mind, as another is in his body, who is either deprived of some of his most essential members, or has lost the use of them. (*Wealth of Nations* Book Five, qtd in Bigelow 48)

Bigelow does address the contradiction more directly a few pages later, when he explains that for Smith, the 'castration threat' of the division of labour is 'a relatively minor problem, correctable by the limited intervention of the state, in providing a standing army and a system of male public education to counteract the erosion of masculine vigor' (63–4). More important for my own purposes, Bigelow also claims that this threat is essentially triumphant in the nineteenth century: 'The demand theory of value, however, embraces the idea that markets are driven by affective responses, by desire. Thus the eighteenth-century threat against which Smith marshals his whole career becomes, in the nineteenth century, the central assumption of economic thought' (64).[81] In other words, 'the fear that the value of a given stock share might rise or fall with the desire or repulsion of common consumers,' which was 'interpreted in the eighteenth century through the metaphor of femininity' (63) has not lost its feminine character in the nineteenth – as the rest of this book demonstrates, this fear has become naturalized, repressed, forgotten, or buried in the pages of the novel. We will see the return of this anxiety, this association of economic perverseness and femininity (along with castration and 'unmanning') in *Adam Bede*'s Hetty Sorrel, *The Mill on the Floss*'s Maggie Tulliver, Michael Henchard in *The Mayor of Casterbridge*, and the central characters in *Tess of the d'Urbervilles*.

We see a similar rhetoric among many economic writers throughout the period as well; just because the new theories of value have become the 'central assumption' of economics does not mean that the threat of feminization they pose has been neutralized. Hobson, the late-century socialist reformer and champion of Ruskin, asserts – in terms strikingly similar to those of Adam Smith – that 'the *dilettanti* workers, in their select fields, fail in actuality, in broad, sympathetic comprehension of the life around them ... The "unnatural" condition of their class-life narrows and emasculates their work of every kind' (*Social* 129). Yet Hobson is not referring to wage workers alienated by the modern division of labour; he is here decrying the feminization of the leisured class, those who enjoy 'property which represents no personal effort' (128). While the condemnation of an effeminate, parasitic, and wasteful aristocracy is certainly nothing new – indeed, has been something of a trope since at least the seventeenth century – what *is* new here is the way that Hobson characterizes these *'dilettanti'*: 'People who are not obliged to "do things for themselves" remain throughout life quite ignorant of many of the common properties and functions of material objects around them, and in particular of the physical capacities of the human body. In other words, they know the material world directly and essentially only as it affects them as "consumers"' (130). The scare quotes remind us that we are in the presence of a new term, and one that Hobson seems to find distinctly distasteful. We see here both the influence of a late-century Ruskinian socialism (elaborated, for example, in the work of William Morris) that decries the alienation of the consumer from the material processes of production, as well as the solidifying of the association between consumption and femininity that is now such a firmly entrenched feature of social life – and such a rich lode for the minings of contemporary cultural critics.

As Klaver argues, Ruskin himself actively took part in this rhetorical feminization: 'The male social actor in Ruskin's text is, in terms of the dominant Victorian discourse of gender, feminized, taking on attributes that the separate-spheres ideology assigns only to women' (172). For Klaver, this move is part of a larger 'two-cultures' shift that assigned the masculine virtues of rationality and impartiality to the new scientific/ mathematical version of economics developing from Jevons's work on marginal utility. However, the very category of demand, and its concomitant emphasis on the affective powers of consumption, is also feminized in the latter decades of the century; while the mathematical character of marginal utility theory may have worked (as Klaver claims) to masculinize the new science of 'economics' (161ff), it also worked to reify the distinction between masculine investigator – economist – and feminized object – consumer.

We can certainly see that a concern with the moral and ethical dimensions of economic thought and practice (which I have discussed as a particularly salient feature of the Ruskinian/historical strain of economic discourse) was viewed as a kind of 'softening' or feminization of political economy as opposed to the supposedly hard-nosed approach of the neo-classicals.[82] Ruskin himself was markedly anxious about the emasculating effect his moral economics may have had on his public persona. In a letter of 1874, later published in *Fors Clavigera*, he indulges in a rather startling passage of gender anxiety:

Because I have passed it [my life] in almsgiving, not in fortune-hunting
... because I have lowered my rents, and assured the comfortable lives of

my poor tenants, instead of taking from them all I could force for the roofs
they needed … finally, because I never disobeyed my mother, because I
have honoured all women with solemn worship, and have been kind even
to the unthankful and the evil – therefore, the hacks of English art and literature wag their heads at me, and the poor wretch who pawns the dirty
linen of his soul daily for a bottle of sour wine and a cigar, talks of the 'effeminate sentimentality of Ruskin.' (*Works* 28:81)

For Ruskin, his ethically admirable economic behaviour is associated,
at least in his own characterization of his public persona, with obey-
ing his mother and 'worshipping' women. From an appreciation of
the feminine and the practice of stereotypically female behaviour (caring about one's tenants and employees) it is a short step to actually
being 'effeminate.' Not only is economic caretaking, as he tacitly acknowledges, the culturally marked out domain of woman, but it also is
simultaneously feminizing and degrading. This is a degradation, as we
have already seen, that Ruskin in turn projects onto the strange, dis-
comfiting, and sexually transgressive feminine figures that populate his
economic writings.[83]

For both Klaver and Bigelow, the perceived feminization of the
ethical/Ruskinian strain of economic discourse goes hand-in-hand with
the domestication of political economy itself. Klaver claims that 'Ruskin
attempts to reconstruct economic knowledge *around* and ground it *upon*
the feminized virtues of domesticity. That is, rather than constructing female figures as carriers of this virtue who can function as com-
plements or antidotes to the immoralities of the commercial sphere,
Ruskin works to domesticate the science – and the functioning – of the
sphere itself' (171, emphases in original). Bigelow notes that in Victorian
separate-spheres ideology the domestic realm provides a sacrosanct
space free from the depredations of the marketplace, in order to support his reading of *Bleak House*, in which 'domestic ideology serves the
same metaphorical functions as the bank … a centripetal force to limit,
order, and regulate the wildness of a total interchangeability' (94). We
have advanced here from the contradiction Bigelow located in Adam
Smith – between an economic sphere shaped by masculine restraint and
a working world full of wage earners emasculated by the division of
labour – which can only be resolved by a governmental 'remasculinization' program of its citizenry. In the *Wealth of Nations* this recommendation amounts to a kind of circular schema 'whereby the responsibility of
contemporary (i.e., feminized) society is to guide its members in their

behavior back toward society's (masculine) point of origin' (Bigelow 48). Klaver also notes that these categories are somewhat unstable, and that 'one way to understand Ruskin's deconstructive project is in terms of not only simply a feminization of the public social sphere but also, simultaneously, a certain remasculinization of the private domestic sphere' (172).

The point here is that it becomes very difficult to untangle the confused metaphorics of gender in these examples. Is the speculator an effeminate gadfly acting only on the whim of transient desires, threatening the stability of the young capitalist economy with his wild gambling? Or is he an avatar of heroic masculinity, swashbuckling his way through the rough-and-tumble of the marketplace? Is the worker under the modern division of labour an emasculated coward who has lost the ability to defend his military honour – and is the rhetoric of financial derring-do a compensation for this perceived loss of masculine prowess on the part of 'advanced' economic man? If the speculator is a dangerous figure, is the perceived threat figured as masculine or feminine? And who should restrain the wildness of his/her behaviour? The 'centripetal force' of a sentimental and feminine domesticity? Or the state, as a repository of wise, prudent, masculine restraint? (Or is the state merely a feminized agglomeration of emasculated workers?) Is the aristocracy a band of effeminate, parasitical wastrels? Or, as we saw in Malthus, a group of potentially rapacious consumers whose luxurious expenditure is the only prop to an economy threatened with a general glut of commodities? Is the political economist a soft-hearted ethicist whining about the unfair allocation of resources? Or a hard-nosed scientific researcher, advancing the cause of (masculinized) knowledge and objective truth?[84] In the readings that follow, I will suggest that this very undecidability functions psychologically – either for individual authors or for the culture at large – to capture and naturalize the uncertainty and instability of the financial world. As critic Paul L. Sawyer notes in his study of Ruskin, the descriptions of sexually transgressive and maternal female images in *Munera Pulveris*, which I discussed in the introduction, are Ruskin's way of converting ambivalence into 'a more tolerable form' through projection and splitting. For Sawyer, this psychological mechanism represents Ruskin's 'struggle toward a new language and an expanded region for that language' (235–6), although it appears on the surface as the yoking of radically disjoined discourses or even the symptom of mental instability.

My task in the remainder of this book is to trace the iterations of these gendered forms in the novels of Eliot and Hardy. I attend particularly to the conflation of certain kinds of economic behaviour and a degraded or debased femininity, while trying to avoid imposing a predetermined schema on the permutations of the feminine (and masculine) in the novels I analyse. Because women traditionally have been associated with consumption and luxurious expenditure – and, since the nineteenth century, with household management and domestic economy – it would seem only natural that they would also be thus associated in the pages of the novel. It would also seem natural, given the nineteenth-century anxiety about economic demand I have been at pains to demonstrate in this chapter, that women as managers and consumers would form the locus of certain kinds of novelistic disquiet.

My goal is to complicate and enrich these commonplace notions of the relationship between gender and economic behaviour in the nineteenth century – in particular, I take aim at the notion that utility as an index of value, which very gradually took hold over the course of the century and was enshrined as the central principle of economic thought at its end, was coterminous with the relaxation of anxiety about the continued robustness of consumer demand, on the part of male or female consumers. Bigelow claims that in the work of DeQuincey, for example, whose early demand theory of value posits a consumer 'equipped with a defining interior principle which exists prior to the encounter with the market' (102), we 'should recognize a historical shift in the symbolic vocabulary of gender' since he 'reverses the symbolic poles of the earlier political economy, claiming what had once been the "feminine" and inconstant affect of the individual as the rock on which the modern market is built' (103). While I agree in general with Bigelow's consistently fascinating analysis, it is the claim for a 'historical shift in the symbolic vocabulary of gender' that I will examine more closely in the pages that follow; this 'shift,' in fact, is something more like a constant shifting back and forth, as the terms of economic debate changed throughout the latter half of the century.

The task of this book is not so much to assume the 'naturalness' of these associations between gender and economic behaviour as to locate them and inquire after their effects. I do not begin with the presumption that the connections between women, degradation, demand, and consumption are transhistorical truths, but instead I will attempt to chart the tiny and beleaguered terrain where different historical strata intersect in the territory of the novel. My object is processes and beliefs that are durable, not necessarily transhistorical; relatively ancient concerns about sex, desire, and economic behaviour take on a very particular shape under the pressures of the burgeoning growth of capitalism in the nineteenth century. That shape can be traced in the novels I now examine.

2 'Fine Clothes an' Waste': Utopian Economy and the Problem of Femininity in *Adam Bede*

The authoress ... does not know how to bring her story to a natural end. When once the point is past to which the whole has been tending, and in which all her strength and intensity have been put forth, she does not care much what becomes of her people. She marries them, or she drowns them, it does not matter which.

(Rev. of *The Mill on the Floss, Guardian* 127)

1 Femmes Fatales

Marriage or drowning – it does not matter which. As her contemporary critics noted, George Eliot is perhaps rather too fond of killing off her heroines for the tastes of genteel mid-Victorian readers. While the motive for the deaths of Hetty Sorrel and Maggie Tulliver remains an unsettling enigma (especially for modern feminist criticism),[1] the symbolic importance of these deaths, and the claims about novelistic form and readerly expectation that they engender, demand that Eliot's first two novels be read against each other. More important, only when we attend to these novels' engagement with contemporaneous economic debates and their pervasive use of economic tropes do their plots become fully legible. In both *Adam Bede* and *The Mill on the Floss*, the metaphor of economic exchange is the guiding principle organizing narrative description, plot structure, and the movement toward closure; it is this organizing construct that occasions the 'sacrifices' of Hetty and Maggie. While this strong claim may be more obviously appropriate to *The Mill on the Floss* – which is, after all, chiefly concerned with a narrative of bankruptcy and regeneration – it also applies to *Adam Bede* insofar as the two novels together are informed by, and form an extended commentary on, governing Victorian ideas of economic organization. Both Hetty and Maggie, as the novels' symbolic loci of problematic consumption and desire, are expelled in a metaphorical process that seeks to eliminate excess; the relative (im)plausibility of their respective deaths is part and parcel of the success of this process. And our sense of this success is in turn inseparable from the very different concerns with economic exchange – particularly the manifestations of the demand function – that the two novels explore.

In arguing that these two novels are informed by specific archetypes of economic organization delineated by classical political economy – that the narratives themselves rehearse, and contribute to, anxieties found in contemporary economic debates – I hope to show that their author's political agenda is rather less conservative, and certainly more conflicted, than traditionally has been argued. But to claim that both *Adam Bede* and *The Mill on the Floss* murder their heroines is to flatten out crucial distinctions between the deaths of Maggie and Hetty; in these distinctions we have the key to understanding both the economic metaphors informing their plots and their difficult and implausible endings. While the fact that Eliot feels compelled to kill off both of these characters is worthy of critical attention, it is necessary to understand the economic logics of the two novels in order to understand fully their different – yet homologous – fatal endings.

Adam Bede is a pastoral reverie, a nostalgic examination of a rural, hierarchical, agrarian society, and as such is governed by the metaphors and characteristics of both the physiocratic model and Herbert Spencer's utopian barter economy analysed in the previous chapter.[2] *The Mill on the Floss*, on the other hand, represents Eliot's attempt to examine the problematic shift from this idealized, utopian economic organization to one characterized by usury, credit, interest, and surplus capital. In that sense, the earlier work can be read as an economic prehistory to the later; while both *Adam Bede* and *The Mill on the Floss* are historical novels (set in 1799 and the late 1820s, but written in 1859 and 1860 respectively), each one engages different features of the contemporary economic milieu that were an ongoing source of anxiety and cultural concern.

While the two novels tackle different historical and cultural questions, both couch their economic concerns in terms of gain and loss. The economy of *Adam Bede*, at both the descriptive and structural levels, envisions a balance between gain and loss, production and consumption, whereas *The Mill on the Floss* is concerned with surfeit or excess. These fundamental concerns inform, and are revealed in, the two novels' plots, endings, narrative voices, and descriptive strategies, but it is in the movement toward closure that they are most evident. Both novels rhetorically invoke endings of all kinds: death, bankruptcy, the ends of their own stories. These endings are continually linked to questions of economic balance, of production/consumption and loss/gain; it is only possible to know, after all, the final status of a balance sheet after all transactions (of trade, of usury, of plot) are finished.[3] The closure of each novel, including – perhaps most importantly – the fate of its heroine, is intimately concerned with these economic questions. And yet the fates of these female characters are inseparable not only from the economic concerns they embody and reveal, but also from the (not so) simple fact of their gender. As I discussed more fully in the introduction and chapter 1, women in the Victorian period are figured simultaneously as objects of exchange and as custodians and governors of economic processes. Eliot's heroines, as women, are thus inextricably connected to the economic metaphors of her novels.

This chapter will examine the first of these two alternative narrative economies, the utopian barter system of *Adam Bede*. With her depiction of the agrarian life of Hayslope, Eliot valorizes a particular kind of economy – both monetary and symbolic – in which the problematic sexuality of Hetty Sorrel is anathema. By invoking and then eliminating the figure who threatens the tightly woven fabric of the familial economic unit, Eliot can both mourn the passing of the pastoral way of life and acknowledge the post hoc inevitability of the ascendance of the credit economy (which is her central concern in *The Mill on the Floss*). It is around the sexualized body of Hetty Sorrel that these issues revolve.

2 Horrors of Excess and the Precredit Fantasy

While nineteenth-century readers of Eliot emphasized the implausibility and technical clumsiness of the death of Maggie in the final volume of *The Mill on the Floss*, they spared the author's first novel from a similar explicit accusation. The reason *Adam Bede* does not immediately seem to have the same problem with closure that troubled readers of *The Mill on the Floss* is that the novel valorizes an economic system which naturalizes and eliminates excess. As Catherine Gallagher notes in her discussion of *Scenes of Clerical Life* (another work that portrays an idealized rural, 'prelapsarian,' and closed society), 'Malthusians tended to stress balance rather than dynamism in the economy' (176). While Gallagher focuses on the fertility and reproduction aspects of Malthusian thought in her analysis, it is also true that in the early stages of her writing career, Eliot is fascinated by the static, balanced, physiocratic model of economic and social organization. The plot of *Adam Bede* seems to evolve and end 'naturally' because the novel's pastoral economic organization does not foreground or problematize irresolvable excesses or failures of demand the way *The Mill on the Floss* does; the strategies of the earlier novel do not incorporate invocations of either surplus or problematic endings nearly to the degree found in the later.

This phenomenon holds true on the more immediately accessible levels of character development, plot movement, and narrative commentary; yet on a deeper level the novel demonstrates doubt and anxiety about the seemingly utopian and natural barter economy it inscribes even as it attempts to authorize it. We can see this anxiety as an effect of the disjunct between a fantasized economy of balance and moderation and the complex credit economy undergoing continued crisis in the years that Eliot was planning and writing the novel. (See my discussion in chapter 1 of the cyclical mania-crash pattern in the first half of the nineteenth century.) Further narrative tension results from a more figurative disjunct between the financial and ethical 'economies' of the novel: Eliot attempts to portray a contained, stable economic system and at the same time condemn the simplistic morality that envisions consequences of actions as containable, which moral delusion is figured as a problem of misreading or misinterpretation. Yet as the novel takes issue with Arthur Donnithorne's ethical naivety, demonstrating the ways in which the repercussions of his actions extend – unstable and uncontainable – beyond his narrow vision of them, it inadvertently problematizes the stability and containment of the pastoral and utopian economy it wants to portray. Although he is writing about *Middlemarch* in particular, D.A. Miller argues that Eliot tends to 'orient [her] texts toward a "utopic" state that is radically at odds with the narrative means used to reach it' (x). This characterization is true of *Adam Bede* as well: the 'utopic' state of balance in pastoral economic exchange is radically at odds with the idea of ethical consequence that Eliot wants to portray.

The novel is able to resolve this contradiction, and restabilize the economic balance of the novel, only by an abrupt and yet oddly downplayed resolution of the problem of Hetty, the figure who is linked to excesses of appetite and uncontainable desire. The economic concerns of the novel are thus linked metonymically to questions of novelistic closure; similarly, the novel groups together questions of consequence (the overriding ethical problem of the novel) with metaphors of reading, misreading, interpretation, and misinterpretation. These two groups of linked tropes – gain and loss/closure and consequence/reading – form the web of complementary and conflicting signs that both construct and deconstruct the image of the utopian 'economy.' Just as the female characters in *Adam Bede* function as the metaphorical loci for economic concerns in their dual roles as managers and objects of exchange, so too do they simultaneously embody and trouble, through the tension between these two roles, the valorization of the pastoral barter economy. As economic actors, tokens, interpreters, and enigmas, the women in this novel bear the symbolic burden of these interrelated pressures.

At the most immediately accessible level, *Adam Bede* seems to endorse quite unproblematically the simple, utopian barter economy that is suggested by the agrarian setting of the novel. (Of course, a pure barter economy as envisioned by Spencer is an ideal; Eliot does not imply that the actual economic organization of the society she depicts is a pure barter economy as much as she invokes or echoes such an ideal. In that sense, the novel is a reverie about the agrarian-based 'balanced' economy of the physiocrats as much as it is a commentary on Spencerian anxieties about the operations of credit.) The narrator and most of the major characters endorse and strive for a state of moderation and balance in which there is no waste or excess – in which what is produced is demanded, and vice versa. Mr Irwine, the novel's voice of reason in this regard, consoles Arthur Donnithorne when the younger man complains that his coming-of-age feast is not splendid enough: 'Never mind, you'll give more pleasure in this quiet way ... In this sort of thing people are constantly confounding liberality with riot and disorder. It sounds very good to say that so many sheep and oxen were roasted whole, and everybody ate who liked to come; but in the end it generally happens that no one has had an enjoyable meal' (254). M. Irwine's comment links moderation in consumption to an increase in pleasure. He is a pseudo-Ricardian and adherent of Say's Law in this regard: his fear is not that the guests' demand is unequal to the imagined bounty, but that they will eat until they hurt. Failure of appetite is not his concern. This consumption/pleasure dialectic is directly connected to the expenditure of capital; Arthur's complaint stems from the fact that his stingy grandfather has not allowed him to spend as much money on the feast as he would have liked: 'I had only a limited sum after all; for though my grandfather talked of a *carte blanche*, he couldn't make up his mind to trust me, when it came to the point' (254).

According to Nancy Armstrong, this marked denigration of aristocratic display is closely allied with rhetorical strategies, dating from eighteenth-century conduct books but not common until later in the nineteenth century, that sought to efface overt signs of hierarchical aristocratic privilege in favour of a horizontal alignment of middle-class interests based on money rather than birth (70–1). In this sense, then, it could be argued that Mr Irwine's comment is quite forward-thinking rather than conservative: his somewhat anachronistic distaste (the novel is set at the very end of the eighteenth century) for traditional forms of obligatory sumptuary display reveals Eliot's own prejudices about older economic organizations, in common circulation much later in the century.

However, Armstrong's argument also reveals a crucial paradox: Mr Irwine's comment about Arthur's celebration, and the rhetoric of moderation in general, also functions metaphorically as a conservative criticism of practices associated with the newer credit economies insofar as it criticizes wholesale the concept of excessive production. The consumption paradigm outlined here actually equates excess with waste, as does the economic logic of the novel as a whole. Georges Bataille likens the sumptuary display of the traditional aristocracy to the premodern gift economy of potlatch, wherein rival tribal chiefs attempt to outdo each other in displays of wealth either given to the enemy or flamboyantly destroyed. According to Bataille, this type of economy creates surpluses of value exactly like a credit economy: 'Wealth is multiplied in *potlatch* civilizations in a way that recalls the inflation of credit in banking economies.'[4] Arthur and Mr Irwine's exchange, occurring as it does at a crucial symbolic juncture of the novel (Arthur's official entrance into manhood and full moral responsibility for the consequences of his actions), reinforces the novel's agenda of praising restraint and moderation by equating excess with waste. In this sense it is aligned with the strain of Victorian economic thought that fears ultimate stagnation and the 'end of capitalism'; Ruskin, for example, takes mainstream Ricardian economics to task for missing this very point: 'I cannot tell you the contempt I feel for the common writers on political economy, in their stupefied missing of this first principle of all human economy – individual or political – to live, namely, with as few wants as possible, and to waste nothing of what is given you to supply them' (*Works* 17:424). The paradox is plain: by indulging one's excessive appetites

– behaviour we would imagine advocated by an underconsumptionist like Ruskin (or Malthus) – one actually courts the creation of excesses and 'waste' – which is, of course, the main fear of the underconsumptionists. (This paradox prefigures the idea of 'demand creating its own supply' which we will later see in *Tess of the d'Urbervilles*.) In *Adam Bede*, this praise of general restraint is even more marked, as we shall see, when contrasted with the narrator's condemnation of Hetty's excessive consumption – and Arthur's own immoderate sexual desires.

The novel's abhorrence of excess, both of production and of consumption, is so marked that it even trumps the other great principle of all of Eliot's early novels: sympathetic identification. In the middle of the first chapter of volume 2, 'In Which the Story Pauses a Little,' an extended explanation of the novel's strategy of sympathetic realism, the proleptic narrator asks an older and wiser Adam to explain the village's dislike of the minister who one day will replace Mr Irwine: the future rector's problem is that he does not live within his income. This causes him to commit the grave and unforgivable sin of haggling with his parishioners: 'He was for beating down prices with the people as worked for him; and his preaching wouldn't go down well with that sauce' (180). His quite literally excessive desires, coupled with an ultimate failure of adequate consumption as indicated by the haggling, cause him to forget the all-important virtue extolled on the previous page: the 'fibre of sympathy connecting [him] with that vulgar citizen who weighs out [his] sugar' (179).[5] Just as the new rector loses his capacity for sympathy in the face of his own immoderate appetites, so too does the novel's project of psychologically sympathetic and insightful character portraiture fail in the face of excessive expenditure. It is only those characters who display immoderate desires who are condemned in the moral framework of Eliot's novels: they are drawn sketchily and without psychological depth, overtly reviled by the narrator, banished, or killed.[6]

Yet it is not merely the prospect of excess per se that horrifies the utopian economic world view of Hayslope. The 'simple' farmers and village inhabitants routinely express their distrust of and scorn for those two unmistakable markers of the modern economy, the inexorable accumulation of surplus capital (which Spencer reminds us is 'ever going on'), and inconvertible goods. Mr Poyser, when faced with the temptation to begin the hay harvest on a Sunday, thinks to himself, 'Had not Michael Holdsworth had a pair of oxen "sweltered" while he was ploughing on Good Friday? That was a demonstration that work on sacred days was a wicked thing; and with wickedness of any sort Martin Poyser was quite clear that he would have nothing to do, since money got by such means would never prosper' (192). His wife read-ily concurs: 'You make but a poor trap to catch luck if you go and bait it wi' wickedness. The money as it got so's like to burn holes i' your pocket' (193). For both of the Poysers, the real deterrent to such a sin is a rather un-Christian, animistic fear of the efficacy of their ill-gotten money to do harm; this is commodity fetishism in a truly anthropologi-cal sense. The blind desire to accumulate more capital, which Victorian political economy implies is the driving engine behind modern credit economies, is checked here not by an ethical consideration, but by a rather primitive and fetishistic superstition supposedly characteristic of a premodern economic organization.[7]

Very shortly after this exchange, the narrator reveals to us the eco-nomic thinking of another rustic inhabitant of Hayslope, the village blacksmith: he has 'an inward scorn of all knowingness that could not be turned into cash' (194). This contempt for the inconvertible good, for the asset that is not translatable into monetary terms, is reminiscent of the difficulty Spencer has in envisioning a pure credit economy without stabilizing and liquidating debt through translation into gold. This sus-picion of goods other than those with exchange value thus aligns the economic world of *Adam Bede* with the Spencerian barter economy, the prelapsarian and utopian system where all transactions are in a state of balance and stability.

Lest we imagine that these views constitute a sort of unconscious (or conscious) contempt on Eliot's part toward her quaint and backward rustics, a similar view is expressed, albeit with more metaphorical so-phistication, by the young squire Arthur Donnithorne: 'I don't think a knowledge of the classics is a pressing want to a country gentleman; as far as I can see, he'd much better have a knowledge of manures' (169). The dismissal of intangible and inconvertible assets ('learning' and 'classics') in favour of a more basic, immediately valuable good ('cash,' which Freud reminds us is metaphorically equivalent to 'ma-nure')[8] characterizes all inhabitants of Hayslope, regardless of socio-economic status.

This suspicion of inconvertible goods is allied to the concern for management and abhorrence of excess that is the overriding charac-teristic of the economic world view of *Adam Bede*. The reason Arthur values a knowledge of manures, he immediately informs his listener, is so that he can put 'the farmers on a better management of their land'

(215). His great dream of benevolent patronage enables him to stabilize the threat of excess, of quite literal waste, in a closed-loop system that turns manure into 'food to maintain scholars' (170). Thus the potentially threatening and destabilizing possibility of excess is neutralized through 'management,' that code word that functions throughout the novel as shorthand for a balance between loss and gain, a system without remainder. In the utopian economic system of *Adam Bede*, perhaps the greatest sin one can commit is to mismanage, whether it be land or sexual desire. Thus the farmer Luke Britton, the brunt of Mr Poyser's contempt, is repeatedly reviled for his poor management skills: he is the ultimate sinner and buffoon.

But why do the characters in *Adam Bede* care so deeply about management, living within their means, effecting a balance between loss and gain? For Lisbeth Bede, the answer is startling and yet somehow completely understandable: 'Decent burial was what Lisbeth had been thinking of for herself through years of thrift' (103). For her, this final expenditure is more important than the substance of the life that went before: while in church at her husband's funeral, she has 'a vague belief that the psalm was doing her husband good; it was part of that decent burial which she would have thought it a greater wrong to withhold from him than to have caused him many unhappy days while he was living' (200). This desire to save money in order to secure a 'decent burial' links the policy of management with death, the ultimate closure or ending, and the notion of a final balance sheet of gain and loss.[9] Lisbeth's preoccupation with funerals necessitates a quite literal concern, on her part, for her final monetary tally: to have lived within one's means and have just enough 'left over' to discharge that final expense converges the practices of good management on an ultimate financial focal point where, hopefully, everything balances out in the end (as opposed to the Dodsons in *The Mill on the Floss*, who want as much left behind them when they die as possible). This linking of closure, economic balance, death, and management forms the complex of interrelated concerns that informs the novel as a whole; it is the drive toward closure and balance that will eventually effect the death of Hetty, the 'poor wanderer.'

It is appropriate that Lisbeth should feel herself responsible not only for her own burial but for that of her husband: it is the women in *Adam Bede* who act as the custodians of economic balance, the true managers both for themselves and for their men and children. Mrs Poyser, that paragon of common sense and housewifeliness, functions as the novel's voice of managerial reason and restraint, continually admonishing those around her who would stray from this sacred principle. It is Mrs Poyser who must keep her husband from approving an economically disadvantageous plan, proposed to them by the old squire, to increase their dairy production. As her husband hems and haws, unable to understand the situation fully enough to make an intelligent decision, she goes right to the heart of the matter:

> How do I know whether the milk 'ull be wanted constant? What's to make me sure as the house won't be put o' board-wage afore we're many months older, and then I may have to lie awake o' nights wi' twenty gallons o' milk on my mind – and Dingall 'ull take no more butter, let alone paying for it; and we must fat pigs till we're obliged to beg the butcher on our knees to buy 'em, and lose half of 'em wi' the measles. And there's the fetching and carrying, as 'ud be welly half a day's work for a man an' hoss – *that's* to be took out o' the profits, I reckon? (346)

Her horror at the unfeasibility of the plan is of course compounded by, if not solely due to, the abhorrent prospect of excess and waste it presents: all of that unwanted butter, gallons of undrunk milk, pigs laid waste before they can be slaughtered! Mrs Poyser endorses a principle of restraint philosophically similar to that of Mr Irwine, yet from a different perspective: she is a quasi-Malthusian, an underconsumptionist invoking the horrifying possibility of a veritable river of wasted dairy products, the result of inadequate demand.[10]

It is incumbent on Mrs Poyser alone to understand the practical and economic ramifications of the plan; her husband is useless in this regard. As she herself claims, her managerial ability gives her the right to make this decision: 'I've a right to speak, for I make one quarter o' the rent, and save th' other quarter' (347). Her importance as the economic custodian of the household gives her both the right to speak and the insight to see the disadvantages of the squire's plan. And even more significant, Mrs Poyser, as Eve Sedgwick points out, appears in her role as managerial dynamo as the apotheosis of the premodern, integrated, and self-contained familial economic unit: 'Mrs. Poyser's personal authority and incisiveness make the warmest of sense in the context of this economically integrated family ... Her say in the production of family goods and power requires no dilation or mystique' (139). Her authoritative voice is the very signal of the idealized economy; she is allowed to be angry with the squire's plan, and to express that anger, precisely because hers is a 'household economy where manual and managerial labor are only barely distinguished' (138). She is one face of the figure I term 'economic woman'; as we shall see, Hetty represents her nightmarish opposite.

Mrs Poyser's ire at the potential disaster of the squire's plan, and her pity and disgust with her husband for being weak enough to consider it, are so strong that she actually castigates the squire to his face, a potentially dangerous transgression of class boundaries. In the famous speech in which she 'has her say out,' it becomes clear that the squire's real sin for Mrs Poyser is not a lack of thrift, but rather the immoderation – in any endeavour – that leads to wastefulness:

> You may run away from my words, sir, and you may go spinnin' underhand ways o' doing us a mischief, for you've got old Harry to your friend, though nobody else is, but I tell you for once as we're not dumb creaturs to be abused and made money on by them as ha' got the lash i' their hands, for want o' knowing how t' undo the tackle. An' if I'm th' only one as speaks my mind, there's plenty o' the same way o' thinking i' this parish and the next to 't, for your name's no better than a brimstone match in everybody's nose – if it isna two-three old folks as you think o' saving your soul by giving 'em a bit o' flannel and a drop o' porridge. An' you may be right in thinking it'll take but little to save your soul, for it'll be the smallest savin' y' iver made, wi' all your scrapin'. (348)

As Mrs Poyser's character portrait implies, the squire's stinginess, which might otherwise be considered a virtue, is so great as to actually lead to wastefulness – to the suggestion of a plan that will lead to overproduction. Just as with the paradoxical situation of the miser who wastes money by hoarding it and thus squandering its true value in purchasing power,[11] or the profligate consumer whose desires lead to waste and excess, so the old squire's stinginess actually costs: the good will of his tenants, the approval of Mrs Poyser, and, potentially, the waste caused by his unworkable plan.

Mrs Poyser has a similar criticism for her 'impractical' niece Dinah, who insists on denying herself worldly comforts as part of her Methodist ministry:

> If everybody tried to do without house and home, and with poor eating and drinking, and was allays talking as we must despise the things o' the world, as you say, I should like to know where the pick o' the stock, and

the corn, and the best new milk cheeses 'ud have to go? everybody 'ud
be wanting bread made o' tail ends, and everybody 'ud be running after
everybody else to preach to 'em, istead o' bringing up their families, and
laying by against a bad harvest. (78)

Although her criticism here is tempered with affection, it is based on
the same basic principle: abstemiousness in too great a degree is actually harmful to the greater economic system as a whole. It is not thrift *qua*
thrift that is the virtue here, but thrift *qua* moderation: as with any other
component of the economic system, it should be pursued only in the
service of balance and stability. As Dinah herself replies, 'It's quite right
the land should be ploughed and sowed, and the precious corn stored,
and the things of life cared for ... We can all be servants of God wherever our lot is cast, but he gives us different sorts of work' (79). While
Mrs Poyser and Dinah may seem to be speaking at cross purposes, each
in her own way is concerned about the larger framework of economic
and social relations in which she is a part; each acts as a custodian of
the greater social good, whether it be her husband's economic interests
or her fellow parishioners' souls. And each is acting as an ideal mouthpiece for Malthusianism, particularly its underconsumptionist strain.

However, Mrs Poyser's characterization of Dinah as impractical and
unmindful of the necessities of managing everyday life is actually belied by the logic of the novel as a whole. The women in *Adam Bede*
are consistently appraised as potential (or actual) wives based on their
ability as financial managers; Dinah is thus compared favourably with
her vain and flighty cousin Hetty. According to Armstrong's now-clas-
sic analysis, the figure of the thrifty and managerial domestic woman
begins to take strong cultural hold in the nineteenth century; women
were explicitly appraised as potential mates in these economic terms:
'[A woman's] desirability hinged upon an education in frugal domestic
practices. She was supposed to complement [the man's] role as an earn-
er and producer with hers as a wise spender and tasteful consumer'
(59).

Thus Dinah Morris is explicitly characterized as an eminently suitable wife; one of the first things Lisbeth Bede says to her new-found
companion, who has come to cheer her after the sudden death of her
husband, is about her thrift: 'I wouldna mind ha'in' ye for a daughter,
for ye wouldna spend the lad's wage i' fine clothes an' waste' (112).
Hetty, on the other hand, is figured as a bad risk for a thrifty husband;
in what will become a devastatingly ironic understatement, Mr Irwine

warns Arthur about flirting too much with Hetty: 'You will spoil her for a poor man's wife' (101). Later in the novel, Irwine advises his young protégé more explicitly about the economic aim of matrimony: 'Mind you fall in love in the right place, and don't get a wife who will drain your purse and make you niggardly in spite of yourself' (170). This advice resonates, for the reader, quite strongly as a 'warning' against Hetty, whom we have already seen in the privacy of her bedchamber trying on the tawdry bangles and earrings she longs to replace with real finery through marriage to a nobleman like Arthur Donnithorne. Hetty longs for the material signs of a profligate and degenerate aristocracy (which in its wanton expenditure stands in, as we have already seen, for the modern credit economy) whereas Dinah's moderate desires are figures for a utopian precredit barter economy where production and consumption are in harmonious balance.

Both Hetty and Dinah, as the novel's two unmarried and marriageable heroines, are thus explicitly assessed as potential financial managers and custodians of their husbands' assets. The irony here is that, although their future managerial roles may bring them a certain degree of autonomy and power (as in the case of Mrs Poyser), they are at present figured quite openly as objects in an economic exchange by men – their potential husbands. Their abilities as economic managers constitute merely a wifely asset, quite literally: their skill in safeguarding their husbands' money is figured as just another one of those assets. Because even the theoretically powerful characteristics of financial management are easily subsumed, in this logic, under the mantle of patriarchal control, the women who are to effect this management are figured as objects of their suitors' desire and assessment. Hetty is continually described in ornamental/sexual terms; just before her pregnancy is revealed, the narrator foreshadows the tragedy by bemoaning the waste of such a potential wife:

> Yes, the actions of a little trivial soul like Hetty's, struggling amidst the serious, sad destinies of a human being, are strange. So are the motions of a little vessel without ballast tossed about on a stormy sea. How pretty it looked with its particoloured sail in the sunlight, moored in a quiet bay!
>
> 'Let that man bear the loss who loosed it from its moorings.'
>
> But that will not save the vessel – the pretty thing that might have been a life-long joy. (340)

Even Arthur, who has no intention of making Hetty his wife but is struggling with the temptation to make her his mistress, describes his desire for her in explicit object/consumer terms: 'However strong a man's resolution may be, it costs him something to carry it out, now and then. We may determine not to gather any cherries, and keep our hands sturdily in our pockets, but we can't prevent our mouths from watering' (167).

The young heroines of *Adam Bede* are thus in a paradoxical position; they are figured both as potential guardians and caretakers of the economic order and as objects in a largely economic exchange. This paradoxical position maintains the appearance of balance central to the concerns of the novel. The avoidance and liquidation of excess is one of the driving forces behind the ethos of 'management' valorized by the inhabitants of Hayslope and the narrator of *Adam Bede*; the prospect of a truly powerful woman would be excess of the most horrifying sort. (We will later see what such a woman looks like in the figure of Mrs Glegg in *The Mill on the Floss*.) The potentially disruptive female managerial forces are carefully balanced or neutralized in the novel: Dinah must stop preaching and Hetty is banished and eventually killed off.

In the most direct balancing of potentially threatening female strength, Mrs Poyser is held in check by the equally acerbic tongue of the archmisogynist Bartle Massey. After being treated to their isolated pearls of wisdom throughout the novel, the reader finally gets to see these two characters confront each other in one of the final chapters:

> [Mrs Poyser]: 'I'm not denyin' the women are foolish: God Almighty made 'em to match the men.'
> 'Match!' said Bartle; 'ay, as vinegar matches one's teeth. If a man says a word, his wife 'll match it with a contradiction; if he's a mind for hot meat, his wife 'll match it with cold bacon ...'
> 'Yes,' said Mrs. Poyser, 'I know what the men like – a poor soft, as 'ud simper at 'em like the pictur o' the sun, whether they did right or wrong, an' say thank you for a kick, an' pretend she didna know which end she stood uppermost, till her husband told her. That's what a man wants in a wife, mostly.' (525)

While they are engaged in a spirited (and ill-natured) disagreement, Mrs Poyser and Bartle Massey are also enacting the very subject of their debate: matching. The effect of this exchange is to both temper the threatening, masculine strength of Mrs Poyser and to undermine the authority of the misogynist comments Massey had been making throughout the novel. Massey does seem to have the last word by proxy, however; it is through the very issue of 'management'. that the schoolteacher questions Mrs Poyser's authority. Craig the gardener tentatively defends her, only to be upbraided by Massey:

> 'Well,' said Mr. Craig ... 'I like a cleverish woman – a woman o' sperrit – a managing woman.'
>
> 'You're out there, Craig,' said Bartle, dryly, 'you're out there ... You pick the things for what they can excel in – for what they can excel in. You don't value your peas for their roots, or your carrots for their flowers. Now that's the way you should choose women: their cleverness'll never come to much – never come to much; but they make excellent simpletons, ripe and strong-flavoured.' (525)

It is her skills in managing that form the basis of Mrs. Poyser's power and authority; by presuming to cleverness in this area, she is actually poaching on what Massey sees as a masculine preserve.[12] However, the other characters in the novel, as well as the narrator, have delineated financial management as the female field of influence; by questioning this view through the words of Bartle Massey, the novel interrogates a potentially destabilizing gender transgression and moves the dynamic back into a state of balance and equilibrium – which of course means patriarchal control.[13]

As central as the issues of female management and exchange are to *Adam Bede*, the striving for balance that characterizes the economic world of the novel is perhaps most strikingly evident in Arthur Donnithorne's ethical dilemma. Arthur's moral economy is one of recompense; he envisions a theoretical balance between harm and good that eventually renders wrongdoing somehow acceptable, or at least tolerable. The narrator reveals this trait in the following anecdote:

> When he was a lad of seven, he one day kicked down an old gardener's pitcher of broth, from no motive but a kicking impulse, not reflecting that it was the old man's dinner; but on learning that sad fact, he took his favourite pencil-case and a silver-hafted knife out of his pocket and offered them as compensation. He had been the same Arthur ever since, trying to make all offences forgotten in benefits. If there were any bitterness in his nature, it could only show itself against the man who refused to be conciliated by him. (310–11)

Arthur imagines that ethical imperatives operate like an economic system, that a loss can simply be offset by a gain somewhere else. This
is not merely his view in regard to Hetty; he is strongly invested in
the idea that the entire world operates according to this principle. His
ethical economy not only leads him to believe that wrong can be com-
pensated with right, but that harm should confine itself to those who
deserve it. He cannot imagine that the consequences of his own 'hob-
ble' could affect anyone other than himself:

> Unhappily there is no inherent poetical justice in hobbles, and they will
> sometimes obstinately refuse to inflict their worst consequences on the
> prime offender, in spite of his loudly-expressed wish. It was entirely ow-
> ing to this deficiency in the scheme of things that Arthur had ever brought
> any one into trouble besides himself. He was nothing, if not good-natured;
> and all his pictures of the future, when he should come into the estate,
> were made up of a prosperous, contented tenantry, adoring their landlord.
> (124–5)

Arthur's visions of worldly prosperity are inseparable from this
good-natured faith in the fairness and balance of consequence; he imagines his success and happiness solely within the context of a world
where consequences operate logically. This glib and naive world view,
Eliot suggests, is a luxury possible only for someone with prospects of
Arthur's kind of prosperity. When Adam and Arthur meet for the second time in the wood after Hetty's trial, Adam is deeply suspicious of
this quality in Arthur:

> Arthur's words had precisely the opposite effect to that he had antici-
> pated. Adam thought he perceived in them that notion of compensation
> for irretrievable wrong, that self-soothing attempt to make evil bear the
> same fruits as good, which most of all roused his indignation. He was as
> strongly impelled to look painful facts right in the face, as Arthur was to
> turn away from them. Moreover, he had the wakeful suspicious pride of a
> poor man in the presence of a rich man. (466)

As the previous two quotations suggest, Arthur's ethical theory is
predicated upon and enabled by his socio-economic status. His escapist
dream of benevolent patronage is intimately linked with his complacent
notions of contained consequence, and his status as a 'rich man' allows
him the luxury of self-soothing indulgence, the ability to avoid facing

the painful facts that Adam cannot avoid. Just as he somehow imagines that a silver knife will make up for a lost dinner, so he is insulated from the harsh realities that make up the world of the labouring poor like Adam. He has no understanding of the unfair operation of consequence because he has been completely insulated from the effects of his actions on those 'beneath' him. Never having had to see how his thoughtlessness affects others – just as he does not have to see Hetty's pregnancy, flight, and child murder – he has no understanding that it does so.

Poverty is no guarantee of the ability to understand the logic of consequence, however. Sensitivity to ethical questions and an understanding of the interrelatedness of human actions is metaphorically linked in this novel not to simple poverty, but to an ability to read and understand narrative. The narrator explains Hetty's ignorance of the dangers of her affair with Arthur: 'Hetty had never read a novel: if she had ever seen one, I think the words would have been too hard for her: how then could she find a shape for her expectations?' (136). The skill that comes with novel-reading, the ability to understand the temporal and causal sequences of narrative, is what enables one to formulate expectations. It is not merely the case that ignorance of narrative does not allow one to formulate expectations, but also that it can lead one to false expectations. Even Adam is not immune from this problem; after Hetty begins her affair with Arthur, Adam misreads her new kindness toward him: 'Hetty, we know, was not the first woman that had behaved more gently to the man who loved her in vain, because she had herself begun to love another. It was a very old story; but Adam knew nothing about it, so he drank in the sweet delusion' (221).

These are not unimportant mistakes. These two delusions – Hetty's formless dreams and Adam's misreading – form the drive train of the causal machinery of the novel; they initiate and perpetuate the entire tragedy of *Adam Bede*. It is through the metaphor of reading that Eliot connects the novel's central ethical concern of consequence with the notion of agency; consequence in this sense does not mean a mindless operation of fate, a text written by an unseen hand, but rather a series of events that can be controlled by will, a text which, being read, can be altered. If Hetty had intuited the plot of her story in advance, and if Adam had been familiar with the fable of deceptive tenderness, then the terrible events that follow would not have occurred.

This combination of inadvertent cruelty and lack of imagination is one that Ruskin reviles in his (in)famous address to young women in *Sesame and Lilies*:

Unless you are deliberately kind to every creature, you will often be cruel to many. Cruel, partly through want of imagination, (a far rarer and weaker faculty in women than men,) and yet more, at the present day, through the subtle encouragement of your selfishness by the religious doctrine that all which we now suppose to be evil will be brought to a good end ... Of course we are ignorant and blind creatures, and we cannot know what seeds of good may be in present suffering, or present crime; but with what we cannot know we are not concerned. It is conceivable that murderers and liars may in some distant world be exalted into a higher humanity than they could have reached without homicide or falsehood; but the contingency is not one by which our actions should be guided. (*Works* 18:41–2)

Ruskin's comments – whose content and moralizing tenor could have come straight from one of Eliot's own narrators – help to draw attention to one of the potential paradoxes of the narratorial rhetoric in *Adam Bede*. While Eliot reviles Arthur for not attending to the future reverberations of his present-day actions, the unforeseen consequences that may attend his petty acts of selfishness and indulgence, she simultaneously ridicules his inadequate attempts at recompense. Yet surely these feeble acts of reparation indicate some sensitivity to causality on the part of Arthur, even if he is not capable of the far-ranging vision of the narrator himself, who is able to foresee – or at least darkly hint at – the future ramifications of Arthur's, Hetty's, and Adam's actions and decisions. Insofar as Arthur's misadventures are meant to serve as a cautionary tale to the reader, it seems a bit of a hard lesson for any reader to internalize: ideally, be omniscient; failing that, never do anything wrong; failing that, for heaven's sake do not try to make up for your wrongdoing. This paradox is one that, as I will discuss further below, ultimately blunts the ethical force of Eliot's prescriptive economics in *Adam Bede*.

This persistent – and paradoxical – concern with characters' agency, imagination, and knowledge aligns the ethical problem of consequence with the novel's problematics of consumption and management. Once again, it is Mrs Poyser who is the pivotal figure: she is presented not only as *Adam Bede*'s foremost manager, but also as its premier manipulator of narrative. She is as close as we get to a character actually able to follow at least some of the lessons set by the narrator: she foresees consequences and she 'narrates' their effects. Mr Irwine characterizes her fluency with story thus: 'She's quite original in her talk ... one of those untaught wits that help to stock a country with proverbs. I told you that capital thing I heard her say about Craig – that he was like a cock who thought the sun had risen to hear him crow. Now that's an Æsop's fable in a sentence' (351). But it is of course her ability to read narrative that marks her as a skilful manager. When Hetty comes down to the family dressed in Dinah's cap, she gives Mrs Poyser a start that causes everyone to laugh; Mrs Poyser, in an attempt to regain control of the situation, claims that Dinah's goodness and charity to those truly in need are no laughing matter. The narrator comments: 'Mrs. Poyser, you perceive, was aware that nothing would be so likely to expel the comic as the terrible' (229). Mrs Poyser understands the subtle workings of narrative, the psychological effects of, and the nuances between, comedy and tragedy, fable and maxim; it is this sensitivity to the exemplary texts that form the template of expectations and consequences that gives her her great strength – her ability to manage those around her so effectively. Skill in reading is crucial to an understanding of consequence, and an understanding of consequence is indispensable to effective management.

The logic of *Adam Bede* thus relates techniques of management, elimination and avoidance of excess and waste, balances of production/consumption, and the possibilities of straightforward interpretation and transparency in reading. Together these organizational or epistemic modes align the novel with the utopian, pastoral barter economy that is imagined to have existed before the onset of industrial capitalism – the rise of which is later examined in *The Mill on the Floss*. However, as I indicated at the beginning of this discussion, Eliot's valorization of this ideal economy of balance and 'wastelessness' is attenuated by a persistent anxiety and mistrust of the possibilities for such a world. This mistrust is evidenced by the narrator's scepticism about Arthur's fantasy of ethical recompense, about the possibility of transparent narratives that can be easily read and interpreted, and about the place of women, especially Hetty, in the economic system of exchange of which they are expected to be a part. It is the figure of Hetty who, in the end, both vividly demonstrates the problems of the utopian economy of *Adam Bede* and functions as a kind of unconscious resolution of those problems.

3 The Ubiquity of Surplus and the Unavoidability of Loss

While Arthur's ethos of compensation and contained consequence is presented as an ideal, economically balanced, closed system, it is in fact questioned and rejected as untenable in the logic of the novel.

When Arthur first learns that his best friend Adam is in love with Hetty (whom Arthur has already seduced), he is confronted with the limits of his moral code; the narrator simultaneously explains and criticizes Arthur's thinking:

> If deeds of gift, or any other deeds, could have restored Adam's content-
> ment and regard for him as a benefactor, Arthur would not only have ex-
> ecuted them without hesitation, but would have felt bound all the more
> closely to Adam, and would never have been weary of making retribution.
> But Adam could receive no amends; his suffering could not be cancelled;
> his respect and affection could not be recovered by any prompt deeds of
> atonement. He stood like an immovable obstacle against which no pres-
> sure could avail; an embodiment of what Arthur most shrank from believ-
> ing in – the irrevocableness of his own wrong-doing. (311)

Adam's pain and suffering are figured here as the irreducible remainder of Arthur's ethical economy, a surplus that cannot be liquidated
through the usual means (translation into 'deeds of gift'). Adam himself, with his great strength, moral righteousness, and threatening masculinity (it is 'above all, the sense of having been knocked down' that
most unsettles Arthur) is the nightmare figure, the figure of pure drive
that cannot be placated by the feminized Arthur with his white hands,
his rich clothes, and his dreams of ethical utopia. It is Adam himself
who mouths the most straightforward and damning condemnation of
Arthur's moral scheme later in the novel: '*Her* ruin can't be undone.
I hate that talk of people, as if there was a way o' making amends for
everything. They'd more need be brought to see as the wrong they do
can never be altered' (459, emphasis in original). Again, Adam speaks
for the irreducible efficacy, the untranslatability, of ethical acts – the decisions that Arthur has made cannot be seen as part of a utopian system
with free-floating and wholly interchangeable signs. Adam represents,
in a sense, a 'founding standard' – the gold specie – of ethical behaviour.
   Yet it is not merely Arthur's ideal of emotional recompense that is rejected in this logic; it is also his notion that the consequences of actions
can be confined to those who 'deserve' them – the actors themselves. As
Mr Irwine explains to Arthur: 'Consequences are unpitying. Our deeds
carry their terrible consequences, quite apart from any fluctuations that
went before – consequences that are hardly ever confined to ourselves'
(172). Not only are the consequences of our actions not confined to ourselves, but it is impossible ever to know how far those consequences

may extend. As Mr Irwine says to Adam later, 'The problem how far a man is to be held responsible for the unforeseen consequences of his own deed, is one that might well make us tremble to look into it' (422). It is this uncertainty and uncontainability (indeed, sublimity), together with the fact that actions are not of the same kind as reparations, that makes the ideal of compensation impossible: because we can never fully understand how far or long the consequences of an act may persist, we can never hope to compensate fully for all the wrong we may have caused – even if unethical acts were of the same currency as amends. The novel's condemnation of Arthur's naive and impracticable moral view thus troubles the idea of a utopian barter ethos in which acts are interchangeable with other, compensatory acts and there is no surplus of undeserved suffering or unpleasure; this condemnation suggests a world in which excess cannot always be eliminated. Just as with Spencer's economic analysis, where epistemological uncertainty is simultaneously a cause and an unavoidable effect of the introduction of credit, so with the moral world of *Adam Bede*: uncertainty about the effects of an ethical choice disrupts the balance and transparency of the barter moral code.[14]

Just as Spencer's analysis suggests that an economy made up of perfectly honest people eliminates epistemological uncertainty, only to reintroduce unintentionally that uncertainty through the concept of credit, so too is Eliot's implied claim that an ability to read and a knowledge of narrative can protect one from unintended consequences belied by the novel's mistrust of transparent interpretation. In apologetically describing the antiquated religious beliefs of Dinah and Seth, the narrator admits that it is possible 'to have very erroneous theories and very sublime feelings' (38); the basis of character judgment should be a person's sympathetic intentions and not her admittedly problematic 'way of interpreting.' This exhortation admits the possibility that one act of misreading (a misguided action based on faulty logic yet sound moral principles) can be counterbalanced by another act of correct reading (the understanding of those sound principles and forgiveness of the action itself).

While this faith in the possibilities of sympathy – both on the part of the actor and on the part of those interpreting her actions – to undo the harm of poor theory or erroneous interpretation seems to cut in the direction of the novel's belief in the possibilities of an ultimate 'correct' reading, there is a deeper sense in which even sympathy cannot guarantee against certain kinds of misreading. Eliot continually points to the problem of family resemblance throughout the novel; there is a profound irony in the fact that relatives may superficially resemble one another and yet be divided by the most insurmountable moral and psychological barriers. On the very next page after the apology noted above, the narrator opines: 'Family likeness has often a deep sadness in it. Nature, that great tragic dramatist, knits us together by bone and muscle, and divides us by the subtler web of our brains; blends yearning and repulsion; and ties us by our heartstrings to the beings that jar us at every moment' (39–40). And yet the question of which signifier to privilege in the mystery of family resemblance, physical appearance or temperamental predisposition, is contested throughout the novel. Mr Irwine and his mother have a disagreement about this very topic:

> 'Don't you remember how it was with Juno's last pups? One of them was the very image of its mother but it had two or three of its father's tricks notwithstanding. Nature is clever enough to cheat even you, mother.'
> 'Nonsense, child! Nature never makes a ferret in the shape of a mastiff. You'll never persuade me that I can't tell what men are by their outsides. If I don't like a man's looks, depend upon it I shall never like *him*. I don't want to know people that look ugly and disagreeable, any more than I want to taste dishes that look disagreeable.' (64–5)

Mrs Irwine's faith in the transparent relationship between inside and outside, between character and physiognomy, is precisely that attitude which is questioned throughout the novel; she serves as a philosophical mouthpiece for the unquestioning worship of physical beauty that proves to be Adam's great mistake about Hetty. As the voyeuristic narrator contemplates Hetty's primping before her bed-chamber mirror, he acknowledges that her beauty, and that of all attractive women, can easily lead men to make such tragic mistakes about character:

> Every man under such circumstances is conscious of being a great physiognomist. Nature, he knows, has a language of her own, which she uses with strict veracity, and he considers himself an adept in the language. Nature has written out his bride's character for him in those exquisite lines of cheek and lip and chin, in those eyelids delicate as petals, in those long lashes curled like the stamen of a flower, in the dark liquid depths of those wonderful eyes. (152–3)

This speech must be read as ironic at this point in the novel; the reader has just been acquainted with the vanity and selfishness in Hetty's character in the very scene in which this commentary appears. To further underscore the point, however, the narrator explicitly gives those reckless misreaders a slap on the wrist on the next page: 'Nature has her language, and she is not unveracious; but we don't know all the intricacies of her syntax just yet, and in a hasty reading we may happen to extract the very opposite of her real meaning' (153–4).

The novel's mistrust of fallible human interpretation in this regard is explained as the greater wisdom – or greater inscrutability – of 'Nature.' This is not a radical questioning of the ultimate interpretability of all texts, for the problem is figured as inherent in the text of Nature itself, not in the reader or the very process of reading. But the existence of an internal or deep entity called 'character' which cannot be represented by external or superficial appearance (or if it can be represented, is represented in such a way that it cannot be readily decoded) belies the idea that skilled reading can protect one from unintended consequences. In a novel with a moral such as *Adam Bede*, this amounts to an almost nihilistic claim; for if the logic of the narrative instructs the reader that sympathetic understanding and a knowledge of consequence can protect against the kind of tragedy that strikes Hetty, Arthur, and Adam, it simultaneously questions the mechanisms that secure this understanding and knowledge: reading and interpretation.

4 Bad Hetty

The plot of *Adam Bede* deepens this scepticism about the possibility of maintaining a balanced moral and epistemological 'economy' by questioning the status of the novel's primary token of exchange: Hetty. While she is, as we have seen, variously figured as a commodity to be assessed in the marriage market and a tempting treat against which Arthur must keep his hands 'sturdily in [his] pockets,' the logic of the novel also resists her characterization as object of exchange by troubling her transfer from Arthur to Adam. The entire burden of Arthur's – and the novel's – plan for ethical recompense rests upon Hetty's deciding to love and accept Adam; she must channel her unruly desires into a more appropriate path in order to undo the damage caused by her affair with Arthur: '[Arthur] persuaded himself that the course was to make the way open between Adam and Hetty. Her heart might really turn to Adam, as he said, after a while; and *in that case there would have been no great harm done*' (315, emphasis added). And Hetty does, in fact, intend to go along with this tidy plan, in a cold-blooded and listless sort of way: 'Why should she not marry Adam? She did not care what she did, so that it made some change in her life' (339). But this easy resolution of the dilemma does not quite happen, and it becomes clear that Hetty is not the unproblematic token of exchange that the novel originally hinted she was. It is her recalcitrance, her stubborn refusal to act as a stable currency in the economic logic of the novel, that seems most sharply to call into question the utopian barter system that the novel, on one level, attempts to invoke.

As we have already seen, the logic of *Adam Bede* critiques the ethical barter system of Arthur Donnithorne; in addition to an implicit claim that the currency of amends cannot be of the same kind as that of injury, the novel also implies that such a system must fail because we can never know the extent of the consequences of our actions. Adam himself takes this idea one step further, and claims definitively that there is no end to the chain of consequence: 'You can never do what's wrong without breeding sin and trouble more than you can ever see ... You never see th'end o' the mischief it'll do' (167).

This claim is echoed by the novel's mouthpiece of misogyny, Bartle Massey, in a somewhat different context. He declares that a 'scolding, nagging woman' – which is, for him, all women – 'go[es] on with the same thing over and over again, and never come[s] to a reasonable end' (261). This despair over the impossibility of a 'reasonable end' is then further echoed, developed, and narrowed by the novel's narrator, who applies it directly to the case of Hetty: 'What will be the end? – the end of her objectless wandering, apart from all love, caring for human beings only through her pride, clinging to life only as the hunted wounded brute clings to it?' (389). This repetitive questioning of 'the end' and Hetty's role in it, coupled with the fact that it is clearly Hetty's problematic inability to go along with the program that occasions all of this agonized hand-wringing in the first place, focuses the full force of the problem of closure on the figure of Hetty. The implied problem here is her status as a woman; it is women who 'can never come to a reasonable end,' who trouble attempts to place them firmly within a system of exchange which will neutralize the havoc they have wrought. It is as if, according to Hélène Cixous, the insistence of the feminine – in this case, Hetty's, Mrs Poyser's, and perhaps even Eliot's herself – in itself troubles closure: 'Her writing can only keep going, without ever inscribing or discerning contours ... [Her language] knows neither enclosure nor death' (259–60). It is Hetty's particularly exaggerated version of cultural femininity – her primping, selfishness and shallow vanity, her abundant curls, high colouring, and 'rounded arms'[15] – which is the focus both of the novel's concern with endlessness and of its disgust with and moralistic condemnation of its heroine.

And, of course, it is the ultimate marker of Hetty's womanliness, her pregnancy, which really troubles the easy resolution of the plot. It is through her pregnancy that her body thwarts both Arthur's attempt to work his ethical recompense and her own status as token of exchange, and of course betrays her 'shame,' her great transgression of the code that enables such exchanges in the first place. Hetty's virginity is the imprimatur of her desirability as a token in this exchange system, and the fact that Adam has unknowingly been robbed of this most important dowry gives Arthur pause: 'Adam was deceived – deceived in a way that Arthur would have resented as a deep wrong if it had been practised on himself' (315). But it is important to note that this is a deception; there is no way for Adam to know the extent of the forbidden relationship until Hetty's flight and child murder. It is only when the 'hidden dread' makes itself manifest that the extent of Arthur's treachery and Hetty's transgression becomes clear; it is only through the uncontainable and relentless workings of her body that Hetty does violence to the orderly and tidy alternative plot that the men had worked out together. It is Hetty's pregnancy – and its seemingly natural extension, her infanticide – which prevents the neat resolution of the dilemma; it is thus her pregnancy and infanticide which are also the enabling events of the novel's 'real' plot. To return to Cixous, it is as if Hetty's body begins to generate an alternative narrative in a way that echoes Cixous's claims for an *écriture féminine:* it is through the very operations of the woman's corporeality itself that a narrative is generated that challenges the stability and readability of the dominant plot.

The subversive potential of this alternative narrative is sharply circumscribed, however; as Sedgwick points out, the 'sexual narrative' of Hetty 'occurs with the overtaking of an active search for power of which she is the *subject,* by an already-constituted symbolic power exchange between men of which her very misconstruction, her sense of purposefulness, proves her to have been the designated *object*' (159). While her transgressions may constitute a challenge to the constraints of Victorian morality, this challenge is readily quashed; it is the uncontainability of the sexual narrative within the constraints of the novel's symbolic economy which seems to necessitate Hetty's banishment and death.

Hetty herself cannot imagine how her story will end; because of her pregnancy she can 'conceive no other existence for herself than a hidden one' (371). Her desperate efforts to hide her pregnancy have siphoned off whatever rudimentary ability she might have had to imagine a course of action and a future for herself: 'After the first on-coming of her great dread ... she had waited and waited, in the blind vague hope that something would happen to set her free from her terror ... All the force of her nature had been concentrated on the one effort of concealment' (365). And here an important paradox is inaugurated: Hetty's pregnancy disrupts the putative 'masculine' plot of exchange that is to be worked out between Arthur and Adam, yet it is important that her pregnancy be revealed in order for the novel's demonstration of ethical consequence to be effected. By attempting to hide her 'transgression,' Hetty threatens to undermine the ethical economy of the novel. Hetty's alternative narrative is one in which concealment would halt the unfolding of consequence that is the author's central ethical and artistic project. Hetty's concealment is not in the service of a plot that will ultimately demonstrate the moral truth of the uncontainability of consequences; it is a selfish motivation that, if successful, would undermine that demonstration.

Hetty's attempts at concealment are important for another reason. As I suggested earlier, it is as a concealer that Hetty wreaks the most damage to the symbolic ethical economy of the novel. She manages somehow to hide her pregnancy for nearly eight months, when she flees Hayslope in her doomed attempt to find Arthur. But it is not just her pregnancy she conceals: the particular method of infanticide she chooses is it to hide the baby in a nest of leaves and cover it – basically to bury it alive – but in her decision to leave it some room to breathe she betrays the fact that it is concealment, and not necessarily murder, that is her chief motive. Under the 1624 statute that would still have been in force at the time of Hetty's crime, an unmarried woman who concealed the death (not necessarily the body) of her infant would have been presumed guilty of murder and thus not tried under common-law rules of evidence.[16]

According to historian Mark Jackson, a woman who enlisted help in her delivery was almost always tried under common law (to her advantage) since this was considered proof that she had not intended to conceal the infant's death. Since there is some ambiguity in Hetty's intent with regard to the baby, and no partial verdict of manslaughter was available in infanticide cases, most juries would have tended to acquit in a case such as Hetty's (*New-Born* 144). There is thus a suggestion that Eliot has dealt much more harshly with Hetty than historical precedent suggests was likely. While, as Jackson argues, the situation is extremely complex, it remains true that 'convictions under the statute were rare in the last half of the 18th century … [and i]n this sense, her conviction was unusual' ('Re: Inquiry'). Eliot 'punishes' Hetty more clearly for her acts of concealment than for her confessed abandonment of her child.

The text itself, at the level of plot, enacts this concern with conceal-ment in the odd non-narration of Hetty's childbirth and murder. The narrator leaves Hetty abruptly in her wanderings, before she has given birth, to return to Hayslope and the panic engendered by her flight. The reader learns of Hetty's imprisonment from a letter that Parson Irwine reads to Adam, and we only learn the details of the birth and murder many chapters later, through the testimony of witnesses at the trial.[17]

However, the birth 'episode' in the novel suggests a different set of complications. Because of the way the narration is structured, so that we hear the account of the midwife figure and the man who discovers the infant's body (which Hetty does not in fact hide until many hours or days later) back to back during the course of the trial testimony, these two episodes – the birth and the concealment/murder – are presented as a single event. Furthermore, the way that the 'concealment' is described by the eyewitness strongly suggests that Hetty has dismembered the body of her child. As the labourer who discovers the baby testifies:

'Just as I was stooping and laying down the stakes, I saw something odd and round and whitish lying on the ground under a nut-bush by the side of me. And I stooped down on hands and knees to pick it up. And I saw it was a little baby's hand … There was a lot of timber-choppings put together just where the ground went hollow, like, under the bush, and the hand came out from among them. But there was a hole left in one place, and I could see down it, and see the child's head.' (434)

We later learn that the body of the infant is intact, but the reader's (and trial-goer's) first impression of the discovery of Hetty's dead baby is that the limbs and head were found in separate places, and that the infanticide was a much more decisive and violent act than the tenta-tive concealment of a live infant in a nest of leaves. The processes of pregnancy, childbirth, and (perhaps) dismemberment – all under the rubric of concealment – are thus seamlessly integrated in the account of Hetty's crime.

Hetty herself (or strictly speaking, Hetty's sexual attractiveness) is consistently associated with dismemberment throughout the novel. When Adam contemplates Arthur's behaviour toward Hetty, he envisions his friend's only options to have been seduction or self-mutilation: 'All for a bit o' pleasure, as, if he'd had a man's heart in him, he'd ha' cut his hand off sooner than he'd ha' taken it. What if he didn't foresee what's happened? He foresaw enough' (423). Arthur's usual failure to foresee the consequences of his actions may have saved him a limb (and rescued the plot), but it cost Hetty her virginal integrity and ultimately her life.

This is not the only time Adam associates the danger of Hetty's charms with the danger of dismemberment. After he has seen Hetty and Arthur embracing in the grove but still thinks they are engaging in a harmless flirtation, he is mistakenly grateful that his discovery has stopped things from going too far: 'It 'ud ha' gone near to spoil my work for me, if I'd seen her brought to sorrow and shame; and through the man as I've always been proud to think on. Since I've been spared that, I've no right to grumble. When a man's got his limbs whole, he can bear a smart cut or two' (325). Little does he know that this particular 'limb' is about to be amputated with the discovery of Hetty's infanticide. Later, after the trial and Hetty's transportation, Adam wonders if he will ever recover from his love of her: 'Now there was ... no moment in the distance when duty would take off her iron glove and breastplate and clasp him gently into rest ... Love, he thought, could never be anything to him but a living memory – a limb lopped off, but not gone from consciousness' (488). The hand of Duty has severed the phantom limb of Adam's delusional attraction.

Hetty's own bodily integrity is also called into question through this persistent focus on extremities. We hear quite a bit about the charms of Hetty's 'limbs' throughout the novel, but perhaps the most striking example is when she contemplates drowning herself after the first onset of her 'hidden dread': 'She clasps her hands round her knees, and leans forward, and looks earnestly at [the pool], as if trying to guess what sort of bed it would make for her young round limbs' (365). Later, after she again decides against suicide in front of another pool, she is delirious with joy and relief: 'The very consciousness of her own limbs was a delight to her: she turned up her sleeves, and kissed her arms with the passionate love of life' (387). Of course, this passionate, life-affirming love of her own limbs presages her later finding a 'sort of bed' for the 'young round limbs' of her newborn child.

In each example I have noted, the threat of dismemberment is fore-stalled: Arthur prefers seduction to self-mutilation; Hetty does not drown herself; her infant is not dismembered but concealed. Even the 'limbs' of Adam's optimism and capacity for romantic love are not ultimately lost, but recovered through his more mature and appropriate love of Dinah. At the very end of the novel, these various thematic threads are neatly tied together when Adam reports having seen Arthur upon the latter's return to England:

> 'It was very cutting when we first saw one another. He'd never heard about poor Hetty till Mr. Irwine met him in London, for the letters missed him on his journey. The first thing he said to me, when we'd got hold o' one another's hands was, "I could never do anything for her, Adam – she lived long enough for all the suffering – and I'd thought so of the time when I might do something for her. But you told me the truth when you said to me once, 'There's a sort of wrong that can never be made up for.'"' (540)

It may have been 'cutting' to see each other, but not quite to the point of dismemberment; the two men can still get 'hold o' one another's hands' and affirm the great moral lesson of the novel, that 'there's a sort of wrong that can never be made up for.' Hetty's sacrifice has enabled the men's ultimate moral 'wholeness'; the great threat of castrating dismemberment she posed has been defused by the narrative parenthesis of her death.

This particular threat can also be read as an economic one. We have seen how Hetty's 'excessive' femininity figures the dangers of economic surplus; as I noted in the introduction, Ruskin also associates perverse feminine economics with castration: in *Munera Pulveris*, the hoarder is likened to a 'money-chest with a slit in it, not only receptant but suctional' (*Works* 17:169). The threat of castration that Hetty poses might also be read as part of the more general fear of emasculation, attendant upon increasing economic specialization, that Gordon Bigelow discusses in his reading of Adam Smith. Bigelow notes that in the *Wealth of Nations*, Smith fears that the division of labour will render the specialized worker a 'coward, a man incapable of defending or avenging himself,' and that this emasculation is figured quite literally (if unintentionally) as a castration: he 'wants one of the most essential parts of the character of a man' and is 'as much mutilated and deformed' as a man 'deprived of some of his most essential members' (*Wealth of Nations* Book 5, qtd in

Bigelow 48). While I would not push this reading of Hetty's castration threat to the point of claiming that she single-handedly represents the encroachment of the modern credit economy on the verdant vales of Hayslope – for one thing, Hetty is aligned with the consumption function in the novel while Smith is concerned with problems of production – I find the connection to Smith's anxieties quite suggestive. Given that in her first two novels Eliot depicts the shift from physiocratic models of balance and moderation to the uncertainties and complexities of the modern credit economy, the fact that Hetty is associated with excessive desires, surplus expenditure, wanton femininity, *and* dismemberment and castration fits well with Smith's fears that a highly specialized, alienated worker will also be an emasculated one. While Adam possesses an almost comically heroic masculinity, there is a whiff of the reaction formation about the narrator's descriptions of his brawny might; he is clearly an avatar of a fantasized, lost generation of self-sufficient economic everymen, at one with his labour and with the landscape. While Hetty's castration threat is forestalled, the reassuring wholeness of both Adam and Arthur at the end of the novel is also tinged with nostalgia and compensation.

Hetty thus embodies simultaneously narrative and economic excess: both the strategy of concealment and the practice of dismemberment have threatened to undermine the novel's depiction of a self-contained ethical economy as well as its financial 'balance.' (While Arthur's mistake is to challenge this ethos of consequence, his erroneous views serve as a demonstration of Eliot's thesis, while Hetty's do not.) The hidden dread of a secret birth becomes a botched and bifurcated 'text,' a baby whose body has perhaps even been dismembered by its mother. Eliot's removal of Hetty from the utopian vision of moral and bodily integrity at the end of the novel also expunges the threats she had posed. As Raymond Williams eloquently notes, Hetty is a 'girl whom the novelist abandons in a moral action more decisive than Hetty's own confused and desperate leaving of her child' (173). Hetty Sorrel, with her obsessive concealment, her unwanted birth, and her disjointed 'text,' is the figure for both an imagined escape from the world of consequence and the threat of a narrative that will never end; as such, she becomes the sacrificial victim to the strictures of both novelistic closure and the self-contained ethical economy.

The logic of the novel thus comes full circle – from a kind of hopeful faith in the possibilities of reading and interpretation, to a deep scepticism about the veracity of physical, bodily characteristics in relation to character, and then finally returning to a complete dependence on the manifestations of the body to reveal the whole story about internal moral qualities. The attempt to revivify this moribund idea is clumsy at best; it is as if Eliot were making a last-ditch attempt to stabilize the ethical havoc wrought by Hetty's almost getting away with it. Wrong will be punished; the dangerous idea that Hetty could partake of marital pleasures and then pass herself off as bride material must be countermanded by her own 'betrayal' of her secret. It is through Hetty's pregnancy that the novel neutralizes the threat to its moral universe that she poses; it is through her banishment (really just an extension of her pregnancy) and death that the novel finally comes to an end. *Adam Bede* set out to argue against the containability of moral consequence while still maintaining the stability and enclosure of a utopian barter ethos; in the figure of Hetty, it got quite a bit more 'uncontainability' than it bargained for. It will take Maggie Tulliver, the heroine of Eliot's next novel, to bring this threat of uncontainability to the modern credit economy into sharper focus.

3 Superfluity and Suction: The Problem with Saving in *The Mill on the Floss*

Our friend Mr Tulliver had a good-natured fibre in him, and did not like to give harsh refusals even to a sister, who had not only come into the world in that superfluous way characteristic of sisters, creating a necessity for mortgages, but had quite thrown herself away in marriage.

(Eliot, *Mill* 77)

In the hands of George Eliot, it begins at the beginning of all things, and stops short at the end of her third volume.

(Rev. of *The Mill on the Floss, Dublin University Magazine* 146)

Why must Maggie Tulliver die? For both contemporary and modern readers of George Eliot's second novel, the abrupt and violent death of her beloved heroine has remained an unsettling enigma.[1] The original readers of Eliot's second novel were no less outraged at Maggie's untimely death than were the professional literary critics of the 1980s who engaged in a protracted debate over the problem of the novel's implausible ending.[2] And yet the real paradox is not the ending itself, but the disbelief and consequent explanatory energy it has inspired. Seen from within the theoretical framework of these very same critics, the problematic ending of *The Mill on the Floss* is an enigma-that-is-not-an-enigma: as much recent feminist criticism has insisted, death as well as marriage represents appropriate closure for the Victorian novel. While Maggie certainly dies too soon, just as her Aunt Moss has 'thrown herself away' in marriage, a heroine's dying young should, in theory, occasion no more aesthetic puzzlement than her marrying precipitously.

The real critical dilemma of *The Mill on the Floss* is not the death of its heroine; a fuller analysis of the novel must consider the critical commentary on the ending as a whole. Numerous readers have also expressed their outrage at the clumsiness and implausibility of Maggie's rejection of Stephen Guest in the third volume, as well as at the great flood at the end of the novel.[3] The discomfort the ending occasions is due to the spectacular and nearly superhuman course of renunciation that Maggie undergoes in her decision to abandon her lover and return to the calumny of St Ogg's. The reason for this discomfort is different for Victorian readers of the novel than for the critics of two decades ago; my contention is that the latter have not adequately accounted for the former. For Victorian readers, the drama that Maggie plays out in her saintly self-denial raises troubling and largely unconscious questions about sexual desire and economic demand – and the relationship between the two – that are invoked by the novel's economic preoccupations as well as by its aesthetic 'mistakes.'

The tendency of modern criticism, where it has attempted to explain the disturbing sacrifice of Maggie, had been to ascribe it to the character's unruly passion and Eliot's unconscious need to eliminate her as an emblem of problematic female desire.[4] My contention is just the opposite: that it is Maggie's renunciation – and the troubling questions about desire and demand that it evokes – that seems to require her elimination. Only when we read the novel, including the plot developments of the final volume, through the lens of Victorian political economy can we make sense of this ostensible paradox; as long as the romantic mini-plot of Maggie's great temptation, renunciation, and death is seen as uncomfortably grafted onto the central story of the Dodsons' bankruptcy and regeneration, the ending, and her death in the flood, will likewise seem an afterthought.

Ironically, this 'grafting' is the explanation many readers have given for the abruptness of the flood: the problem of the ending of *The Mill on the Floss* has been blamed on the structure of the novel itself.[5] The bifurcation of the novel into two separate narratives – the economic story of bankruptcy and regeneration, and the romantic story of Maggie's courtship and temptation – necessitates, according to this argument, the abrupt and apocalyptic melding of the two plots in the redemptive waters of the flood: in the end, thus, the narrator can proclaim (of the siblings and of the plots) that 'they were not divided.' Yet this attempt to fuse the two separate plots is usually characterized as a failure; not only is the ending clumsy and unbelievable, but it does nothing to alleviate our sense that the novel itself is awkwardly divided between two unintegrated stories.[6]

While I certainly agree that the novel is bifurcated into two separate narratives – the 'Tom' plot of economic striving and the 'Maggie' plot of sentimental struggle – I would further argue that these are not simply separate stories, one about economics and one about love, but two entirely different modes – of language, ethics, narration, political economy, and closure. The two narrative modes, even as they seem to describe alternatively a world taken up with economics and one from which such concerns are banished, instead engage contradictory strains within Victorian economic thought as a whole. While in her first novel, *Adam Bede*, Eliot was concerned with a precredit barter economy, in her second novel she extends her analysis to the early phases of capitalism in the industrial town of St Ogg's. Here she engages directly the various anxieties attendant upon the contradictory nature of Victorian economic thought: the obsession with monetary representation, the fetishism of objects of 'inherent' value, and the fascination with hoarding that are all the results of the deep, repressed conflict between the optimistic and pessimistic strains of Victorian political economy.

This conflict is reinscribed in *The Mill on the Floss* as the differing modes of language and ethics in the novel's two narratives: the plain meanings and straightforward consequences of Tom and the Dodsons, and the metaphorical viewpoint and complex ethical interdependence of Maggie's world view. In this chapter I will examine the role of political economy in the two different plots, specifically the relationship between the ethical and linguistic modes of Tom and Maggie on the one hand, and the novel's concern with growth, accumulation, and demand on the other. These different modes – especially the rhetorical preoccupation with excess and superfluity surrounding the activities and descriptions of Maggie – engender conflicting notions of proper closure and timely endings. The traumatic ending of *The Mill on the Floss*, I contend, is an end to both the 'economic' and 'romantic' plots; until it is read this way, it will always seem awkward and implausible. While it perhaps does not wholly succeed in suturing the rift between the two narratives, it certainly is successful as a resolution to the thematic problems inaugurated by the novel's economic preoccupations. The novel's aesthetic failure is its conceptual success.

In chapter 1, I traced the strains of thought that constitute the two competing narratives of capitalism: the unshakable faith in the good of accumulation and the bright and limitless future of economic growth, versus the apocalyptic doom of failures of demand and inevitable stagnation. One the one hand, it is fairly easy to see how these conflicting predictions about the fate of the English economy might be manifested in a mid-Victorian novel, notorious for its diametrically opposed plots, largely devoted to a narrative of bankruptcy, recovery, and ultimate disaster. However, while one could argue that the different narratives devoted to Tom and Maggie thus represent, in a fairly straightforward way, the two conflicting Victorian interpretations of capitalist growth, this reading flattens out some important subtleties in the bankruptcy plot devoted to Tom's struggle and the financial preoccupations of his family.

The Dodsons and Tullivers together are, as I will argue, the very embodiment of dominant nineteenth-century economic thought – and, as such, they also demonstrate the conflicting attitudes and obsessions that constitute that thought. We can thus read within the economic or 'Tom' plot, in the minds and habits of the families themselves, the contradictory strains of optimistic striving and pessimistic fetishism found within laissez-faire economics. The 'Maggie' plot, on the other hand, stages a much more troubling and direct challenge to the superficially complacent Victorian economic world view. Maggie's story, inextricably bound up with questions of appetite, demand, and transgressive desire, presents an uncomfortable alternative to the prevailing economic theory from which all questions of effective demand have been banished. The reign of Say's Law within the novel, which nullifies one side of the economic equation by pronouncing that supply creates its own demand, is troubled by Maggie's insistence on foregrounding questions of demand, appetite, and renunciation. Furthermore, the Maggie plot, which invokes sudden, dangerous, and chaotic endings of all kinds, links questions of appetite and desire to questions of closure and metaphorical death, underscoring the threatening and problematic role of economic demand in the broader optimistic view of Victorian political economy.

The differing concerns of the two plots have, as I have suggested, ramifications beyond the immediate economic preoccupations which constitute them as separate modes of narration. Tom's narrative of bankruptcy and regeneration is one in which there are plain meanings, strict cause and effect, linear time and history, plausible events, and unlimited economic growth. The narrative belonging to Maggie, on the other hand, has a different allegiance and grounding metaphorical pre-

occupation: her world view – ethical, linguistic, historical, and economic – is complicated by her sense of endlessly multiplying and potentially
limitless possibilities. This constant multiplication and accumulation of
meanings, choices, and potential actions has its economic analogue in
her persistent invocation of the concepts of 'excess' and 'superfluity.'

Thus the optimistic, laissez-faire view that there can never be too low
a level of demand or too great an accumulation of surplus to threaten
steady and continuous growth – the conventional promise of the Tom
plot – and the warning rumblings against these very possibilities – the
dangerous promise of Maggie's – are brought into direct conflict in the
economic universe of *The Mill on the Floss*. The unstable compromise
that Victorian political economy has wrought between Ricardian optimism and the 'Twilight-of-the-Gods' view of ultimate stagnation[7] is
dramatized – and problematized – by the economic concerns of the Tullivers and the denizens of St Ogg's as a whole, while the metaphorical economy of Maggie exposes and destabilizes the delicate balance
between the two. This, I will argue, is why she is so deeply disruptive,
and why she cannot be contained within the town of St Ogg's or the
plot of *The Mill on the Floss*.

One final note before I turn to a concentrated discussion of the novel
itself. The question of 'historicizing' *The Mill on the Floss*, and especially
of making claims about the economic and cultural milieu of which we
can see traces in the text, is particularly vexed because the novel was,
of course, written in 1859–60 and set in 1829–44 (precisely between the
two greatest economic crises of the Victorian age: the Companies Mania of 1825–6 and the Great Railway Mania of 1844–7). Many of the
economic issues discussed in chapter 1 were specific to the 1820s and
1830s: the crash of 1825–6, which had not yet been naturalized into an
explanatory framework of business 'cycles'; the uncertainty immediately following the return to the gold standard and the resultant wave
of bank failures; and the great influence of Malthusian economics chief
among them. However, as I hope I have convincingly demonstrated in
the earlier chapter, the deeper cultural anxieties attendant upon these
issues were still present until late in the century (if not beyond). Debates
over the gold standard persisted and even intensified; a new wave of
crises, including the railway mania of 1844–7, kept the issues of credit
and inflationary paper very much alive; and the spectre of consumer
demand was never entirely exorcised, but 'lived on furtively, below the
surface' (Keynes 32) until the rise of the marginal utility school in 1870.
As Boyd Hilton points out,

The important ideological questions dividing Malthus and Ricardo were not ... [value, rent, wage, and trade], but the former's physiocracy and the latter's confidence that, in favourable conditions, Say's law of markets would operate to ensure that supply created its own demand. On these points Ricardo, who died in 1823, is seen to have triumphed posthumously over Malthus ... It seems likely, however, that whatever professional economists thought, the Malthusian perspective retained a hold over 'Christian economists' and over the 'official mind' until the 1850s. (*Age* 65)

Because of this continuity, the line between Eliot as indulgent commentator on an earlier age and Eliot as mouthpiece for her own times is a blurry one indeed – and one, quite frankly, which it is not that important to draw. Eliot chose to set *The Mill on the Floss* during a very particular epoch in recent Victorian economic history, one that enabled her to portray such 'quaint' customs as hoarding and a fear of speculation, but one which also resonated quite strongly with her own time. The issues with which her characters grapple in the novel were, by and large, also her own.

1 Two Worlds of Ethics; or, 'The Simple Rule of Renunciation'

As the narrator makes abundantly clear from nearly the first page of the novel, the Tullivers – with the notable exception of Maggie – have a great deal of trouble with figurative language. Our first glimpse of the Tulliver parents involves a comical misunderstanding about an emblematic man with a mole on his face: Mrs Tulliver, of course, does not understand that her husband is using a figure of speech (10–11). We are given many examples, throughout the novel, of Mr Tulliver's own clumsiness with language, from his admission that the initial conjugal misunderstanding might have been his own fault ('I meant it to stand for summat else; but niver mind – it's puzzling work, talking is') to his frequent lament that the lawyers always get the best of him because of their facility with words ('Things have got so twisted round and wrapped up i' unreasonable words, as aren't a bit like 'em, as I'm clean at fault, often an' often' [20]). Most suggestively, the narrator even implies that Tulliver's inability to understand metaphor is an important source of his proclivity for 'lawing' to begin with: it is the 'principle that water was water' (154) that goads him into the disastrous suit over water rights with Mr Pivart.

Yet it is with the Tulliver children, of course, that the distinction between literal-mindedness and facility with metaphor is thrown into sharpest relief.[8] We find that Tom has a great deal of difficulty with wordplay – 'in his coolest moments a pun would have been a hard nut' (136) – and with the special linguistic skills involved in learning Latin. He is, more generally, a 'boy born with a deficient power of apprehending signs and abstractions' (169), possessing a 'narrow tendency in his mind to details,' attributes which affect likewise his abilities in Latin, his appreciation of landscape, and, as we shall see later, his capacities for sympathy and love. Maggie, on the other hand, has quite a facility with language – metaphorical and figurative language in particular. In a famous passage describing her visit to Tom at Mr Stelling's school, the precocious Maggie informs Tom that 'almost every word' means several things at once, and her understanding of Latin 'secretly astonishes' her brother (145). Maggie's sense of the possibilities of language is underscored in the even more famous passage on metaphor where the narrator indulges in an ironic 'lamentation' on the necessity of figurative speech in all human expression. Here, Aristotle's notion that the understanding of metaphor is a mark of intelligence is juxtaposed to the necessity of using metaphor in intelligible speech: 'We can so seldom declare what a thing is, except by saying it is something else' (140).[9]

While a differing attitude toward metaphorical language is certainly emblematic of a profound difference between the 'Tom' and 'Maggie' modes of narration, it is the guiding light of ethical responsibility that throws their differences into sharpest relief.[10] In its examination of ethical method, the novel performs its trickiest balancing act between potentially conflicting philosophical allegiances: it is the narrator's simultaneous prescription of deprivation and fascination with uncontrollable appetite that gives the plot of *The Mill on the Floss* its self-contradictory character. And this ambiguity is, as I hope to demonstrate, closely allied to the competing imperatives of Victorian political economy that I have already described.

For Tom, of course, questions of right behaviour are simple and easily decided – while to say that Maggie has difficulty deciding between competing ethical imperatives would be to reduce to an aphorism the entire premise of the novel. Even as children, the siblings demonstrate this crucial difference: 'If Tom had told his strongest feeling at that moment, he would have said, "I'd do just the same again." That was his usual mode of viewing his past actions; whereas Maggie was always wishing she had done something different' (53). A short while later, during the bitter hair-cutting episode, this description of the young siblings' respective ethical codes is refined and developed:

> She could see clearly enough, now the thing was done, that it was very
> foolish ... for Maggie rushed to her deeds with passionate impulse, and
> then saw not only their consequences, but what would have happened if
> they had not been done, with all the detail and exaggerated circumstance
> of an active imagination. Tom never did the same sort of foolish things as
> Maggie, having a wonderful instinctive discernment of what would turn
> to his advantage or disadvantage. (65)

Maggie's 'active imagination,' her ability to see many meanings and possibilities at once, is here pinpointed as the main source of her childish pain: it is because she can see so clearly the consequences and foreclosed possibilities of any action that she is doomed to a 'bitter sense of the irrevocable' (65). It is, of course, this active imagination and alertness to possibility that is likewise the source of her facility with metaphorical language.[11] That imagination, 'always rushing extravagantly beyond an immediate impression' (344), keeps many meanings and possibilities before her at once, while the dullard Tom, who cannot see beyond the primary sense of a word, is also unable to see beyond the fact of an action being done, and a possibility past and over.

Maggie's sense of her own difficult lot, her own painful struggle under deprivation and inappropriate desire, is thus due not so much to her circumstances being genuinely different from the norm, but rather to her heightened sensitivity to possibility. Because she can see farther into both consequences and possibilities than those around her, she suffers more than they; Tom's greatest comfort is his narrow focus and single-minded, conventional sense of right and wrong. As the narrator tells us in the course of describing Mr Wakem, there are 'men who can be prompt without being rash, because their motives run in fixed tracks, and they have no need to reconcile conflicting aims' (251). Maggie's main problem is, of course, the fact that she is always doomed to 'reconciling conflicting aims.' And the reason she is so condemned is, as I have suggested, that her aptitude with metaphor – her ability to multiply meanings and possibilities, both in language and in ethics – is precociously developed.

To have this picture of possibilities always before one, in all its indefatigable glory, is, according to the narrator of *The Mill on the Floss*, the special prerogative of the ethically sensitive. As we are reminded again and again, the correct and admirable understanding is one which encompasses 'a large vision of relations, and to which every single object suggests a vast sum of conditions' (272–3). However, the narrator also cares to remind us that a broad 'observation of human life' (273) should never devolve into a formulaic or axiomatic understanding. This is the famous warning against the 'man of maxims':

> All people of broad, strong sense have an instinctive repugnance to the man of maxims; because such people early discern that the mysterious complexity of our life is not to be embraced by maxims, and that to lace ourselves up in formulas of that sort is to repress all the divine promptings and inspirations that spring from growing insight and sympathy. (498)

The narrator somewhat fudges the issue here. In attempting to endorse the 'broad' vision he has elsewhere privileged, he carefully distinguishes his own (and Maggie's) ethical method from the broadest and most encompassing vision of all – the generalizing scope of the maxim. From one perspective, of course, the 'perpetual reference to the special circumstances that mark the individual lot' (498) can be seen as the narrowest vision of them all, while the attempt to understand broad patterns of human behaviour that distinguishes the epigrammist may seem admirably far-sighted and comprehensive. In fact, the actual result of the narratorially privileged descriptive method can, in practice, become quite constricting indeed. The narrator feels the necessity to invoke his great scope of vision as a justification for the shape of his storytelling project; when the focus of the novel starts to seem unbearably narrow, hovering obsessively over the bonnets and tablecloths of the Sisters Dodson, the narrator instructs his readers in patience, informing them that this restrictedness is actually in service to the broader view of human interdependence: 'I share with you this sense of oppressive narrowness; but it is necessary that we should feel it, if we care to understand how it acted on the lives of Tom and Maggie ... There is nothing petty to the mind that has a large vision of relations, and to which every single object suggests a vast sum of conditions' (272–3).

But my goal is not to turn this distinction into a sophistical one. The point is that the narrator has some degree of difficulty remaining consistent in his own epigrammatic interventions and axiomatic asides. This difficulty becomes even more pronounced when we consider the various moments where the narrator discusses how these ethical principles are to be enacted, in actual judgments of characters' actions. As we have already seen in chapter 2, Eliot's narrators are quite interested in proving that the only right basis for ethical judgment is the consequences of actions; good intentions are never to excuse behaviour that has deleterious effects on one's neighbours. In a passage deleted from the final version of the novel, the narrator notes that this process may even work in reverse; we may later come to excuse rash or thoughtless behaviour when it is seen 'through the softening medium of desirable consequences.'[12] (Eliot may well have deleted this passage in a desire to avoid the logical conclusion of her doctrine of ethical consequence; however, the fact that she deleted the passage does not change the fact that this kind of ex post facto rationalization *is* its logical conclusion.)

However, at another point, the narrator is quite sarcastic about attempts to rationalize behaviour through an appeal to consequence. In condemning Philip's plan of subterfuge in continuing to meet Maggie in the Red Deeps, the narrator opines:

> If we only look far enough off for the consequences of our actions, we can always find some point in the combination of results by which those actions can be justified: by adopting the point of view of a Providence who arranges results, or of a philosopher who traces them, we shall find it possible to obtain perfect complacency in choosing to do what is most agreeable to us in the present moment. (330)

What has happened to that happy confluence of broad vision and an unflinching sense of far-reaching results? The same attributes so lauded in the abstract are here roundly condemned when seen in the service of an individual character's personal desire. 'In the abstract,' of course, should be read 'in the narrator.' What the logic of the passage really condemns is Philip's presumptuousness in taking on the perspective of that far-seeing narrator: it is because he dares to adopt the 'point of view of a Providence who arranges results, or of a philosopher who traces them' that Philip is chastised. What better description of a narrator do we have, than of an intelligence that arranges and traces results within the world of the novel (especially in Eliot novels, which are notorious for being uncomfortably divided between action and narrative commentary)?[13]

But the demagoguery of the narrator does not end there. He also sees fit, later in the novel, to condemn the gossips in St Ogg's – the 'world's wife' – who judge Maggie based on the results of her actions rather than her intentions:

> We judge others according to results; how else? – not knowing the processes by which results are arrived at. If Miss Tulliver, after a few months of well-chosen travel, had returned as Mrs Stephen Guest ... [public opinion] would have judged in strict consistency with those results. (490)

Here the narrator condemns the principle of ethical judgment that looks only at consequences without regard to intentions. Once again, a behaviour praised as the ethical ideal in the abstract – or when practiced by the narrator – is condemned when found in the practices of actual characters.

As we have seen, the narrator has some degree of difficulty maintaining consistent principles for both ethical behaviour and judgment. If some of the philosophical inconsistencies of *Adam Bede* can be traced to Eliot's attempt to depict simultaneously a self-contained barter economy and a world where the consequences of actions extend, potentially infinite, beyond their agents, then in *The Mill on the Floss*, Eliot seems to be attempting to avoid the logical problems inherent in a stringent insistence on limitless consequences – a qualification of her earlier stance that seems to lead only to a philosophical muddle.

However, there is a deeper underlying principle at work here, one which is belied – and denied – by the narrator's self-description, but which is nonetheless borne out by the logic of the examples I have given. We can find a clue to this principle at the very end of the novel: 'Conscientious people are apt to see their duty in that which is the most painful course' (512). In each of the instances of ethical decision-making quoted above, which we must find hopelessly contradictory if we accept their principles as those the narrator gives us, there is in fact one guiding standard of correct behaviour: self-denial. What is wrong with Philip's actions is that he is thinking of his own pleasure. What is wrong with the judgment of the wives of St Ogg's is that it condemns Maggie's heroic self-denial in turning down Stephen's proposal. Even Riley's recommendation of Stelling is suspected, in a long passage that remains in the novel, because he may gain some possible advantage from it in the future. The reason that the ethical rules invoked throughout the novel seem so confused is because they are mere chimeras, excuses cobbled together after the fact, masking the real guiding principle behind narratorial approval, which is the same in every case.

But why? Why is the single fact of self-denial, the heroic striving to curb appetites and restrain desires, the sine qua non of acceptable behaviour according to the narrator of *The Mill on the Floss*? To answer this question, we must examine the crucial relationship between the ethical and economic modes of the novel. As I have already mentioned, the obsessive focus on self-denial by the narrator of *The Mill on the Floss* is part of a larger concern, on Eliot's part, with the examination of conflicting strains of Victorian economic thought: it is the ultimately destabilizing character of 'demand' in all its forms that effects Maggie's struggle and eventual death.

But at this point it is only necessary to note that the rhetoric and logic of the novel itself explicitly liken the operations of ethical consequence to a monetary economy. Maggie continuously refers to the ethical obligations she strives to honour as 'debts'; at one point she beseeches Stephen to 'remember what we both felt – that we owed ourselves to others, and must conquer every inclination that could make us false to that debt' (475). Similarly, Tom gets to Maggie's soft spot when he tells her to consider the effects of her actions on Lucy: 'Go and see the return you have made her' (485). Filial obligations, as so many things in this novel, are intelligible primarily in terms of an economy of debt and repayment – not an unimportant metaphor given the nature of the novel's central narrative of bankruptcy and regeneration.[14]

This master trope of ethical economy is present from the very first pages of the novel, where the description of Riley's thoughtless recommendation of Stelling – again – serves as an occasion for narratorial commentary:

> It is easy enough to spoil the lives of our neighbours without taking so much trouble: we can do it by lazy acquiescence and lazy omission ... We live from hand to mouth, most of us, with a small family of immediate desires – we do little else than snatch a morsel to satisfy the hungry brood, rarely thinking of seed-corn for next year's crop. (25)

This metaphor is particularly striking because it seems to condemn without clear instruction. If living from hand to mouth, with a 'small family of immediate desires,' is clearly what the narrator wants to denounce, then what does he implicitly advocate? That we narrow our desires even further, curbing them and reining them in to the point where we completely efface our own needs in the face of more compelling claims? Or rather that we broaden and enlarge them, increasing our appetites to the point where we start accumulating things that will satisfy them, hoarding against times of privation? Should we strive to be Ricardians or Malthusians?

The ethic of self-denial that seems to underlie all of the narrator's character judgments seems, of course, to demand the former. However, it is this very ambiguity – between an ethic of deprivation and a fascination with uncontrollable appetite – that fuels the narrative of *The Mill on the Floss* and gives it its self-contradictory and baffling character. And it is this same ambiguity, as I have already suggested, that will ultimately bring about the 'elimination' of Maggie. For her great sin is not to have greater demands than others, nor is it to be deficient in self-denial; it is rather to raise the very spectre of 'demand' to begin with.

2 Victorian Versions of Capitalist Growth: Economic Narratives and the Problem of Debt

The ethical logic of *The Mill on the Floss* tends to reduce judgment to terms of debt and repayment. In fact, everything in the town the novel depicts, we are told repeatedly, is related to a grounding principle of practical economy. In a long passage laying out the history of St Ogg's, the narrator tells us that the three main fears of the townspeople are 'Catholics, bad harvests, and the mysterious fluctuations of trade' (118). While the last two of these are obviously a direct part of the 'money-getting' ethos of the town, even the first is seen, by its estimable citizens, in terms of the great questions of trade and economy: the real reason the Catholics are feared, we learn, is because they can lay hold of property, not because anyone in St Ogg's is in danger of becoming a papist (118). Dissent, similarly, is viewed as 'a foolish habit that clung greatly to families in the grocery and chandlering lines,' while those who bothered themselves with thinking about these things in political terms are regarded as 'dangerous characters: they were usually persons who had little or no business of their own to manage, or, if they had, were likely enough to become insolvent' (118–19). Every great question of the day is reduced, in this prosperous burg, to the terms of business and trade; even the upheaval of the late Napoleonic wars is remembered simply as a 'past golden age, when prices were high' (118).

The great virtue praised above all others in St Ogg's is, of course, thrift and good management, which are repeatedly characterized as maintaining a balance between expenditures and income. To live beyond one's means is the greatest sin and foolishness: while 'there are people in St. Ogg's who made a show without money to support it,' these people are spoken of 'with contempt and reprobation' (189). The narrator seems to enter into the spirit of the town's preoccupations in his own descriptions of various of the novel's characters. Poor Mr Stelling's main function in the novel – since he can barely educate Tom – seems to be as punching-bag for the narrator's own 'contempt and reprobation' of improvident habits. He is invoked repeatedly as the type of striving young man whose boundless confidence in his eventual prosperity leads him to spend beyond his means: since he cannot yet afford the accoutrements of affluence he so desires, 'it followed in the most rigorous manner, either that these things must be procured by some other means, or else that the Rev. Mr Stelling must go without them – which last alternative would be an absurd procrastination of the fruits of success, where success was certain' (135).

While the spectre of failure haunts the psyches of the inhabitants of St Ogg's, and their ethos of management and thrift is the ruling standard of economic behaviour, this disposition does not preclude their vigorous striving and admiration of successful speculation. There is an uneasy truce between the respective virtues of minimal wants and great incomes; while the goal is always a balance between what comes in and what goes out, it is not always clear which end of the equation should be adjusted when this balance is lacking. While on the one hand, the narrator sarcastically comments that people like Mr Stelling are somehow morally lacking because when faced with such a disproportion, they tend to conclude that 'since wants are not easily starved to death, the simpler method appear[s] to be – to raise their income' (167), he also comments (ironically, but not without some degree of approbation) that the desire to better one's lot is a national, if not human, characteristic: 'Is not the striving after something better and better in our surroundings the grand characteristic that distinguishes man from the brute – or ... that distinguishes the British man from the foreign brute?' (152).

But whether the virtue of good management is characterized as striving or starving, and whether it is ultimately the unique province of human beings, the British, or residents of St Ogg's, it reaches its apotheosis in the Dodson and Tulliver families.[15] It is the economic world view of these families that is the philosophical source of the Tom narrative of economic regeneration. The family traditions include (and these are certainly not the least important of the list) the 'hoarding of coins likely to disappear from the currency [and] the production of first-rate commodities for the market' (274). Here, again, the narrator invokes the different aims of saving – effectively equivalent to limiting demand – and production. All the members of the family share these managerial habits; it is a point of pride with the Dodsons (and spouses) to think of nearly all things in terms of economical management. Mrs Glegg herself, of course, is the supreme monarch of this little saving nation; her husband, who chose his bride as the 'embodiment of female prudence and thrift' (121), finds her 'household ways a model for her sex' (122), displeased though he may be with their state of conjugal warfare.

The Dodson family are, in fact, the very embodiment of the dominant concerns of mid-Victorian political economy. On the one hand, they demonstrate a great faith in the benefits of accumulation and an unquestioning belief in capitalism's infinite growth, which we see in their veneration of 'capital,' interest, and profits, as well as in their professed faith in the continuing and limitless prosperity of the new industrial economy. On the other hand, their habits and predilections demonstrate the deep suspicion of credit and memoranda of debt – and the concomitant obsession with gold and objects of supposedly inherent value – that we also saw in Spencer's laissez-faire account. This suspicion manifests itself particularly in the Dodsons' obsession with saving, their fetishistic desire to have their money physically before them, and their old-fashioned notions of debt and deficit. While both ideas are present in the preoccupations of the Dodsons, the latter does not constitute a real challenge to the prevailing nineteenth-century ideology of capitalist striving; the anxiety over credit and debt in the Victorian 'public mind' coexists, as we saw in the case of Spencer, with a belief in the efficacy of Say's Law. While the Dodsons may demonstrate a nascent fear of an end to capitalism, it will be up to Maggie, with her huge appetites and melodramatic self-denial, to mount a real (Malthusian) challenge to this comfortable faith in accumulation and effective economic demand.

Let us begin with the first set of Dodsonian economic issues: the Dodsons and Tullivers are creatures of their times in their great faith in the continued growth of the capitalist economy, and the unalloyed benefits thereof. The very concept of 'capital' is revered by everyone concerned – so much so that its lack is seen as a moral failure, a sign of insufficient economy or striving. When he wants to steel himself to cash in his bond with his sister, Mr Tulliver whips himself into a state of indignation over his brother-in-law Moss's deficiencies in this regard: 'He got up a due amount of irritation against Moss as a man without capital' (77). This unfortunate lack even trumps, for Tulliver, the great virtue of diligent work: when Moss protests that there 'isn't a day-labourer works harder' than himself, Mr Tulliver rejoins with, 'What's the use o' that ... when a man marries, and's got no capital to work his farm but his wife's bit o' fortin?' (82). Similarly, Mr Tulliver understands on some level that the very invocation of this word will help smooth over any familial protestations about his plans for Tom's schooling: 'Tom's eddication 'ull be so much capital to him.' Regardless of whether or not this assertion is true (and subsequent events demonstrate that it is not), the magic word certainly goes over well with Mr Glegg: 'Ay, there's something in that,' he puts in, inspired enough to break into a little poem (71).

This veneration of capital extends into other venerations as well – of profits and interest. Again, this principle is seen chiefly in the fear of its opposite; Mr Glegg is so deeply committed to the idea of profiteering that he cannot abide the idea of Bob's wanting to help Tom speculate on Laceham goods without taking a cut for himself: 'Well, but it's nothing but right you should have a small percentage ... I've no opinion o' transactions where folks do things for nothing. It allays looks bad' (315). The Dodsons, in fact, do everything at interest; Mrs Glegg refuses to lend money to Tom for this same speculation on anything other than those terms: 'I mean you to pay me interest, you know – I don't approve o' giving' (324). This focus on the bottom line, to the expense of even familial obligation and fellow-feeling, shows the Dodsons and Tullivers in sway to the great Victorian faith in economic progress, growth, and accumulation.[16]

All of this optimistic faith in striving can be read as the family's confidence in the promise of Say's Law – the tenet that unlimited growth is possible and that there will always be an effective demand for all goods produced. Mr Deane himself gives a neat summary of this philosophy in an impromptu lecture to Tom: 'Ours is a fine business – a splendid concern, sir – and there's no reason why it shouldn't go on growing; there's a growing capital, and growing outlets for it' (397). In this same lecture he also echoes the narrator, telling Tom that the very pace of economic growth is far greater than it was when he was starting out: 'The world goes on at a smarter pace now than it did when I was a young fellow' (395). In this little homily, Mr Deane speaks as the very figure of the prosperous Victorian man of business: growth is strong, will only get stronger, and the narrative of progress seems to have no end.

Yet both the Dodsons and Tullivers also evince, simultaneously, the equally prevalent Victorian fear of profiteering and speculation: they are, of course, nearly maniacal about the virtues of saving for the sake of saving.[17] The narrator specifically mentions this attribute as an example of the family's economic old-fashionedness: 'This inalienable habit of saving, as an end in itself, belonged to the industrious men of business of a former generation, who made their fortunes slowly ... it constituted them a "race," which is nearly lost in these days of rapid money-getting' (121).[18] This paradigm explicitly opposes the possibilities for accumulation characteristic of the modern capitalist age to the more sober methods that are suspicious of speculation, and places the Dodsons firmly on the side of the latter. They are the embodiment of Malthus's hoarding capitalist, squirreling money away for the provision of dependents. This characterization is borne out by the central importance of the family chest and tin money box in the mind of Mr Tulliver. As he lies seemingly near death after the initial shock of bankruptcy, it is the sound of the chest clanging shut that alone can rouse him:

> Perhaps there was something in that sound more than the mere fact of the strong vibration that produced the instantaneous effect ... In the same moment when all the eyes in the room were turned upon him, he started up and looked at the chest, the parchments in Mr Glegg's hand, and Tom holding the tin box, with a glance of perfect consciousness and recognition. (221)

The sound of the great chest, which is home both to the money box and his sister Gritty's note of debt, is of such deep-seated import in Tulliver's thrifty, money-saving unconscious that it can awaken him from a state in which he could not even recognize the members of his family.

The Dodsons' great faith in saving is closely allied with their need to have their money physically before them: this is their fetishistic counterpart to the ubiquitous Victorian obsession with gold and suspicion of promises-to-pay. During the long process of saving to pay back the family's creditors, Mr Tulliver becomes fixated on the idea of having the growing pile of money in the house where he can see it and touch it: 'The little store of sovereigns in the tin box seemed to be the only sight that brought a faint beam of pleasure into the miller's eyes' (278). Similarly, even after Tom informs his father that he has earned the money to pay off all the debts – significantly, through speculation and not the slow process of saving – his father cannot believe it until he lays eyes on the cash: '"I wish you'd brought me the money to look at, Tom," he said, fingering the sovereigns on the table; "I should ha' felt surer"' (351). Mr Tulliver's need for the present, physical object of value is characterized as unnecessary over-caution in the logic of the novel. When Tom approaches his father about investing in that same speculation that eventually allows them to pay off their debts, he refuses: 'Mr Tulliver would not consent to put the money out at interest lest he should lose it' (311). It turns out he is dead wrong in this fear, but the characterological point is made: he is truly of the old-fashioned school of 'money-getting.'

The family's obsession with the physical nature of money can reach even greater, downright bizarre, proportions. In a curious passage describing Mrs Glegg's secret economic fixations, we are told that her romantic vision of life after her husband's death (and his handsome provision for her), is

> to have sums of interest coming in more frequently, and secrete it in various corners, baffling to the most ingenious of thieves (for, to Mrs Glegg's mind, banks and strong-boxes would have nullified the pleasure of property – she might as well have taken her food in capsules). (126)

Here the need for direct contact with money is described as a physical pleasure, akin to the sensuous enjoyment of food. (The pun on the word 'secrete' strengthens the sense of the money as a direct outgrowth of Mrs Glegg's own body – it is almost a bizarre physical product of some bodily process.) Mrs Glegg is a fetishist of the first order.

While the need for the object of 'intrinsic' value (sovereigns in a tin box, money secreted in corners) is paramount, in its absence its signifier (the note or promise-to-pay) takes on an almost equal significance. Victorian anxieties about the liquidation of memoranda of debt – occasioned, as I have argued, by the epistemological uncertainties attendant upon the growing credit economy – is admirably demonstrated by the Dodson family. When Tom informs the family council gathered about Mr Tulliver's sick-bed that his father's wish was to release Gritty from her debt to him, he naturally suggests that they destroy the note so that it will not fall into the hands of Tulliver's creditors. While everyone present agrees on the justice of this plan, they are almost comically reluctant to perform the actual deed. Uncle Glegg's 'good feeling led him to enter into Tom's wish, but [he] could not at once shake off his habitual abhorrence of such recklessness as destroying securities,' while even hidebound Mrs Glegg approves of Tom's sentiment and yet is still secretly horrified at 'this wicked alienation of money' (219). The destruction of the promise-to-pay uncomfortably evokes the fear of an unstable correspondence between paper and gold: the flip side of a note without an inherently valuable good to liquidate it is the senseless destruction of the sign that stands for that valuable good in the first place.

The final indication of the Dodson family's economic anxieties is their marked concern with maintaining a perfectly circular and self-contained balance between income and expenditure: they have a very horror of debt, deficit, and waste. As we learn at one point, they have the narrow and petty habit 'of regarding life as an ingenious process of nibbling out one's livelihood without leaving any perceptible deficit' (122). This strict adherence to the goal of self-contained economy, literally without surplus or deficit, marks the family as true inheritors of the Victorian suspicion of the credit economy and its unstable value correspondences and inflationary issues.

The narrator himself comments on this familial predilection, pointing out its archaism:

> These narrow notions about debt, held by the old-fashioned Tullivers, may perhaps excite a smile on the faces of many readers in these days of wide commercial views and wide philosophy, according to which everything rights itself without any trouble of ours: the fact that my tradesman is out of pocket by me, is to be looked at through the serene certainty that somebody else's tradesman is in pocket by somebody else; and since there must be bad debts in the world, why, it is mere egoism not to like that we in particular should make them instead of our fellow-citizens. (279)

Once again, the family's suspicion of the operations of the modern credit economy is seen as quaint and old-fashioned – and that old-fashionedness is valorized. What is particularly interesting about this passage is the way in which it links ethical and monetary economies. The narrator again excoriates the 'wide view' of the greater web of consequence that he reviles in Philip: just as we saw earlier, the real standard of ethical behaviour is self-denial, a mode of conduct that would shoulder the burden of debt without recourse to a larger balance of claims and consequences.

And yet, here as before, the narrator contradicts his own claims of capacious judgment in the interests of that ethos of self-denial. In an atypical endorsement which marks it rather the thought of the narrator than of the man himself, Mr Glegg at one point reminds Tom of the interconnectedness of all financial transactions, and of the importance of taking this wider view of his own deeds: 'But there's a deal o' things to be considered, young man ... when you come to money business, and you may be taking one man's dinner away to make another's breakfast' (220). Sometimes the wide view is praised, sometimes it is reviled: the narrator's real motivation is an unswerving endorsement of self-denial, and whichever 'scope' of examination will answer that end at the given moment is the one he promotes.

And yet, while the narrator's approval of self-denial in general is quite pronounced, the logic of the narrative itself – at the level of plot – has a somewhat more conflicted ethical agenda. While Maggie's restraint in refusing Stephen is strenuously praised by the narrative voice, we must still account, of course, for her spectacular sacrifice in the flood at the end of the novel. Maggie's great sin is not as straightforward as it may seem: the reason she is so ruthlessly eliminated at the end of the novel, while usually declared to be her unruly and inappropriate desires or 'demonic' nature, may in fact equally be her heroic restraint and denial of those desires.[19] The real reason criticism of the novel has had such a difficult time answering the question of Maggie's 'failure,' the reason she must die at the end of the book, is that it is the wrong question: Maggie does not die because she fails either in her self-denial, or alternatively in her embrace of life. The real 'problem' of Maggie is that she succeeds in questioning too closely the dearly held assumptions of her economic time, ostentatiously staging a debate between the virtues of economic demand and self-restraint – a debate that the ruling ideology of Victorian economic thought was not prepared to consider or countenance.

3 Very Irregular Polygons: Maggie's Desires and the Problem of Economy

For many critics of *The Mill on the Floss* the problem with Maggie is her immoderate appetites and great wants. This reading seems intuitive; it is certainly the one that is offered and supported by the narrator in his descriptions of Maggie, particularly in her childhood. From our very first glimpses of Maggie as a young girl, her inordinate appetites are getting her into trouble. In the notorious jam puff scene, for example, she inadvertently angers Tom because she fails to donate part of the 'best bit' of the puff that she has won in the guessing game. While she is more than willing to give Tom the larger piece without the pretence of competition, once she has won it she loses herself in enjoyment of the treat: she eats her share 'with considerable relish as well as rapidity' and is 'lost to almost everything but a vague sense of jam and idleness'

(46). Tom, of course, pounces on her as soon as she is done, denouncing her as greedy for not giving him some of her share, being quite 'conscious of having acted very fairly' in dividing it in the first place.

What is particularly striking about this scene is the way in which it conjoins questions of appetite and ethical behaviour; it is our first example of Maggie's comportment under a strong sense of desire and conflicting imperatives. While she seems quite selfless in her initial desire to give Tom the best piece of pastry, the narrator 'fear[s] she cared less that Tom should enjoy the utmost possible amount of puff, than that he should be pleased with her for giving him the best bit' (45). Even Maggie's impulse to 'self-denial' is in the interest of a greater need: for Tom's approval and love. Once she has made this point, she can give in to a more immediate appetite and devour the puff with impunity, little knowing that Tom is under the sway of a different ethical imperative altogether. For Maggie, the goal is to appear self-sacrificing, while for Tom it is to appear scrupulously fair: 'If I go halves, I'll go 'em fair – only I wouldn't be a greedy' (46). Tom's 'economic' viewpoint demands that he evenly divide 'that very irregular polygon into two equal parts' (45), while Maggie's viewpoint mutates from an appearance of sacrifice in a gambit for love, to genuine enjoyment of her prize. At this early stage of Maggie's ethical development, the appearance is of greater importance than the charity; as odious as we may find Tom's behaviour, he is right in exposing Maggie's generosity as a sham: she promptly forgets about him and his inferior piece of puff once her point has been made.

It is, as I noted, in the service of gaining Tom's approval that this point is made. Perhaps Maggie's most striking attribute is her boundless desire for love. The narrator comments on this aspect of her character on several different occasions; one of the times she hides in the attic after a scolding from Tom, she can stay only for 'five dark minutes' before she longs to be with him again: 'The need of being loved, the strongest need in poor Maggie's nature, began to wrestle with her pride, and soon threw it' (37). Even at this early stage, Maggie's craving for love is figured as something she strives to subdue, one aspect of a great and ongoing struggle. Yet the craving is nearly always the winner: 'It is a wonderful subduer, this need of love – this hunger of the heart – as peremptory as that other hunger by which Nature forces us to submit to the yoke, and change the face of the world' (38–9).

The language of this passage evokes that of Adam Smith in *The Theory of Moral Sentiments*.[20] Smith returns to this idea repeatedly throughout the work (1.2.4.1, 1.2.5.1, 2.3.2.2, 3.1.7, and 3.5.8); for example, 'There is satisfaction in the consciousness of being beloved, which, to a person of delicacy and sensibility, is of more importance to happiness than all the advantage which he can expect to derive from it' (1.2.4.1). As Charles L. Griswold notes in his study *Adam Smith and the Virtues of Enlightenment*, 'Without much exaggeration, one could say that *The Theory of Moral Sentiments* is generally about love: our need for love and sympathy' (148); he also points out that 'even in *The Wealth of Nations*, our loves are thought to be very important in explaining our behavior' (148–9). In the later work Smith also uses the word 'love' more generally to refer to the motivations behind all economic operations; for example, the 'love of present ease and enjoyment' (5.1.2.2) among the poor is seen as an impediment to their proper functioning in civil society (it causes them to 'invade property' rather than labour productively for their own goods).[21] This language is very similar to that of Malthus when he attempts to explain the underconsumption of commodities – human beings naturally prefer indolence to products. Certainly in the jam-puff scene Maggie prefers – at least initially – the love of Tom to luxurious enjoyment. The emphasis on love as a driving force behind economic decision-making – where it always seems to interfere with consumption – seems to unite Smith, Malthus, and Eliot. Erotic and economic 'consumption' are imbricated for these authors, but in ways that seem at times to suggest a zero-sum mentality.[22] (Certainly this reading is consonant with the Malthus of the *Essay on Population* as well; in the idea of eroticism distracting one from proper consumption we can see another possible solution to the seeming 'paradox' of Malthus's two major works – sex leads to less food through greater population.) I will return to this question, as it relates to Maggie's romantic story, shortly.

These great appetites of Maggie's childhood do not disappear with her youth. Despite the influence of Thomas à Kempis on our heroine, the novel's rhetoric of desire and appetite increases sharply during Maggie's young womanhood. Maggie is conscious of her uniqueness in this regard: she thinks it is 'part of the hardship of her life that there was laid upon her the burthen of larger wants than others seemed to feel' (288). Later, she reveals this interpretation of her own character to Philip, claiming that the problem she had as a child is with her still: 'I was never satisfied with a *little* of anything. That is why it is better for me to do without earthly happiness altogether' (328). Her self-description is particularly poignant since it suggests that all her experimentation in self-denial has failed to give her relief; it is particularly telling because it indicates that her sense of abnormal appetite is primeval, if not innate – not an effect of her family's later privation.

It seems that there is no arena of life safe from Maggie's immoderate appetites; her catalogue of dissatisfactions is, to say the least, idiosyncratic: she wants 'books with *more* in them' (286), 'more instruments playing together,' voices that are 'fuller and deeper' (328). In fact, the danger is that Maggie's appetites may, theoretically, never be fulfilled. The narrator claims that restraint is an all-or-nothing proposition for her: once she has forsaken that 'simple rule of renunciation,' she is under the sway of 'the seductive guidance of illimitable wants' (325). Maggie cannot even renounce in moderation; her self-denial must be greater, more absolute, than anyone else's.

While Maggie's own rhetoric thus locates her 'problem' in her immoderate appetites, the novel persistently suggests that it is Maggie's attempts to deny her desires that are the real source of her anguish. At first, this interpretation comes from the mouth of Philip, in a lecture he delivers to Maggie in the Red Deeps: 'It is mere cowardice to seek safety in negations ... You will be thrown into the world some day, and then every rational satisfaction of your nature that you deny now, will assault you like a savage appetite' (329). Both the logic of the narrative, of course, and Maggie's own subsequent admissions affirm this interpretation. Later, Maggie unequivocally endorses Philip's view after she has gone to stay with Lucy Deane: 'So many things have come true that you used to tell me ... You used to say I should feel the effect of my starved life, as you called it, and I do' (413–14). And during her great struggle with romantic temptation, we are told, in a dramatic interjection that is poised between the consciousness of the narrator and the consciousness of Maggie, that 'it seemed to her as if all the worst evil in her had lain in ambush till now, and had suddenly started up full-armed, with hideous, over-powering strength!' (458). (This language foreshadows the situation of another of Eliot's avatars of self-denial, Dorothea Brooke, whose marriage to Casaubon is figured repeatedly throughout *Middlemarch* as a 'sacrifice,' particularly since it strikes all concerned as utterly unerotic.)

The problem with Maggie's (as well as Dorothea's) plan of renunciation, as I have suggested, is that it is itself immoderate. Eliot seems to have an unconscious horror of Maggie's plan of self-deprivation. One of the reasons for the extremity of this plan seems to be her misreading of Thomas à Kempis. From the very beginning of her acquaintance with *The Imitation of Christ*, when she first encounters the 'little, old, clumsy book' and begins to read where the 'quiet hand pointed' (289), she misunderstands the real concept of renunciation: 'Maggie was still panting for happiness, and was in ecstasy because she had found the key to it' (291). Maggie's project of self-denial is just one more manifestation of her great appetite and large desires.[23] This particular kind of misreading is one against which John Ruskin warns his young female interlocutors in *Sesame and Lilies*: he laments that current methods of education encourage young people to

> endure both their own pain occasionally, and the pain of others always, with an unwise patience, by misconception of the eternal and incurable nature of real evil. Observe, therefore, carefully in this matter; there are degrees of pain, as degrees of faultfulness, which are altogether conquerable, and which seem to be merely forms of wholesome trial or discipline ... But you cannot carry the trial past a certain point ... Let heart-sickness pass beyond a certain bitter point, and the heart loses its life for ever.
> Now, the very definition of evil is in this irremediableness. It means sorrow, or sin, which ends in death. (*Works* 18:41–2)

The last sentence of this warning seems eerily prescient when applied to the fictional situation of Maggie Tulliver.

One way of reading *The Mill on the Floss*, of course, is as a kind of Bildungsroman wherein Maggie undoes this mistake Ruskin warns against, and comes to understand the real meaning of Thomas à Kempis and to embody it in her renunciation of Stephen. This seems to be the interpretation she herself (and perhaps Eliot as well) prefers: 'Philip had been right when he told her that she knew nothing of renunciation; she had thought it was quiet ecstasy; she saw it face to face now – that sad patient loving strength which holds the clue of life – and saw that the thorns were for ever pressing on its brow' (471). This reading actually emphasizes the intractable nature of Maggie's appetites; her real nature has not changed, she is still 'abnormal' in her desires, which are greater and more inappropriate than other people's – they do, after all, occasion her death. She may, in the course of the novel, have learned better how to accept the pain of her unique burden, but the persistent sense of Maggie as exceptional, even monstrous, is not touched by this didactic reading.

In fact, Maggie's monstrous childhood desires merely mutate into monstrous sexual desires. The 'savage appetite' Philip warns her against is the return of her childish craving for love in a new form.

This is a development we can see foreshadowed in the novel's earlier echoes of *The Theory of Moral Sentiments* and the *Wealth of Nations*. As I discussed above, sexual desire and the desire to consume, for Smith and Eliot, are both expressions of the same (erotic) energy and seem to exist in a zero-sum relationship: the repression of the latter erupts, in the case of Maggie, into the violent passion of the former. Maggie is perhaps the most obviously sexual of Eliot's heroines (the transgressive Hetty excepted); as Margaret Homans has noted, the novel dwells almost obsessively on highly sensual descriptions of Maggie's 'large round arms,' 'queenly' hair, and well-developed physique ('Dinah's Blush' 176–7). This type of narratorial attention begins with – just as her entrance into womanhood is marked by – Maggie's visit to her cousin Lucy's house, with its musical parties, boating expeditions, and courtly gentleman callers. (The novel is conspicuously silent about the austere intervening years Maggie spends as a teacher, which one might think would warrant attention given the narrator's supposed concern with her developing spirituality and quietism.)

The new earthly and sensual temptations Maggie experiences at the Deanes' are markers for her blossoming sexuality; rather than inaugurating a new set of wants and needs, her entrance into the Deane household merely betrays the perdurable nature of her early childish appetites: 'She had slipped back into desire and longing ... she found the image of the intense and varied life she yearned for, and despaired of, becoming more and more importunate' (374). This desire and longing, we are told, takes as one of its chief forms the craving for admiration: 'Life was certainly very pleasant just now; it was becoming very pleasant ... to feel that she was one of the beautiful things of this springtime. And there were admiring eyes always awaiting her now' (401).

This heightened sense of her own sexual attractiveness is accompanied by a heightened sense of her own bodily sensations generally; Maggie is fairly consumed, at the Deanes' house, with the enjoyment of music, which is persistently linked to primal and bodily processes: she often plays scales rather than melodies, in order to 'taste more keenly ... the more primitive sensation of intervals' (401). Similarly, the enjoyment of music, and in particular the satisfaction of hearing intervals and chords, is explicitly described in sexual terms: 'The sense of fulfilling expectation just at the right moment between the notes of the silvery soprano, from the perfect accord of descending thirds and fifths, from preconcerted loving chase of a fugue, is likely enough to supersede any immediate demand for less impassioned forms of agreement'

(368). A short time later, when we are told that Maggie has 'little more power of concealing the impressions made upon her than if she had been constructed of musical strings' (410), we cannot help but read this as a statement about Maggie's sexual eagerness and impressionability.

And yet, as I insisted earlier, this newly kindled sexual longing is seen as a reformulation of her childhood cravings, not as a new thing. As Lucy points out to Maggie, she has always been susceptible to the pleasures of attention: '"Why, dear Maggie," she interposed, "you have always pretended that you are too fond of being admired"' (377). She has Maggie's specific tastes in mind when preparing her room, filling it with prints, drawings, and flowers: 'Maggie would enjoy all that – she was so fond of pretty things!' (370). It seems as though Maggie's tastes and cravings are no secret, regardless of the years of self-denial she has supposedly practised. The intervening period of 'renunciation' cannot break the continuity of Maggie's yearning nature. It is this sense of the continuity of her great needs and cravings that aligns her sexual attraction to Stephen with the wild appetites of her girlhood.

This persisting sense of Maggie's putatively unreasonable desires – both her childish cravings for love and her 'inappropriate' adult sexuality – foregrounds the question of demand and consumption that is banished from the laissez-faire plot of the Dodsons and Tullivers, where it exists only in its denial. The entire sexual/romantic narrative, as I have suggested, is a nightmare version of the failure of Say's Law. The real transgression of the Maggie plot of temptation and renunciation is the way it stages the confrontation between conflicting Victorian narratives of the trajectory of capitalism. As I discussed more fully in chapter 1, the 'pessimistic' strain of Victorian economic thought which predicts the end of capitalism is in direct conflict with Say's Law, the axiom that supply must create its own demand – yet this strain of thought persists at the margins of Victorian political economy, a dark possibility whose effects on the public mind we see in the obsession with gold, a fear of inflationary issues, and an insistence on a one-to-one correspondence of monetary value. Maggie's monstrous appetites and her spectacular renunciation are potentially disturbing because they bring this repressed content to light; they reintroduce the question of demand into an economic equation that insists on its unimportance. If the function of the economic narrative of Tom and the Dodsons is to embody the striving, optimistic face of Victorian political economy (even as it unconsciously rehearses the possibility of failure and stagnation), then Maggie's immoderate demands – and worse, her attempt to starve those demands

– are a radically destabilizing influence on the narrative of progress and growth that the Tom plot sketches. It is Maggie's sexual narrative – both her secret engagement to Philip Wakem and her precipitous flight with Stephen Guest – that twice directly threatens the economic plot Tom has so carefully managed.

One of the ways we can trace these concerns is through the persistent repetition of the concept of superfluity – indeed, in the repetition of the very word 'superfluous' – in association with Maggie and her desires. In order to strengthen his resolve to call in his brother-in-law's debt, for example, Mr Tulliver ruminates not only on his untoward lack of capital, but also on the problematic existence of his sister: Gritty had 'come into the world in that superfluous way characteristic of sisters' (77). Of course, we are explicitly told to read this entire episode as a metaphor for Tom's feelings for Maggie (84); we are not, in any case, in need of much more evidence that Tom sees Maggie's life as a troublesome burden to him, and her appetites as dangerous and excessive: 'You're always in extremes ... and will not submit to be guided' (392). He also finds Maggie's entire narrative 'mode' excessive and problematic as well; when Maggie falls into the irritating habit of making up little stories about the animals and insects they come across in their play, Tom registers his 'profound contempt for this nonsense of Maggie's' by smashing an earwig 'as a superfluous yet easy means of proving the entire unreality of such a story' (99). It is unclear how destroying the subject of Maggie's fanciful tale proves the tale untrue, but it is clear that it is her very habit of make-believe and imaginative narrative that the prosaic Tom finds profoundly superfluous.

The source of this word can be found in one of the passages Eliot quotes from Thomas à Kempis:

> Forsake thyself, resign thyself, and thou shalt enjoy much inward peace ...
> Then shall all vain imaginations, evil perturbations, and superfluous cares
> fly away; then shall immoderate fear leave thee, and inordinate love shall
> die. (290, ellipsis in Eliot's quotation of original)

The notion of cares – in the sense of desires as well as worries – being superfluous is, of course, at the root of Maggie's ethic of renunciation. It is this very characterization that Philip protests when he says that there are 'certain things we feel to be beautiful and good, and we *must* hunger after them' (303, emphasis in original). The advice of Thomas à

Kempis promises Maggie a way to rid herself of what is 'superfluous' or excessive, and it is indeed her sense of her own excessiveness from which she is in such desperate flight – the way of resignation is supposed to lead to the death of 'inordinate love,' the very thing tormenting her throughout the novel. (In this sense, perhaps one could argue that Maggie did not, after all, misread Thomas à Kempis by hoping for the very end of desire instead of a peaceful resignation under its painful burden.)

The word 'superfluous,' with its etymological affinities to both 'surplus' and the flood, links the economic plot of Tom, the renunciation plot of Maggie, and the anomalous ending of the novel. In the most obvious sense, the concept of surplus refers to the economic accumulation that is the driving force behind the capitalist system and Tom's plot of regeneration and striving. Yet, as I argue, this 'optimistic' economic world view represses the crucial question of demand – and it is the marginalized, underconsumptionist version of capitalism that rehearses both excessive accumulations of surplus and insufficient demand. By persistently displaying uncontrolled demands of all kinds – immoderate desires, unruly appetites, inordinate loves – and then ostentatiously renouncing those demands, Maggie simultaneously invokes the repressed side of the economic equation and explicitly raises the possibility that demand may fail, that surpluses may go unconsumed, that excesses may flood the delicate balance of the marketplace. Her real problem is that she attacks that balance on both sides, with her excessive wants and then her 'unconsumed' superfluity. As Tom criticizes her, she is 'always in extremes,' at one time 'tak[ing] pleasure in a sort of perverse self-denial,' at another without even the 'resolution to resist a thing that [she] know[s] to be wrong' (393).

But Maggie's excesses – of both kinds – are most strikingly evoked by the great flood that takes her life. Literally 'superfluous,' the flood waters seem supernatural as well, called into being by the very desires and torments of the novel's heroine. And it is also, ironically, the great flood that is so often criticized as excessive within the art and propriety of the novel itself; in this way, the superfluity of the Floss brings together the problems of economy, death, and closure that are at the heart of the novel. But in order to understand how the 'excessive' ending of *The Mill on the Floss* illuminates the economic concerns discussed above, we need first to examine the curious way in which the very notion of death operates in the novel.

4 Proper Funerals, Improper Closure, and Implausible Floods

The Mill of the Floss brings a great deal of attention to bear on the question of balance sheets and deficits – how a plan of economy 'turns out' in the end. We saw this concern operating within the ostensibly self-contained economy of *Adam Bede*, and we see it in Eliot's second novel as well, in a greatly intensified form. The most consistently invoked balance sheet in the novel is, of course, the financial state of the Tullivers after the bankruptcy: the slow saving of the debt and the obsessive counting of sovereigns in the little tin box take on the solemnity of a religious rite. This concern with the familial ledger sheet is nearly always invoked in the context of Mr Tulliver's imminent demise. Mr Tulliver's real concern is that he and Tom pay off the creditors before his death, presumably – although apparently this is so obvious it need not be explained – because he wants to die an 'honest' man. When the narrator first describes the agonizingly slow process of accumulating the precious sovereign coins and the 'faint beam of pleasure' that the sight of them brings to Mr Tulliver's eyes, he also notes that the pleasure for the miller is 'faint and transient, for it was soon dispelled by the thought that the time would be long – perhaps longer than his life – before the narrow savings could remove the hateful incubus of debt' (278). The uncertainty of the debt being paid before Tulliver's death weighs heavily on both him and Tom; the latter attempts to encourage his father by saying, 'But perhaps you will live to see me pay everybody, father' (258), while the miller himself gloomily predicts, 'But you're like enough to bury me first' (350).

This fixation on the end-of-life balance sheet has a striking analogue in the Dodson sisters' obsession with their own wills and funerals. In his descriptive catalogue of the familial characteristics, the narrator declares that for the Dodsons, to 'live respected, and have the proper bearers at your funeral, was an achievement of the ends of existence' (274). Of course, the only thing that can rival the proper funeral is the proper will; as the narrator goes on to say, the effect of the funeral would be nullified if 'on the reading of your will, you sank in the opinion of your fellow-men, either by turning out to be poorer than they expected, or by leaving your money in a capricious manner, without strict regard to degrees of kin' (274). This strict kinship-code of money-leaving, a veritable hermeneutic of wills, is of momentous concern to the Dodsons, trumping almost every other consideration. Even after the great insult Mrs Glegg suffers at the hands of her brother-in-law Tulliver, she does not consider for a moment trifling with this canon: 'Mrs Glegg did not alter her will in consequence ... for she had her principles. No one must be able to say of her when she was dead that she had not divided her money with perfect fairness among her own kin' (129).

The great principle of the will is paramount in the Dodsons' ethical and economic universe; it overrides all the other concerns that are, in other contexts, of such great importance to the sisters: family feeling, profit, and propriety. When Mr Glegg urges his wife to help the Tul-livers after the bankruptcy, she sarcastically retorts: 'And I'm to alter my will, or have a codicil made, and leave two or three hundred less behind me when I die' (214). (The irony of refusing to give money to relatives so that there will be more to leave to those same relatives is also pointed out by Tom in this same scene [213].) Even when given a chance to make a tidy profit in the Laceham goods venture – and simultaneously help Tom – Mrs Glegg rationalizes her reluctance by claiming that Tom will 'see some day as his aunt's in the right not to risk the money she's saved for him till it's proved as it won't be lost' (319). And finally, the somewhat comical reason given for Mrs Glegg's support of Maggie after the abortive elopement is that 'lightly to admit conduct in one of your own family that would force you to alter your will, had never been the way of the Dodsons' (498–9). In each case, the unblinking focus on the metaphorical balance sheet of her life – the sum left behind her when she dies – keeps Mrs Glegg from any other consideration. The Dodsons' obsession with wills and funerals depicts their view of death as a great final summing-up, a logical extension of a measured, prudent, and frugal life.

Unlike the Dodsons' sensible and judiciously planned ends, death for Maggie is continuously figured as irrational and sudden. There are hints from the very beginning of the novel that Maggie may not follow the course her aunts have mapped out for themselves: her mother has a perpetual fear, we are told, that the young Maggie will meet an un-timely death in the river and be brought in 'dead and drownded some day' (103). The problem of drowning, both literal and metaphorical, is one with which Maggie must contend her whole life; even her effort to renounce Stephen is figured as 'the convulsed clutch of a drowning man' (510).

In this potential for untimely, accidental death, Maggie contravenes, as we have seen, the mortal plan of the Dodsons. As the sisters com-plain at one point, the whole Tulliver family has gone far astray in this regard; the threat of sudden death is simply the culmination of a long and troubling plan of subversive economy: 'There was never failures, nor lawing, nor wastefulness in our family – nor dying without wills ... No, nor sudden deaths' (455). This imminent threat is particularly associated with Maggie, of course, and her problematic conduct and immoderate desires; after she returns from her trip with Stephen, her mother allows herself one moment of complaint: 'It's gone from bad to worse, all of a sudden, just when the luck seemed on the turn' (501). It is her suddenness that unsettles those around her; the Maggie who is 'always rushing extravagantly beyond' what is proper and judicious would be just the kind of person to die an untimely death in some natural disaster. Maggie herself fears this propensity for bad timing as she tries to reach Tom with her boat during the 'final rescue' on the flooded river: 'Great God! there were floating masses in it, that might dash against her boat as she passed, and cause her to perish too soon' (519). 'Perishing' in general does not seem to be the issue here, but dying too soon certainly does – a curious concern given that minutes before she was lamenting, 'But how long it will be before death comes! I am so young, so healthy' (515).

What all of this rhetoric of timely and untimely death does, of course, is foreground the issue of narrative closure. Maggie's death in the flood is so frequently deemed 'inappropriate' not because it is an unseemly or unlikely way to die but because it brings the novel to an unsatisfying, abrupt, or implausible end. What Maggie's vision of 'the end' does, in fact, is challenge and subvert the Dodsons' notions of proper closure – just as she challenges and subverts their notions of political economy. The Dodsons and Tullivers have very definite ideas about proper closure writ large – how things (lives, destinies, stories) should end in a seemly, prudent, and frugal way. Maggie is much more concerned with feeling than she is with appropriateness; she sentimentalizes the version of proper endings given by her family, and in so doing reinscribes the conflict between passion and propriety already at work in the novel's depiction of political economy.

The Dodsons and Tullivers worry about things ending both too late and too soon. We have already seen the way in which Mr Tulliver fears dying before his debts are paid; in a comic reversal of this fear, his wife frets that all her 'best things' will be sold into strange people's houses and 'wore out before I'm dead' (203). Tom evinces his own anxiety about timely endings when he wonders about his choice of future career and, by extension, the viability of his own projected narrative of striving and repayment: 'There seemed so little tendency towards a conclusion in the quiet monotonous procedure of these sleek, prosperous men of business' (227). What the Dodsons and Tullivers really seem to fear is the possible failure of convergence between things that should, ideally, all end at the same time: to live on past the lives of your tablecloths, to die while still in debt, to be stuck 'writing ... for ever to the loud ticking of a time-piece' while commercial opportunity passes you by – these are the horrors of improper closure that the Dodsons envision.

This failure of convergence, the fear of improper ends, is felt by the Dodsons as a very real and painful possibility. After Maggie loses control and shouts at her aunts for not helping the family in their bankruptcy, Mrs Tulliver is faced with this acute fear: 'Mrs Tulliver was frightened; there was something portentous in this mad outbreak; she did not see how life could go on after it' (215). The poignancy of this description is quite striking; Mrs Tulliver, for all her pathetically narrow little concerns, is quite sensitive to the possibility of tragedy in Maggie's 'portentous' outburst. It is the finality and melodrama of the eruption that raises the spectre of an untimely or improper end; it seems as though everything must likewise come to an end, that life cannot go on after it. We are similarly alerted to the real stakes of proper closure in the passage that describes Mr Tulliver's borrowing money from Wakem's client, the decisive act that will eventually place the mill in the hands of his bitter enemy: 'Mr Tulliver had a destiny as well as Œdipus' (130). The narrator sees fit, in these passages, to remind us that the issue of endings is no small or unimportant matter; the story of the Tullivers has possibilities for real tragedy, a tragedy that may be caused – rather than merely described – by an untimely or improper closure.

This ideal of proper convergence in closure is metaphorically echoed by the image of the river; for all rivers, we are assured, there is 'the same final home' (402), a melding of waters where the 'loving tide' meets the hurrying, onrushing current (7). Unfortunately, this reassurance does little to alleviate the threat of untimely closure in the novel; it is Maggie's destiny that is likened to the river in this passage – not that of Œdipus – and it is her destiny, of course, that poses the problem for proper closure to begin with. (It almost goes without saying that it is the river itself that brings about that very destiny and untimely end.)

Maggie poses a problem for this vision of proper closure throughout the narrative; just as the flood is relentlessly foreshadowed throughout the novel, so Maggie is persistently figured as a threat to the Dodsonian ideal of convergence. She subverts and reverses her family's striving for proper endings at every turn. In a telling outburst, Maggie echoes her mother's concern that the family should not have their possessions about them when they die; however, for her, it is a question of sentiment rather than of propriety: 'The end of our lives will have nothing in it like the beginning!' (239). This tendency to sentimentalize the notion of closure is also present in her oft-cited rejection of Philip's copy of *Corinne*:

> 'I didn't finish the book,' said Maggie. 'As soon as I came to the blond-haired young lady reading in the park, I shut it up, and determined to read no further. I foresaw that the light-complexioned girl would win away all the love from Corinne and make her miserable. I'm determined to read no more books where the blond-haired women carry away all the happiness.' (332)

Maggie not only predicts the ending of the novel ('I foresaw'), but recognizes its lack of satisfaction – lack of propriety – for her own perspective. (It is quite striking how Maggie anticipates not merely the end of her own story, but also the critical reaction to the ending of *The Mill on the Floss* itself.) Maggie's sentimental reading refuses the strictures of closure; she feels fit to reread and to rewrite the ending of the tale based on her own romantic agenda.

Maggie's tendency to sentimentalize, rewrite, and subvert the imperatives of closure also leads her to a certain blindness to causation, an ignorance of narrative movement. She herself signals this propensity when she expresses envy of Tom, who has 'something to do on which he could fix his mind with a steady purpose' (288): Tom is able to adhere strictly to linear development, to the forward movement of narrative tending to a proper end. It is, of course, the 'economic' narrative on which Tom's mind is fixed that Maggie envies; as she laments to Philip, she wishes she could make for herself 'a world outside [loving], as men do' (413). The first type of narrative adheres to strict causal development, a proper end, and 'steady purpose,' while the second leads only to tragedy and 'sudden deaths.' This lack of purpose is likewise indicated in the passage about Maggie's destiny examined earlier. The metaphorical river of Maggie's fate is 'at present hidden' and 'unmapped,' and while it may eventually lead, in the broadest possible sense, to the 'same final home' (all novels end just as all people die), it is nonetheless dangerously uncertain and perhaps out of control: 'Under the charm of her new pleasures, Maggie herself was ceasing to think ... of her future lot' (402).

It is, as this last quotation indicates, the sexual nature of the 'Maggie' plot, combined with the inordinate appetites of its heroine, that lends it this improper character, this uncertain movement, this threat of an untimely end. The pleasures of romantic attraction are figured as exclusive of a reading of narrative movement or an awareness of closure: 'Each was oppressively conscious of the other's presence, even to the finger-ends ... Neither of them had begun to reflect on the matter, or silently to ask, "To what does all this tend?"' (403).

In fact, the problem of Maggie's mis- (or non-) reading can be seen, generally, as an effect of the 'romantic' or 'sexual' narrative and its idiosyncratic hermeneutic (endings are ignored, meanings conveyed silently, feelings signalled through musical chords, etc.). This way of reading bleeds over, for Maggie, into its attempted opposite: the sexual narrative is, in a profound way, hopelessly entangled with the plan of renunciation – not set over against it. Just as the problem with Maggie's program of self-denial is that it merely recapitulates her great appetites ('Maggie was still panting for happiness' [291]), so she conflates the implications of the separate narratives of romantic fulfilment and renunciation. Both are immoderate, both are attempts after pleasure, neither is the result of 'judgment and self-command' (392). In a crucial moment, Maggie even reads the two central texts of her alternative destinies in the same way. She 'reads' Stephen's pleading missive ('She did not *read* the letter: she heard him uttering it') the same way she had 'read' Thomas à Kempis (she was 'hardly conscious that she was reading – seeming rather to listen while a low voice said – ') (514, emphasis in original; 290).[24] Even the great summa of the novel, the justification for all her striving toward self-abnegation – 'In their death they were not divided' (522) – has already been echoed by Stephen Guest in his proposal in the boat: 'Let us never go home again – till no one can part us' (465).

Under the pressure of her own great desires, Maggie is continually led into acts of misreading (or rather, acts of non-reading), moments where her ability to foresee the end of her own 'narrative' is forestalled or foreclosed. This striking inability – in one with such a facility for language and reading – is a result of her confusion of the implications of the narrative of sexual fulfilment with those of the narrative of renunciation and self-denial. And it is this very confusion that is so deeply threatening to the Victorian economic world view of the other characters. Maggie confuses the imperatives of striving and starving – the optimistic and pessimistic Victorian narratives of capitalism – and in so doing foregrounds the problem of demand repressed elsewhere in the novel, and in the culture generally. Her subversion of proper closure is part of this general problem: while the Tom plot has no trouble marching blithely forward, with 'steady purpose,' toward its proper end, the Maggie plot continuously ignores the imperatives of forward movement and proper closure and unconsciously subverts the entire project of narrative propriety.

Thus her spectacular death – her much-maligned elimination – is metaphorically linked to her inappropriate demand. She dies, and becomes the agent of Tom's death, in order to resolve the tensions inaugurated by her great and improper desires. She is the victim not so much of her self-denial or of her appetites alone, as of her confusion of the two; the economic imperatives of the novel require and bring about her elimination along with her symbolic and threatening appetites. It is, after all, not the unrestrained, symbolically sexual waters of the flood that kill her, but rather the giant pieces of industrial machinery broken free of their moorings and rushing down the river. She is sacrificed to the 'ingenious machine' of optimistic capitalism, 'which performs its work with much regularity [and] is guilty towards the rash man who, venturing too near it, is caught up by some fly-wheel or other, and suddenly converted into unexpected mince-meat' (247).

4 'All Was Over at Last': Epistemological and Domestic Economies in *The Mayor of Casterbridge*

Men apply themselves to the task of growing rich, as to a labour of providential appointment, from which they cannot pause without culpability, nor retire without dishonour.

(Ruskin, *Works* 16:138)

She had her own way in everything now. In going and coming, in buying and selling, her word was law.

(Hardy, *Mayor* 377)

1 The Family Drama of the Novel

What does it mean for the heroine of a Victorian novel to supplant her father in the patriarchal role of 'buying and selling'? For her word to be law, to have 'her own way in everything'? For if this trajectory in *The Mayor of Casterbridge* is a marked reversal of the usual psychoanalytic narrative of the Œdipus complex, in which the boy is promised the ultimate ascendance to his father's position of phallic authority and privilege, it is also a rather startling reversal of the usual narrative of the Victorian novel, in which the girl's ultimate reward comes from the proper marriage.[1] Elizabeth-Jane's ending seems, in this light, every bit as perverse as Maggie Tulliver's. Elizabeth-Jane does make the proper marriage, of course – but she also ends up with much more. As John Goode has pointed out, Elizabeth-Jane not only accedes to her father's position of authority, but also directly competes with him as privileged narratorial perspective in the novel: it is her 'narratorial mode,' or acute gaze and finely grained depiction of events, that supplants Henchard's cruder and more broadly sketched description at key points in the narrative (77–94).

While Goode claims that Elizabeth-Jane's temporary coup is ultimately neutralized by the ascendance of Henchard as newly made man by the end of the novel, I would argue that there is a much deeper sense in which the daughter finally supplants the father. Elizabeth-Jane, through the persistence of her vision of sympathetic domestic arrangements, undoes Henchard's old-fashioned insistence on the patriarchal mode of ownership: his 'economy' of patrilineal descent and the exchange of women among men is thwarted by Elizabeth-Jane's newer vision of chosen families and bourgeois marriage-for-love. By seizing control of the economic narrative of the novel, and by denying the importance of patrilineal inheritance and biological kinship in the formation of familial ties, Elizabeth-Jane threatens the old order which Henchard embodies and promotes. Her father's 'law' of 'buying and selling' – typified by the infamous wife sale that opens the novel – is domesticated and feminized by novel's end.

However, as we shall see, this relatively straightforward novelistic process is undermined in two directions: first, through the complicated figure of Donald Farfrae, whose economic world view is markedly more modern than Henchard's, but who also is a destabilizing figure. He embodies the contradictions of Adam Smith's specialized labourer, whose narrow expertise, at certain points, also seems to feminize and domesticate him. The second complication arises from the fact that Elizabeth-Jane, whose perspective is triumphant at novel's end, is a character without desire – she ultimately represents just as great an economic problem as did Maggie Tulliver. In a sense, the novel overcorrects the economic issue it set out to address: the character with outlandish and perverse economic (and sexual) desires is displaced by a character without any, who is married to a soft and domestic man.

The perverse and outlandish end of the econo-erotic spectrum (that is, Henchard's) is presented to us quite insistently in the very opening pages. In the logic of the novel, the wife sale is simultaneously imprimatur of Henchard's misogyny and part and parcel of his atavistic economic practice: the two are inseparable. The contemporary understanding of the wife sale is particularly interesting from an economic standpoint. From 1861 to 1884, three articles on wife selling appeared in popular Victorian periodicals. While all the writers profess consternation and embarrassment at the paltry sums English wives seem to have fetched in sales from the sixteenth century to the then-present day (see

'Better-Half Barter,' 'The Sale of Wives,' and 'Wife-Selling'), the writer of the latest article – the only one published after the rise of the marginal utility school – develops an elaborate series of economic metaphors to explain the low 'value' of wives on the open market. He waggishly notes that the low prices for wives in the eighteenth century must have been due to the fact that 'the wife-market … [appeared] to have been in a very depressed condition, and to have fallen to a very low level at that time' ('Wife-Selling' 256). He also notes that low prices in 1841 must have been due to the fact that the 'value of a wife seems to have been mostly held in light esteem' (258), and claims that by the time of a sale that took place in 1882, the 'tariff would seem to be on a downward-sliding scale as we advance in the century' (259).

While all three writers seem disturbed at the low 'value' of these women, this writer alone attributes it, however jokingly, to sluggish demand and a depressed 'market.' Even on this humorous register, the transgressive economic practices of Henchard are condemned from the more modern, late-Victorian, demand-driven perspective. Of course, Henchard's handling of the wife sale is doubly perverse (above and beyond the inherent perversity of the act itself, that is): he conducts the auction in reverse, first demanding one guinea for his wife, and then when there are no takers, raising the price to three, again to four, and finally to five guineas – at which 'price point' he finally receives an offer. While there is a certain bizarre sophistication in his conduct of the sale (he seems unconsciously to have grasped the concept of mimetic desire – and, in fact, his technique ultimately works), he clearly has failed to understand the concept of marginal utility as determinant of price. As we shall see, the process of economic feminization he undergoes is intimately connected to his chastisement as outmoded businessman, as a practitioner of perverse and emotion-driven economics.

Critics Elaine Showalter and John Goode have convincingly argued that Henchard's education is a process of indoctrination into the traditionally feminine mode of sympathetic understanding and insight; he becomes the repository of feminine knowledge – and concomitant weakness and degradation – by the end of the novel. As I argue further, the feminization of Henchard is not confined to the arguably positive and desirable process of becoming a sympathetic and skilled observer of fellow human beings; it bleeds over into the same kind of transgressive, uncontainable, and ultimately punished sexuality that we saw in Hetty and Maggie. While Henchard's transgressive sexual exploits – the wife sale as well as the affair with Lucetta – take place before the expansion of his powers of sympathy that mark him as feminine, the unintended exposure of these transgressions is inseparable from the feminization process, as well as from his economic practices. The two spheres of 'private' sexual behaviour and 'public' business practices furnish metaphors for each other, and in the end come to seem nearly inextricable.

While Henchard begins the novel as the enthroned and unimpeachable locus of knowledge, the only one who has access to all information and all secrets about the other characters, he is supplanted in his epistemological privilege through the publicity of his scandalous past. The plot of The Mayor of Casterbridge is a complex web of deceptions, concealments, and secrets, which circulate according to a definable internal and gendered logic; while Henchard initially controls the flow of secret information in the novel, he is finally undone by the exposure of his own sexually transgressive past. It is not merely his supposed economic downfall at the hands of Farfrae which does him in, but his usurpation as controller of the circulation of secret information. For the question of Henchard's defeat, the designation of his tragic flaw, is much more complicated than is usually acknowledged. While the economic narrative is clearly crucial to an understanding of this defeat, it is finally subsidiary to the real symbolic work of the novel, which is the family drama between Elizabeth-Jane and Henchard. And this reworked and seemingly reversed Œdipal crisis is itself in service to the same drama of punished transgressive femininity we have seen elsewhere. He is penalized for his perverse economics every bit as Maggie Tulliver or Hetty Sorrel are. From sole repository of knowledge, to economic combatant, to banished 'daughter,' Michael Henchard is an eerily familiar and simultaneously defamiliarized figure.

2 The Overdeterminacy of Failure

Traditional criticism of The Mayor of Casterbridge has focused markedly on the opposition between Henchard and Farfrae – not on that between Henchard and Elizabeth-Jane – as the ruling dynamic of the novel.[2] The competition between the two men has been figured variously as a tension between tradition and innovation, between agrarian and urban economies, even between metaphor and metonymy. The problem with the traditional Henchard-vs-Farfrae critical move, however, is that this opposition, once invoked, invariably implies that Henchard is somehow doomed from the very beginning, a dinosaur whose economic methods are unsound and who is inevitably and necessarily supplanted by the younger and more dynamic Farfrae: 'Michael Henchard, the embodiment of tradition, and Donald Farfrae, the agent of technological change, are pitted against each other in what becomes virtually an allegory of technology's defeat of traditional values centered in the countryside' (Ingersoll, 'Troping' 60).

While this reading has an undeniable intuitive force, it ignores a crucial fact about the economic competition between the two men. It is not the old-fashionedness of his business methods that undoes Henchard, but the exact opposite, his unthinking embrace of the decidedly newfangled methods of selling short and buying on credit:

> Henchard had backed bad weather, and apparently lost. He had mistaken the turn of the flood for the turn of the ebb. His dealings had been so extensive that settlement could not long be postponed, and to settle he was obliged to sell off corn that he had bought only a few weeks before ... Much of the corn he had never seen. (261)

There is a sense in which the problem here is Henchard's decision to muck around with newer, 'non-representational' methods of business. The fact that he has 'never seen' the corn, that he has resorted to the new and vaguely dangerous business of trafficking in goods that he did not grow, does not touch, never lays eyes on, becomes as important as the fact that he has made foolish buying decisions; this insight is underscored later by the narrator's comment that Henchard's real downfall comes when he 'fail[s] to preserve that strict correspondence between bulk and sample which is the soul of commerce in grain' (291).[3]

Yet Henchard not only resorts to newer (and therefore questionable) ways of doing business; he also consults a soothsayer to help him predict the weather. And he not only consults a soothsayer to help him predict the weather, but he then fails to trust his advice completely and sells off his corn before the predicted rainstorms ruin the harvest. Of course we have already seen how he conducts the wife-sale 'auction' in reverse. In other words, it is nearly impossible to locate the 'real' source of Henchard's problem, in his old-fashionedness or his new-fashionedness, his inability to maximize the new methods of the credit economy or his betrayal of the old ways. It is as much a distortion to argue that Henchard represents tradition and Farfrae innovation as it is to say that one represents metaphor and the other metonymy.[4]

This difficulty is underscored when we consider that while Henchard

violates the rule of 'strict correspondence between bulk and sample,'
Farfrae does not: immediately after the younger man shows Henchard
his method for restoring grown wheat, the latter expostulates, 'I tell
you, young man, if this holds good for the bulk, as it has done for the
sample, you have saved my credit, stranger though you be. What shall
I pay you for this knowledge?' (116). While we might be tempted to
read this difference between the two men as, again, a definitive cause
of Henchard's downfall, Hardy confuses matters by ascribing the 'new-
fangled' methods equally to the two rivals: while Farfrae has the technological know-how, Henchard (despite describing himself as a 'rule o'
thumb sort of man' [117]),[5] is the one who insists on paying cash for the
restoration of his 'credit,' an offer Farfrae gracefully declines by insisting that the demonstration was an act of pure, impulsive generosity –
as well as one that he does not 'value.'

This indeterminacy is not confined to the question of business methods and Henchard's failure in trade; the entire plot is larded with alternative endings and other possibilities – what Gillian Beer refers to
as Hardy's 'ghost plots' (239). This sense of what-might-have-been is
fostered and nurtured by the narratorial voice; it is the narrator who
continually foregrounds other possibilities, who incessantly reminds
the reader that things might have turned out differently 'if only ...'[6] It
is thus impossible to sketch a chain of causation in *The Mayor of Casterbridge*; just as the narratorial second-guessing seems to reach a climax,
an apotheosis of possibility – here is the final, absolute, incontestable
reason for Henchard's downfall – another 'final' reason is presented
which undermines (or at least complicates) the former.

And it is important to note that all of this plot-commentary is indeed
directed at the question of Henchard's failure and does indeed function as an attempt to locate and understand his 'tragic flaw.' There is
certainly a reason that the novel's critics have trod this well-worn path.
But there is likewise a reason to take issue with this type of criticism,
as I noted before, for while the narrator's obsession with presenting
alternative plots invites this critical preoccupation with locating the final cause of Henchard's tragedy, it ironically thwarts all such attempts
through its sheer prodigiousness. In the end, there are too many possibilities to allow any particular one to be preferred to the others, especially since all are treated roughly the same by the narrator – as equally
valid, or at least equally viable, ways for things to have turned out.

Another reason to question the characterization of the novel's plot
as a straightforward son-usurping-father narrative is that the role of

Farfrae's 'extraordinary' abilities in Henchard's downfall is quite complex. As we will consider later in greater detail, Farfrae is far from a sympathetic character, and far from a uniformly skilled or admirable personage. Our first hint that Farfrae may not be everything he appears to be comes shortly after he is introduced, during the scene of his great singing triumph at the Three Mariners: 'He was to them like the poet of a new school who takes his contemporaries by storm; who is not really new, but is the first to articulate what all his listeners have felt, though but dimly till then' (122–3). This characterization places the responsibility for Farfrae's great success, and subsequent great popularity, squarely on the shoulders of the townsfolk themselves, who after all already possess those qualities of mind (and 'sentiment') that they come to admire in the newcomer.

But even more damning for the commonplace picture of Farfrae as an enfant terrible whose overwhelming character charms all before him is the fact that many of the traits which the novel comes to valorize (in Elizabeth-Jane and later, as we shall see, in the changed and humbled Henchard) – sympathy, discernment, sensitivity, and depth of attachment – are sorely and conspicuously lacking in the Scotchman. We are reminded again and again of his callousness toward Elizabeth-Jane, most markedly in his convenient forgetting of the courtship he had begun and his later complete inability to understand how it might pain her to watch him woo Lucetta. Similarly, Donald's general thick-headedness in reading the motivations and feelings of those around him is frequently remarked upon, particularly in the scene where Elizabeth-Jane attempts to warn him that Henchard may want to hurt him – 'Every word cost her twice its length of pain[, a]nd she could see that Farfrae was still incredulous' (312) – but more generally in the narrator's understated comment that Donald's relationship with Henchard encompasses 'meanings that [are] not very plain to him' (172).

To further complicate this schema, however, we must note that while Donald is conspicuously lacking in the feminine qualities of sympathy and discernment, his gender signification is complex and shifting. During the Three Mariners ballad-singing scene, for example, we are told that 'the singer himself grew emotional, till [Elizabeth-Jane] could imagine a tear in his eye as the words went on – "It's hame, and it's hame, hame fain would I be, / O hame, hame, hame to my ain countree!"' (120). (Interestingly, this scene forms a symbolic contrast to the opening passages of the novel, where we see Michael Henchard reading a ballad-sheet as he strides along, pointedly ignoring his wife and child. Donald is able here to put into practice – into actual music – that which Michael can only contemplate.) Farfrae's singing is admired by the gathered drinkers, yet this introductory scene marks him as sentimental, emotionally labile, and a bit histrionic – qualities we will see borne out in his actions throughout the rest of the novel. This scene also takes on an added interest when we remember the condemnatory words of Bartle Massey in *Adam Bede*, that 'the Scotch tunes are just like a scolding, nagging woman ... They go on with the same thing over and over again, and never come to a reasonable end' (307).

This scene, in fact, is part of a longer section of the novel which is focalized through Elizabeth-Jane. When she takes Donald his supper in his room at the inn, we are treated to this rather startling passage of physical character description: she 'saw how his forehead shone where the light caught it, and how nicely his hair was cut, and the sort of velvet-pile or down that was on the skin at the back of his neck, and how his cheek was so truly curved as to be part of a globe, and how clearly drawn were the lids and lashes which hid his bent eyes' (113). Donald is described here in markedly feminine terms; furthermore, this very action of lovingly detailed description objectifies him in ways that are usually reserved for female characters – in fact, if we were to change the gendered pronouns here, this passage could be airlifted straight into *Tess of the d'Urbervilles* where it would serve nicely as a description of that novel's heroine.

Furthermore, after Farfrae comes to work for the mayor, we are reminded over and over again that his new-fangled business methods are rather unmasculine: as he observes the younger man performing a bookkeeping task the 'corn-factor's mien was half admiring, and yet it was not without a dash of pity for the tastes of any one who could care to give his mind to such finnikin details' (146). (I will return to this moment in my discussion of the narratorial modes of the novel later in this chapter.) It is not just Donald's highly specialized skill with numbers, but the 'dexterity' (146) with which he records financial details that amazes his observer, who had 'received the education of Achilles, and found penmanship a tantalizing art' (146). We see later in the novel how important the gendering of penmanship is for Henchard, when he angrily condemns Elizabeth-Jane for the 'splendid round, bold hand of her own conception, a style that would have stamped a woman as Minerva's own in more recent days' (201). Donald's managerial style is also noticeably softer and more humane (notwithstanding his general personal callousness) than Michael's; for example, his 'entertainment' triumphs over Henchard's because he has anticipated the comfort of his guests, and he inadvertently humiliates his employer by refusing to allow him to humiliate Abel Whittle in the 'de-pantsing' episode. The fact that Donald – particularly in his business practices – is thus marked as feminine complicates further the standard Farfrae Triumphant reading of the novel.

But the final blow to the reading that sees Farfrae prevail over Henchard because of his superior abilities and talents comes in a quite offhand comment of the narrator's that disavows such an interpretation: 'Whether it were that his northern energy was an over-mastering force among the easy-going Wessex worthies, or whether it was sheer luck, the fact remained that whatever he touched he prospered in' (185). The one half-hearted stab the narrator makes at an explanation of the ascendance of Farfrae cannot even decide between character and luck, cannot definitively interpret the novel as a cautionary tale or a story without a moral.[7]

In place of this traditional way of understanding *The Mayor of Casterbridge* as a son-overthrows-father narrative, we can instead substitute a more nuanced analysis of characterological 'power dynamics' in the novel, dynamics that I contend are both gendered and thoroughly imbricated with economic concerns. As I noted earlier, Goode persuasively argues that the vision and experience, or narratorial mode, of Elizabeth-Jane are as important to understanding this novel as Henchard's.[8] Elizabeth-Jane's 'narrative domination' (87) in the second part of the novel gives us an entirely new perspective on events; she allows us to see what Henchard cannot, 'that at the centre of Casterbridge is the "human," historical world of romantic love, practical marriage and improving machinery' (Goode 87). This perspective is in marked contrast to the 'primitive, scriptural parameters' of Henchard's own experience (85); yet Goode's description does not require that one mode triumph over the other, but rather that a new understanding of narration and character grow out of the conflict between the two:

Thus *The Mayor of Casterbridge* is not the reproduction of an impasse but the representation of conflicting modes of narrative totalization ...

In presenting these two readings as at once mutually exclusive and equally valid it is forced to produce a third concept of character. (90)

This third concept is the perspective of the *'misérable'* – nameless, genderless, classless – the feminized man and former of representations who comes to look suspiciously, Goode hints, like the author himself. Because the *misérable* is the synthesis of the two conflicting modes of being that are represented by Elizabeth-Jane (womanly in the sense of sympathetic, insightful, and truthful) and Henchard before his downfall (manly in the sense of 'unmarked' – objective, genderless, classless), Goode's analysis functions as a narratorial dialectic of the sort that Jonathan Culler has described: 'One can attempt to establish a coherent causal series, in which disparate incidents are read as stages towards a goal, or a dialectical movement in which incidents are related as contraries whose opposition carries the problem that must be resolved' (222). This latter reading method helps clarify certain puzzling aspects of the novel's structure; if we were to read the plot as a process leading inexorably toward Henchard's decline and death (an interpretation that is only available to us, as numerous structuralist critics will point out, in view of having read the end),[9] then we could not make sense of the shifts in narratorial perspective that occur throughout the novel; only if we read the novel dialectically, as an attempt to synthesize elements that are in seeming conflict, do these shifts begin to make sense.[10]

This approach is important for two reasons: it not only provides a model for a reading which seeks to synthesize disparate and seemingly contradictory elements of the novel, but it also foregrounds the perspective of Elizabeth-Jane. This emphasis on the experience of the heroine (or as close to a heroine as we can come in this thoroughly masculine novel) is crucial for my purposes, since the questions I ultimately want to ask about *The Mayor of Casterbridge* have to do with the ways in which women in general, and Elizabeth-Jane in particular, function within the symbolic system of exchange inaugurated between Henchard and Farfrae. How does Elizabeth-Jane's status as token differ from that of the other heroines I have discussed? How are the symbolic economies operating in Hardy's novel similar to or different from those in Eliot's novels? How and in what ways are they gendered – i.e., specifically male? And finally, how does the narrative mode inaugurated by Elizabeth-Jane, the 'discerning silent witch' (243), undo both these gendered economies and the very 'dichotomization' of the novel that so many critics have depended upon? In order to answer these questions, however, we first need to closely examine the symbolic economies that are at work in the novel, and in order to do this we must consider how Hardy's use of differing narratorial perspectives, and his concomitant elaboration of a particular epistemological subject-position, relate to the economic issues of credit, barter, and exchange that I have elaborated elsewhere.

3 The Soul of Commerce: Synecdoche, (Mis)Representation, and the Economy of Lies

Literature certainly is in rather a bad way, but perhaps a time will come
when a scientific system of reviewing will be adopted, & books no longer
condemned in their entirety for some such reason as that the critic finds a
slip in an accent, quotation, or date. My last novel was sneered at by the
Saturday because of a sentence describing a rather unlikely way of improving bad flour, *which had scarcely anything to do with the story.*

(Hardy, 'To Edmund Gosse' 24 Dec. 1886, 159, emphasis added)

Any reader of *The Mayor of Casterbridge* would certainly raise a sceptical
eyebrow at the last part of this protest of Hardy's; the tale of how Donald Farfrae restores Michael Henchard's grown wheat is quite obviously central to the novel, both plot and theme. If Farfrae had not passed
by the King's Arms Hotel that day, and had not happened to overhear
the Town Council upbraiding Henchard, and had not happened to
have a scrap of paper on which to scribble his note to the mayor, and
had not happened to ask the same waiter who delivered the note for
the name of a good hotel, and all this had not happened to take place in
front of Elizabeth-Jane and her mother ... It is quite clear that the chain
of extraordinary coincidences that constitutes the plot of *The Mayor of
Casterbridge* is set in motion by this crucial meeting between Henchard
and Farfrae over the bad wheat; it is what Roland Barthes would call a
'kernel' (no pun intended) or a structuring action of the plot ('Introduction'). We can go further and say that it is an enabling one, which both
allows and necessitates the events which follow.

And perhaps more important, it is the nature of this meeting – the
fact that Farfrae has some new-fangled technical knowledge to pass
on to the older and more traditional corn-factor – that sets the tone for
their entire relationship; it is the beginning of a long series of events
that convinces Henchard that Farfrae is out to usurp his privilege and
authority, a conviction which in itself becomes a crucial motivation
of the plot. But what is perhaps most astonishing about this denial of
Hardy's is that the narrator of the novel, who we can assume is closely
allied with the author as interpreter of the story, himself asserts the
centrality of this first meeting between the two rivals: he comments
that Farfrae may not have stopped to listen at the King's Arms at the
beginning of the story 'had not his advent coincided with the discussion on corn and bread; in which event this history had never been
enacted' (106).

Why, then, would Hardy deny the central importance of this plot twist in a letter to his friend? The most obvious answer comes from the context of the quotation in which the denial occurs: he is in the process of condemning the practice of critics who would dismiss an entire novel based on one improbable plot element (or on any single element, for that matter). His outrage at what he sees as an over-hasty generalization leads him to momentarily misread the plot of his own novel, to deny what is undeniable in his desire to disavow a potential critical bugbear: that the chain of possibility and event that is central to *The Mayor of Casterbridge* is enabled and necessitated by this first, crucial meeting.

And in denying so vehemently, Hardy acknowledges the importance of that which he claims to disavow: the relationship between part and whole, between plot element and novel, as a compelling way of reading. He has elsewhere even encouraged this synecdochic method of reading his own novel: the narrator asks us to read the whole of Casterbridge through its marketplace and streets, the whole of Elizabeth-Jane through her features, the whole of the town merchants through their clothing and gestures, and the whole of Henchard through his basket of tools. But more interesting is the fact that the narrator condemns Henchard for failing to adhere to this method in not preserving a 'strict correspondence between bulk and sample' (291) in selling his grain.

Let us return to this last, crucial moment of narratorial commentary. This failure of correspondence is presented as yet another of those final and ultimate reasons for Henchard's downfall, and I insisted earlier that the plot of this novel is resistant to such instrumental readings. Yet the fact remains that as an attempt at explanation it has more causal force than many of the others proposed by the narrator, and it bears closer consideration as a recurring motif. For one thing, this failure is the final blow which leads Henchard into bankruptcy, which event is the last before he is led to haunt the bridge of the '*misérables*' where he will ultimately remake himself as the newly sympathetic man (292–7). And for another, the misrepresentation is proposed as something over which Henchard has no real control (it is one of his men who misrepresents the grain to his buyers), in much the same way that Hardy has no real control over the critical response to his novel. As Hardy repeatedly complains in his letters and journals, the method by which novels are judged is not 'scientific,' or is unfair, or is random (startlingly similar, in fact, to Henchard's business practices). At one point he implores Robert Louis Stevenson to 'write something on the art of criticism. Meredith says somebody who has produced creative work ought to do it – so that the critics may get some rudimentary knowledge of the trade they profess' ('To Robert Louis Stevenson' 147). At another he proposes to Edmund Gosse

a strong argument against anonymous journalism. I have suffered terribly at times from reviews – pecuniarily, & still more mentally, & the crown of my bitterness has been my sense of unfairness in such impersonal means of attack, wh. conveys to an unthinking public the idea of an immense weight of opinion behind, to which you can only oppose your own little solitary personality: when the truth is that there is only another little solitary personality against yours all the time. ('To Edmund Gosse' 19 Oct. 1886, 154)

What all of these examples have in common is Hardy's horror at the idea of misreading a whole from one of its parts: a whole novel from an implausible plot element, the bulk of corn from a sample, the condemnation of the entire reading public from the opinion of a single critic. And this fear of misrepresentation, and attendant concern with honest representation, is everywhere in *The Mayor of Casterbridge*. In his initial descriptions of the businessmen of Casterbridge, Hardy carefully explains how their facial expressions and bodily gestures form an honest and complete picture of their states of mind:

The yeomen, farmers, dairymen, and townsfolk, who came to transact business in these ancient streets, spoke in other ways than by articulation. Not to hear the words of your interlocutor in metropolitan centres is to know nothing of his meaning. Here the face, the arms, the hat, the stick, the body throughout spoke equally with the tongue ... Chicanery, subterfuge, had hardly a place in the streets of this honest borough. (130)

This is a utopian description of a world of perfect representation, a world almost without language where meanings are evident on surfaces (bodies and clothing) and do not have to be decoded. Without 'articulation' there are none of the problems attendant upon interpretation or translation: no misunderstanding, no slippage between signifier and signified, no possibility of falsehood or 'subterfuge.'

This description should sound familiar – it is remarkably similar to the terms in which Herbert Spencer delineates his two ideal economies, the worlds of all liars and all honest men:

Among unmitigated rogues, mutual trust is impossible. Among people of absolute integrity, mutual trust would be unlimited ... Given a nation made up of liars and thieves, and all trade among its members must be carried on either by barter or by a currency of intrinsic value ... On the other hand, given a nation of perfectly honest men – men as careful of others' rights as of their own – and nearly all trade among its members may be carried on by memoranda of debts and claims. ('State-Tamperings' 326)

In a world of perfect epistemological transparency, where not only everyone is honest but everyone knows that everyone is honest, business can be transacted in an atmosphere of trust, and credit may be extended with impunity. Hardy wants us to believe that this is the case in Casterbridge, that 'honest borough,' and we would certainly expect this, would we not, since Hardy has already told us that all the businessmen here are perfectly transparent?

And yet this does not seem to be exactly true:

All over-clothes here were worn as if they were an inconvenience, a hampering necessity. Some men were well-dressed; but the majority were careless in that respect, appearing in suits which were historical records of their wearer's deeds, sun-scorchings, and daily struggles for many years past. Yet many carried ruffled cheque-books in their pockets which regulated at the bank hard by a balance of never less than four figures. In fact, what these gibbous human shapes specially represented was ready money – money insistently ready – not ready next year like a nobleman's – often not merely ready at the bank like a professional man's, but ready in their large plump hands. (224)

There are many different, overlapping, and complex sign-systems invoked in this passage, and not all of them have to do with perfect honesty and epistemological transparency. On the surface, the acts of representation described here are the same kind as those found in the earlier description of Casterbridge. Clothing speaks eloquently of the men who wear it, bearing visible marks of labour and serving as 'historical records of [its] wearer's deeds.'[11] The ubiquity of cash serves to underscore the idea of the traders' honesty; all trade is carried out in 'a currency of intrinsic value,' money is not merely ready but 'insistently ready,' not merely available in a bank account but present in cash, not merely accessible in wallet or pocket but visible in 'large plump hands,' all but leaping after commodities of its own free will. (While some of these traders do carry 'ruffled cheque-books,' the narrator insists that their money is more immediately available than that 'merely ready at the bank like a professional man's' – perhaps because in this case, the bank is 'hard by.') There is no possibility of subterfuge or dishonesty here; everything is what it seems to be; workers look like workers; money is money and the fact that it is visible and available creates an atmosphere in which all transactions can be trusted.

And yet not everything here is necessarily as it appears on the surface. One of the first things we notice about the denizens of the marketplace upon closer examination of the passage is that their clothing belies their real wealth, and cannot be trusted as an accurate marker of their class. Although their suits may bear the marks of hard work and age, the traders are not the labouring poor, but instead have four-figure chequing accounts. What happened to those businessmen whose very hats and sticks could be trusted to speak eloquently of the true nature of their bearers? Similarly, we must question, in light of Spencer's commentary, Hardy's insistence that these men carry out their business solely in the medium of ready money: surely if these men were as honest, open, transparent, and readable as Hardy claims they are, there would be no need to insist so vehemently on the fact that they transact all business in cold hard cash?

In order to make sense of this seeming contradiction, I would like to pay special attention to Hardy's use of the word 'represented' in this passage. He claims that what these businessmen themselves 'represented' was 'ready money.' What is curious about this assertion is that usually only one thing is said, in itself, to represent ready money, and that is those 'memoranda of debts and claims' – promises-to-pay, currency, and cheques – that Spencer notes are the special province of honest men. It is as though Hardy is remapping the representational relationship between 'real' money of intrinsic value (precious metal) and the certificates said to represent it (paper currency and promises-to-pay) onto the bodies of the Casterbridge traders. And it is indeed their very bodies, their 'gibbous human shapes,' which bear the metaphorical weight of this representational relationship; it is their bodies which are analogous to paper promises in their ability to stand in for ready money.

This strange image seems to belie an anxiety, not only about the so-called honesty of these perhaps not-so-transparent men, but more important, about the economic system which allows the circulation of substitutes for 'real' money. In attempting to shift the burden of monetary representation away from paper currency and promises-to-pay (the medium denigrated as 'ready next year') and onto the bodies of the men who hold the cash in their hands (or whose banks are at least 'hard by'), Hardy seems to be attempting to simplify the complex and uncertain relationship between gold and paper. Having already established that the bodies of these traders are incapable of lying, are by their very nature utterly readable, Hardy then attempts to substitute these transparent signs for the more troubling and difficult signs of promises-to-pay.

And yet this substitution does not quite work. For one thing, the relationship Hardy describes between the traders' bodies and their cash is a metonymical one, not a metaphorical one as is the relationship between gold and paper.[12] The bodies of the traders represent money because they are associated with money in physical space – they hold it in their hands and can produce it upon demand. Just as the clothing of the traders bears the signs of work, and thus represents labour metonymically (by virtue of its contiguity to labour, by having been physically present as labour took place), so the human shapes of the traders become associated with cash.

And the similarity does not end there, for both metonymical relationships also have in common the fact that they break down at some point, fail to represent accurately, and cannot bear the full burden of honest disclosure that is placed upon them. The businessmen's clothing lies because it does not tell the full story about its wearers – that many of them have bank accounts in four figures. And the businessmen's bodies lie because the mere presence of cash does not ensure the honesty of the person holding it. Metonymical relationships (especially synecdochical relationships, like the ones I have already discussed) are potentially problematic in that the metonymic sign bears no necessary relationship to the object it represents, and is therefore rife with possibilities of misrepresentation and misprision.[13]

It is here that we can see the real divergence between Spencer and Hardy. In Spencer's account, the apprehension of one's trading partners as honest or dishonest occurs prior to the decision to transact business in either cash or on credit; we choose one method over the other because we know the natures of those with whom we are doing business. For Hardy, the presence of cash seems to function, paradoxically, as a marker of honesty; one cannot help but be honest if one does not have the means of being dishonest – just as the transparency of the businessmen's gestures in the first passage guarantees honesty since deceit is impossible where everything is readable. And this insistence on describing the structures which make dishonesty impossible – thereby guaranteeing a sort of ethically empty honesty-by-default – betrays Hardy's concern with misrepresentation and lying.

And with good reason – his eponymous character (one of them, anyway) is a liar. Henchard's life story is chock-full of lies, deceptions, concealments, omissions; his ability to lie becomes, as we shall see, the enabling condition of the plot of this novel. And yet he is presented to us, time and again and with much fanfare on the part of the narrator, as a scrupulously honest man. Here is what the senior commissioner has to say about him at his bankruptcy hearing:

> I am bound to admit that I have never met a debtor who behaved more fairly. I've proved the balance-sheet to be as honestly made out as it could possibly be; we have had no trouble; there have been no evasions and no concealments. The rashness of dealing which led to this unhappy situation is obvious enough; but as far as I can see every attempt has been made to avoid wronging anybody. (293)

That is unless you count his wife, his daughter, his mistress, his former business partner ...

The truth is that Henchard is both honest and dishonest: he ultimately goes bankrupt because he lies about his grain, but the lie was not his fault. And if Henchard's problem is misrepresentation, if he is sometimes honest but sometimes cannot be trusted to represent things accurately, then he is the true avatar of what Spencer calls the 'mixed currency' of credit and barter: 'In a nation neither wholly honest nor wholly dishonest, there may, and eventually will, be established a mixed currency – a currency partly of intrinsic and partly of credit-value' ('State-Tamperings' 326–7). And in representing Henchard as the embodiment of a new business practice – not simply the traditionalist opposed to the modernist Farfrae – Hardy is choosing to examine a new way of being, a new epistemological subject-position (which term I will clarify later on).

In the plot of *The Mayor of Casterbridge* Hardy is concerned with economies of knowledge – how knowledge, truth, and information circulate and are exchanged – as opposed to Eliot's concern, in her first novel, with economies of consequence. Just as Eliot's project in *Adam Bede* is to demonstrate how the consequences of actions extend beyond their owner's ability to contain them – which only undermines her simultaneous attempt to nostalgically depict a closed system of economic exchange – so Hardy's project in this novel is to demonstrate how Henchard's actions, and particularly his attempts at recompense, involve him further in the intricacies of falsehood which are, ironically, his real source of power. In this scheme Elizabeth-Jane and her 'narrative domination' (Goode 87) function as a sort of standard or template of honesty (and ignorance) against which we measure Henchard's manipulations of truth and his control of the flow of information around him. Each inhabits a radically disparate epistemological position, and each position is presented as the prevailing narrative point of view for various parts of the novel, as Goode has pointed out. My analysis differs importantly from Goode's in that I see Henchard's position ultimately valorized as the main point of sympathetic identification in the novel, while Elizabeth-Jane's claims to truth prevail. It is this disjunct that renders the closure of the novel so unsettling: the triumph of Elizabeth-Jane, as we shall see, feels hollow and forced, and this feeling of let-down blunts the force of the economic and ethical critique that Hardy seems to want to mount.

But how do we know, first of all, that Hardy is so concerned with the issue of truth-telling, epistemological uncertainty, and misrepresentation when it comes to the plot of *The Mayor of Casterbridge*? To answer this question, let us return briefly to the concept of 'ghost plots' that Beer discusses in her section on Hardy in *Darwin's Plots*:

> Deterministic systems are placed under great stress [in Hardy]: a succession of ghost plots is present. The persistently almost-attained happy alternatives are never quite obliterated by the actual terrible events. The reader is pained by the sense of multiple possibilities, only one of which can occur and be thus verified in time, space, and actuality. (239)

Beer does not spend much time explaining exactly how this sense of happy alternatives is achieved, beyond noting that one of the levels of plot operating in a Hardy novel is 'the optative plot of the commentary, which often takes the form "Why did nobody" or "had somebody ..."' (240).

While there are certainly numerous instances of this kind of narrative questioning in *The Mayor of Casterbridge*, by far the most persistent and common type of narratorial comment takes the form of 'If only So-and-So had told the truth.' We are treated to this particularly painful post-hoc chastisement at three crucial points in the novel: when Henchard accidentally misrepresents his grain in the market; when the facts of Henchard's wife sale are made public in the town; and when Farfrae discovers Lucetta's affair with Henchard. In the first of these commentaries on the plot, we are informed that it is not Henchard's poor grain that undoes him, but rather the fact that he appears to have misled his buyers about it: 'The produce if honestly offered would have created no scandal; but the blunder of misrepresentation, coming at such a moment, dragged Henchard's name into the ditch' (292). A similar protestation is made regarding the furmity woman's publicizing of the wife sale: 'Had the incident been well known of old and always, it might by this time have grown to be lightly regarded ... But the act having lain as dead and buried ever since, the interspace of years was unperceived; and the black spot of his youth wore the aspect of a recent crime' (291). And again, we are helpfully informed that had Lucetta only been honest with Farfrae about her past affair with Henchard, all might have turned out for the best: 'Had she confessed all to Donald in their early acquaintance he might possibly have got over it, and married her just the same – unlikely as it had once seemed' (322).

What is striking about these three protestations, all of which occur around key points in the narrative, is that they are utterly unbelievable. The narrator explicitly invites us to perform that action of imagining 'counter-texts,' or different (and impossible) outcomes, that Barthes has noted is crucial to the process of understanding plot.[14] Yet in each case we can say that the happy outcome is an implausibility, that the narrator is taunting us with an unattainable idea of a happier ending – for surely we can extrapolate what would have happened in each of those instances (if we imagine for a moment the novel as a fully realized world) had the person in question been entirely truthful. Henchard may not have been denigrated as a liar, but no one would have bought his inferior grain nevertheless, and he still would have gone bankrupt. Donald surely would not have consented to marry a woman who had had an illicit affair with his arch-rival (or probably anyone, for that matter – we need only turn to *Tess* to get an idea of how a deliberate and passionless man reacts to the news of his wife's unfortunate past in a Hardy novel). And one cannot even imagine how Henchard would have gone about being honest and open about the facts of the wife sale (drop it casually into conversation, tell the story in front of the crowd at the Three Mariners, make an announcement at his mayoral inauguration?), let alone that the results would have been as benign as the narrator assures us they would have been.

The effect of Hardy's insistence on these alternative 'truthful' plots is to impress us, as readers, with how crucial lies are to this story. Starting with Henchard and Newson's joint de facto lie to Susan that she is bound by the terms of the wife sale, through to Henchard's lie to Newson that Elizabeth-Jane is dead, the whole armature of the novel is built upon a foundation of falsehoods. Without these falsehoods, the story could not have happened – which the narrator as much as admits by inviting us to imagine the results had everyone told the truth. 'This history had never been enacted' could just as easily be appended to any one of these narratorial interventions as to the description of Farfrae's initial meeting with Henchard.

And these are not just any falsehoods, but falsehoods with one thing – or rather person – in common: Michael Henchard. It is he alone who knows all of the following: the story of the wife sale, his history with Lucetta, the facts of Elizabeth-Jane's parentage, the fact that Newson is still alive, and the fact (which he conceals from Newson) that Elizabeth-Jane is alive. Certainly other characters know some of these things, but Henchard alone has privileged access to all the truth in this story. (The one instance where this perfect knowledge is threatened, the truth of Elizabeth-Jane's parentage, is quickly neutralized by Henchard's 'accidental' opening of Susan's death-bed testament – but this is an important incident which I will examine later in greater detail.) And not only does Henchard have access to all available information, but the fact that no one else does is directly due to his own lies and omissions: his position of epistemological privilege goes hand in hand with his history as a liar.

The plot of *The Mayor of Casterbridge* is a web of deceptions and concealments, which circulate according to a definable internal and gendered logic. Much of this circulation is carried on through the medium of writing – particularly women's writing – but the ultimate control over that circulation belongs to Henchard (although he engages in acts of symbolic exchange with other men in the novel). It is he who directs and intercepts the two key texts which bear the greatest burden of secrecy – and therefore truth – in this novel: Susan's written death-bed confession and Lucetta's packet of love letters to Henchard. It is he who is the key trader in this symbolic economy of truth.

The very plot of *The Mayor of Casterbridge* is thus fuelled by lies, so much so that we can say that truth – or rather, the revelation of truth – undoes the narrative, is opposed to narrative. My sense of the forward notion of plot as depending on these enabling falsehoods is informed by the work of both Barthes and Peter Brooks. In *Reading for the Plot*, Brooks elaborates on what Barthes terms 'passion' for meaning, which keeps the reader reading and attempting to integrate the various elements of narrative into a coherent and satisfying whole (Barthes, 'Introduction' 124). For Brooks this notion of passion, or desire, is important not only for understanding our synthetic operations as readers but also for understanding the sources of narrative itself (48). For Brooks, one such source is the Freudian 'masterplot,' which he extrapolates from *Beyond the Pleasure Principle*: plot, just as the organism for Freud, is propelled forward by the death drive, the drive toward the end and the release of tension. The desire for meaning that is the impetus behind narrative, what causes plots to begin, also demands discharge, demands that the plot/organism return to a state of quiescence (103). For Freud, the self-preservative instincts, as opposed to the death instincts, work 'to assure that the organism shall follow its own path to death, and to ward off any possible ways of returning to inorganic existence other than those which are immanent in the organism itself' (*Beyond* 33). These instincts manifest themselves in narrative, to return to Brooks, as various postponements or detours (repetitions) which ensure that the proper ending is reached: 'The improper end indeed lurks throughout narrative, frequently as the wrong choice ... The development of the subplot in the classical novel usually suggests ... a different solution to the problems worked through by the main plot, and often illustrates the danger of short-circuit' (104).

While I am not prepared to accept wholeheartedly every nuance and implication of Brooks's argument, I do feel that the basic model of narrative he has outlined is a compelling one, particularly for *The Mayor of Casterbridge*: an initial 'excitation' of desire, often taking the form of ambition (39), which seeks its release, ultimately in death, by way of a series of repetitions and detours. To apply this model in greater detail, then, I would argue that the 'death drive' of the plot of this novel is the drive toward the revelation of truth: as soon as all the secrets that Henchard knows are revealed, as soon as all of his private knowledge is made public, he dies and the novel ends. But this is to work backwards, of course – to argue teleologically that whatever happens at the end of the novel is necessarily what the 'drive' of the plot was moving toward. We could leave it at this, that this novel, as perhaps every narrative, is necessarily about a simultaneous movement toward revelation and death: as Walter Benjamin reminds us, 'Not only a man's knowledge or wisdom, but above all his real life – and this is the stuff that stories are made of – first assumes transmissible form at the moment of his death' (94). But not only does the plot end with Henchard's death and the revelation of the lies he has told; it also performs numerous 'detours' along the way, even at the expense of plausibility, precisely whenever Henchard's monopoly on the circulation of knowledge is threatened.[15]

For example, there are two crucial points in the novel where the course of events threatens to allow female characters an uncomfortable control over the flow of information. The first is when we learn that Susan has kept the secret of Elizabeth-Jane's true parentage from Henchard; he learns about it, of course, when he reads the letter that she dictated on her deathbed. In the course of one evening, the epistemological landscape of the novel alters dramatically, as a course of seismic shocks ruptures and alters the surface of both what the characters know and what the reader knows. It is worth tracing in painstaking detail: if we designate the fact that Elizabeth-Jane is Newson's daughter as the 'truth,' we can see that at first, Susan and Elizabeth-Jane know the truth but not Henchard or the reader; then, after Henchard's disclosure, Susan alone 'knows' the truth (she is dead by this point); and finally, after Henchard reads the letter, he and Susan and the reader all know the truth but not Elizabeth-Jane. (This is ignoring, for the sake of simplicity, complications such as the fact that Elizabeth-Jane's initial truth is really a double falsehood, since she has no knowledge of Henchard and Susan's past relationship at all.)

What Henchard's reading of the letter does is give him access to the truth, and what his earlier disclosure to Elizabeth-Jane does is ensure that he alone has this access. In a double gesture, he has removed both women from a position of privileged knowledge: had he merely made the disclosure, Susan alone would have known the truth, and had he merely read the letter, Elizabeth-Jane and Susan both would have known. It is only through the improbable combination of reading a posthumous letter, in which the writer can have no more possible claim to epistemological privilege, and having just made an erroneous disclosure to his 'daughter,' that Henchard can resecure his position as final arbiter of knowledge in this novel. And lest we lose sight of the fact, it is indeed an improbable combination of events – so much so that the narrator feels compelled to justify what has happened in one of the very rare instances in Hardy where we are informed that things had to have happened this way:

Henchard, like all his kind, was superstitious, and he could not help thinking that the concatenation of events this evening had produced was the
scheme of some sinister intelligence bent on punishing him. Yet they had
developed naturally. If he had not revealed his past history to Elizabeth he
would not have searched the drawer for papers, and so on. (197)

Here speaks the voice of an author suddenly concerned with the plausibility of his text; these narratorial justifications, so common in Eliot,
rarely occur in Hardy and thus signal moments of extreme pressure
and uncertainty.[16]

The reason Hardy takes such a risk with his readers' credulity, I would
argue, is that the overwhelming motivation in the logic of the novel, at
this point, is to preserve Henchard's position of epistemological privilege. It is through this preservation, as we shall see, that Henchard remains our primary point of identification and sympathy, as well as our
primary source of knowledge in reading the text; as Elizabeth-Jane's
perspective begins to take over in the second part of the novel, this monopoly on both identification and information shifts noticeably.

But before we get to this shift, let us look at the second crucial moment when a woman threatens to gain control over the circulation of
knowledge in Casterbridge. Lucetta's love letters to Henchard serve as
physical evidence of her impropriety, her non-maidenhood, her Past; to
allow her to destroy this evidence would be to allow her a dangerous
measure of control over knowledge of this past, a control that she would
specifically exercise over her husband, Farfrae. She never achieves this
authority, of course, because it is Henchard who maintains control over
this crucial information throughout (even at the moment of its 'relin-
quishment,' as we shall see, he still maintains this power).

Because this is information which is of primary interest to Farfrae,
we can see the effective exchange of the letters between the two men
as another instance of Henchard and Farfrae's symbolic economy of
exchange (an economy whose primary token up until this point has
been Elizabeth-Jane). In order to understand how Henchard maintains
effective control over this crucial information, let us look closely at the
passages which describe how both key documents – Susan's will and
Lucetta's letters – come to be wrongfully read:

Mrs Henchard, though more patient than her husband, had been no practical hand at anything. In sealing up the sheet, which was folded and

> tucked in without an envelope, in the old-fashioned way, she had overlaid
> the junction with a large mass of wax without the requisite under-touch of
> the same. The seal had cracked, and the letter was open. (195)

And similarly, the packet of Lucetta's letters which Henchard hands
over to Jopp to deliver to her:

> The pen and all its relations being awkward tools in Henchard's hands he
> had affixed the seals without an impression, it never occurring to him that
> the efficacy of such a fastening depended on this. (327)

In each instance we have a failed seal, a sheaf of papers literally flap-
ping open, unable to contain the damaging contents therein – or perhaps even eager to publicize those contents. Our first reaction upon
reading these two passages is of an utterly pragmatic nature: why on
earth did Henchard not learn about the importance of proper seals,
since it was a poor seal which had already given him information he
would have preferred not to know? But the corollary of this question
is, of course, that Hardy is interested in depicting his protagonist as not
wanting to conceal this information – he supposedly already knew to
carefully seal it if he meant it to remain private. Regardless of the depth
of his animosity toward, and bitterness of his rivalry with, Farfrae, the
trade route of information – and women – which has already been established between them is supremely powerful. What Gayle Rubin has
called the 'traffic in women' is thus exposed as the real motivation behind the purely 'economic' exchange over which the two rivals struggle: patriarchal kinship exchange is a deeper and more fundamental
concern than the circulation of more mundane goods such as corn. As
Hardy depicts him, Henchard at some level meant for Farfrae to learn
of his new wife's past.[17]

This apprehension becomes even more striking if we consider the nature of the information so circulated. Both exemplary texts – Susan's will
and Lucetta's packet of letters – are emblems of their writers' shame,
markers of their inappropriate sexuality outside of marriage. (We are
continually reminded of Lucetta's fallen status; when she moves into
High-Place Hall, for example, the event is described in these Ruskinian
terms: 'Men had still quite recently been going in and out with par-
cels and packing-cases, rendering the door and hall within like a public
thoroughfare' [210].[18] Elsewhere, in a letter to Henchard, she refers to
herself as a 'woman you meet in the street' [319].) As markers of the

two women's transgressive sexuality, Susan's will and Lucetta's letters begin to stand in for the women's bodies themselves; the loose seals become a fantasy of unlimited male access, both to information about these women's bodies and to the bodies themselves. There is no way to distinguish the two: the words contained in these texts, which leak out unbidden, are uncontainable and have consequences far beyond the borders of the paper on which they are written. And so they become emblems of their writers' desire itself, unbound by their bodies and beyond the control of the bourgeois institution of marriage and the men who are their husbands. Henchard's unstoppable (unsealable?) access to these texts is an ultimately failed attempt to recontain this dangerous sexuality, to harness its energy to the ends of the masculine system of symbolic exchange. It ultimately fails because it is through a similar revelation of his own scandalous past that Henchard's privileged position, in the town and in the novel, will ultimately come to an end.

Thus we can see that the novel's primary goal, at this point, is to maintain Henchard as the character of supreme epistemological privilege. This motivation is so strong that it distorts and warps the plot itself, causing implausible events and unlikely actions in order to keep this enthronement secure. To return to Brooks, it is as if the plot were delaying the point where Henchard's viewpoint is no longer coterminous with the available information in the novel in order to achieve the 'proper end' of his death; as soon as he loses his position of authority and privilege, the novel comes to a close. It is as if there is nothing left to say as soon as Elizabeth-Jane replaces Henchard as the privileged centre of the novel and the holder of available knowledge; this evacuation of the narratable goes hand in hand with the narratological ascension of a character without (economic) desire. Elizabeth-Jane's 'mode' prevails on one level – or rather, as we shall see, Henchard and Elizabeth each take on the knowledge of the other. But in order to understand how this realignment takes place, we must first trace more carefully the ways in which our two narrative modes inform and affect each other, how Henchard and Elizabeth-Jane must learn to be like their opposites.

4 Symbolic Exchange and the Problem of Sympathy

The Mayor of Casterbridge inaugurates two distinct – and to a certain extent competing – modes of narrative: Henchard's and Elizabeth-Jane's. Henchard's point of view, which dominates the first part of the novel, is the mode of 'energy,' the 'primitive, scriptural' mode of brute force,

crude understanding, theatricality, and the possibility of tragedy. Elizabeth-Jane's, on the other hand, is above all else 'discerning': she sees
deeply into the psyches and motivations of those around her, is capable
of fine distinctions, and 'knows that what she sees is too small for Henchard' (Goode 89).

The reader is quite clearly encouraged to favour Elizabeth-Jane's
mode over Henchard's. As the narrator comments at one point, the
corn-factor was not a man 'who could care to give his mind to such
finnikin details ... He was mentally and physically unfit for grubbing
subtleties from soiled paper' (146). This characterization can be read
as differentiating Henchard either from Farfrae (to whom the passage
ostensibly refers) or from the narrator/author himself. It is commonly
noted that Hardy's narrators differentiate themselves from mere 'ordinary' observers by emphasizing the subtlety and discernment of
their observations.[19] The viewpoint of the discerning narrator, minding
finnikin details, and the author, grubbing subtleties from paper, is continually held up as the standard against which to measure skills in ob-
serving. And the ability to understand events at the level of individual
psychology, and fluency in the language of emotions, are skills that are
valorized not only by (and in) the narrator but by the events of the plot:
the fact that Henchard is, as several critics have pointed out, feminized
in the course of the novel lends a certain intuitive force to the idea that
Elizabeth-Jane's way of seeing is the telos toward which he must move
in the course of becoming fully human.[20]

However, we must be careful not to take this insight too far: it is
certainly not the case that Elizabeth-Jane's perspective is privileged in
terms of access to secret information and knowledge of deceptions, as
I have shown. This kind of 'insight,' this epistemological prerogative,
is the province of Henchard. Julie Grossman's observation that 'in *The
Mayor of Casterbridge*, Elizabeth-Jane's observations are an extended
metaphor for divining the truth' (619) is thus both right and wrong.
It is right in the sense that the novel sees the 'truth' as that feminine
'excluded knowledge' that Henchard takes on by the time of his death;
it is wrong in that Elizabeth-Jane is, quite frankly, completely in the
dark for much of the novel. There is a disjunction here between mode
of observation and epistemological perspective: Elizabeth-Jane is given
the language of truth to speak, and yet she is deceived throughout the
novel, unaware of basic information to which both Henchard and the
reader are privy.

There are thus two different modes of truth operating in the novel: knowledge and discernment. But Grossman is right again, although in a way that she does not intend, when we consider that the full disclosure of Henchard's secrets – and most especially to Elizabeth-Jane – constitutes the horizon of the novel. We can thus say that Elizabeth-Jane and Henchard trade places during the course of the book: he takes on the mantle of sympathy, insight, and discernment that she had worn, and she moves toward the centre of privileged knowledge (of secrets, of events) that he had occupied. This is how the novel rewrites the Œdipal drama as a quasi-economic exchange.

While Goode claims that a 'third concept of character' (90) is created from the clash of the feminine mode of Elizabeth-Jane and the masculine mode of Henchard – Henchard as the figure of the *misérable* – we must note that the process of 'switching' that the two characters undergo transforms Elizabeth-Jane as well. Instead of taking on the 'voice of the oppressed' (Goode 92) as does Henchard, she takes on the voice of narratorial authority; her perspective becomes all-encompassing, wise beyond her years and sweepingly vast in its comprehension:

> The finer movements of her nature found scope in discovering to the narrow-lived ones around her the secret (as she had once learnt it) of making limited opportunities endurable; which she deemed to consist in the cunning enlargement, by a species of microscopic treatment, of those minute forms of satisfaction that offer themselves to everybody not in positive pain ... And in being forced to class herself among the fortunate she did not cease to wonder at the persistence of the unforeseen, when the one to whom such unbroken tranquillity had been accorded in the adult stage was she whose youth had seemed to teach that happiness was but the occasional episode in a general drama of pain. (410)

The persistent vocabulary of the first part of this passage – finer, scope, narrow, limited, enlargement, microscopic, minute – demonstrates the extent to which Elizabeth-Jane's perspective has broadened to the parameters of the narrator's. Her discernment is now no longer merely the ability to see much smaller objects than most other people, but also the power to magnify those objects until they reach the horizon of perception – which operation has been, up until this point, the sole province of the omniscient narrator. When we combine this power with the second part of the passage, which demonstrates the content of her marvellous perceptive ability – a balanced and understanding view of the painful nature of human existence – we can see that Elizabeth-Jane has taken on the powers, abilities, and voice of narratorial authority. She now combines discernment (which she has all along) with knowledge (which she gains at the end of the novel).

It is Elizabeth-Jane who is specifically accorded the power of 'magnification,' whose discernment has never been in question, and who is given the last words (through free indirect discourse) of the novel. Thus Goode's comment that Henchard's education 'takes him far beyond that feminine awareness which is the education of Elizabeth-Jane' (93) strikes me as not quite right: while it is true that Elizabeth-Jane's perspective is to a certain extent marginalized and not necessarily triumphant over Henchard's, she does have the final word. Henchard and she may switch places, but Hardy still valorizes her perspective: perhaps it is simply easier to learn what one had not known, which is what Elizabeth-Jane's education consists in, than to take on a whole new set of skills, which is what constitutes Henchard's. Elizabeth-Jane's remains the chosen perspective, at least at the bare level of authorial attention: there is a sense in which Hardy is trying very hard, as we can see in this last passage, to merge her perspective with that of the novel itself.

If Elizabeth-Jane's perspective is ultimately valorized and merged with that of the narrator, then we can see that her status as object of exchange must be quite complex and problematic. At the beginning (and through the middle) of the story, Elizabeth-Jane is shunted back and forth between Susan, Henchard, Farfrae, and Lucetta like an unwanted Christmas fruitcake; the actions of 'giving back' and 'accepting' Elizabeth are the phonemes of a complex language of betrayal and reconciliation among the other characters in the novel. She is traded as daughter, fiancée, housekeeper, and friend, and for the most part effects very little control over the traffic in her affections and loyalty.

Elizabeth-Jane's role as token of exchange is inaugurated at the very opening of the story. When Henchard and Susan agree to part after the wife sale, she is mentioned as one of the objects of contention in their transaction; Henchard declares: 'She [Susan] shall take the girl if she wants to, and go her ways. I'll take my tools, and go my ways' (76–7). The significance of this gesture as a transfer of 'ownership' is underscored in the next scene, where, upon awakening, he laments the fact that he has given up his rights to his daughter: 'She'd no business to take the maid – 'tis my maid; and if it were the doing again she shouldn't have her!' (80). As Showalter notes, the sale of Elizabeth-Jane is every bit as important in the logic of the novel – even more so, perhaps – as the sale of Henchard's wife (103).[21] Henchard's habit of thinking of his daughter as chattel which can be given up or withheld in order to gain advantage in other relationships continues in his dealings with Farfrae. When he first quarrels with the Scotchman he immediately forbids him paying addresses to his daughter; later, when he feels burdened with the fatherhood of a girl who is not his own, he regrets this decision: 'Henchard was sitting up, thinking over his jealous folly in forbidding Farfrae to pay his addresses to this girl who did not belong to him, when if he had allowed them to go on he might not have been encumbered with her' (206). So he immediately dashes off a note to Farfrae allowing him to court Elizabeth-Jane, echoing the note he had written previously forbidding it.

But it is too late: by this time, of course, Farfrae is about to become smitten with Lucetta, and a whole new economy of exchange is about to commence – between Lucetta and Henchard. Elizabeth-Jane becomes the token they trade back and forth to communicate: to signal their interest in each other, to punish and reward each other. Lucetta initially uses Elizabeth-Jane as a draw to Henchard; she has Elizabeth come and stay in her house as her companion in order that Henchard may visit her (Lucetta) without arousing suspicion in the town (which move Henchard characterizes as an 'adroit and pleasant manœuvre' [221]). When Lucetta later discovers that Henchard hates his daughter and that her presence may in fact be a deterrent to their romance, she decides that 'Elizabeth-Jane would have to be got rid of – a disagreeable necessity' (226); later, when she stops caring about Henchard's opinion due to her kindled interest in his rival, she suddenly 'no longer [feels] strongly the necessity of getting rid of the girl for her stepfather's sake' (236). There is no pretence here that Elizabeth-Jane is ultimately much more than a pawn in Lucetta's courtship game, first with Henchard and later with Farfrae. Yet just as with the exchange of Lucetta's letters, it is ultimately Henchard who has control over the circulation of Elizabeth-Jane – his pleasure or displeasure that dictates where she lives, his rivalry with Farfrae that weaves the complex web of loyalty and betrayal that decides where she ends up.

So Elizabeth-Jane functions as a token of exchange in *The Mayor of Casterbridge*: this is fairly obvious and incontestable. How does this insight fit in with the question with which we began, the fact that it is her viewpoint, her narrative 'mode,' her voice that Hardy ultimately attempts to valorize at the end of the book? Whoever heard of a symbolic object rising up – or even quietly persisting – and taking charge of the whole operation of which she had been a mere token? By the end of the novel her word is law: not only has she replaced the father, she has become the father. One is reminded of Lévi-Strauss's comment that the symbolic economies in which women are exchanged among men are different from, for example, the symbolic economy of language, because women can in turn affect the processes which are affecting them: 'Words do not speak, while women do; as producers of signs, women can never be reduced to the status of symbols or tokens' (61). Two things must be going on here: Elizabeth-Jane must somehow be speaking in order to become the centre of authorial attention, and Henchard must be silenced in order to be eliminated from the symbolic economy of the novel.

We have already seen the way Hetty 'speaks' in response to her attempted exchange between Arthur and Adam – with her body, her problematic and uncontainable pregnancy – and the way Maggie 'speaks' with the eloquence of the flood. Elizabeth-Jane in turn 'speaks' with her silence, her patience, her resignation. She has given up all rights to happiness and instead relies upon her very lack of desire to allow her to function in a world where she gets nothing she wants:

> Yet her experience had consisted less in a series of pure disappointments than in a series of substitutions. Continually it had happened that what she had desired had not been granted her, and that what had been granted her she had not desired. So she viewed with an approach to equanimity the now cancelled days when Donald had been her undeclared lover, and wondered what unwished-for thing Heaven might send her in place of him. (250–1)

The paradox is that this attitude of non-caring ultimately garners her what she (ostensibly) wants; she gets Donald back and she takes her place at the centre of the epistemological economy of the novel. Her detachment is what enables her to speak with the voice of authority at the end of the story, and it is her very lack of desire that allows her this detachment.[22] This is radically different from Hetty's and Maggie's responses to similar uses of them as tokens of exchange; their rage and desire (in Maggie's case, her excessive desire for desirelessness) end up losing them everything, including authorial attention and their lives (which in *Adam Bede* and *The Mill on the Floss*, of course, are the same thing).

But there is one thing that Hetty and Elizabeth-Jane, unlike Maggie, do not win at the end of their stories: the reader's sympathy. What is most striking about Elizabeth-Jane as narratorial perspective, or broadly speaking Elizabeth-Jane as heroine, is that she is a miserable failure as a figure of sympathetic identification. One does not care what happens to her. She remains a figure at a distance, a theoretical heroine, a silent lurker who strikes the reader as rather more annoying and peckish than anything else. As Marjorie Garson notes, 'The Mayor of Casterbridge has no compelling female character' (83).[23] One reason for her insipidity, I would argue, is that Elizabeth-Jane is a character utterly without desire. We see this shortcoming particularly in her rather lacklustre acts of consumption; after she has come to live with the wealthy Henchard, she resists what would be the temptation of most girls in her position, and does not start tricking herself out in fancy dress:

> It might have been supposed that, given a girl rapidly becoming good-looking, comfortably circumstanced, and for the first time in her life commanding ready money, she would go and make a fool of herself by dress. But no. The reasonableness of almost everything that Elizabeth did was nowhere more conspicuous than in this question of clothes. To keep in the rear of opportunity in matters of indulgence is as valuable a habit as to keep abreast of opportunity in matters of enterprise ... Her triumph was tempered by circumspection, she had still that field-mouse fear of the coulter of destiny despite fair promise, which is common among the thoughtful who have suffered early from poverty and oppression. (158)

This laudatory commentary – 'to keep in the rear of opportunity in matters of indulgence is as valuable a habit as to keep abreast of opportunity in matters of enterprise' – is, in the logic of the novel, rather unconvincing. This is the standard version of good feminine domestic economy, the trait that, in Adam Bede, is praised in Dinah and whose lack is lamented in Hetty. Yet just as its effects were mixed in that novel (Dinah's parsimony was rather too severe), so it does not seem to serve Elizabeth-Jane very well. When we are given a glimpse of her actual person in the next paragraph, we learn that this lovely eighteen-year-old woman has been dressing herself like a widow, in 'a black silk bonnet, velvet mantle or silk spencer, dark dress, and carrying a sunshade' (158). When Lucetta appears on the scene, Elizabeth-Jane is eclipsed; in fact, it is only when the very Hetty-like Lucetta is removed from the erotic economy of the novel that our putative 'heroine' is once again noticed, by either Donald or the narratorial gaze. Her underconsumption has left her unfit to compete in the erotic marketplace of Casterbridge.

When we contrast our reactions toward Elizabeth-Jane (or Hetty) with those toward Maggie or Tess, for example, or even toward Farfrae or Henchard, we can see the difference between engaging with a character and binding up our process of reading with his or her fortunes, and feeling as though she is being thrust upon us by an author with a particular agenda. Hardy clearly wants Elizabeth-Jane's 'mode' to prevail; by giving her the power of discernment, the knowledge from which she had been excluded, and the voice of the narrator, he attempts a coup against Henchard that he cannot quite pull off. Henchard remains the character we care about, the one with whom we sympathize, the one whose fortunes we feel we are following as we read – just as in *Adam Bede* our sympathy remains with Adam, although he is also one of the men whose desires control the fortunes of the heroine. This situation is different in both *The Mill on the Floss* and *Tess of the d'Urbervilles*: Maggie and Tess, while still circulated as tokens among men and relatively powerless to affect these symbolic transfers, occupy the centres of sympathy in their novels in a way Hetty and Elizabeth-Jane do not.

Another possible explanation for this failure of sympathy comes to us, in a roundabout way, from Ruskin. In '*A Joy For Ever' and Its Price in the Market*, he theorizes:

> Something of the same temper which makes the English soldier do always all that is possible, and attempt more than is possible, joins its influence with that of mere avarice in tempting the English merchant into risks which he cannot justify, and efforts which he cannot sustain; and the same passion for adventure which our travellers gratify every summer on perilous snow wreaths, and cloud-encompassed precipices, surrounds with a romantic fascination the glittering of a hollow investment, and gilds the clouds that curl around gulfs of ruin. Nay, a higher and a more serious feeling frequently mingles in the motley temptation; and men apply themselves to the task of growing rich, as to a labour of providential appointment, from which they cannot pause without culpability, nor retire without dishonour. (*Works* 16:138)

For Ruskin, as for Henchard and Adam Smith (and Hardy?) as well, investment, speculation, and financial enterprise are marked by a heroic and romantic masculinity. Henchard has features of the Smithian figure of economic wholeness, who supposedly roamed free before the feminizing depredations of the modern division of labour wrought their havoc. It is an obvious point, but one that is so familiar that it perhaps needs to be repeated: it is no coincidence that Henchard's unmanning is coincident with his financial ruin. The arena of the marketplace has been for him the arena of manly striving – the stuff of plot, of narrative interest. When the economic mode of the novel shifts to the demure sphere of household management, the narrative interest flags as well. This is the novel's fundamental drive toward closure: while the narratorial perspective merges with that of a character without demands, the narrator at least seems deeply ambivalent about this merger. Once again, to be without desire is to risk stagnation: in this case, both (lack of) readerly interest and (violated) economic imperative converge.

It is, in other words, extraordinarily difficult to sympathize with someone without desires. The ascendance of the heroine's perspective in *The Mayor of Casterbridge* is felt as a failure because the anomic Elizabeth-Jane is every bit as much of an economic 'threat' as Maggie Tulliver – to renounce desire is to pose an uncomfortable challenge to both novelistic and fiduciary economies. While Henchard is punished for his economic transgressions – through banishment and death, as was Hetty – in *The Mayor of Casterbridge* the economic situation is rather more complicated than in the Eliot novel. While Hetty was purged as an avatar of surplus, whose elimination allowed a nostalgic and compensatory closure on a scene of idealized physiocratic wholeness, Henchard's elimination feels somewhat like a mistake. As we have seen, his economic practices were perverse, but they were perverse in a heroic, masculine, risk-taking way: he was something like the (morally challenged) Adam Bede of the marketplace before his risk-taking unmanned him.

The economic message of the novel may seem 'correct' (do not sell your wife, or corn on the margin) just as it was in *Adam Bede* (do not confuse ethical and economic compensation) and *The Mill on the Floss* (do not misread Thomas à Kempis and stop desiring things), but unlike in these other novels, in *Mayor* the ending seems economically 'correct' but really is not – the character without desire is left in the triumphant position. The scene of closure in *The Mayor of Casterbridge* is on a compensatory marriage between an always-already feminized, 'specialized' labourer and a bloodless, depressed heroine with whom it is nearly impossible to identify.

In the next novel I will examine, Hardy also depresses us by murdering off the character we like best, but the economic questions become rather more complicated as we move – just as we did in the case of Eliot's first two novels – from a simpler rural economy to a more complex modern one. (This characterization may seem initially a bit odd, given the setting of *Tess of the d'Urbervilles*, but as we shall see, the novel indeed engages many of the late-century economic concerns I delineated in chapter 1: demand, utility, and consumption.) In the case of *Tess* the question of character identification is inextricably bound up with the process of internalization and focus on the individual economic actor that the novel inaugurates. And this process leads us back to question the types of exchange in which Tess is engaged, and ultimately to examine the different types of symbolic economies inaugurated in Hardy's antepenultimate novel.

5 Self-Sacrifice, Skillentons, and Mother's Milk: The Internalization of Demand in *Tess*

Earthly life, therefore, has no share in the general system of the universe. It is a little episode, so to speak, in the poem of creation ... The disappearance of all our race would, to the physical universe, be less than the crushing of the tiny insects, to which all the world they know is but a drop of water.

(F.W. Johnston, 'The Circulation of Matter' 560)

To her, and to her like, birth itself was an ordeal of degrading personal compulsion whose gratuitousness nothing in the result seemed to justify, and at best could only palliate.

(Hardy, *Tess of the d'Urbervilles* 344)[1]

Few people will deny the terrible dreariness of this tale, which, except during the few hours spent with cows, has not a gleam of sunshine anywhere.

(Rev. of *Tess of the d'Urbervilles*, *Saturday Review* 190)

1 Internalization and Sacrifice

The novels I have examined thus far have shared, along with their economic predilections, a rather cold-blooded willingness to sacrifice their protagonists. The term 'sacrifice' is, at first blush, particularly appropriate in the case of *Tess of the d'Urbervilles*. As many of Hardy's contemporary and modern readers have noted, Tess is consistently figured as a sacrificial victim throughout the novel, from her parents' callous surrender of her to Alec d'Urberville to her final capture on the altar at Stonehenge. The necessity of this abandonment is variously figured, in both the novel and its criticism, as the inexorability of Fate, the doom of hereditary impulse, the impersonal workings of Nature, or some combination thereof. As J. Hillis Miller has noted, it is nearly impossible to resist the impulse to answer the question 'Why does Tess suffer so?' (*Fiction* 128). Always present behind this question, its ghostly consequence and unacknowledged cause, is the assumption that Tess is done *to*, wrought *upon*, sinned *against*: that Tess is, in short, ruthlessly and thoroughly sacrificed.[2]

Countless readers, reviewers, and literary critics have commented on the mechanistic nature of the Hardyan universe; particularly in his later novels (although certainly to a greater or lesser extent throughout his career), Hardy is interested in tracing the often devastating effects of deterministic factors – both biological and social – on the lives of his hapless characters. As Hardy wrote in 1878 (sounding very much like literary naturalist Émile Zola), 'a Plot, or Tragedy, should arise from the gradual closing in of a situation that comes of ordinary human passions, prejudices, and ambitions' (*Early Life* 157). Certainly this sense of fatality and grim determinism was one that his contemporary reviewers returned to over and over again: as one such critic opines about *Tess*, 'Mr. Hardy here works determinedly in his most fateful vein' (le Gallienne 193), while another writes: 'Prof. Huxley once compared life to a game of chess played by man against an enemy, invisible, relentless, wresting every error and every accident to his own advantage. Some such idea must have influenced Mr. Hardy in his narrative of the fortunes of Tess Durbeyfield' (Rev. in *Athenaeum* 197).

While this powerful sense of determinism and the inexorability of fate in Hardy's novels is not one with which I would care to argue (even were it possible to do so), I would like to examine more closely the etiology of this impression, and its particular effects in *Tess*. My contention is that the sacrificial impulse in *Tess*, while originating outside, beyond, over there, from above, is internalized and transformed into an impulse to self-sacrifice on the part of the heroine. Furthermore, this transformation is but one aspect of a more general dynamic pervading the novel as a whole: *Tess of the d'Urbervilles* consistently effects a process of internalization wherein natural, social, economic, and even rhetorical operations are envisioned as taking place within the individual, and are in turn relocated physically within the human body.

This internalization process is figured as one of the key causes of Tess's tragedy. Many critics have noted that Hardy inveighs against the consequences of internalized social norms and mores throughout his novelistic career; what is not noted as often is that this ethic is part of a larger project of delineating the effect on the individual of internalized collective processes in general: natural, economic, and linguistic, as well as ethical. In the case of *Tess* this movement of internalization within the individual – and specifically within the individual body – crystallizes economic forces and compulsions that traditionally had been depicted as originating outside the individual, at the level of the social and collective.

There are several obvious ways in which economic processes are underscored in the novel: the Durbeyfields' dependence upon Alec d'Urberville's patronage, Tess's concomitant sense of obligation toward her 'cousin,' her own work history. But there is yet another way in which these concerns are related in the text. *Tess of the d'Urbervilles* is one of the first novels to explore thematically the consequences of a radical paradigm shift in Victorian economic thought – the ascendance of the marginal utility school.[3] While *The Mayor of Casterbridge* is also written after the rise of the new economics in 1870, in its exploration of early nineteenth-century rural England it is more concerned with those preoccupations of early industrial capitalism I have delineated elsewhere: the problem of inflationary issues, the epistemological uncertainties of the credit economy, the correspondence between value and sign. *Tess*, on the other hand, is much more concerned with mapping economic (and other collective) processes at the individual level. Just as both the historical and marginal utility schools begin to examine the effect on the economic system as a whole of individual demand and consumption decisions, so *Tess* greatly advances a process already underway in the novel generally: a greater scrutiny of the individual consciousness, the examination of the internal state and the effect on that state of broader social networks.

This concern with mapping the intersecting territory of the collective (including deterministic forces at the social level) and the individual (including the problem of free will) was certainly part of the late-Victorian zeitgeist. Much of the energy of this enterprise came from political economy, particularly the work of marginal utility theorists such as W. Stanley Jevons. The starting point of Jevons's work was the translation of mechanistic and mathematical techniques into the social sciences, particularly economics; he did so, as Harro Maas notes in his fascinating study of Jevons in the context of nineteenth-century thought, by 'shifting the "basis" of political economy from ... psychology to physiology,' which enabled him to 'reframe the "laws of human wants" in terms of mechanics' (154). Or, as Gallagher puts it, 'physiological stimuli as registered in the sensorium were asserted to be the primary motivators of economic activity'; furthermore, Jevons 'believed prices were the objective data recording psychophysiological phenomena' (*Body* 124, 127). As several critics have discussed, Jevons struggled to reconcile the implications of this mechanistic model with the emphasis on individual desires and decision-making that is the basis of marginal utility theory.[4] This issue, of course, was part of a larger struggle on the part of Victorian scientific thinkers to reconcile the notion of free will with the image of human automata that seemed to be implied by new biologistic theories of psychology and motivation. (T.H. Huxley's work, particularly the 1874 essay 'On the Hypothesis that Animals are Automata, and Its History,' was particularly provocative in this regard.)[5]

As Maas discusses, Jevons indeed struggled with this issue ('it is clear from his scattered remarks on the free will issue that it was a matter of serious concern to him' [155]), yet his adoption of the statistical methodology of Adolphe Quetelet (who developed the concept of the 'average man') in his work on marginal utility allowed him ultimately to sidestep the question. According to Maas, 'Jevons thought about laws in terms of aggregates or mean values, while maintaining freedom of will on the level of observation of individuals' (155).[6] Jevons's 'emphasis on the "ordinary procedures" of averaging in the other sciences gave him a way out of the free will conundrum. Laws were always about average or mean values; individual observations were inevitably loaded with errors in measurement' (175). Or, as Jevons himself put it, 'As regards science free will is simply chance; it represents a cause acting sometimes one way and sometimes another but concerning which we have no information' (qtd in Maas 175). Jevons's focus on statistical averaging inaugurates something of a paradox for marginal utility theory: while the driving engine of economics is the desires, demands, and tastes of individual consumers (the subjective/psychological strain of the theory), the 'individual' is really an aggregate or average of a mass of economic actors (the mechanistic strain).[7]

This tension between mechanistic models of human behaviour and the problem of the individual is one with which Hardy is also deeply engaged, particularly in his later novels. While for Jevons the social scientist, free will is 'simply chance' – a disrupting variable that must be controlled through a focus on aggregates and averages – for Hardy the novelist, chance is of course the exact opposite – an inexorable antagonist to human hopes and desires. Yet the tension between the two explanatory mechanisms is certainly not resolved for Hardy; it structures the entire plot of *Tess of the d'Urbervilles*. My reading rather stacks the deck on the side of determinism, an interpretation with which I believe even the most casual reader of Hardy must agree. Yet we can see traces of this struggle, particularly its economic valence, through- out the text, in the form of a dialectic of externalized compulsion and internalized impulses. While Hardy drew the external-causation strain from contemporary trends in the social sciences (including economics) – as well as a concomitant anxiety about the status of free will – *Tess of the d'Urbervilles* works through this anxiety, as I will show in the re- mainder of this chapter, by examining the internalization of social proc- esses. Tess is described by her narrator as 'an almost standard woman' (96) – a Jevonsian aggregate or average – yet her desires are insistently felt at the level of the individual. Internalization is a trope that allows Hardy to capture this tension between the external and the internal, the collective and the individual, and thus to work through some of the contradictions inherent in the new economics.

Tess of the d'Urbervilles consistently refigures the relationship between internalized impulses and external compulsion as a tension between the individual and the family. Consider this sampling of quotations from the early chapters of the novel:

1. On an evening in the latter part of May a middle-aged man was walking homeward from Shaston to the village of Marlott …The pair of legs that carried him were rickety, and there was a bias in his gait which inclined him somewhat to the left of a straight line. (13)

2. There still faintly beamed from the woman's features something of the freshness, and even the prettiness, of her youth; rendering it probable that the personal charms which Tess could boast of were in main part her mother's gift, and therefore unknightly, unhistorical. (25)

3. 'Pooh – I have as much of mother as father in me!' she said. 'All my pret- tiness comes from her, and she was only a dairymaid.' (108)

The first two quotations treat Tess's father and mother respectively. What does it mean, in the logic of this relentlessly tragic work, for Tess's fate to be divided evenly between the paternal and the maternal im- pulse, for her to have, as the third epigraph claims, 'as much of mother as father' in her? For her to be composed equally of the 'rickety' and the 'fresh'?

The two parental goads to Tess's fate – her fresh, pretty maternity and her knightly, historical paternity – reinscribe the possibilities for Victorian womanhood envisioned by Ruskin in *Munera Pulveris* (as well as by the canonical Victorian novel): motherhood and death. As we have already seen, Ruskin proposes an alternative to the degraded body of the meretricious hoarder whose death he imagines releasing stores of purloined currency, and that is 'the circulation of wealth … soft, steady, strong, far-sweeping, and full of warmth, like the Gulf stream' (*Works* 17:208). The untroubled circulation of fluid sustenance, metaphorical mother's milk, is counterposed to the castrating genitalia of the hoarding 'money-chest with a slit in it' (169) whose death the reader can presumably only welcome. Of course, in Ruskin's metaphor the womanly body is the vehicle, while monetary policy is the tenor; in Hardy's novel the specificity and reality of women's bodies are central to his plot and theme.

The actual trajectory of Tess's career manages to encompass both alternatives Ruskin invokes – motherhood and degradation/death. Ruskin's conflicted warnings – that the 'natural' state of circulation, modelled on the nurturant maternal body, simultaneously demands a degree of intervention for its maintenance – are inscribed in Hardy's novel as both a recurring concern with economic demand and the technological processes of dairy production (which will be a focus of this chapter), and an anxiety about the paradoxical fertility of the maidenly or pure body. The two opposed types of bodies in Tess are not the mother and the virgin – since Hardy is at such pains to deconstruct that particular opposition – but rather the mother and the barren corpse (or 'skillenton'). The real unconscious horror of *Tess of the d'Urbervilles* is not impurity, but the possibility of an interruption in the circulation of milk, due either to barrenness (in the case of mother's milk) or a cessation of consumer demand for cow's milk. I would suggest that for both Ruskin and Hardy, the metaphor of lactation (or 'free-flowing fluid sustenance') is so attractive because milk is the only product whose supply is completely determined by, and entirely dependent upon, demand.

But before I discuss the question of economic demand in *Tess* in more detail, I would like to examine the structure of the novel more generally, particularly the configuration of binary oppositions that I suggested Hardy is at pains both to create and to question. The logic of the novel itself proposes two equally important and determining factors in Tess's tragedy: the social, collective imperatives which condemn her 'impurity,' and the individualistic, regenerative impulses of 'nature' and sex, which are the root cause leading to her impurity in the first place.[8] These two opposed forces are depicted as Tess's dual inheritance from her father and mother respectively, yet even as the events of the plot and the structure of the novel insist on the equal importance of these two causative structures, the rhetoric of the narrator represses and denies the maternal legacy as a coequal determinant of events.

The discourse of the paternal (the social, historical, and ethical imperative) is everywhere in *Tess*, and is most insistent, as I will show, in the ubiquitous figure of the palimpsest, or the layering process of historical event. The operations of history constitute the novel's privileged causative term. It is only with an analysis of the economic logic of the novel, with its emphasis on the role of individual desires in consumption and demand, that we can recuperate the lost half of the causative equation. It will thus be necessary to discuss the establishment of the maternal/paternal binary in *Tess*, and how it is subsequently denied by the narrator, before we can arrive at the question of the political economy of the novel. My intent here is not so much to deconstruct the founding opposition between paternal and maternal qualities (although such a deconstruction will be an inevitable by-product of my analysis, as, for example, when the operations of the historical palimpsest are seen at work on the 'natural' human body) as it is to recuperate the lost explanation that the novel itself suggests and then forgets. The operations of the maternal and the paternal come together in the very notion of internalization – the work the social and the bodily perform together.

The trajectory of *Tess* as the career of Tess is concerned with this internalization process at every level. As social creature, Tess takes within herself the imperatives operating around her – economic, linguistic, ethical. As heroine, Tess takes within herself the imperatives of the novel of which she is a function. She is the native force behind the 'death drive' of the novel;[9] it is her compulsion to self-sacrifice that effects the fatal closure that has seemed to come 'from without' in the previous novels I have examined. This internalized impulse is the direct result of a novelistic project that seeks the effects of the social and collective upon the individual character, and the (attenuated, internalized) desire of the individual upon the historical event. In Hardy's antepenultimate novel, this means the almost merciless laboratory experiment perpetrated upon the body of his favourite heroine: the great question of how the larger designs of history, economics, and narrative come to be traced upon the 'feminine tissue' of one pure woman.

2 As Much of Mother as of Father: Inescapable Heredity and the Scapegoat of History

One of the most striking things about contemporary (and for that matter, modern) criticism of *Tess* is its perfectly contradictory character. A perusal of a collection of contemporary reviews of the novel garners the following pairs of antithetical evaluations: the events of Tess's history are absolutely inexorable and could not have happened any other way, and everything that happens to Tess is her own fault and could easily have been prevented through her own wise action; Tess is pure, virtuous, sinned-against-not-sinning, and Tess is coarse and 'defiled'; the scenes of peasant life in the novel have never been more real, and 'there is not one single touch of nature' in any character in the book; and so on.[10] While there is certainly nothing unusual about disagreement over a controversial novel like *Tess of the d'Urbervilles*, it is unusual for reviewers to be so perfectly at loggerheads about even the remotest detail of the story – at times even quoting the exact same passages as evidence in support of diametrically opposed readings.

There is something about *Tess* that invites these striking disagreements: the novel itself is built upon an armature of binary oppositions. These antitheses (modern/primitive, Christianity/paganism, rape/seduction, Alec/Angel) are subsumed under one guiding, overarching opposition which is continually invoked by the narrator and borne out by the attitudes of the characters and the events of the novel. This is the opposition between the socio-historical (family names, ethical norms, historical determination) and the natural (the body, the regenerative impulse, the 'appetite for joy'). The natural or bodily is the maternal inheritance and the social or historical is the paternal: Tess gets her looks from her mother and her ancient name from her father.[11]

The qualities aligned with these two poles – the remembrance of history and attention to ethical law versus the forgetfulness of the body and the desire for joy – are continually at work upon Tess. She is depicted as perpetually torn between these two impulses, neither of which can decisively claim her allegiance (a short and far from inclusive catalogue of these impulses would be her repulsion/attraction to Alec, her sense of shame/desire for a fresh start at Talbothays, her desire/inability to tell Angel her history). The novel reminds us that these impulses originate outside and prior to Tess, and are found everywhere in human hearts; even at 'starve-acre' Flintcomb-Ash they are still operative: 'So the two forces were at work here as everywhere, the inherent will to enjoy, and the circumstantial will against enjoyment' (278).

Yet even as the novel is capable of reminding us – occasionally – that these forces are universal, it at the same time insists upon locating them within the character of its heroine and as the legacies of her two parents. We are told, during the passages describing Tess's summer romance with Angel Clare and her consequent struggle with her conscience, that within Tess a 'spiritual forgetfulness co-existed with an intellectual remembrance' (195). The inherent will to enjoy become the spiritual forgetfulness, the circumstantial will against enjoyment become the intellectual remembrance: Tess is continually figured as the apotheosis of these general traits.

Of course, there would be nothing odd about this characterization if Hardy did not particularize these traits so markedly in Tess alone; it only makes sense that a quality at work 'everywhere' should also be at work in his heroine. But he does particularize them; he explicitly describes them as her unique inheritance, and reminds us again and again where each trait comes from. No other character in the novel, not even the ones who are depicted with internal struggles and conversions of their own – Angel, Alec, Izz Huett – is ever described in these binary terms or as torn between these same two impulses. We may hear about one or the other of them (Angel's pagan scepticism, Alec's sensuality, Izz's torturous desire), but it is for Tess alone to be the pull-toy between 'society' and 'nature.' The external processes of history and nature (genealogy and body) are internalized in the single character of Tess, reinscribed as the individualistic qualities of family name and physical appearance.

It is important to remember that, within the logic of the plot if not explicitly within the narration, both of these inheritances are equally responsible for Tess's 'downfall'; we are instructed that either one of them alone would not have been sufficient to effect her tragedy. (On the very simplest level, for example, if Tess had not been a d'Urberville she would not have been sent to Alec, and had she not been beautiful she would not have been subject to d'Urberville's criminal desire.) The first two chapters emphasize the mutual dependence of these two determinative forces; in a doubling of what D.A. Miller calls the 'incitements to narrative' found in the opening passages of a novel (ix), there are two initiatory chapters in *Tess*, one devoted to each of the two threads that are woven to form its heroine's destiny. In the first we have the fateful meeting of Parson Tringham and the haggler John Durbeyfield, in which the former, against his better judgment, tells the latter about his recently discovered illustrious genealogy. Lest we not immediately recognize that this knowledge will be of great import in shaping the narrative to follow, we are treated to the sight of Durbeyfield reclining luxuriantly upon the grass and informing the first passer-by that his heritage is 'recorded in history all about me' (16). (And just in case we still have not got it, we are frequently reminded, by various characters and in agonized tones, that had that parson just not informed Durbey-field, none of this story would have happened.)

The second inaugurating chapter is the May dance on the green, where Angel spies Tess for the first time. Kaja Silverman has insightfully described the voyeuristic nature of this episode: the supposedly undis-covered territory of Blackmoor Vale traversed by the three knapsacked rovers out on a walking holiday becomes a figure for the relentless 'in-scription' that the narrative works upon the figure of Tess (Silverman 5–6).[12] The episode also, of course, sets in place the causal machinery which will constitute the second great force vying for Tess later in the novel: it is because of this first meeting that Tess and Angel are destined to fall in love later; it is this meeting that inaugurates the bodily, natural, appetite-for-joy impulse in Tess that is her maternal legacy.

I emphasize the word 'maternal' here because it works in more ways than one. Tess's beauty and physical nature come to her from her moth-er, and the chapter that establishes these aspects of her character is re-plete with maternal imagery. The vale is described in terms of a fertile, motherly body: it is 'engirdled and secluded,' 'rich,' 'fertile and shel-tered' (18). The insistent fertility and nurturant capacity of this land-scape – in which 'the fields are never brown and the springs never dry' – is in direct contrast to its concomitant characterization as virginal and 'untrodden' that Silverman notices. It is, in this way, doubly a figure for Tess herself: virginal, untouched, 'pure,' yet simultaneously fertile and maternal. Similarly, we are told in the next chapter that the young Tess frequently assumes a 'deputy-maternal attitude' (28) in the family. She is described repeatedly as the only responsible member of the ne'er-do-well Durbeyfields, the one who must shoulder responsibility and even mother her wayward parents when they stray repeatedly to the neigh-bourhood pub. From the very beginning of the novel, her maternal ca-pacities are insisted upon – those very capacities which, being a part of her physical inheritance, are appropriately enough on her mother's side of the hereditary equation.

The first two chapters of the novel thus establish the twin forces at work in Tess's physical make-up and character. As human specimen, she constitutes a particular kind of physical presence (which is, as many readers have noted, almost obsessively described by the narrator throughout the novel) caught in a network of historical and genealogical determination. Both of these factors are insisted upon, and both are given equal time in the opening moves of the narrative. The 'trump card' that Tess has to play in trying her fortune is not merely her face, as her mother appropriately enough insists (55), but is also her noble blood, as Angel notes much later in the novel: 'It is a grand card to play – that of your belonging to such a family' (194).

Having established that both the maternal and paternal 'strains' in Tess are of equal importance in determining her fate, we must now ask why, then, the novel thoroughly represses one of these causal explanations in favour of the other? For it is the paternal, historical forces at work upon Tess that are overtly blamed for her unhappiness and bad luck; Hardy deliberately opposes the characterological consequences of this inheritance in Tess – the propensity to repeat, the impulse to tell her history, the compulsion to remember, the 'death drive' – to the life-giving, regenerative powers of nature and sex. It is as though the initial opposition between historical remembrance and bodily forgetfulness, both of which are responsible for Tess's tragic situation and ultimate execution, are reinscribed as the difference between the impulses of death and life.

We first see this repressive move when Tess is beginning to reawaken to the possibilities for happiness in a new situation after the death of her baby. She starts to allow herself to imagine being young and happy again, and directly opposes this lightening of spirit to the deathly legacy of her ancestors:

> Not so very far to the left of her she could discern a dark patch in the scenery, which inquiry confirmed her in supposing to be trees marking the environs of Kingsbere – in the church of which parish the bones of her ancestors – her useless ancestors – lay entombed.
>
> She had no admiration for them now; she almost hated them for the dance they had led her. (108)

This regenerative life-force, in opposition to her deathly and 'useless' ancestry, is explicitly invoked a few paragraphs later: 'There was, it might be said, the energy of her mother's unexpended family, as well as the natural energy of Tess's years, rekindled after the experience which had so overwhelmed her for the time' (110).

The responsibility of Tess's ancestry for her downfall is insisted upon by others in the novel as well. During the aftermath of Tess's wedding-night confession, Angel laments to her that 'the parson who unearthed your pedigree would have done better if he had held his tongue' (229). This is curious logic on Angel's part: why, at this point, would he wish that Tess had never learned of her noble lineage? Does he feel that her own knowledge of her ancestry has somehow contributed to her downfall? (This is the conclusion the reader is encouraged to draw earlier in the novel: if Tess had not known she was a d'Urberville, she would never have gone to Trantridge, etc.) But Angel seems to have something else in mind: 'Heaven, why did you give me a handle for despising you more by informing me of your descent!' Angel characterizes the problem of Tess's ancestry as an epistemological one; if she had not known, he would not have known, and thus would have less cause to despise her. (He clearly wishes that Tess had 'held her tongue' as well, not merely the absent Parson Tringham.)

Yet from this relatively reasonable – at least understandable – wish never to have known about Tess's ancestry, Angel makes a logical leap to desire that Tess actually had not been of noble blood: 'He was embittered by the conviction that all this desolation had been brought about by the accident of her being a d'Urberville' (254). The problem mutates from an epistemological to an ontological one. Rather than being a mere matter of mischief wrought through dangerous knowledge, Tess's ancestry becomes a problem somehow inherent in her very being: 'I cannot help associating your decline as a family with this other fact – of your want of firmness. Decrepit families imply decrepit wills, decrepit conduct' (229).

In his analysis of Tess in Fiction and Repetition, J. Hillis Miller argues that there are five answers proposed, in the passage describing the violation in The Chase, to the question 'Why does Tess suffer so?' – each of which is then rejected by the logic of the novel as the ultimate cause of Tess's tragedy (129). One of these answers, Tess's noble ancestry, is proposed ('One may, indeed, admit the possibility of a retribution lurking in the present catastrophe' [Tess 119]) only to be denied, according to Miller, because the story of Tess as 're-enactment of the family tradition reverses its elements' (130).

While I agree with the thrust of Miller's argument that the novel does not allow its readers the satisfaction of one final, ultimate cause for Tess's tragedy, I disagree with his reasoning on this point: the narrator makes a concerted attempt to posit the mechanical operations of history – including the weight of family tradition and the law of heredity – as the real cause of Tess's downfall. The logic of the narrative itself certainly belies this single-cause interpretation, as I have argued, but the narrator is committed to it. Far from being dismissed by an ironic reversal as Miller claims, the family-history explanation of Tess's woes reappears much later in the novel, again with the imprimatur of the narrator:

> Thus the Durbeyfields, once d'Urbervilles, saw descending upon them the destiny which, no doubt, when they were among the Olympians of the county, they had caused to descend many a time, and severely enough, upon the heads of such landless ones as they themselves were now. So do flux and reflux – the rhythm of change – alternate and persist in everything under the sky. (338)

Thus the method of the novel: one side of the causal equation (the role of Tess's maternal inheritance) is effaced and repressed in the narrative rhetoric, while it is borne out as a crucial element by the events of the plot itself. Perhaps the most striking example of this operation of repression is the way in which Alec, the representative of historical inevitability associated with the deathly d'Urbervilles, is squarely blamed for Tess's tragedy while Angel, the child of nature and regenerative joy associated with sunny Talbothays, gets off relatively lightly.

But here again the narrator's interpretation is at odds with the logic of the narrative: there is a persistent collapsing together of Angel and Alec – at the 'unconscious,' metaphorical level of the novel – as the agents of Tess's destruction. First of all, Angel's persistent proposals to Tess, his unwillingness to credence her repeated refusals, is disturbingly similar to Alec's insensitive wooing of Tess as Trantridge. His proposal to her after he returns from visiting his parents is nearly an exact recapitulation of the scene in The Chase: '"Dear, darling Tessy!" he whispered, putting his arm around her, and his face to her flushed cheek. "Don't, for Heaven's sake, Mister me any more. I have hastened back so soon because of you!"' (172). He returns from his trip, just as Alec had returned from his reconnoitring mission in the forest, to physically accost a 'waiting' Tess and lay his face against her cheek ('He knelt and bent lower, till her breath warmed his face, and in a moment his cheek was in contact with hers' [77]). Angel's own language with regards to Tess also recapitulates the language of Alec. His calling her 'my Pretty' (173) during this first proposal is uncomfortably close to Alec's nickname for her, 'my Beauty' (both imply a possession that Tess herself does not countenance). But perhaps most damning of all is his repetition of Alec's worst mistake with Tess: the refusal to believe the plain words she herself speaks about her feelings. Just as Tess threatens to knock Alec out of his gig in her anger when he refuses to acknowledge that 'what every woman says some women may feel' (82), so Angel immediately begins to muse to himself, after Tess's refusal, that with women 'the negative often meant nothing more than the preface to the affirmative' (176). Likewise, each man uses similar language to reveal his aversion to Tess's working while she is 'married' to him. 'You must not work like this ... You are not my servant; you are my wife,' Angel declares (237); while Alec later expostulates to Tess while she tends her family's garden plot, 'I come to protest against your working like this' (337).

It is not just in the similarity of their attitudes toward Tess, however, that Angel and Alec are aligned as agents of Tess's destruction. The very logic of the plot argues that Angel is, on some level, the one responsible for Tess's misguided murder of Alec (the real cause of her 'downfall' in a way that the seduction is not). After Angel learns of Tess's past, and is in the process of condemning her, he plants the suggestion that later reaches fruition in her desperate murder: 'How can we live together while that man lives? – he being your husband in Nature, and not I. If he were dead it might be different' (239). Much later in the novel, Tess confirms this fatal suggestion when she sobs to her husband, 'Angel, will you forgive my sin against you, now that I have killed him? I thought as I ran along that you would be sure to forgive me now that I have done that. It came to me as a shining light that I should get you back that way' (372).

As perverse as this suggestion may seem, Tess is actually right in her instinct. Angel, does, in fact, take her back after the murder and he had, in fact, told her that one of the conditions of his doing so was the death of Alec d'Urberville.[13] Once again, Angel's supposedly avant-garde modern notions falter under the influence of his earlier training: the idea of the forgiveness of sin (by a worshipped and god-like creature, no less) through the murder of a sacrificial victim is certainly the same mechanism as the 'untenable redemptive theolatry' that Angel condemns elsewhere in the novel (120). Finally, there is some suggestion that Tess could have continued, not unhappily, in her arrangement with d'Urberville had Angel not returned: 'I hate him *now*, because he told me a lie – that you would not come again; and you *have* come!' (366, first emphasis added).

Angel's speech and actions are not the only signs of his conflation with Alec. Tess herself betrays her awareness of their similarity when she gives in under his relentless blandishments and decides to accept him. Tess experiences identical linguistic breakdowns immediately before her murder of d'Urberville and at the point of her acceptance of Angel. 'Oh my heart – O, O, O!' she cries when she finally decides to marry Clare (180), while the landlady at The Herons hears the following emanating from Tess and Alec's shared room immediately before the murder:

> One syllable, continually repeated in a low note of moaning, as if it came
> from a soul bound to some Ixionian wheel –
>   'Oh – Oh – Oh!'
> Then a silence, then a heavy sigh, and again –
>   'Oh – Oh – Oh!' (367)[14]

Tess associates the two men, and her sense of desperation in the face of their indefatigable desire, at the deepest prelinguistic level. All men, no matter how civilized and genteel they may seem outwardly, are, according to Tess, capable of becoming 'rough and brutal,' 'bloodthirsty' savages running amuck among 'their weaker fellows in Nature's teeming family' (271). It is their problematic desire and relentless pursuit that effects this transformation; as Tess says later of her cruel boss at Flintcomb-Ash, 'He won't hurt me. *He's* not in love with me' (309).[15]

Thus the culpability of Angel is elided and the misdeeds of Alec underscored in the rhetoric of the narrative, while the events of the plot suggest that Angel is perhaps even the more responsible party. It is, as I noted before, the historical, 'knightly' half of the novel's causal machinery which takes most of the narratorial blame for events, just as it is the paternal inheritance of the d'Urberville blood that is blamed for Tess's misfortunes.

What is particularly striking about the way in which this operation of history is described in *Tess of the d'Urbervilles* is its markedly spatial character. The processes of history are figured as a layering, a palimpsest, a superimposition of recent events on more ancient ones, which are never completely obscured by the process.[16] This historical layering is evident in many Hardy novels, the most obvious example perhaps being the passage in *The Mayor of Casterbridge* that describes the unearthing of buried Roman skeletons in Casterbridge residents' back yards: 'Casterbridge announced old Rome in every street, alley, and precinct. It looked Roman, bespoke the art of Rome, concealed dead men of Rome' (*Mayor* 140). In *Tess*, this process is ubiquitous. It occurs on every register of the narrative: the economic, the natural, the historic.[17] The new residents of Tess's family cottage, who move in after the death of John Durbeyfield and the great economic 'depopulation' force the rest of the family to vacate their lifehold, are completely unaware of the former inhabitants' existence:

> The new residents were in the garden, taking as much interest in their new doings as if the homestead had never passed its primal time in conjunction with the histories of others, beside which the histories of these were but as a tale told by an idiot. They walked about the garden paths with thoughts of their own concerns entirely uppermost, bringing their actions at every moment in jarring collision with the dim ghosts behind them. (360)

Similarly, the very landscape of Wessex bears the scars of historical sedimentation. The land around Talbothays is 'a level landscape compounded of old landscapes long forgotten, and, no doubt, differing in character very greatly from the landscape they composed now' (114), while the resort town of Sandbourne, a 'new world in an old one,' is superimposed directly on an ancient tableau: 'Within the space of a mile from its outskirts every irregularity of the soil was prehistoric, every channel an undisturbed British trackway' (363). Likewise, the operations of heredity, both paternal and maternal, trace superimposed designs upon ancient materials. The paternal characteristics of the ancient d'Urbervilles are still present in Tess, her features being 'unquestionably traceable' in the 'exaggerated forms' of the family portraits (215), while her own physical history, the maternal inheritance of her beautiful face, is still present in all its permutations beneath her more recently acquired womanly exterior: 'You could sometimes see her twelfth year in her cheeks, or her ninth sparkling from her eyes; and even her fifth would flit over the curves of her mouth now and then' (21).

While this process of superimposition or palimpsest occurs at least occasionally, as I noted, on every register of the novel, when it is associated with the socio-historical thematic I delineated earlier – the realm of culture, history, family lineage, and social norms – it takes on a very particular and traumatic character. As Silverman notes, the operations of the historical are seen as vertical superimpositions, while the life-force of nature, the body, and sex is thematically associated with lack of boundaries, 'loss of margin,' and horizontal movements as opposed to vertical (15–17). All of the moments representing what I term the 'death drive' of the novel, the moments 'associated with a terrifying coercion of people and events' (Silverman 15), are for Silverman associated with the 'vertical axis,' while 'the great utopian moments of the novel consist of tableaux in which ... horizontal movements take priority over vertical ones' (15–16). Thus, the 'coercive' operations of history are almost always figured as vertical superimpositions or 'tracings' (like the design Alec traces upon Tess in The Chase),[18] and would include by extension the ubiquitous historical palimpsests I discuss. This palimpsestic drive to blur – never obliterate – the outlines of the past is not always an impersonal one, however; at one of the many moments when Tess decides that she will disown the past, the narrator imagines that she 'trod upon it and put it out, as one treads on a coal that is smouldering and dangerous' (193).

The vertical, layering motions of historical events in *Tess* are also associated both with the impulse to narrate and with the 'death drive' within the novel and of the novel itself (which is intimately related to the problematics of narrative closure). As Gillian Beer notes in her analysis of evolutionary narrative in Hardy, his novels generate the two distinct levels of 'plot' or narrative (the 'intolerable apprehensions of what future events may bring') and 'writing' (which 'awakens us to sensations full of perceptual pleasure') (238). These two modes are aligned with the two types of causation I have discussed: the sense of inexorability of the narrative itself, from origin to closure and cause to effect, is associated with the historical and social, while the purely sensual and non-linear pleasures of description are associated with the life-force of regenerative nature and sex. While Silverman and other critics note that writing, or the graphic production of marks on a blank surface, is the trope of coercion, mastery, and historical inevitability in *Tess*, it is in fact the broader impulse of narrative itself, of delineating cause and effect and historical sedimentation, that is associated with the death drive in the novel. (And thus Beer distinguishes plot, or linear narrative, from writing, or description.)

This narrative impulse is in turn associated with vertical movements, stratifications, and images of historical sedimentation. So, for example, the narrator notes that in the first moments after Tess's disclosure on their wedding night, Angel remains in a state of incomprehension: 'the intelligence had not even yet got to the bottom of him' (225). The operations of narrative take place on a vertical plane, a sifting through layers of accreted material, even as the eye of the narrator can strip away the strata of history (landscape, dwellings, facial features) to expose the ancient formations beneath: 'These and other of his words were nothing but the perfunctory babble of the surface while the depths remained paralyzed' (226).

The 'intelligence' that Tess relays to her husband is depicted as an irresistible impulse, an inexorable drive toward her own destruction. Time and again Tess is reproached – by the narrator, by other characters, by the logic of the plot itself – for not keeping silent about her 'history.' (Tess's real problem, as so graphically illustrated by the hot-house strawberry incident at Trantridge, is her inability to keep her mouth shut – in more ways than one.) Her mother is chief among the castigators in this regard; she advises Tess against, and then reproaches Tess for, telling her history throughout the novel. 'Many a woman – some of the Highest in the Land – have had a Trouble in their time; and why should you Trumpet yours when others don't Trumpet theirs? No girl would be such a Fool, specially as it is so long ago' (192), she writes to Tess at Talbothays. (The reader is tempted to ask, indeed, why would Tess be such a fool?) And after she learns that Tess has ignored her advice and told Angel everything, prompting his desertion, her mother roundly chastises her: 'I'm sure I don't know why children o' my bringing forth should all be bigger simpletons than other people's – not to know better than to blab such a thing as that' (251).

It is particularly telling (no pun intended) that the harshest critic of Tess's 'blabbing' should be her mother: it is, after all, the 'appetite for joy' aligned with her maternal inheritance that would seem to demand Tess's silence, while that deathly d'Urberville instinct, associated with 'histories' of all kinds, is what prompts her to tell her own. Mrs Durbeyfield characterizes this self-destructive instinct very much as a problem of heredity: she cannot understand particularly why children of her 'bringing forth' should be compelled to tell their painful histories. And indeed she is right: it is the d'Urberville in Tess that works this irresistible disclosure. As Tess herself acknowledges, 'Her mother did not see life as Tess saw it' (192); Tess's mother does not have that strain in her that turns the 'passing accident' of the past into the 'haunting episode' of Tess's own experience.

Yet the castigation of Tess is certainly not left to her mother alone. Any voice in the novel that has a stake in the 'appetite for joy' of forgetfulness and regeneration gets in on the act. The narrator himself notes that Tess tells Angel many things 'that would have been better left to silence' (229). And that comic-storyteller-cum-Greek-choragus Dairyman Crick, whose ribald tales form an ironic commentary on the events of Tess's own past, pipes in with some salubrious advice when Tess is caught sitting a bit too close beside Angel near the fireside: 'If so be you hadn't told us, I am sure we shouldn't ha' noticed that ye had been sitting anywhere at all in this light ... That shows that folks should never fancy other folks be supposing things when they bain't' (197). Once again, Tess would have done better to keep her mouth shut. Even Angel himself reminds Tess that she should have kept silent, both by his hint about her ancestry we saw earlier (wishing the parson – and by extension Tess – had 'held his tongue') and by his own actions (deserting her for her honesty). And finally, both Angel and the narrator make explicit, in a way the events of the narrative only imply, that the source of Tess's narrative impulse is at odds with the self-preservative life-force. The narrator comments, after one of Tess's failures of nerve at Talbothays, that 'her instinct of self-preservation was stronger than her candour' (189). And, of course, in a memorable comment he makes to Tess after her disclosure, Angel echoes this sentiment when he notes that her previous silence was due to a 'mood of self-preservation' (227).

The impulse to narrate, to relate the events of the past and to draw linear, cause-and-effect patterns, is thus associated both with a process of historical superimposition or palimpsest and with the 'death drive,' the force at odds with self-preservation and regeneration. The self-destructive instinct displayed by Tess is also the drive toward closure of the narrative itself; it is in this way that she 'internalizes' these drives and pressures. As a preliminary sketch of a later, fuller discussion of this process, I would like to draw attention to the way in which these various concerns come together, at the end of the novel, in the scene indicating Tess's execution. The chapter opens with a long and detailed description of the city of Wintoncester, and then locates Angel and Liza-Lu within its environs. We are then treated to a lengthy passage describing the view of the two watchers from the hill, which elaborates upon the perspectival superimposition of landscapes we have seen before:

> The prospect from this summit was almost unlimited. In the valley beneath lay the city they had just left, its more prominent buildings showing as in an isometric drawing – among them the broad cathedral tower, with its Norman windows and immense length of aisle and nave, the spires of St Thomas's, the pinnacled tower of the College, and, more to the right, the towers and gables of the ancient hospice, where to this day the pilgrim may receive his dole of bread and ale. Behind the city swept the rotund upland of St Catherine's hill; further off, landscape beyond landscape, till the horizon was lost in the radiance of the sun hanging above it. (383–4)

It is immediately after this description that the viewers catch sight of the sign of Tess's execution: the black flag raised atop the prison staff. In this way, the death of Tess – brought about in part by her own narrative impulse – the superimposition of landscape upon landscape and building upon building, and the 'horizon point' of the novel itself are brought together in one striking image. Palimpsest, closure, and death are here aligned; and lest we forget what ancient force is behind this sad ending, the ancestors of the hapless murderess themselves are invoked as absent 'witnesses' of the scene: 'the d'Urberville knights and dames slept on in their tombs unknowing' (384).

3 The Carapace of the Body

The superimposition process of history (and by extension, narrative) in *Tess of the d'Urbervilles* is certainly striking, and has not gone unnoticed in the novel's criticism. But what is equally striking is the way in which this process is so frequently rewritten onto the surfaces and depths of the characters' bodies themselves, so as to quite graphically illustrate the psychological mechanism of internalization. Again and again, this 'death force' of history and social convention is imagined as occurring somehow within, inside, the corporeal shells of the novel's characters. The process of palimpsest thus works in both directions: just as the eye of the narrator strips away layers of historical stratification to reveal ancient bedrock, so the weight of history and social norms are impressed into the inner materials of the individual to form the layers that can then be revealed. When Angel wonders whether or not his instinct to separate from Tess is the correct one, he demonstrates this remarkable tendency of visualization:

> He waited in expectancy to discern some mental pointing ... He thus beheld in the pale morning light the resolve to separate from her; not as a hot and indignant instinct, but denuded of the passionateness which had made it scorch and burn; standing in its bones; nothing but a skeleton, but none the less there. Clare no longer hesitated. (245)

Angel literally searches within himself, within his own body, denuding his corporeal infrastructure of the passion that is associated with life and regeneration, to find the deathly 'skeleton' of the social imperative laid bare.

This conceptualization of the skeletal infrastructure as coming from without, as the end result of a process of internalization rather than a framework upon which the outer integument is draped, would not necessarily have seemed perverse to the Victorian reader. As one contemporary naturalist explained:

> As we gaze on the solid framework of bone, presenting in so distinct an outline the contour of the living form, it seems to us as if it had been laid down as a basis on which the creature's structure was built up; that the bones were first marshalled in their place, and then clothed with flesh, like the dry bones in Ezekiel's vision. But it is clear that nothing can be more false than this impression. So far from the bones being laid down first, they are altogether a secondary formation: they are rather a deposit from the growing tissues than a framework on which they are built. ('A Meditation; on Skeletons' 622)

What we mistakenly view as a primary infrastructure may turn out to have been built up later, as a 'secondary formation,' just as the social imperative that prompts Angel to reject Tess may be deeply internalized but still not necessarily 'natural': 'Within the remoter depths of his constitution, so gentle and affectionate as he was in general, there lay hidden a hard logical deposit, like a vein of metal in a soft loam' (237). The secondary formation is one whose deathly origin is not immediately obvious:

> But not only can we thus recognize the skeleton as a derived and secondary structure, built up within themselves by the living parts around, but we can trace in thought (though our senses cannot follow it) the mode of its origin. Here again our natural ideas would mislead us. Speaking according to our impressions, we should assign its production to the action of the vital force, and regard it as a direct exhibition of the formative power of life. But the truth is the very opposite again of this. Bone is formed in living structures by a precipitation of solid matter, which is virtually a process like that of excretion, or the casting off of waste materials ... The production of bony matter is a result of the loss and failure of vitality. (622–3)[19]

This opposition of the 'vital force' and 'processes of decay' (622) is everywhere in *Tess*. The skeletal nature of Angel's ethical impulse renders it, in the logic of the novel as well as in the broader cultural context, deeply suspect.

The graphically corporeal basis of Angel's rejection of Tess is made even clearer when the narrator notes that it is Angel's own internalized moral imperative, his own niceness, which is really the root of his dismay: 'Even if these assumed reproaches were not likely to be addressed to him or to his by strangers, they might have reached his ears from his own fastidious brain' (240). There is something slightly gruesome about these images – denuding skeletons, messages travelling on an internal closed circuit from brains to ears – that underscores the deathly genesis of the ethical impulse. (How else, after all, does one have visual access to skeletons and brains except in death?)

The novel returns to this image of bodily layering again and again. When Alec comes to visit Tess at her lodgings in Flintcomb-Ash, and reaches the final stage in his reconversion back to his old profligate ways, he undergoes a physical transformation before her very eyes: 'The corpses of those old fitful passions which had lain inanimate amid the lines of his face ever since his reformation seemed to wake and come together as in a resurrection' (313). The face of Tess's erstwhile seducer is a living palimpsest: traces of his former character are visible in the old tissues, never to be completely erased by fresh markings. Again, it is the deathly, degenerative forces in the novel that are depicted as a superimposition, a layering, and by extension as an internalization within the human body.

Tess herself is capable of this kind of thinking. When she is travelling home to Marlott after her parents have taken ill, she enters the sleeping town of Nuttlebury before dawn and passes the local inn: 'Under the thatched roofs her mind's eye beheld relaxed tendons and flaccid muscles, spread out in darkness beneath coverlets made of little purple patchwork squares, and undergoing a bracing process at the hands of sleep for renewed labour on the morrow' (333). Muscles and tendons 'spread out' upon beds – this is quite an image for Tess to have in her 'mind's eye'! It is as though, under the pressure of her final return home to her birthplace, she suddenly develops the kind of X-ray vision that has been the narrator's prerogative all along. Just as Angel is capable of this kind of visual feat under the pressure of crushing internalized ethical obligation, so Tess is capable of it as the gathered weight of historical – and narrative – imperatives comes to bear upon her wearied frame.

Two intertexts demonstrate the extent to which Hardy is here underscoring the epiphanic or even mystical nature of Tess's sudden penetrative vision. In *Sartor Resartus*, Thomas Carlyle's whimsical German-idealist subject, Diogenes Teufelsdröckh, indulges in a similar rumination on the sleepers beneath the eye of heaven: 'Oh, under that hideous coverlet of vapours, and putrefactions, and unimaginable gases, what a Fermenting-vat lies simmering and hid ... Upwards of five-hundred-thousand two-legged animals without feathers lie all around us, in horizontal positions; their heads all in nightcaps, and full of the foolishest dreams ... All these heaped and huddled together, with nothing but a little carpentry and masonry between them ... But I, *mein Werther*, sit above it all' (13–15). Elsewhere Hardy himself draws a startling parallel between this kind of penetrative vision, the specialized skills of the author, and the force of social imperative; the passage, from his essay 'The Profitable Reading of Fiction,' is worth quoting in full:

> Education has as yet but little broken or modified the waves of human impulse on which deeds and words depend. So that in the portraiture of scenes in any way emotional or dramatic – the highest province of fiction – the peer and the peasant stand on much the same level ... In the lapse of countless ages, no doubt, improved systems of moral education will considerably and appreciably elevate even the involuntary instincts of human nature; but a present culture has only affected the surface of those lives with which it has come in contact, binding down the passions of those predisposed to turmoil as by a silken thread only, which the first ebullition suffices to break. With regard to what may be termed the minor key of action and speech – the unemotional, every-day doings of men – social refinement operates upon character in a way which is oftener than not prejudicial to vigorous portraiture, by making the exteriors of men their screen rather than their index, as with untutored mankind ... In the one case the author's word has to be taken as to the nerves and muscles of his figures; in the other they can be seen as in an *écorché*. (124–5)

Tess's ability to see the figures in the Nuttlebury cottages 'as in an *écorché*' underscores the extraordinary emotional pressure of this moment. She has indeed taken on the prerogatives of the author, as I mentioned above, but it seems as though this ability is available wherever superficial 'social refinement' is stripped away (literally) by scenes 'emotional or dramatic.'

As a final example of this metaphorically somatic process, I would note the novel's obsession with 'skillentons' in general. Of course, John Durbeyfield never shuts up about the illustrious bones in his 'gr't-family-vault-at-Kingsbere,' much to the humiliation of his eldest daughter. This is perhaps the most literal way in which the historical, d'Urbervillean strain of the novel is associated with the interiors of bodies. Tess herself demonstrates this preoccupation when, after fleeing the unwanted attentions of a fellow traveller on her way to Flintcomb-Ash and taking cover (significantly, in a 'nest' of leaves yet again), she is at the depths of her despair: 'The wife of Angel Clare put her hand to her brow, and felt its curve, and the edges of her eye-sockets perceptible under the soft skin, and thought as she did so that a time would come when that bone would be bare' (270). Tess, at least, realistically associates the process of stripping away bodily tissue down to the bone with death. (In a sort of precipitation of this process, she 'mercilessly nip[s] her eyebrows off' [272] in the novel's next scene – laying bare the skin beneath, if not yet the bone beneath the skin.)

What is significant about this persistent imagery is the way in which it makes quite literal a process that is usually conceived metaphorically. If, as the narrator keeps insisting, the problem with Angel Clare and the others who would condemn Tess (including Tess) is the fact that they have internalized a wrong-headed social imperative that is at odds with the promptings of nature, then what better way to demonstrate this process than by a literal internalization within the physical body? It is the ethical law, the 'law of the father' associated with heredity and the socialization into preexisting networks of relationship and coercion, that is taken into the bodies of the characters Hardy describes: it is, literally, the paternal name of d'Urberville.

Yet there is a problematic and unstable exchange between the different layers of the palimpsest in this schema. In the examples of vertical superimposition associated with the natural, maternal pole of the novel, there is a reliable and orderly layering which can be read in a fairly straightforward way: landscape upon landscape, older facial feature upon younger. Yet in the examples demonstrating the death drive or the degenerative processes of history, this sedimentation becomes radically unstable. Things are taken within bodies, tissues are stripped away in a traumatic manner, older images (the facial 'corpses' of d'Urberville's old passions) unexpectedly reemerge, buried signs are not allowed to float easily to the surface where they can be read alongside their more recent counterparts.

This sedimentation is the cause of the trouble that so many of the characters seem to have in reading the visible marks of one another's faces. There are the oft-cited examples where Angel goes wrong in trying to construe the face of his bride: 'He argued erroneously when he said to himself that her heart was not indexed in the honest freshness of her face' (232), and 'Nature, in her fantastic trickery, had set such a seal of maidenhood upon Tess's countenance that he gazed at her with a stupefied air' (234). (Similarly, even before they are married, the befuddled Angel attempts to understand Tess's refusals by 'conn[ing] the characters of her face as if they had been hieroglyphics' [176].)[20]

It is not only Angel who has trouble in this regard. Early on in the novel, during one of his first bouts of describing Tess, the narrator coyly notes that she had a 'luxuriance of aspect, a fulness of growth, which made her appear more of a woman than she really was. She had inherited the feature from her mother without the quality it denoted' (45). Presumably the narrator is referring to her mature breasts, which he seems to imply denote a potential for maternity incongruous in an adolescent girl (since both she and her mother are sexually mature women, there is a residue of signification in this 'fulness of growth' that could only be captured by motherhood). Tess's very body belies her internal qualities in both directions: on the one hand, making the virginal appear matronly, on the other, making the deflowered appear virginal.

The unstable correspondence between inner and outer is most marked in the case in which the stakes are highest: the reading of Alec d'Urberville. When Tess first meets Alec preaching near Evershead, she is forcibly struck by the contrast between outer signification and inner spiritual state (in his case, certainly not the outward and visible sign of an inward and spiritual grace). The incongruity strikes her as a 'ghastly *bizarrerie*':

It was less a reform than a transfiguration. The former curves of sensuousness were now modulated to lines of devotional passion. The lip-shapes that had meant seductiveness were now made to express supplication; the glow on the cheek that yesterday could be translated as riotousness was evangelized to-day into the splendour of pious rhetoric ...

The lineaments, as such, seemed to complain. They had been diverted from their hereditary connotation to signify impressions for which nature did not intend them. (297–8)

When she sees this transformed face, Tess thinks to herself, 'Yet could it be so?' – the very question that Angel asks when confronted with the stark lie of her own countenance. In each case, the narrator wants to indicate a substratum of 'reality' – Tess's purity, Alec's profligacy – that is belied by the superficial signs with which others attempt to read those depths. In each case, there is an unease, an uncanniness on the part of the reader that signals that he or she is getting it wrong: Tess supposedly accepts Alec's conversion but somehow knows it to be shallow and false; Angel rejects Tess but has a nagging feeling he is missing something about her real 'purity' (when he leaves her he 'hardly knew that he loved her still' [248]).

Much later in the novel, after Angel has returned from South America – he returns both wasted from illness and chagrined by his former harsh judgment of Tess, conditions whose intimate connection is both strongly suggested and never fully explained[21] – the narrator describes him thus:

> You could see the skeleton behind the man, and almost the ghost behind the skeleton. He matched Crivelli's dead *Christus*. His sunken eye-pits were of morbid hue, and the light in his eyes had waned. The angular hollows and lines of his aged ancestors had succeeded to their reign in his face twenty years before their time. (356)

On the one hand, this rather startling image hints at a kind of moral retribution: Angel is being punished for his adherence to the 'skeletal' social imperative by having to wear its disfiguring marks openly on his countenance. On a broader level, it also sketches a kind of teleology of ancestral skeletons that is mystified by the descriptions of Tess's inherited characteristics. While both Tess and Angel are horrified by her resemblance to the portraits of the sepulchral d'Urberville ancestors they see on their honeymoon after Angel has more or less recanted his judgment of Tess in Brazil, he thinks of this same resemblance in very different terms: 'In recalling her face again and again, he thought now that he could see therein a flash of the dignity which must have graced her grand-dames; and the vision sent that *aura* through his veins which he had formerly felt, and which left behind it a sense of sickness' (330–1). While the previous 'aura' had been occasioned not by the portraits but by contemplation of Tess's freshness and beauty at Talbothays (152–3), this ghostly revisitation is brought about by precisely the opposite characteristic: Tess's ancestral markings, the skeletal signifiers of her ancient race. The narrator is ambiguous about whether the 'sickness' is brought on by Angel's regret at his harshness, or by the same kind of horror that had wracked him in front of the ancestral portraits. Whenever the narrator contemplates the surfacing of ancient facial characteristics, he is consistently surprised at the instability of the signification process. Tess's ancestral features are occasions of both disquiet and softened regret; Angel's ancestors are surfacing twenty years ahead of their time. Ancestral resemblance (especially when it means looking like a skeleton) is at best unsettling, and at worst, occasion for tragic mistakes and acts of misreading.

What Hardy suggests most consistently, in effect, is that the events of a character's life may change his or her superficial impressions, attitudes, and desires – and change his or her outer integument in accord – but the most ancient layers of sedimentation, the skeletons of early belief and habits, always threaten to resurface.[22] When Angel returns home to the vicarage to ask his parents' blessing of Tess, the narrator notes that they see a great change in him physically: 'He was getting to behave like a farmer; he flung his legs about; the muscles of his face had grown more expressive; his eyes looked as much information as his tongue spoke, and more' (162). Yet Angel has not become one of those carefree, sensual 'nymphs and swains' he is beginning to resemble, of course. At the crucial moment, his old prejudices and ethical imperatives reemerge and cause him to condemn Tess; the facial muscles, legs, eyes, and tongue give way to the bare bones and 'fastidious brain' of his early training – they are at the deepest level and thus the most intractable.

The image of Angel's new farmerly behaviour is strikingly similar to the descriptions of the Casterbridge farmers we have already seen: 'Here the face, the arms, the hat, the stick, the body throughout spoke equally with the tongue ... Chicanery, subterfuge, had hardly a place in the streets of this honest borough' (*Mayor* 130). With the simple people 'of the soil,' supposedly, there is a trustworthy and transparent correspondence between inner state and outer sign; in becoming like a farmer, Angel takes on this characteristic of readability, his body giving as much information as his tongue speaks. Yet this easy and straightforward state of affairs is complicated in two directions: Angel's seeming transparency, his communion with the values and mores of the farmers and workers of Talbothays, turns out not to be true – just as we have already seen that the supposed transparency of the trader turns out not to be true in the case of Casterbridge.[23]

In *The Mayor of Casterbridge*, I argued, this unconscious anxiety about correspondence, and the remapping of the gold-paper relationship onto the bodies of the traders, whose 'gibbous human shapes' are representative of 'ready money' (130), is part of a larger concern on

Hardy's part with epistemological uncertainty, readability, and lying. In *Tess*, this same concern is there in the form of problematic inner-outer correspondences and the sudden resurfacing of buried traits and predilections, but it has to do more specifically with the relationship between the individual and the social than it does in the earlier novel. In *Tess*, it is the social and historical imperative that is the deepest, most thoroughly internalized level of the individual, and it is, as I have argued, the explanation for events that the narrator most consistently offers. Yet there is something incomplete about this explanation, just as there is something incomplete and unstable about the bodily surfaces of the characters who have undergone transformations due to outside pressures.

For one thing, the attempt to blame Tess's tragedy on the hypocrisy of societal norms inaugurates an irresolvable logical paradox. Hardy cannot both exonerate Tess by appeal to her purity and condemn the very standards which establish the category 'pure.' In order for us to have a sense of Tess's tragedy, we must feel it deeply wrong that she should be deflowered, and in order to feel this as a deep wrong we must share in the standards of female purity Hardy supposedly condemns.[24] If, as Hardy persistently hints, the standards for female purity among the peasantry are different than those among the upper classes, then in order to feel Tess's seduction as a real loss we must tacitly admit that she is being judged by those reviled bourgeois standards. In addition, in attempting to valorize the appetite for joy and the sexual instinct as 'natural' and then counterpose them to the artificiality and cruelty of ethical norms, Hardy has walked into a trap wherein he must praise Alec for his sensuality and condemn Angel for his hypocrisy (the latter of which he sometimes does, the former of which he most decidedly does not).

There must, in other words, be something going on in the explanatory machinery of the novel beyond the mere condemnation of socially imposed standards of behaviour. Because the truth is, we do feel Tess's tragedy, including her seduction, as deeply wrong, even as we might want to join Hardy in critiquing Victorian standards of female purity. Just as the events of the plot and other indications in the novel (metaphorical associations, characters' speech, etc.) belie the narrator's proposed socio-historical explanation for Tess's general tragedy, there must be another way in which the repressed, maternal function has a shaping role in determining events. The other pole of the novel – the natural, regenerative force – is repressed by the narrator's insistence on the culpability of social law and historical determination, yet it is this individualistic force, the self-preservative instinct, that is perhaps even more important in determining events than the 'd'Urbervillean' force of history (just as Angel is perhaps even more to blame for Tess's tragedy than Alec). It is this half of the causal machinery of the narrative that betrays the economic concerns the novel seeks to resolve. The internalization process I have described inaugurates – and is a result of – the novel's emphasis on the individual in the two systems of 'law' it describes: the ethical and the economic.

4 Internalized Economies and the Role of Demand

As a novel, *Tess of the d'Urbervilles* is interested in the workings of the individual, on both the ethical and economic planes, in an unprecedented way. As a contemporary reviewer of the novel notes, Hardy 'is fond of showing ... how much cruelty, how much bitter suffering, your would-be hero may inflict by sticking too consistently and religiously to his rôle.'[25] While I would argue that this suffering is perhaps due more to individuals' insistence on continually changing their roles, I agree that Hardy is ultimately interested, in *Tess of the d'Urbervilles*, in delineating individual responsibility as it intersects with the mechanisms of fate, history, and heredity.

This is in stark contrast to Eliot's project of describing ethical 'consequences' in *Adam Bede* and *The Mill on the Floss*; Hardy obsessively resorts to the rationalization of intent throughout *Tess*, while for Eliot this justification is meaningless in the face of the effects of our actions on others. Hardy is consistently concerned with examining the intersection of individual responsibility and external determination in the form of internalized social imperatives. This internalization process operates in a homologous manner in both the economic and the ethical realms: just as the social law is taken within the individual and becomes a personal moral imperative (or hypocrisy), so the regimenting and coercive economic relationships in which the characters find themselves enmeshed become internalized and personalized as well.

As I discussed at the opening of the chapter, this new interest in the role of the individual in economic processes is the inheritance of a shift in economic thinking in the late nineteenth century – the rise of the marginal utility school and a revitalized interest in the demand function. Before I turn to the thematics of internalization in *Tess of the d'Urbervilles* and a new consideration of Say's Law, I would like briefly to examine the ways in which the novel depicts those larger economic relationships on the plane of the social and collective.

There are several obvious ways in which *Tess* signals an interest in economic relationships. One of the many tragic questions posed by the novel (in addition to Miller's over-arching 'Why does Tess suffer so?') is the question of why the Durbeyfields', as well as Tess's, economic fortunes are so unfortunate. The novel proposes several solutions to this enigma. From the very beginning of the narrative, the reader is subjected to numerous narratorial laments over the Durbeyfields' poor domestic economy. From a description of Mrs Durbeyfield's slovenly housekeeping habits – 'The interior ... struck upon the girl's senses with an unspeakable dreariness ... There stood her mother amid the group of children, as Tess had left her, hanging over the Monday washing-tub, which had now, as always, lingered on to the end of the week' (25) – the novel moves to a condemnation of Mr Durbeyfield's earning prowess: 'Durbeyfield was what was locally called a slack-twisted fellow; he had good strength to work at times; but the times could not be relied on to coincide with the hours of requirement; and, having been unaccustomed to the regular toil of the day-labourer, he was not particularly persistent when they did so coincide' (39). The final condemnation of the Durbeyfields' economic management comes toward the end of the novel, when Tess returns home from Flintcomb-Ash to find that her family members have eaten the seed potatoes, 'that last lapse of the improvident' (334). From this perspective, the economic misfortunes of the Durbeyfields are entirely of their own making, their own laziness or poor judgment (or perhaps overenthusiastic, anti-Malthusian childbearing).[26]

Broadening the scope of this analysis a bit, we notice that the novel's examination of economies moves outward to consider the larger socioeconomic networks in which the family is enmeshed – the relationship between landowners and tenants, changing at the historical moment in which the novel's action takes place. According to the narrator, as landlords increasingly decided not to renew the leases of lifeholders, copyholders, and small freeholders when they came due, those families of 'an interesting and better-informed class' than the farm labourers, families like the Durbeyfields, were forced to move to larger cities: 'A depopulation was going on ... These families, who had formed the backbone of the village life in the past, who were the depositaries of the village traditions, had to seek refuge in the large centres; the process [was] humorously designated by statisticians as "the tendency of the rural population towards the large towns"' (339).

This analysis locates the source of the Durbeyfields' trouble on a somewhat broader plane; it is an historical movement, a demographic shift, a more general – if unfortunate – mechanism in which individual families find themselves entrapped. And yet, even as the narrator begins to shift the source of the Durbeyfields' problems somewhat farther from the epicentre of individual responsibility, he quickly collapses it back to the level of personal blame, if not just bad luck. Immediately after the passage cited above, as Tess sits ruminating at the window of her family cottage on their last night in Marlott, her eyes come to rest 'on the web of a spider, probably starved long ago, which had been mistakenly placed in a corner where no flies ever came' (340). As a figure of economic improvidence, this hapless spider is squarely blamed for its own starvation. Such things are at worst stupidity, at best dumb luck: one 'mistakenly' makes a wrong decision, and one pays the price, without any consideration of larger patterns or historical shifts into the bargain.

Regenia Gagnier suggests another interesting parallel between individualism and the kind of intense pessimism we see in this novel: '[Herbert] Spencer's idea that all progress was progress toward individualism instilled at the broadest cultural levels fears of anomie, isolation, and egoism that had gone well beyond [Adam] Smith's idea of "self-interest" leading to the social good' ('Law' 106). Certainly the image of Tess staring at the starved spider – a moment of intense melancholic projection – seems a perfect example of this side effect of economic progress. Gagnier ties this fear of 'selfish individualism' directly to the rise of marginal utility economics (which is 'inextricable from ... social individuation' [106]); this connection is clearly visible in the novel, where historical and broader economic processes (which under Smith's regime would constitute the very fabric of the 'social good') are continually referred back to the level of individual responsibility.

Similarly, at other times when the novel makes a token attempt to examine economic determination on a broader scale, it cannot maintain its scope and quickly collapses back to the level of the individual. In the notorious scenes where the novel examines the impact of the new agricultural machines upon farm labour, there seems to be some attempt to document a larger economic pattern – and even some attempt to demonize, for example, the mechanical thresher at Flintcomb-Ash, the 'red tyrant' (314) that seems to make work for the individual labourers more difficult than before, not less (even as it undoubtedly increases the profit margin of the farm owner).

However, the problem with the machinery, within the logic of the novel, is not the coercive or unbalanced economic relationships it inaugurates – its function as capitalist means of production – but rather that its integrity and tenacity is not matched by the bodies of the people hired to run it: the thresher at Flintcomb-Ash, for example, makes a 'despotic demand upon the endurance of their muscles and nerves' (314). Insofar as the labourers' individual duties are determined by their ability to keep up with the machine (Groby does not like Marian to spell Tess because she is not as fast a feeder), the 'problem' with the machine is reinscribed as a potential 'problem' with the bodies of the workers themselves; they are deemed fit or unfit based on a new standard set by the machine. This intersection of the mechanistic and the individual body powerfully recalls the tensions of marginal utility theory discussed above. (Intriguingly, the narrator indicates that 'for some probably economical reason it was usually a woman who was chosen for this particular duty' of feeding the thresher [317]. The narrator indicates that an external force is at work here – 'economical reasons' – yet his insistence, throughout the scene, on parsing the women according to their strength and ability relocates responsibility within the individual physical body.)[27]

There is a similar dynamic at work in the other famous scene where a farm machine makes a prominent appearance – the passage where we see Tess nursing her new baby while at work in the field. The scene opens: 'But of all ruddy things that morning the brightest were two broad arms of painted wood, which rose from the margin of a yellow cornfield hard by Marlott village.. They, with two others below, formed the revolving Maltese cross of the reaping-machine' (92). The 'margin' of the field has given birth to the machine; it has arisen from that portion of the cornfield that has been 'opened' by hand-cutting, thereby literalizing the intersection among different, historically gradated kinds of work: the natural growth of the wheat, the old-fashioned hand labour involved in cutting the field's borders, the mechanized reaping. The chronological development is manifest here; once again, we can see a process of superimposition or replacement of ancient methods by new.

This juxtaposition would seem to locate the margin of the field as a space where we can read the effects of the deindividuating labour inaugurated by the machine, and yet in the next passage the narrator makes it clear that there is something inherent in the workers themselves – specifically women, since once again it is 'mainly women' who work in conjunction with the machine – that causes this depersonalization: 'a field-woman is a portion of the field; she has somehow lost her own margin, imbibed the essence of her surrounding, and assimilated herself with it' (93). The active nature of the verbs here is somewhat incongruous: *she has* lost, imbibed, assimilated. The responsibility for the deindividuation brought about by the mechanization of labour is located within the wills of the labourers themselves. In both cases where Hardy describes the introduction of machinery, the same trajectory applies: an initial gesture toward the workings of external economic pressures, an acknowledgment that it is women whose labour is primarily affected by these pressures, and then a relocation of responsibility for the effects of those pressures within the workers. The initial attempt to locate blame at the socio-historical pole of causation is undermined by an insistence on the role of the individual and 'natural.'

Tess herself, as an individual, is depicted by the events of the plot as existing within a network of coercive economic relationships. Most obviously there is her dependence upon Alec d'Urberville – a dependence which is present throughout her career and cannot even be ameliorated by her marriage to another man. Tess herself can be adamant (at times) about locating the source of her trouble with Alec in the compulsory nature of their relationship. After one of their tiffs at Trantridge, Alec asks her why she has never told him when he makes her angry, and Tess replies: 'You know very well why. Because I cannot help myself here' (73). Tess recognizes her own helplessness in the face of her economic dependence upon Alec; however, it is more her sense of duty to her family, and their dependence on his patronage, that binds her. Time and again, d'Urberville uses this weak spot to manipulate and coerce Tess. As she laments to him after he tells her he has sent Mr Durbeyfield a new horse: 'I didn't know – you had ever sent them anything ... I almost wish you had not – yet, I almost wish it ... It – hampers me so!' (75). And much later in the novel, during d'Urberville's second round of manipulation and blandishment, Tess again expostulates to her seducer: 'Don't mention my little brothers and sisters – don't make me break down quite ... If you want to help them – God knows they need it – do it without telling me' (324).

Tess is not without her reasons for feeling responsible for her family's economic well-being; they themselves do much to inculcate this sense of duty in their eldest daughter. After the untimely death of the family's horse, her mother begins to pressure Tess to go to Trantridge and 'claim kin' with the spurious d'Urbervilles there. As always, Tess would prefer to maintain her independence – 'I'd rather try to get work' she mur-

murs (39) – but her family's appeals and her own sense of guilt are too strong: '"Well, as I killed the horse, mother," she said mournfully, "I suppose I ought to do something"' (40). The economic pressures on Tess are thus located at two levels beyond her own individual responsibility: the ambitious pressure of her parents and the unavoidable pitfalls of her family's class position and concomitant dependent status.

This depiction of Tess as enmeshed in determining and coercive relationships beyond her control is insisted upon throughout the novel; even when she comes across the 'tex' painter on her way back from Trantridge, the narrator reminds us of her general condition of helplessness: 'The man turned as he spoke to an opening at the roadside leading into a pasture. "If you'll wait a moment," he added, "I shall not be long." As he had her basket she could not well do otherwise' (85). Tess is continually finding herself in positions were 'she could not well do otherwise'; throughout the novel, people with various sorts of designs upon her hold her metaphorical 'basket' hostage, forcing her to do that which she might not otherwise have done.

And yet, the same process of internalization operates with Tess here as it does elsewhere in the novel. Her dependence on d'Urberville – whose coercive nature she tacitly acknowledges – she simultaneously insists on characterizing as her own weakness: 'If I had ever sincerely loved you, if I loved you still, I should not so loathe and hate myself for my weakness as I do now ... My eyes were dazed by you for a little, and that was all' (82–3). A bit later, the narrator again relates Tess's own thinking on the subject: 'She had dreaded him, winced before him, succumbed to adroit advantages he took of her helplessness; then, temporarily blinded by his ardent manners, had been stirred to confused surrender awhile' (87). In each case, Tess's account of events begins with a description of the forces acting on her from without, and in each case it ends with an insistence on her own responsibility – and weakness – in surrendering to her seducer. Tess's nascent sense of external economic coercion is complicated by her own internalized sense of responsibility and guilt.

This internalized responsibility is most clearly signalled by the economic metaphor that both she and d'Urberville use to describe their relationship. During the scene when d'Urberville drives Tess home to Marlott after her disastrous tenure on the poultry farm, he (briefly) acknowledges his own fault and declares to Tess: 'I am ready to pay to the uttermost farthing' (83). Much later, when Tess contemplates confessing her past history to Angel on their wedding night, she steels herself to the odious task: 'She would pay to the uttermost farthing; she would tell all, there and then' (220). This 'payment' refers, in small part, to her somewhat dishonest withholding from her fiancé; however, it refers in main to the events of her past history itself. She has transferred Alec's words describing his own culpability wholesale to her own case.

This is not the only way in which Tess fails to see the larger economic patternings in which she is enmeshed. When she goes to work at Flintcomb-Ash farm, she does 'task work,' being paid only for what she accomplishes, not by salary or even hours worked. This kind of payment system makes the exploitative nature of the owner-labourer relationship starkly clear; the surplus value due to the differential between a commodity's price and the cost of labour required to produce it is located at the very level of the individual good. Yet when Farmer Groby tries to mystify this exploitative relationship by telling Tess that his real goal is the completion of the work (even while declaring 'we'll see which is master here' [282]), Tess feels responsible for her slowness and volunteers to stay longer to finish the threshing: 'I am going to work all the afternoon instead of leaving at two as the others will do' (283). When she breaks down under the unaccustomed strain of the work, and the farmer reenters the barn at that moment and chastises her for resting, Tess pleads to him: 'But it is my own loss ... Not yours' (284).

The effect of Tess's insistence on relocating responsibility for her own plight at the level of the individual agent – herself – is to make her economic position and her sexual position (virgin, mistress, wife, mistress) mutually dependent and determining. Tess's sexuality – the supposedly private, inner, and protected sphere – is made public through a process which confounds the types of 'work' she performs throughout the novel: the overtly exploitative and wage-based (farm work) with the less obviously so (the sexual work of mistress and wife). When the novel, and Tess's logic, refuses to acknowledge the ways in which she is coerced into sexual relationships, and instead makes these relationships seem of her own free will and choosing, it makes them seem like wage labour.

The novel performs this conflation in ways other than Tess's own insistence or the sheer facts of her dependent position. During the famous lament describing the violation in The Chase, the narrator comments: 'An immense social chasm was to divide our heroine's personality thereafter from that previous self of hers who stepped from her mother's door to try her fortune at Trantridge poultry-farm' (77). And much later in the novel, Angel comically wonders as he goes to search for Tess in the glittering resort town of Sandbourne, 'Where could Tess possibly be?... Were there any cows to milk here? There certainly were no fields to till' (363). Both of these comments equate Tess's 'trying her fortune' with the sexual labour she ends up, in both cases, performing for Alec d'Urberville. Her wage work is put in a sexual light, and her relationship with d'Urberville is put in an economic one.[28]

Tess of the d'Urbervilles thus displays a recurrent concern with the role of the individual (the maternal mode of the novel) in economic and ethical relationships. This thematic is a departure from the previous three novels I have discussed, which are primarily concerned with delineating larger social patterns: the self-contained ethical economy of *Adam Bede*, the familial political economy of *The Mill on the Floss*, and the symbolic kinship relations of *The Mayor of Casterbridge*. Each of these novels betrays a certain anxiety about truthful correspondences and readability which I have claimed is the inheritance of a widespread concern with the functioning of surplus value and the possible stagnation of the burgeoning mid-Victorian credit economy. *Tess*, on the other hand, signals the beginning of a shift away from these prevailing concerns. While it certainly has not abandoned the issues I have located in the other novels, it adds to the mix – in its insistence upon the role of personal responsibility in economic and ethical relationships – a nascent concern with the influence of the individual on larger social processes.[29]

One of the ways to see this shift is by examining a scene in *Tess* which seems to recapitulate, in a different form, the economic concerns of Hardy's earlier novel *The Mayor of Casterbridge*. As we have already seen, there is a key passage in the latter which describes one of the main problems with Henchard's trading practices: 'His dealings had been so extensive that settlement could not long be postponed, and to settle he was obliged to sell off corn that he had bought only a few weeks before ... Much of the corn he had never seen' (261). The problem here is Henchard's abandonment of the strict correspondence between valuable goods and promises-to-pay: there is a pressure to liquidate, to 'settle,' which is undermined by his failure to follow the old rules of barter exchange. The real issue is that he has not seen the corn, that he maintains a problematic distance from the fundamental processes which undergird economic exchange: the soil, the growing, the harvest.

Similarly in *Tess*, the consumers of the milk and butter from Talbothays are removed from its production:

'Londoners will drink it at their breakfasts to-morrow, won't they?' she asked. 'Strange people that we have never seen.'

'Yes – I suppose they will. Though not as we send it. When its strength has been lowered, so that it may not get up into their heads.'

'Noble men and noble women, ambassadors and centurions, ladies and tradeswomen, and babies who have never seen a cow ... Who don't know anything of us, and where it comes from.' (188)

The issue of not seeing the goods and of being removed from the processes of production, which in the earlier novel is a problem of trade, is here remapped onto the consumption function. (Significantly, it is Tess, the novel's most relentless 'internalizer,' who notices and comments upon this state of affairs.) The anxiety about correspondence and unstable value relationships that in *The Mayor of Casterbridge* is the especial province of exchange has become, in *Tess*, a problem of demand. And this reconfigured problem is the thematic analogue to the new concern with consumption inaugurated by the marginal utility school and the demise of Say's Law.

Classical political economy, as we have already seen, chiefly concerned itself with questions of accumulation and growth, thus expanding the older physiocratic models of self-contained circulation. The marginalist revolution, to put it very simply, returned to the questions of distribution posed by the earlier economics, largely ignoring the questions of accumulation and equilibrium inaugurated by classical economists.[30] Stanley Jevons puts it this way: 'The problem of Economics may, as it seems to me, be stated thus: – *Given, a certain population, with various needs and powers of production, in possession of certain lands and other sources of material: required, the mode of employing their labour which will maximise the utility of the produce*' (267, emphasis in original). As I have already discussed extensively throughout this study, one of the most important consequences of this shift in thinking is the ascendancy of the demand function in economic analysis: 'Consumption, not accumulation, appears in marginalist economics as the mainspring of economic activity. The new system, so to say, substitutes "consumers' sovereignty" for "capitalists' sovereignty." Thus the phenomenon of demand ... comes to occupy the pride of place in the marginalist system' (Dasgupta 80).

As we have seen, Say's Law, which argues the impossibility of overproduction by ignoring fluctuations in demand – claiming that there can be no general overproduction because any produced good indicates a desire on its manufacturer's part to purchase another good of the same price – is unceremoniously unseated by the new economic thinking. Demand comes to take 'pride of place,' and in so doing inculcates a new fear for the continuation of consumer demand on the part of manufacturers.[31] In *Tess*, thus, a process is analysed and made explicit that was hidden and repressed in, for example, *The Mill on the Floss*.

5 Breasts, Bones, Mothers, and Fathers

As I suggested earlier, in order to understand the role of economic demand in *Tess* we must consider the novel's fascination with milk – from the narrator's obsession with the bucolic utopia of dairy farms, to the constant reminders that Tess's mother was 'only a dairymaid,' to the suggestive passages dealing with Tess's own status as nursing mother. Milk is the only product that actually comes into being as a direct result of consumer desire; as merchandise it is a unique manifestation of the vigour of demand, and as metaphor it is an index of anxieties about the possibility of demand's failure. As one Victorian commentator eloquently noted: 'Our mother's milk is one of the few articles of food we ever swallow without its having cost a money payment or an equivalent for a money payment. It comes exactly *when* we want it; and its quality, at its first coming, is exactly *what* we want' ('Milk' 126).[32]

Milk is, of course, also a metaphor of maternal nurture, and it functions this way as well in *Tess*. We see in the novel's treatment of dairy products and dairy farming another permutation of the ubiquitous maternal/paternal binary: there is an organic relationship, beyond the merely metaphorical, between maternal milk and paternal bones. The novel also insists on opposing Tess's labour as a dairymaid to her 'labour' as a nursing mother. In order to tease out the connections between these various figurative oppositions and the larger issues of economic demand and women's labour, we must look more closely at the cultural meanings of milk and lactation at the end of the nineteenth century.

The technological processes of dairy farming and milk production were of particular civic interest during this period. During the last quarter of the nineteenth century, there was a great increase in the demand for, and consumption of, dairy products. Most contemporary commentators attributed this upsurge in consumption to the use of various types of machinery. With the advent of rail transit, it became possible for the first time to ship milk into cities and other sites far removed from its production before it had time to spoil.[33] In addition to the railroad, mechanized production techniques also played an important role: 'Milk separators, and all the newest and most improved machinery, are in constant use ... Whether as a result of the use of these Dairy Companies in London, or not, the consumption of milk in the Metropolis has enormously increased' ('Our Milk-Supplies' 799). This consumption-production cycle was a self-perpetuating one. As a result of increased demand for liquid milk in urban centres, dairy farmers began to alter their production patterns: in 1875, J.P. Sheldon, an influential writer on agricultural issues, advised that shipping liquid milk by rail to cities was by far the most profitable way of disposing of it (270).[34]

Along with the surge in dairy consumption among city-dwellers came a growing concern with the quality and safety of milk. This concern took two different forms: anxiety either about the adulteration of milk by unscrupulous dairy farmers and distributors, or about natural contamination by disease-bearing bacteria. The first concern, that milk available in cities was commonly adulterated with any number of nasty additives (the most benign of which seems to have been chalk), had been widespread at least since early in the century.[35] Many writers on the dairy trade in popular journals argued strenuously and repeatedly that such fears were unfounded, and that most city milk was adulterated with nothing more virulent than water.[36] (Bad enough, we might say!) One optimistic commentator even argued that the advent of new machinery had eliminated that ancient bugbear of the urban consumer, watered-down milk:

> Instead of the primeval plan of bringing in the cow wherever she may be wanted, and supplementing the supply, whenever it may happen to be unequal to the demand, by calling in the aid of the pump, railways have rendered it practicable to keep the cow wherever it may be most expedient to do so, and telegraphs have put it in the power of our purveyors to supplement a deficient supply from one source by making an extra demand on another ...The facilities of railways and telegraphs, have called into existence some of the most remarkable organisations of modern commerce. ('Curiosities' 652)

(It is interesting to note that this writer conceives of the milk production cycle as being entirely driven by consumer demand.) The sheer number and repetitiveness of these claims eloquently attest to the intractability of this popular fear; whether or not the widespread use of adulterating agents by crooked dairy distributors was reality, the fact remains that much of the public seems to have assumed it was true.[37]

Other writers concerned themselves not with urban legends about adulteration, but with the real risk of disease from contaminated milk – and with good reason. Mass shipping of milk by rail predated widespread pasteurization by about seventy years: between 1850 and 1920, more disease-bearing milk was made available to more people than ever before. Between 1878 and 1908, for example, there were no fewer than 317 outbreaks of milk-borne typhoid and scarlet fever in England (Enock 74). While the first guidelines for pasteurization times were given in 1890, the technique was not in widespread commercial use at the end of the century, and the term 'pasteurization' was not given legal meaning until the Milk and Dairies Amendment Act of 1922 (Enock 113).

Numerous contemporary commentators decried the dangers of milk shipped far from its site of production, either in the interest of advocating pasteurization or simply to argue that city-dwellers' 'vast demand' for milk is 'outside its natural functions' ('Something About Milk' 821). The great majority of these warnings insist that there is no excuse for ignorance regarding the dangers of widely transported milk: 'It is a fact, now well known to everyone, that milk often contains those deadly pathogenic bacteria which give rise to such malignant diseases as consumption, cholera, typhoid fever, scarlet fever, and diphtheria' (Aikman 768); 'There is now no longer any question as to the great and continual risk of spreading disease which is run by the consumption of unboiled milk' (Frankland, 'Boiling' 454); 'Scientific authorities agree that milk is a great carrier of disease, and that nothing is more liable to pick up disease germs' (Wallace 657); and 'As an active agent in the spread of scarlet fever, diphtheria, and enteric (typhoid) fever, milk is well known, and the risks run by the public in this respect are not imaginary' (Fincham 549).

These appeals to scientific authority were frequently leavened with more colloquial – and colourful – warnings: '[Milk's] chemical composition makes it a food for bacteria as perfect as it is a food for infants' ('Sterilized Milk' 197); 'It will almost always be observed that milk when it is consumed is richer in bacteria by far than the sewage of our large cities' (Frankland, 'Milk Dangers' 469); and 'Who would not thankfully exchange ... the tumbler of dust-laden, germ-swarming milk which is handed round at our railway stations ... for a flask of milk guaranteed to be sweet and free from all contamination?' (Frankland, 'Boiling'

459). One further example deserves particular attention, since it revisits the anxieties about stagnation and superfluity that I have argued are of such importance in the Victorian imagination:

> If we consider how cows become covered with dirt and slime, that obstinately adheres to them when they wade through stagnant ponds and mud, and realise the chance thus afforded for malevolent microbes to exchange their unsavoury surroundings for so satisfactory and nourishing a material as milk, then indeed precautions of cleanliness, however troublesome, will not appear superfluous. (Frankland, 'Milk Dangers' 465–6)

Victorian reformers were concerned not just about the safety of milk, but also with the social meaning – and cost – of such a significant shift in the patterns of national food circulation. Commentators in popular periodicals warned that shipping so much milk into urban centres might starve the rural poor. The irony of country neighbours of dairy farmers suddenly unable to get milk, and having to subsist on the new-fangled product tinned condensed milk, was not lost on George Brodrick, who in 1881 lamented that 'there are many villages in which labourers cannot buy fresh milk for their children at any price, though it is often given to pigs, and Mr. Bear states that "even on farm-house tables it is not uncommon to see condensed milk all the way from Switzerland"' (296). This particular irony is analogous to the widely reviled problem of wet nurses who slowly starve their own babies in order to provide high-priced breast milk to the children of rich urbanites (an issue to which I will return shortly).

The thread that runs through all of these interlocking concerns is the conundrum of economic demand. While it is interesting to note that milk is a product brought into being entirely by consumer demand, this is not to say that the production side of the equation has no influence on that level of demand. Of course city dwellers could not have a meaningful 'demand' for liquid milk if it were simply not available to them; their desire is partially brought into being by the new possibilities of supply. The continued demand for liquid milk was not seen as unproblematic or guaranteed: commentators worried about disease, poor quality, and high prices affecting the delicate desires of comparatively dainty urban consumers. As the agricultural writer Brodrick put it, 'The consumption of milk in England might well be multiplied tenfold, and … where it is now sold by the spoonful it might be sold by the pint, if the mass of people should recover the habit of drinking it, and could rely on obtaining a regular supply at a moderate price' (295–6).

The fickle desires of finicky consumers are repeatedly invoked as a central cause of fluctuations in the dairy trade: 'The consumer is always ready to advise the farmer … But the vagaries of the consumer are strange indeed' (Wallace 657–8). One writer went so far as to imagine the consumption of dairy products as the linchpin in a self-contained and self-perpetuating economic cycle: 'The better milk is, the more will be consumed; the more there is consumed, the more cows will have to be kept, and the greater will be the resulting quantity of manure, which is the backbone and mainstay of agriculture' ('Milk' 129). The quality of dairy products affects demand, and demand affects the farmer's livelihood – therefore, the farmer must cater scrupulously to the tastes of the urban consumer. As another writer warned, 'A butterman … must have uniformity of quality in order to satisfy his customers, who of course complain, and perhaps leave him, if he sends them "strong" or rancid stuff for the "best fresh"' ('Dairy Produce' 305).

This is an anxiety we see repeatedly in *Tess*. The novel makes the new concern with the consumption end of the economic cycle explicit in several passages from the Talbothays section. Dairyman Crick, a new style of businessman from the hidebound Michael Henchard – sublimely unconcerned about the townspeople's reaction to his grown wheat – evinces a special sensitivity to the opinion of his potential consumers: 'For Heaven's sake, pop thy hands under the pump, Deb! Upon my soul, if the London folk only knowed of thee and thy slovenly ways, they'd swaller their milk and butter more mincing than they do a'ready; and that's saying a good deal' (135–6). The bottom line is the demand of the consumer – a thoroughly modern consumer who is removed from the site of production, and whose removal is only underscored by the impossible image of his somehow knowing the hygiene habits of a Wessex dairymaid. The novel reminds us again, even more forcefully, of the power of this consumer when the dairy is thrown into an uproar over a faint 'twang' of garlic in the butter: can there be any more powerful testimony to the all-mighty consumer than the image of a whole dairy's labour force on its hands and knees crawling through a mead, searching for a few strands of bitter herb?

But perhaps the most blatant evidence for this shift in economic priority is the passage where the narrator explains Crick's insistence on milking the dairy's few hardest cows himself, lest they not be thoroughly milked and eventually dry up: 'It was not the loss for the moment that made slack milking so serious, but that with the decline of demand there came decline, and ultimately cessation, of supply' (113). This off-hand statement is nearly an exact reversal of the law of effective demand that had held such sway over British political economy for the majority of the nineteenth century. Crick's concern, in metaphorical form, with the continuation of a certain level of demand is an exact replication of the new concern with consumer demand attendant upon the rise of the marginal utility school. While not a radical departure from the economic concerns of its predecessors, *Tess of the d'Urbervilles* nonetheless complicates the prevailing issues of value and correspondence with a new concern with the individualistic process of demand.[38]

The themes of individualism and demand (and even anxiety over the quality of milk) present in the novel's treatment of dairy farming are recapitulated in its descriptions of nursing. Before Tess is a dairymaid, she is of course a nursing mother – and the connection between the two kinds of 'labour' is an important one in the logic of the novel. The labour that Tess performs as a new mother, as opposed to the utopian idyll of her work at Talbothays dairy, is not particularly successful or rewarding. While the reader never learns the specific cause of death of Tess's young son, whom she baptizes 'Sorrow,' the narrator intimates that its demise is at least complicated, if not entirely caused, by malnutrition: 'The baby had been suddenly taken ill since the afternoon. Some such collapse had been probable, so tender and puny was its frame' (97).

The contemporary reader of *Tess* would certainly have associated this description with undernourishment. The public furore over wet nursing was at its height immediately before the novel's publication, and medical periodicals of the time were full of screeds decrying the selfishness of wealthy (mostly urban) mothers who bought working-class women's breast milk at the expense of the latter's babies.[39] A correspondent to the *British Medical Journal* in 1871, for example, wrote:

Why should a mother be allowed to sacrifice her child – to subject it to a slow process of disease and death – in order to make a handsome profit out of her nursing powers? And then, again, what right has a wealthy mother to purchase these services – to have her own child fed to the destruction of the infant whom her own supplants?[40]

While Tess does not work as a wet nurse, the popular image of the poor woman's baby dying through lack of nourishment is one that was etched into the popular consciousness by such debates, and would reach its full elaboration with the publication of George Moore's novel *Esther Waters* in 1894, which featured a young mother's encounter with a wicked 'baby-farmer' who offers to allow her infant to die through neglect so that she might work as a wet nurse for a wealthy family. According to Valerie Fildes's study *Wet Nursing*, a field woman like Tess would not necessarily have to be peddling her milk in order to endanger the life of her own infant:

> In the summer months, during which, in many areas, wet nurses worked hard, long hours in the fields, it is unlikely that they had a sufficient, good quality diet, or the necessary amount of rest which are essential for a good supply of milk. Also, the number of feeds they gave to the child (often only two or three times a day) would be insufficient to maintain adequate lactation, or to stimulate further milk production if their milk supply was failing. (227–8)

Even if Tess were not selling her own milk as a wet nurse, the arduousness of her labour in the fields, combined with the fact that she could only feed her baby once during the working day (the narrator explains that Tess's sister Liza-Lu must bring the infant all the way from their house to the field during Tess's one noon-day break [94–5]) would certainly have been enough to bring about the insufficiency Fildes describes.[41] In a rather bizarre passage, Hardy describes Tess nursing her child in the fields; she has just taken her noon-day break along with the other labourers, the men passing around cups of ale filled from a stone jar while they eat lunch:

> When she [Tess] had deposited herself a man in a rabbit-skin cap, and with a red handkerchief tucked into his belt, held the cup of ale over the top of the shock for her to drink. But she did not accept his offer. As soon as her lunch was spread she called up the big girl, who was her sister, Liza-Lu, and took the baby of her ... Tess, with a curiously stealthy yet courageous movement, and with a still rising colour, unfastened her frock and began suckling the child.
>
> The men who sat nearest considerately turned their faces towards the other end of the field, some of them beginning to smoke; one, with absent-minded fondness, regretfully stroking the jar that would no longer yield a stream. (95)

In addition to the suggestion that this last absent-minded field worker longs for nothing so much as to return to suckling at the breast, the passage also implies that Tess herself is 'dry': she has refused to take ale, she nurses her child, and then we are told that the stone ale jar is empty. As Alicia Carroll has noted in her discussion of the novel, Hardy's narration here seems to suggest that Tess herself 'no longer yields a stream' (182). In other words, a lack of supply due to failure of demand – of the exact nature that Dairyman Crick warns against in the milking of his cows – contributes, more or less directly, to Sorrow's demise.[42]

In addition to a problem of supply, the quality of what little milk is available to the infant during such times of privation doubtless would have been substandard. Fildes continues: 'Further evidence of the quality of milk and/or diet provided by the wet nurses is shown in the extra payments made to nurses, 1856–1900, whose foster children under 12 were diseased or infirm; the largest category for which nurses received such payments was consistently the deficiency disease rickets' (228). There was thus both a scientific and a thematic connection between mother's milk and bones. As early as 1651, medical writer Francis Glisson noted that milk had something to do with the strength and straightness of one's bones, and that a deficiency of milk in infancy was a cause of rickets (Fildes, *Breasts* 112). He also noted that rickets was more common among the rich than the poor (193) – until the nineteenth century, milk was drunk mainly by rural labourers (387), which perhaps explains the higher incidence of rickets among wealthy urban populations.[43]

Attempts to understand the etiology of rickets were haphazard throughout the seventeenth through early twentieth centuries; in fact, according to Fildes, 'bad' milk from wet nurses was often used as a scapegoat for rickets as well as other diseases (193ff). Before the metabolism theory of nutrition was promulgated in the early twentieth century it was popularly believed that the human body was made up directly of ingested materials: the calcium in milk turned into the calcium in bones (Guggenheim 99–100). Until 1912 there was no understanding of the role of vitamins in nutrition (McCollum 217), and thus no understanding of the importance of vitamin D in the absorption of calcium and the formation of a healthy skeleton. In the popular consciousness, milk equalled bones.[44]

The skeleton, in both its healthy and diseased incarnations, was an important economic metaphor for the Victorians; the thrifty use of animal bones, literally the basest level of waste product, was a figure for wise and provident economic management. As one Victorian commentator opined, 'While the Russians export or simply waste all their bones, other more thrifty people boil them, to extract their grease and gelatine; convert them into charcoal, to be used in refining sugar; pass them on to the turner, to be made into knife-handles and a thousand other useful articles; or grind them up to supply phosphate of lime for the farmer's crops' ('Rubbish' 598–9). In his 1853 essay 'The Circulation of Matter' (which I discuss in more detail in the introduction), chemist F.W. Johnston also turns to exotic examples of bodily thrift: 'The priests at Leon, in Nicaragua, sell the burial-ground around their churches for the use of their occupants for periods of from ten to twenty-five years, "at the end of which time the bones, with the earth around them, are removed, and sold to the manufacturers of nitre"' (550). An early-century Swiftian parody of misers, 'Elements of Save-all-ism,' takes this waste-not advice one step further by bringing it home to England: 'The human carcase is a valuable mass of materials, and ought not to be suffered to undergo a useless decomposition in a deep grave' (527). Most valuable of all are the skeletons of the dearly departed: 'Professor Bumgroschen states himself to be an economical osteologist, and converts the bones of the departed into a material for fertilizing the land ... "By adopting this manure, we shall obtain double crops; famine will become an obsolete term, and the land will flow with milk and honey"' (529). Not only does milk build bones, but bones can even create milk! While the author's desire here is to mock the overly thrifty, miserly impulse that is at odds with consumption, he does not stray far from the age-old physiocratic fantasy of a self-contained economy without waste – in this case, bones. This sentiment is echoed nearly fifty years later by Johnston: 'As we have no property in, so we ought to have no foolish affection or reverence for dead ashes; and certainly we ought to have no fear that they can ever long be withheld from connecting themselves, in some form or other, with new phases of vegetable and animal life' (558).

Decades later, John Ruskin also uses the figure of the skeleton to critique prevalent economic thought. While excoriating the classical model, which assumes a heuristic rational economic agent and then deduces all its insights from this dubious starting point, he imagines the flip-side of economic man – what we might call 'boneless man.' The passage is worth quoting in full:

> Observe, I neither impugn nor doubt the conclusions of the science if its terms are accepted. I am simply uninterested in them, as I should be in those of a science of gymnastics which assumed that men had no skeletons.

It might be shown, on that supposition, that it would be advantageous to roll the students up into pellets, flatten them into cakes, or stretch them into cables; and that when these results were effected, the re-insertion of the skeleton would be attended with various inconveniences to their constitution. The reasoning might be admirable, the conclusions true, and the science deficient only in applicability. Modern political economy stands on a precisely similar basis. Assuming, not that the human being has no skeleton, but that it is all skeleton, it founds an ossifiant theory of progress on this negation of a soul; and having shown the utmost that may be made of bones, and constructed a number of interesting geometrical figures with death's-head and humeri, successfully proves the inconvenience of the reappearance of a soul among these corpuscular structures. I do not deny the truth of this theory: I simply deny its applicability to the present phase of the world. (*Works* 17:26)

Ruskin here opposes the skeletal (the selfish, rational, 'economic' impulse) to the spiritual (fellow feeling, sympathy, and Christian charity). We can see here the economic analogue to the opposition that Hardy locates within his own characters, between a deathly moral pressure to judge and condemn and a life-affirming impulse toward forgiveness and new beginnings. Ruskin puts this same bones-soul opposition to work in an explicitly economic context.

We might say that the very infrastructure of *Tess of the d'Urbervilles* is a bony one: the thematic skeleton of the novel is skeletons. We are invited to think of Mr Durbeyfield in terms of his bones from the second sentence of the novel, quoted earlier: 'The pair of legs that carried him were rickety, and there was a bias in his gait which inclined him somewhat to the left of a straight line' (13). Immediately after this description of Tess's father as ricketic – as having particularly problematic bones – he learns of his noble ancestry from the passing parson and proudly declares, 'And to think that I and these noble d'Urbervilles were one flesh all the time ... There's not a man in the county o' South-Wessex that's got grander and nobler skillentons in his family than I' (16). Durbeyfield immediately makes a connection between the bones in the family vault and his own (they are 'one flesh,' yet of course his ancestors are now pointedly fleshless), a droll bit of irony given that we have just been told he is ricketic. The irony is, however, an important one, borne out by the novel's persistent fascination with skeletons – as well as its suspicion of the value of noble family lineage. In fact, the bones in the vault turn out to be worthless; they garner Durbeyfield and his family precisely nothing in terms of prestige, fungible inheritance, or even luck. While Durbeyfield's association of his own crooked bones with his ancestors' reads as structural irony, it in fact makes sense that he would conflate the mouldering markers of a useless inheritance with his own rickety frame.

In fact, the Durbeyfields almost never think of their newly discovered ancestors as anything other than 'skillentons,' as bones in the 'gr't-family-vault-at-Kingsbere' (20). One of the few times Tess is invited to contemplate her ancestors as something other than corpses is on her honeymoon in a 'fine manorial residence' that had been 'the property and seat of a d'Urberville' (214). She and Angel come across the disturbing and unpleasant portraits of her female forbears: 'The long pointed features, narrow eye, and smirk of the one, so suggestive of merciless treachery; the bill-hook nose, large teeth, and bold eye of the other, suggesting arrogance to the point of ferocity' are unfortunately still visible in Tess's 'fine features' (215). Again, the disquieting bones of the d'Urbervilles, with their long, pointy skulls and prominent teeth, mock the pretensions to gentility of a humble Durbeyfield. Both Tess and Angel are discomfited by the traced resemblance; the memory of those unpleasant skulls seems to haunt Tess later when in a burst of despair and self-loathing she feels the edges of her own eye-sockets and imagines a time 'when that bone would be bare' (270).

As if the link between skeletal remains and the burdens of history were not clear enough, Durbeyfield himself explicitly makes the connection when he boasts once again about his 'folk lying there ... as genuine county bones and marrow as any recorded in history' (252). The rather gruesome repetition of skeletal metaphors, which are always associated with the paternal, d'Urbervillean strand of the novel, signals another way in which the maternal thematic – milk, sustenance, nurture – is privileged in the logic of the narrative: without milk, bones are impossible. It is not mere coincidence that the two substances most consistently associated with the dual 'inheritances' at work in Tess's history, maternal milk and paternal bones, share an organic connection. They also share an important metaphorical burden: the rickety nature of the paternal skeleton calls into question the social imperative – 'the resolve to separate from her' – that Angel found 'standing in its bones' the morning after his bride's confession. Yet as I have already insisted, the maternal side of the causative structure, while not foregrounded by the narrator, is just as important a determinant of tragedy in the logic of the plot. The individualist impulse in the novel, the life-affirming, free-flowing 'appetite for joy,' is a force about which the novel is deeply conflicted: the very concept of 'appetite' in *Tess* is one fraught with ambiguity and danger.

Just as the knowledge that the credit economy is dependent upon the efficacy of promises-to-pay engenders a certain anxiety about correspondence and readability in the earlier novels I discussed, so in *Tess* this new sensitivity to the role of consumer demand in economic equilibrium inaugurates a new set of concerns. The scenes which insist upon the importance of demand are marked by a nagging anxiety, a sense of imminent chaos – invading germs, rank produce, dried-up cows – that have almost the eloquence of biblical plagues. The anxiety demonstrated by a depiction of the demand function is no less acute than the anxiety attendant upon unstable value correspondences.

In its restless shifting back and forth between diametrically opposed models of causation, *Tess of the d'Urbervilles* attempts to negotiate between these two visions of chaos. The novel begins by dividing the source of causation into two realms – the socio-historical associated with Tess's paternal inheritance, and the natural, bodily, and individualistic associated with the maternal – and then proceeds to privilege the explanatory force of the former even as the events of the plot bear out the (greater) importance of the latter. Those events which bear witness to the importance of the individual are intimately bound up with the novel's depiction of political economy; it seems that because the consequences of a new economic focus on demand are so uncertain, so chaotic, the narratorial insistence on the d'Urbervillean strain of the historical and social are maintained. It is with a redoubled vigour that the novel brings these forces to bear on its hapless heroine; Tess is sacrificed by her narrative as surely as the other perverse 'economists' we have examined. It is Tess's great sin to embody – quite literally – the novel's experiment in individual responsibility and the internalization of social and ethical imperatives; in her case, then, this sacrifice takes on a special new valence.

6 Giving No Sign or Sound: The Internalization of Closure in *Tess*

Just as with the other processes in the novel – work, economy, historical causation – Tess as character internalizes and makes personal the imperative of narrative closure. This internalization takes the form of an impulse to self-sacrifice and an urge to self-destruction: the plot's 'death drive' or movement toward closure is refigured as Tess's own eagerness to die.[45] The novel initially signals this figuration in a curious passage wherein Tess wonders about the date of her own death:

> She suddenly thought one afternoon, when looking in the glass at her fairness, that there was yet another date ... that of her own death, when all these charms would have disappeared; a day which lay sly and unseen among all the other days of the year, giving no sign or sound when she annually passed over it. (102)

The two events, death and narrative closure, are coterminous: the very last event related by the novel is the raising of the black flag indicating Tess's execution. Tess's suicidal desires are her own 'narrative impulse'; as we saw earlier, her instinct of self-preservation (her initial silence about her past) is at odds with this impulse to narrate (her inability not to relate her history). The historical, knightly d'Urberville in her wins out, and by so winning claims as its victim our heroine.

Hardy's conflation of closure and death in this novel is indicated by his insistence on undermining the usual horizon of the Victorian novel – the marriage for love. Our appetite for this ending is whetted not simply by the weight of novelistic convention which demands it (although this is certainly the main contributing factor). The narrator himself encourages this expectation when he describes the aftermath of Angel's first declaration to Tess (the moment that is described repeatedly as occurring beyond the range of vision of Dairyman Crick):

> In the interval since Crick's last view of them something had occurred which changed the pivot of the universe for their two natures; something which, had he known its quality, the dairyman would have despised, as a practical man; yet which was based upon a more stubborn and resistless tendency than a whole heap of so-called practicalities. A veil had been whisked aside; the tract of each one's outlook was to have a new horizon thenceforward – for a short time or for a long. (154)

A 'new horizon' is herein invoked: the horizon of closure intersecting with the trajectory of love and bourgeois marriage. This new horizon comes into being through the workings of that natural force, the 'stubborn and resistless' regenerative/sexual impulse, which is explicitly opposed to the realm of 'practicality' represented here, momentarily, by Dairyman Crick – and presumably also to the realm of the paternal and historical which would demand a marriage based on lineage and social class.

Hardy is invoking a whole set of expectations here, dealing with romantic love, the irresistibility of sexual attraction, the moral superiority of marriages based on affection rather than practicalities, the proper ending of a novel. And yet there is a deep irony here: it is the realm of Dairyman Crick which will ultimately hold sway in the logic of the narrative, attractive as its alternative may be. The marriage of Tess and Angel is a false ending, a foreshortened horizon, a perspectival mistake: the real ending must wait for the 'lost horizon' of 'landscape beyond landscape' beyond the hill of St Catherine – the false martyr – and the prison where Tess is hanged. It is for Dairyman Crick's style of narration to prevail: 'Dairyman Crick's stories often seemed to be ended when they were really not so, and strangers were often betrayed into premature interjections of finality; though old friends knew better. The narrator went on ...' (138).

The narrator does go on, in *Tess*, to quite a new sort of ending. The many false marriages in the novel (the 'natural' marriage to Alec, the marriage-in-name to Angel, the re-'marriage' to Alec, the 're-marriage' to Angel) are so many false endings, so many ironic rehearsals for the real ending of sacrifice that Tess herself effects. She is a 'good girl,' as Angel comments at one point, and her goodness extends even to the point of shouldering the burden that Hetty, Maggie, and Henchard all demanded their narrators accept: her own elimination. It is Tess's unique function to straddle the worlds of mid-century economic imperatives, associated with horrors of surplus and dreams of a self-contained economy, and the new regime of the demand function, with its tension between 'average man' and the importunate desires of the individual. In *Tess* the internalization process we have seen operating throughout the novel, signalling the era of the new economic agent, the desiring consumer – both lauded and reviled – has begun.

Notes

Introduction: Demand; or, the Cephalopod

1 I have in mind here particularly Gagnier's *Insatiability of Human Wants*, Gallagher's *Body Economic*, and Poovey's *Genres of the Credit Economy*. I will discuss these works, as well as many other important and influential recent studies in this vein, elsewhere throughout this book.

2 The denial of private ownership is an idea to which Johnston returns repeatedly in his essay: for example, he reminds us that molecular materials are 'never really the property of any, and never linger ... long in one stay' (553); and '[a]s we have not property in, so we ought to have no foolish affection or reverence for dead ashes' (558); etc.

3 One might argue that Sol and Cuttle's inability to lay immediate hands on cash is one of the indications of their moral superiority to Dombey, who of course has plenty of liquid assets. Certainly the narrator hovers lovingly over the objects in the instrument-maker's shop and returns obsessively to the quaint mementoes weighing down Cuttle's pockets. Yet it is this very sentimentality, I would argue, that marks these 'goods' as problematic, troubling, in need of explanation and assimilation. At the very least, they brand Sol as (in his own words) 'old-fashioned, and behind the time' (142).

4 Indeed, 'hoarding' of products other than currency was, according to Ruskin, beneficial and even necessary under certain strictly controlled conditions:

> There ought to be government establishments for every trade ... At these government manufactories the discipline should be strict, and the wages steady, not varying at all in proportion to the demand for the article, but only in proportion to the price of food; the commodities produced being laid up in store to meet sudden demands, and

sudden fluctuations in price prevented ... When there was a visible tendency to produce a glut of any commodity, that tendency should be checked by directing the youth at the government schools into other trades; and the yearly surplus of commodities should be the principal means of government provisions for the poor. (*Works* 16:112–13).

Note, however, that even as Ruskin is endorsing the idea of accumulation, it is still in the interest of managing – and avoiding – potential gluts, which seem to be his central concern here.

5 It is tempting to read this passage as an echo of Thomas Carlyle's sardonic query in *Sartor Resartus*: 'Are we Opossums; have we natural Pouches, like the Kangaroo? Or how, without Clothes, could we possess the master-organ, soul's seat, and true pineal gland of the Body Social: I mean, a PURSE?' (43–4).

6 *Fors Clavigera*, vol. 1 (1871), letter 5, 'The White-Thorn Blossom.' In *Works* 27:80. Compare the use of the aquatic-creature metaphor in the work of feminist writer Frances Power Cobbe:

What reason can be alleged, in the first place, why the male of the human species, and particularly the male of the finest variety of that species, should be the only animal in creation which maltreats its mate, or any female of its own kind?* [footnote:] *With the exception, perhaps, of the Seal. Mr. Darwin gives a sad picture of amphibious conjugal life: 'As soon as a female reaches the shore ('comes out,' as we should say in 'society'), the nearest male goes down to meet her and coaxes her, until he gets between her and the water so that she cannot escape him. Then his manner changes, and with a harsh growl he drives her to a place in his harem.' – *Descent of Man*, vol. ii. p. 269. What an 'o'er true tale' is this of many a human wooing and of what comes later; the 'bowing and coaxing' first, and the 'harsh growl' afterwards! I am surprised Mr. Darwin did not derive from it an argument for the Descent of Man from the Seal. (56)

7 For a discussion of the meaning of Lydgate's desire to 'collect' Rosamond, see Wormald, 'Microscopy and Semiotic in *Middlemarch*,' esp. 506.

8 For seminal discussions of the ideology of Victorian household management and motherhood, see, for example, Armstrong; Homans, *Bearing the Word*; Poovey, *Uneven Developments*; and Davidoff and Hall.

9 This rhetoric has its roots in the eighteenth century (and earlier); as Mac-Kenzie notes in his study *Be It Ever So Humble*:

The poor embody, for example, the available supply of surplus labor – labor whose yield is surplus value – so essential to increased wealth.

From Quesnay on, surplus value had become a central tenet of political economy. The abstraction of labor required for such a model enables a conception of the poor as a reservoir of labor in potential – labor that is deferred and not yet used up. Over this supply the poor woman has several kinds of influence: She is its source – literally its mother ... she is a manager – 'when a labourer is thus blessed with a frugal, industrious, and intelligent wife, he shews his attachment and good sense by leaving all domestic concerns to her prudent and superior management' (Cowe 86); she is an educator – 'as teachers ... British women had established a newly prominent social role by the beginning of the nineteenth century' (A. Richardson 167); and she provides the laborer with the object for which he strives and aspires – 'he who does not make his family comfortable, will himself never be happy at home; and he who is not happy at home, will never be happy anywhere' (Bernard 284). (MacKenzie)

10 Of course, women are figured just as consistently as objects of exchange in the Victorian novel. For example, in Dickens's *Dombey and Son*, the narrator rhetorically asks: 'But what was a girl to Dombey and Son! In the capital of the House's name and dignity, such a child was merely a piece of base coin that couldn't be invested' (13). Yet the trajectory of the plot is oriented toward the transformation of Florence Dombey from object of exchange to household manager: the moral pressure of the novel demands that her father learn to accept her as economic agent. I discuss a similar process in *The Mayor of Casterbridge* in chapter 4.

11 Thomas DeQuincey, a nominal Ricardian who became much more critical of the tenets of laissez-faire capitalism in the 1840s, employs a similar image to describe the 'natural' workings of free-flowing capital:

If our human vision were fitted for detecting agencies so impalpable, and if a station of view could be had, we might sometimes behold vast arches of electric matter continually passing and repassing between either pole and the equatorial regions. Accordingly as the equilibrium were disturbed suddenly or redressed, would be the phenomena of tropical hurricanes, or of auroral lights. Somewhat in the same silent arches of continual transition, ebbing and flowing like tides, do the re-agencies of the capital accumulated in London modify, without sound or echo, much commerce in all parts of the kingdom. Faithful to the monetary symptoms, and the fluctuations this way or that, eternally perceptible in the condition of every trade, the great moneyed capitalist standing at the centre of this enormous web, throws over his arch of capital or withdraws it, with the precision of a fireman directing

> columns of water from an engine upon the remotest quarter of a con-
> flagration. (170)

For DeQuincey, the process seems more ejaculatory (or mictatory?) than
lactational, but the recourse to an image of bodily processes is striking.
Also of interest is the vision of the 'moneyed capitalist' as omniscient
narrator, standing in the centre of a vast 'web' whose full operations are
visible only from his vantage point – an image that George Eliot would
doubtless appreciate.

12 Of course the Victorian 'virgin-whore' dichotomy is a commonplace, and
    not only for modern readers; its pervasiveness was also visible to contem-
    porary feminists like Frances Power Cobbe:

> Stripped of the euphemisms of courtesy with which we generally
> wrap them up, it cannot be denied that the sentiments of a very large
> number of men towards women consist of a wretched alternation of
> exaggerated and silly homage, and of no less exaggerated and foolish
> contempt. One moment on a pedestal, the next in the mire; the woman
> is adored while she gives pleasure, despised the moment she ceases to
> do so. (63, n.)

My goal here is not to retrace well-known arguments about Victorian
womanhood *tout court*, or about the hypocrisy of nineteenth-century attitudes toward female sexuality, or even about the ideology of the 'separate spheres.' It is, instead, to consider the very specific – and heretofore
unexamined – intersection among Victorian ideologies of womanhood, the
rhetoric of classical political economy, and the novel.

13 There have been many insightful studies of the relationship between the
    development of capitalism and the novel. Some of the authors whose
    works have most influenced and helped me are Patrick Brantlinger, Jeff
    Nunokawa, and Regenia Gagnier. At the time of the original composition
    of this study, however, there had been no sustained analysis of political
    economy and the form of the novel. In the interim, Gallagher's *The Body
    Economic* and Poovey's *Genres of the Credit Economy* appeared in print; I
    discuss several important aspects of both arguments in the chapter that
    follows. As will become clear, I have quite strenuous objections to the
    methodology and conclusions of Poovey's work.

14 I discuss the work of the physiocrats at greater length in chapter 1.

15 See Backhouse and Medema for a discussion of the provenance of the
    term.

16 See Sowell, *Classical* 21–4.

17 Whether or not the writers were fair or just in these characterizations of
    Smith and Ricardo is another issue; see Henderson 37. For a representa-

tive late-Victorian discussion of the waning of classical laissez-faire, see
Foxwell's 1887 article 'The Economic Movement in England': 'Every one
can see that *laissez faire*, formerly a foregone conclusion, is now scarcely
even a presumption' (101–2), and 'The teaching which was supposed to be
summed up in the doctrine of *laissez faire* fell into hopeless discredit' (87).
I discuss the relationship between the marginal utility school and laissez-
faire toward the end of the first chapter.

18 This is an attitude that, incredibly, persists well into the twentieth century.
As former U.S. Federal Reserve chairman Alan Greenspan opines in a
book coauthored with Ayn Rand, 'The gold standard is an instrument of
laissez-faire and ... each implies and requires the other' (101). As this quotation implies, he strongly advocates the resumption of specie convertibility.

19 Only one other literary critic, as far as I can ascertain, has discussed the
fact that the demand theory of value was inaugurated by Malthus in
the early decades of the nineteenth century. Gordon Bigelow writes: 'A
number of writers in the 1820s argued, against Smith and Ricardo, that
exchange value was wholly unconnected with the larger system of production and exchange, and was a function only of consumer demand. The central figure of this reaction was Malthus' (59–60). One of the main concerns
of Bigelow's study *Fiction, Famine, and the Rise of Economics in Victorian
Britain and Ireland* is the 'odd precursor[s] to neoclassical economics' (4),
which means that he is attentive to the appearances of demand theories of
value throughout the century. I will discuss other aspects of his very helpful study in subsequent chapters.

20 Feminine, or most precisely, feminized, sexuality is not exclusively confined to women, as my chapter on *The Mayor of Casterbridge* will attempt to
demonstrate.

21 As Poovey goes on to say, she does examine some reviews of Martineau
and Charles Reade's work elsewhere in her study, but she does not use
them to generate interpretations of texts based on contemporary readers'
sense of the aesthetic successes or failures of these works. Furthermore,
when she at last turns to her own readings of novels, she specifically disavows this reading technique in favour of 'historical description.' For a
recent article on Martineau that includes a thorough discussion of her contemporary reviews (an article that Poovey for some reason does not cite),
see Annette Van, 'Realism, Speculation, and the Gold Standard in Harriet
Martineau's *Illustrations of Political Economy.*'

22 I am indebted to Walsh and Gram's *Classical and Neoclassical Theories of
General Equilibrium* (15) for introducing me to this helpful distinction, and
to the work of Schumpeter in general.

23 As Gillian Beer points out in the introduction to her *Darwin's Plots*, in the case of a hugely influential paradigm such as natural selection – or, I would argue, classical political economy – 'Who had read what does not fix limits' (6). As she goes on to claim, however, a richer and more nuanced exploration is possible when one confines one's study to those novelists whom we know to have read the works in question; this is another reason I have limited my analysis to novels by Eliot and Hardy.

1 Popular Demand: Surplus and Stagnation in Nineteenth-Century Political Economy

1 As one historian puts it, 'classical economists' analysis of the process by which capital, technology and labour grow over time led them to a common conclusion, motivated by different causes – that the process of economic growth was gradually self-attenuating and ended in a state of stagnation (the "stationary state")' (Cameron). As I will discuss later in this chapter, while the Ricardians and their critics take different paths to get there, both groups ultimately reach the same destination: stagnation.

2 Although a detailed reception history of this law is beyond the scope of this chapter, I will briefly note its most salient points. First is the question of the general applicability of Say's Law to a static economic model. Most modern economists consider the law to hold true for barter economies, where it is consonant with Walras's Law, a general equilibrium postulate formulated later in the century by Léon Walras, one of the leading lights of the marginal utility school. However, it runs aground when money is introduced: essentially, an 'over-demand' for money (the kind of hoarding Ruskin warns against, as discussed in the introduction) can create a glut or oversupply of goods. Second is the question of applicability over time: the mainstream consensus among historians is that while the version of the law later termed 'Say's Identity' – that there can never be a general glut at any time – is not true, the version termed 'Say's Equality' – that there cannot be general gluts in the long run – is true. In other words, Say was wrong in the short run but correct in the long run, wrong for monetary economies but correct for barter ones. This is of course a gross simplification; the question of where one stands on Say's Law and the possibility of underconsumption is something of a litmus test for one's economic (and political) philosophies, just as it was in the nineteenth century. Few economic principles have garnered such heated debate over the years: for a recent overview of opinions, see Kates's edited volume *Two Hundred Years of Say's Law*. More important for my purposes, much of the modern

discussion of the Malthus-Ricardo debate on general gluts has focused on the question of who interpreted which version of Say's Law in what way, and thus who deserves to be vindicated for getting the question right. See Blaug, *Economic* 143–71; Davis; Maclachlan; and Sowell, 'The General Glut Controversy Reconsidered' and *Classical* 35–52.

3 Malthus did support the principle of free trade in the abstract, but with important conditions that put him squarely at odds with the mainstream Ricardian laissez-faire theorists. Beyond simply advocating humanitarian government intervention as a corrective to the depredations of rampant money-getting, he also questioned, on a deeper theoretical level, the notion that the principle of capital accumulation would necessarily lead to the fairest or even best social organization. See Winch's discussion in his study *Malthus* 59–61, 76–7.

4 This omission, I believe, is due to the fact that Gallagher has chosen – for obvious reasons – to focus on the Malthus of *The Essay on Population*, who foresees the day when there are too many people and not enough food, as opposed to the Malthus of the *Principles*, who worries about general gluts of commodities. She goes on to delineate some of the other 'lost' strains of Malthusian thought in her Afterword, but does not dwell on the implications of 'Malthus's chief concerns – defense of unproductive consumption, respect for empirical data, and advocacy of the stimulating effects of government spending' (189) that are the very corollaries of the demand function that interest me. She does note that marginal utility theory 'absorbed important elements of Malthus's bioeconomical thought without leaving any lasting interdisciplinary residue' and that 'Malthus's critique of the orthodox theory of value ... was read by Jevons as an argument for the priority of demand, and as such it partly inspired his reformation of the discipline' (188–9), but she does not attend to the actual sources of the 'priority of demand' and fears of underconsumption in Malthus himself. For a helpful reconsideration of the debate between Malthus and Ricardo, see Maclachlan, 'The Ricardo-Malthus Debate on Underconsumption.'

5 For summaries of the work of the physiocrats, see Vaggi, *The Economics of François Quesnay*; M. Beer, *An Inquiry into Physiocracy*; and Walsh and Gram 18–44. The beginning sections of Marx's *Theories of Surplus Value* are also quite helpful.

6 This exact phrase was never used by Say himself (in any language), but it has become almost a slogan for those advocating a hands-off approach to economic intervention. According to Steven Kates, the phrase has its origins in the work of John Stuart Mill but was coined by John Maynard

Keynes, a sharp critic of (his characterization of) the Law. See Kates's article '"Supply Creates Its Own Demand"' for a fuller discussion.

7 All quotations throughout are from Malthus's *Principles of Political Economy* unless otherwise noted.

8 Malthus's exact position on the question of value has been something of a vexed issue for his modern exegetes. One common interpretation is that Malthus became converted to the labour theory of value in his *Measure of Value* (1823) and maintained this position in the second (posthumous) edition of the *Principles* (1836). This is the interpretation forwarded by, among others, V.E. Smith and, more recently, John Pullen, in the introduction to the Variorum edition of Malthus's *Principles of Political Economy*. However, as Christopher Herbert points out, while Malthus accepts with qualifications the notion that labour commanded can serve as an index of value, he rejects Ricardo's claim that a commodity's value is directly equivalent to the value of the labour expended in its production. Furthermore, as Herbert claims, 'All Malthus's subsequent argument hinges upon the proposition that measurable relative value is a function not of labor but of desire' (119–20).

9 Hilton takes a somewhat different view of this issue in Malthus's work; according to his account, Malthus 'did not prescribe measures to stimulate demand for productive labour,' emphasizing instead economic self-restraint and 'diminishing production, both of people and of things' (*Age* 70). This is one way of resolving the seeming paradox in Malthus's work between warnings of overpopulation and a fear of underconsumption. However, as I think I have demonstrated, Malthus was quite concerned to examine ways in which consumer demand, particularly among 'unproductive' consumers, might be stimulated and encouraged. (Thus yielding another possible solution to the paradox: geometrically increasing numbers of the poorer classes will not provide the kind of consumption necessary to stave off gluts.) This is the dimension of Malthusian thought that Christopher Herbert emphasizes in his discussion (116–28).

10 For a good overview of the two sides of the debate, and a very convincing argument that Malthus did not believe that savings equalled investment, see John Pullen's discussion in the *New Palgrave Dictionary of Economics*.

11 Important questions regarding the specifics of these claims are still under discussion by historians of economic thought: Was Malthus employing a long-run or short-term model? Dynamic or static? Could uninvested savings include money that was simply hoarded, or did they simply reflect a time lag before suitable investments could be found? The settlement of these questions does not, as I trust I have shown, affect the larger point

that Malthus was deeply pessimistic about the self-regulating capacity of the economic system.

12 It could be argued that this is a somewhat uncharacteristic thread of utilitarian thinking in Malthus: a contradiction in the desires of the worker between the 'disutility' of work and the ultimate 'utility' of consumption.

13 Herbert also sees this principle at work in Malthus's earlier *Essay on Population*, wherein even the famous Malthusian will to procreate is checked by human beings' fundamental laziness. See Herbert 111–16.

14 Adam Smith, *Wealth of Nations* 2.2.2.19, quoted in Malthus, *Principles of Political Economy* 468.

15 See Hilton, *Age* 64–70.

16 As I noted earlier, while I agree with Gallagher's isolation of a strain of heterodox economic writing from Malthus through to Ruskin and Dickens, my sense of the sources of that critique is somewhat different. While Gallagher makes the very helpful point that 'although [Malthus] certainly feared overpopulation, he gave (at least in the first edition of the *Essay*) no definition of value that can distinguish it from flesh,' and therefore 'Malthus was the originator of the very sentiments that Ruskin thought of as *anti*-Malthusian when rhetorically connecting economic and bodily health through etymology' (88), she does not, again, discuss Malthus's underconsumptionism or fear of gluts, which is the similarity with Ruskin that most interests me here.

17 See, in particular, Austin, Fain, Shell, and Sherburne. Klaver's *A/Moral Economics* contains a particularly helpful discussion of the moral and ethical dimensions of Ruskin's economic critique.

18 I have included here only two emblematic moments from Ruskin's oeuvre. It would probably be impossible to count the number of times he excoriates the 'law of supply and demand'; he criticizes it liberally and frequently, in works on topics as disparate as architectural theory, female education, the hiring of servants, and iron-mongering. He nicely summarizes his career-long battle against this 'law' in an 1873 letter to the editor of the *Scotsman*: 'I have simply stated that ... no "law of supply and demand," as expounded by Professor Hodgson and modern economists, ever did or can exist' (*Works* 17:503). See also *Fors Clavigera*, vol. 1, Letter 11 (*Works* 27:192ff.)

19 Craig also considers how Ruskin's ethics of consumption influences his theory of value, and vice versa: 'Instead of grounding "effectual value" in "intrinsic value" as he appears to do, a better, and indeed, a more accurate reading of his ethics of consumption takes "effectual value" as the regulative concept. This reformulation makes "intrinsic value" a matter of

the considered judgments of individuals actively seeking out good lives for themselves and others through certain cultural activities' (286–7).

20 For Ruskin, discussions of the ethics of consumption and the proper role of the artist and workman bleed into one another; he often refers to paintings, architecture, and literature as products whose 'supply and demand' should also be regulated by the same ethical principles he discusses in relation to more mundane products like iron, cloth, or crops. A full discussion is beyond the scope of this chapter, but significant discussions of the ethics of the demand for art may be found in the following passages: *Works* 14:121–2; 16:82; 16:151; 16:438 (on mechanical modes of production); 17:390; 20:26; 22:471; 34:276 (demand for fiction); 36:25 (demand for literature); and, of course, throughout *The Stones of Venice*, but particularly the following passages: 9:289–90; 10:103–4; 11:15–17.

21 Indeed, as a much later commentator on Ruskin's political economy opines: 'If consumption is thus all-important, we find, working backwards, that production is to be judged by the consumption to which it leads' (Devas 31). Thus Ruskinian principles are enshrined by the marginal utility theorists writing at the end of the century (I discuss this phenomenon more fully in the following paragraphs).

22 This comment is part of a longer diatribe against John Stuart Mill and Ricardo regarding the demand for labour: 'The most curious error in Mr. Mill's entire work, (provided for him originally by Ricardo,) is his endeavour to distinguish between direct and indirect service, and the consequent assertion that a demand for commodities is not a demand for labour' (*Works* 17:102). For another treatment of the same question, see the longer discussion in *Fors Clavigera* (*Works* 27:31ff.).

23 For fuller overviews of the reaction among 'orthodox' political economists to Ruskin's work, see Fain, Rosenberg, and Spear.

24 The modern commentator James Sherburne concurs with these fin-de-siècle sentiments; according to him, Ruskin's insights have 'been incorporated into the fabric of professional economics. They include his emphasis on demand as a determinant of price; his awareness of psychological factors in changing currency values, his rejection of the gold standard; and his view of currency as an instrument to be "managed" for prosperity' (124). For a summary of other Ruskinian influences on later economists, see Henderson 27–8, 37–40. Henderson goes even further than Sherburne in noting that Ruskin's views were 'vindicated by the social legislation which was initiated at the turn of the century. His works, celebrated in two centenary events, were then seen to have this "reservoir" of ideas relevant to the reform of capitalist society along lines determined by wider notions of social welfare' (38–9).

25 In her recent study *Genres of the Credit Economy*, Poovey makes a sharp
    distinction between the writers she terms economic theorists and those
    she terms economic journalists (or popularizers). (See 221–3 and 243–7.)
    This distinction, while important for Poovey's overall discussion of the
    development of economics as a profession, seems to me both artificial and
    not entirely necessary. A writer like Ruskin, for example, does not fit neatly
    into either camp; while he tackled head-on the theories of writers whom
    Poovey would consider 'professional,' such as John Stuart Mill, he was
    never taken entirely seriously by those he continually attacked. Moreover,
    he was quite a popular writer, especially among the middle classes. I am
    primarily interested in the 'public mind' of these classes, since it is from
    these ranks that the authors I discuss, and their readers, are drawn. Thus
    while I use the term 'popularizer' throughout this study, I do not mean
    thereby to imply a sharp distinction between different types of pre-1870
    economic writing.

26 See Gordon's two helpful overviews of the debates in the economic jour-
    nals: 'Criticism of Ricardian Views on Value and Distribution in the British
    Periodicals, 1820–1850' and 'Say's Law, Effective Demand, and the Con-
    temporary British Periodicals, 1820–1850.' Historian Frank W. Fetter goes
    even further, claiming that it is in the columns of the *Quarterly Review* and
    Blackwood's Magazine, 'and not in the writings of Malthus, that one finds
    in the 1820s and 1830s the most consistent exposition of the idea that the
    operations of demand do not automatically guarantee full employment' .
    ('Economic' 436).

27 In her article 'DeQuincey, Malthus, and the Anachronism-Effect,' McDon-
    agh supplements this analysis with a description of DeQuincey's calls for
    luxurious expenditure among the poorer classes as a way of propping up
    the economy (74–5) – a distinctly Malthusian recommendation, as I have
    shown. However, McDonagh oddly characterizes this strain in DeQuincey
    as counter to his Malthusian leanings; by attending only to the Malthus of
    the *Essay on Population* (there are too many poor) and not to the Malthus of
    the *Principles* (we are in danger of gluts), McDonagh misses a golden op-
    portunity to make her case for DeQuincey's Malthusianism even stronger.

28 He also notes that historians of economics – with the notable exception of
    Mark Blaug – have consistently and erroneously characterized DeQuincey
    as a staunch Ricardian throughout his career.

29 Quoted in Hilton, *Age* 65.

30 For an excellent discussion of the popular reception of the 'laws' of politi-
    cal economy in the nineteenth century, see Freedgood's article 'Banishing
    Panic' and Klaver, esp. 53–77.

31 This is a matter of some controversy. For historians who believe that

Ricardianism is in abeyance by the 1830s, see Fetter, 'The Rise and Decline
of Ricardian Economics,' and Meek, 'The Decline in Ricardian Economics in England.' For those who stress the ongoing influence of Ricardo
through 1870 – the position I myself agree with, as I assume has become
clear – see Blaug, *Ricardian Economics*; Hollander, *The Economics of David
Ricardo*; and of course Keynes. Fetter, in particular, is quite scathing of
those who claim that Ricardian value theory – in particular, his neglect of
effective demand – was the dominant force in pre-1870 British political
economy, or that Ricardo's debate with Malthus over Say's Law was the
defining disagreement of nineteenth-century British economic theory. (He
blames Keynes for latching onto this reading and influencing a subsequent
generation of historians.) However, as Fetter himself acknowledges, it is
John Stuart Mill who was one of the greatest promulgators of this reading,
which clearly had enough sway pre-Keynes that Stanley Jevons, one of the
first generation of marginal utility theorists, was to write in 1879:

> When at length the true system of Economics comes to be established,
> it will be seen that that able but wrong-headed man, David Ricardo,
> shunted the car of Economic science on to a wrong line, a line, how-
> ever, on which it was further urged towards confusion by his equally
> able and wrong-headed admirer John Stuart Mill. There were econo-
> mists, such as Malthus and Senior, who had a far better comprehen-
> sion of the true doctrines (although not free of Ricardian errors), but
> they were driven out of the field by the unity and influence of the
> Ricardo-Mill school. (*Theory* lvii)

Fetter also admits, confusingly: 'When Schumpeter wrote that in 1831 "it
is clear that Ricardianism was ... no longer a living force," he must have
had in mind the Ricardianism of this formal model, and not the Ricardianism that inspired the Bank Act of 1844, contributed to the repeal of the
Corn Laws two years later, or according to Keynes "conquered England
as completely as the Holy Inquisition conquered Spain"' (Fetter, 'Rise'
78), thus contradicting his own argument by acknowledging the ongoing
importance of the Ricardian model after 1831. Given these inconsistencies,
and the fact that I am particularly interested, in this study, in what the
Victorians themselves (e.g., Mill and Jevons) saw as the leading economic
questions of the day, I see no reason to revise my reading based on Fetter's
claims.

32 I have in mind Hilton's discussion of economists William Whewell and
Richard Jones, who on the one hand believed that the 'facts of life, *once
properly ascertained,* would assuredly illuminate the wit and wisdom of the
deity' and that 'apparent evils would show up in their true if paradoxi-

cal light as *real* benefits, further evidences of divine contrivance' (*Age* 51, emphases Hilton's), and on the other 'rejected Say's Law and anticipated crises of underconsumption or gluts' (52).

33 This is a somewhat different view than that presented by Barbara Weiss in her study of bankruptcy in the Victorian novel; Weiss chooses to focus on the more secular meanings of bankruptcy, seeing it, indeed, as a 'kind of providential life force that exposes the reality which lies below the surface of Victorian society' (86), but a largely secularized one, which represents not the hand of God but a 'threat to the idea of self' (87), as well as functioning as a structuring element in the mid-Victorian realistic novel.

34 The other is William Wilberforce's *Practical View of Christianity*. G.M. Young 29, quoted in Hilton, *Age* 3–4.

35 One of the key components to this theory is the adherence to Thomas Malthus's population thesis, which states that the population tends to increase faster than food supply. See his *Essay on Population*.

36 There is a raging debate, still ongoing, over whether Ricardo believed that this stagnation was inevitable under any circumstances, or only under the agricultural protection of the Corn Laws. See n. 38, below. I am indebted, for the simplified summary above, to Landreth 100–1.

37 One of the more amusing moments in modern political economy must be the end of Marx's *Theories of Surplus Value*, where he graciously extends Ricardo enough rope with which to hang himself. The entire last section of Marx's book consists of juxtaposed quotations from Ricardo which demonstrate the glaring inconsistencies between Say's Law and what Marx terms the 'bourgeois "Twilight of the Gods,"' the doctrine of the falling rate of profit. After these many, long, and contradictory quotations, Marx glosses: 'Such are Ricardo's views on accumulation and the law of the falling rate of profit' (427). End of book.

38 Piero Sraffa, editor of the definitive edition of Ricardo's works, is responsible for the so-called 'corn model' view of Ricardian economics. This interpretation claims that Ricardo based his entire economic model – including the conclusion of the falling rate of profit – on the agricultural sector. Modern writers on Ricardo largely define their own interpretations either in accordance or disagreement with Sraffa's reading (and thus in accordance or disagreement with the hypothesis that Ricardo's model was constructed almost solely to defeat the protectionist Corn Laws). Maxine Berg takes a somewhat different approach in her analysis of machinery and Victorian political economy, claiming that Ricardo believed that technological change could also stave off the problem of falling profits (43–74). For an overview of recent Ricardo criticism, see Peach's chapter 'Interpretations

of David Ricardo' in his *Interpreting Ricardo*, and also the recent articles on the Ricardo controversy in the *Cambridge Journal of Economics* by Peach; Kurz and Salvadori; and Hollander.

39 This summary is my own; however, for a Victorian analysis of this process, see J.S. Mill's *Principles of Political Economy*, esp. Book 3, chaps 11–13 (3:527–69).

40 For a helpful prehistory of the nineteenth-century debates over the gold standard, see Dick's '"The Ghost of Gold."' Dick anticipates Poovey's argument in *Genres of the Credit Economy* by demonstrating that for Shelley, literature begins to function as a type of standard of value in the context of the forgery trials of the early nineteenth century.

41 Of course, traders would still be exchanging paper currency as mere promises to pay the gold itself, but presumably every certificate would in theory be redeemable for gold upon demand and at any time. This condition was fulfilled by the Bank Charter Act of 1844.

42 Spencer, 'State-Tamperings' 326. Unless I indicate otherwise, all quotations from Spencer in the following section are from this essay.

43 My claim here depends on a notion of the inevitable slippage between a 'measure' of value and a 'standard' of value. It is, I contend, impossible to invoke coin as a conventional measure in exchange transactions without importing the notion of its primacy as standard against which all other values are measured. The problem of an unavoidably 'transcendental-seeming' founding standard can be found throughout nineteenth-century economics – for example, in Ricardo's search for a fixed measure of value – as well as in the insights of deconstruction. See, especially, Derrida 19–20. Jean-Joseph Goux discusses three registers of money – as standard of value, as measure of value, and as medium of exchange. Goux's analysis, however, tries precisely to rescue the distinctions among these three terms. See *The Coiners of Language* 33–7 and, more generally, *Symbolic Economies* 9–63.

44 This very apprehension – of the radically contingent or 'proportional' nature of value – was described several decades earlier by Thomas Malthus (see his *Principles of Political Economy*). Yet, as with almost everything Malthus argued, this insight was virtually forgotten for much of the century.

45 This is a concern shared by the other model economist of this chapter, John Ruskin: 'Much occasional work may be done in a state or society, by help of an issue of false money (or false promises) by way of stimulants; and the fruit of this work, if it comes into the promiser's hands, may sometimes enable the false promises at last to be fulfilled ... but all such procedures are more or less unsound' (*Works* 16:136). And later in the same essay: 'no

merchant deserving the name ought to be more liable to 'panic' than a soldier should; for his name should never be on more paper than he can at any instant meet the call of, happen what will' (137). As usual, the strictly technical problem for Spencer (and other political economists) becomes an ethical one for Ruskin: 'by far the greater number of the transactions which lead to these times of commercial embarrassment may be ranged simply under two great heads – gambling and stealing' (138).

46 Even Ruskin acknowledges this potentially salutary function of promises-to-pay: 'I am not sure whether some quantity of false issue may not really be permissible in a nation, accurately proportioned to the minimum average produce of the labour it excites' (*Works* 16:136). However, Ruskin does not agree with Spencer that the accumulation of capital will ultimately redress these imbalances.

47 By way of emphasizing the laissez-faire theorists' conflation of credit and accumulation, I will briefly note J.S. Mill's treatment of the credit-barter distinction. Although Mill is supposedly adamant about distinguishing the extension of credit from the increase of capital ('Of Credit, as a Substitute for Money,' *Principles* 3:527–37), in the chapter 'Of Excess of Supply' in his *Principles of Political Economy*, he argues that the introduction of credit can lead to oversupply, since traders can use money as a store of value instead of trading directly for other goods, thereby causing a disjunction between goods for sale, credit, and money supply (a situation that is impossible in a strict barter economy). However, since Mill's book is mainly concerned to support laissez-faire policies and defend Say's Law against its critics, he goes on to argue that such gluts are temporary and will eventually adjust according to the operations of the law of markets. In his attempt to defend Say's Law, then, he actually raises the intractable issue of gluts and stagnation, demonstrating, once again, not only the inability of the laissez-faire theorists to deny this dire possibility, but also their inability to refrain from continually invoking it.

48 As Dick points out, strictly speaking England did not go 'off' the gold standard because it was never legally on it before 1816. See '"Ghost of Gold"' 385.

49 See, for example, Landes 204–6. Poovey also discusses the cyclical mania-crash pattern at some length in her recent study *Genres of the Credit Economy*. She argues that it is primarily political economy's popularizers – financial journalists and pamphleteers, as opposed to the authors of treatises aimed at more specialist audiences – who focused on the mania-crash issue and attempted to 'neutralize' the fears of an anxious public. See 219–83.

50 Hobsbawm 112–13. I am grateful to Kristin Samuelian for bringing this passage to my attention ('"A Mine of Pure, Genial Affections"').
51 Although the question of the wider cultural meanings of credit, debt, and value is fascinating, a detailed discussion is beyond the scope of this chapter. Two very helpful studies have informed my thinking on these issues: Goux's *The Coiners of Language*, and the more recent *Fictions of State* by Brantlinger.
52 Hilton, *Age* 224; Parry 105.
53 For a helpful summary, see Schwartz, 'Banking School, Currency School, Free Banking School.'
54 Hilton, *Corn, Cash, Commerce* 43–8. This study contains an excellent précis of the bullionist controversy in Parliament.
55 This incident is discussed in Russell's *The Novelist and Mammon* 46–7.
56 This is the impetus behind the Bank Charter Act of 1844. See the brief discussion on page 246n41.
57 In a footnote, he describes his reasoning thus: 'For example, suppose an active peasant, having got his ground into good order and built himself a comfortable house, finding time still on his hands, sees one of his neighbours little able to work, and ill-lodged, and offers to build him also a house, and to put his land in order, on condition of receiving for a given period rent for the building and tithe of the fruits. The offer is accepted, and a document given promissory of rent and tithe. This note is money. It can only be good money if the man who has incurred the debt so far recovers his strength as to be able to take advantage of the help he has received, and meet the demand of the note; if he lets his house fall to ruin, and his field to waste, his promissory note will soon be valueless: but the existence of the note at all is a consequence of his not having worked so stoutly as the other. Let him gain as much as to be able to pay back the entire debt; the note is cancelled, and we have two rich store-holders and no currency' (*Works* 17:205). What Ruskin's account fails to take into consideration, of course, is that the promissory note is not really money in the sense of being perfectly liquid: it is not perfectly liquid and in fact was created provisionally by the poorer peasant specifically as a claim against his future labour. It is not a store of value in the sense in which Mill discusses.
58 For a discussion of this same anxiety in Harriet Martineau's writings, see Van, esp. 121–3. For a scathing – and amusing – critique of Ruskin's monetary policy from a contemporary, see Cairnes, 'Mr. Ruskin on the Gold Question.' For a helpful discussion of Ruskin's attitude toward monetary police and the gold standard, see Craig 317–27.
59 At one point Ruskin acknowledges the potentially confusing nature of his

treatment of credit and promises-to-pay, and attempts to set the record straight; in an 1877 letter to the editor of *The Socialist*, he laments: 'I observe ... the assertion by your correspondent of his definition of money as if different from mine. He only weakens my definition with a "certificate of credit" instead of a "promise to pay." What is the use of giving a man "credit" – if you don't engage to pay him? But I observe that nearly all my readers stop at this more or less metaphysical definition, which I give in *Unto This Last*, instead of going on to the practical statement of immediate need made in *Munera Pulveris*' (*Works* 17:487).

60 I have in mind here Gagnier's study *The Insatiability of Human Wants*; *The Commodity Culture of Victorian England* by Richards; *Novels Behind Glass* by Andrew Miller; Nunokawa's *Afterlife of Property*; *Shopping with Freud* by Bowlby; *Consuming Desire* by Birken; and *Fiction, Famine, and the Rise of Economics in Victorian Britain and Ireland* by Bigelow.

61 For a brief discussion of the divide between inductive and deductive methodologies in classical political economy, see Klaver 4–5: 'A small but influential number of nineteenth-century scientists and philosophers, including notably David Ricardo, continued to make arguments for the necessity, if not inevitability, of a priori forms of thought.'

62 See Leslie, esp. 433–4; Shaw, esp. 211; and Godkin, for example. This was a charge that the immediate contemporaries of Ricardo made as well: 'He proceeds, says M. Say, "by absolute principles, as if writing on geometry: but in political economy this method is full of peril, and ought to be distrusted"' ('Ricardo on Political Economy' 429–30).

63 See, for example, Nicholson.

64 See also Geddes, *John Ruskin, Economist*.

65 Much ink has been spilt on the question of how the theory could have cropped up at the same time in three different places. For a good discussion, see Blaug, *Economic* 277–92.

66 J.E. Cairnes, writing in 1872, put it this way: '[Marginal utility theory] has diverged from the beaten track in two directions – on the question of the method by which political economy ought to be cultivated, and also on some of its substantive doctrines. As regards method, he [Jevons] thinks that economic principles may be best developed by means of mathematics; while he has propounded, on the subject of value in exchange, as well as on some other doctrines of the science, some views of more or less novelty' ('New' 72). Another commentator agreed a few years later: 'It is quite obvious that it [political economy] admits of indefinite development in two directions: first, as regards the accuracy of calculation in the required deductive reasoning; and, secondly, as regards more and more completeness

in admitting all the causes which co-operate in actual history to produce economic results' (Solly 473).

67 Smart's essay also acknowledges what we might call a more 'Ruskinian' strain in the new economics as well: 'We say that the old individualistic conception of the business man as a selfish being … is out of date at a time when the old Christian conception of the solidarity of the human race is coming into prominence again' (287).

68 This same author, interestingly, also claims that consumer demand is not of great economic importance: 'If the demand for the produce of a large manufacture were to cease so universally and so abruptly that all the produce in stock was wasted, the cessation of the demand would have the effect of deducting that amount from the wealth to be spent in employment. But, as a rule, the amount of capital devoted to employment depends on the possessor of capital, not on the consumer' (205). How much the rhetoric will have changed in just a few years!

69 According to Blaug, 'English historicism was as indigenous growth, whose roots go back to Carlyle's and Ruskin's protests against the narrow scope of classical political economy' (*Economic* 283).

70 Although he does also acknowledge that 'wherever there was a historicist bias – a pervasive bias in Germany and a widespread one in England – marginal utility economics was dismissed together with English classical political economy as excessively abstract and permeated with implausible assumptions about human behaviour' (292). For a fascinating discussion of seventeenth-century economists, in whose work we can also see some of the precursors of a full-blown demand theory of value, see Finkelstein, *Harmony and the Balance*. Economic theorist Nicholas Barbon in particular reads like a proto-marginalist: he 'believed that humans were subject to "Wants of the Mind" that were as necessary to them as were the "Wants of the Body," (food, clothing, and shelter) and, in fact, were economically more useful to the state because, being "infinite," psychic wants prompted humanity to ever increasing efforts to attain them, increasing the true wealth of the nation … In Barbon's hands the "infinity of wants" became a necessary complement to an "infinity of supply"' (Finkelstein 211–12).

71 Of course this leaves aside the question of the intellectual or even political stakes of these interpretations for modern writers of the history of economic thought – a question beyond the scope of my analysis. For an interesting discussion, however, see the beginning passages of Winch's essay 'Marginalism and the Boundaries of Economic Science.'

72 Although – as I discuss shortly – my general sympathies tend to be with the 'continuity' group, I strongly disagree with the claim that marginal

utility theory represented an intensification of laissez-faire. First of all, the rhetoric in popular journals and economic treatises alike in the last decades of the century (and beyond) was markedly and vociferously anti-laissez-faire. Furthermore, and more important, Jevons himself was a sharp critic of the blind application of the principle. As he opines in an 1876 lecture entitled 'The Future of Political Economy,' 'It seems to me, while population grows more numerous and dense, while industry becomes more complex and interdependent, as we travel faster and make use of more intense forces, we shall necessarily need more legislative supervision ... We need a new branch of political and statistical science which shall carefully investigate the limits to the *laissez-faire* principle' (203–4). In his 1882 work *The State in Relation to Labour*, he famously refers to the 'metaphysical incubus' of a priori adherence to a doctrine of individual rights, including laissez-faire (16ff). For modern discussions of the marginals' antipathy to laissez-faire, see Hutchison 96–102 and 256–61; and Greenleaf 127–31.

73 For a helpful discussion of the differences between Jevons and Ruskin, see Maas 213–16.

74 In fact, Gagnier goes on to complicate this claim in a later footnote (*Insatiability* 49n), along similar lines to those of my argument in this section.

75 See Solly 475; Blaug, *Economic* 283; Maloney ('of [classical orthodoxy's] two main potential heirs, marginalism and historicism, it was the historicists who were more in tune with the general intellectual climate of the time'); and Caird ('the sense of social responsibility has been growing in a way which makes it impossible to isolate the economical problem from the ethical, as the tendency formerly was to isolate it' [214]).

76 I also find a bit problematic Klaver's claim that historians of economic thought have noted that 'the classical political economy of Ricardo and Mill, in retrospect, looks inclusive, even holistic, compared to the neoclassical economics founded in part by Jevons and the marginalist revolution' (164). This reading is supported by a footnote to only a single historian, Donald Winch, whose essay could best be interpreted as claiming the exact opposite: 'For the historian of economic thought one of the ironies about some current revivals of interest in classical-Marxian modes of analysis is that they frequently require us to admire holistic features of the classical economists' approach which contemporary critics condemned them, as well as their marginalist successors, for neglecting. The shift from classical to neoclassical entailed an accentuation – not the invention – of economic individualism' (Winch, 'Marginalism' 343). More important, the late Victorians, through Keynes and beyond, squarely blamed Ricardo – whether fairly or not – for the callousness and excesses of laissez-faire policy. Klav-

er also quotes Gagnier in support of this reading, although Gagnier herself includes a footnote which considerably complicates this view (*Insatiability* 49n).

77 Winch notes that it was primarily the historical-school practitioners who wanted to bridge the perceived gap between their approach and the marginal utility school, not the other way around ('Marginalism' 332). Perhaps this is a case of the institutionally weaker party seeing the advantage of association with the stronger? This view is complicated by the (in)famous *Methodenstreit* between Austrian marginal utility theorist Carl Menger and German Historical School author Gustav von Schmoller. While Schmoller had the full institutional and governmental backing of the German state and university system, he nonetheless is seen to have 'lost' the battle of methods with Menger – between an approach that emphasizes deduction from universal laws of behaviour and one that stresses the importance of empirical, historical research and economic history. Yet the fact that in defeat, Schmoller became the first economist to attempt a theoretical (conciliatory?) integration of historicism and marginal utility theory, in his *Grundriss der allgemeinen Volkswirtschaftslehre*, perhaps supports my point about the weaker reaching out to the stronger. See Shionoya 10–14.

78 Another early critic of the Ricardian theory of value, Samuel Bailey, has also been consistently described as 'individualist' by modern historians of economic thought. Unfortunately, space does not allow a full treatment of every heterodox critic of Ricardo in the early decades of the nineteenth century, but the interested reader is directed to Bailey's 1825 work *A Critical Dissertation on the Nature, Measures and Causes of Value*, and its modern exegesis by Rauner, *Samuel Bailey and the Classical Theory of Value*. Gagnier mentions Bailey very briefly (*Insatiability* 47), and Peter Groenewegen discusses Bailey in the course of tracing the influence of Turgot on early nineteenth-century heterodox theories of value ('Turgot's Place' 597–9).

79 Gagnier discusses this same trend in Spencer in *The Insatiability of Human Wants* (95–9) and at greater length in 'The Law of Progress and the Ironies of Individualism in the Nineteenth Century.'

80 Klaver discusses this phenomenon as well (183). For a very helpful article delineating the history and stakes of holism versus 'methodological individualism' – a term Schumpeter claims to have invented – in economics, see Kincaid, 'Individualism versus Holism.' According to Kincaid's analysis, in one important way the historical school is even more 'individualist' that the marginal utility theorists: 'Much explanation in economics that might seem individualist in spirit is really nothing of the sort. One case in

point is the widespread use of representative agents who are not flesh and blood individuals and who cannot be legitimized as reasonable aggregations of individual behaviour. Another is the widespread practice of taking household and firms as basic entities. These are social, aggregative entities that, when treated as black boxes, *belie a commitment to individualism*' (emphasis added). In addition, Kincaid claims that Schumpeter was wrong in characterizing even the classicals as methodological individualists, since Adam Smith in particular 'explicitly acknowledged that invisible hand processes work against a background of social institutions, customs, and the like.' On this same point, see Klaver 6–13 and Gagnier 21–7, 64–8; for a fuller discussion of both the Smithian 'paradox' and the history of individualism in the nineteenth century, see Gagnier, 'The Law of Progress,' and her review of Poovey's *Making a Social Body*, entitled 'Methodology and New Historicism.' It is precisely the sense of the 'messiness' of these strains and counterstrains, which Gagnier emphasizes in her review, that I am trying to capture here.

81 For a fuller discussion, which places Smith's fears in the context of eighteenth-century philosophy, see Barker-Benfield's chapter 'The Question of Effeminacy' in *The Culture of Sensibility*.

82 Klaver also discusses this 'feminization' process in the work of Harriet Martineau as Ricardo's great popularizer. See 53–77.

83 Of course, Ruskin's misogyny is legend – and takes on a particularly pointed tone when he is addressing young women who need to be 'educated,' especially in wise domestic economy. In *Sesame and Lilies*, for example, Ruskin addresses his young female interlocutors – whom he will shortly urge to 'resolve to do every day some [work] that is useful in the vulgar sense' and to learn 'first thoroughly the economy of the kitchen' – thus: 'Of all the insolent, all the foolish persuasions that by any chance could enter and hold your empty little heart, this is the proudest and foolishest – that you have been so much the darling of the Heavens, and favourite of the Fates, as to be born in the very nick of time, and in the punctual place, when and where pure Divine truth had been sifted from the errors of the Nations' (*Works* 18:36).

Perhaps Ruskin's crowning statement on his chequered career with women occurs in the same essay: 'As years have gone by, it has chanced to me, untowardly in some respects, fortunately in others (because it enables me to read history more clearly), to see the utmost evil that is in women, while I have had but to believe the utmost good' (47).

84 Some of this 'gender dysphoria' works its way into Bigelow's account in the form of some rather confusing examples. At one point, he notes that in

Jevons, economic relations are seen as acts of free will and therefore non-coercive:

> Within this system, poverty – whether individual or national – can be explained implicitly as a matter of choice ... It is with this final turn that the metaphysical dangers of basing value on desire are finally reduced to acceptable levels. Imprudent, excessive, destructive, or selfish desires – which were seen in the eighteenth century as both dangerous and inevitable in finance capitalism – are completely marginalized here, contained with an orientalized femininity. (71)

But it is in marginal (not 'marginalized') utility that we see the enthronement of desire at the centre of economic discourse, as Bigelow himself has acknowledged. And why in the eighteenth century is 'orientalized femininity' figured as a threat to the smooth workings of the financial system, but here it is safely marginalized?

Elsewhere Bigelow returns to this trope of 'feminization' in another somewhat confused gesture. In his reading of Walter Bagehot's critique of Dickens's prolixity, he claims that the 'feminized excesses of Dickens's imaginative overproduction do, in Bagehot's view, lead to a kind of glut of Dickens's products on the literary market,' but that Bagehot acknowledges that 'Dickens can hardly be blamed for this, given the unrestrained demand for his writing from an equally feminized English reading public' (105). How does unrestrained demand cause gluts? (Gallagher notes the same paradox in Eliot, for whom 'in the literary marketplace, the laws of supply and demand simply do not work to prevent overproduction' [*Body* 120], but whereas Gallagher links this fear to the influence of the marginal utility school, obviously this explanation cannot pertain in the case of Dickens.) Even more interestingly, why are both production and consumption figured here as 'feminine'?

My aim here is not to nitpick what is generally an extremely admirable and fascinating study, but rather to point out the extraordinary entanglement – nay, confusion – of gendered economic metaphors in this period. Even literary critics are not immune to their snares.

2 'Fine Clothes an' Waste': Utopian Economy and the Problem of Femininity in *Adam Bede*

1 I discuss and cite the feminist consternation with these endings more fully in an endnote to chapter 3.
2 As Williams argues in *The Country and the City*, the collective fantasy of an integrated rural society which existed thirty or so years before the present

– a utopic 'Old England' – is one found in every generation. The pastoral fantasy is, of course, one which serves particular ideological ends at particular historical moments. For Eliot, as I hope to show, the pastoral reverie is a socially normative backdrop against which the problems attendant upon industrialization and privatization are examined. See Williams's discussion of Eliot in 'Knowable Communities' 165–81.

3 This idea is akin to the saying attributed to Solon, 'Call no man happy until he is dead,' quoted by Herodotus in his *Histories* and discussed by Aristotle in the *Nicomachean Ethics* (1.10). For a discussion of Aristotelian ethics in George Eliot, see Markovits 87ff.

4 He goes on to explain: 'It would be impossible to realize all at once the wealth possessed by the total number of donors resulting from the obligations contracted by the total number of donees' (122). (This should sound familiar – the impossibility of simultaneous liquidation is also the definitive feature of a credit economy.) Potlatch is likened to sumptuary display because both engage in profligate expenditure outside the bounds of the 'self-contained' economy imagined by earlier political economists. What is significant about sumptuary display, Bataille argues, is the 'positive property of loss – from which spring nobility, honor, and rank in a hierarchy' (122). Since inflation of credit and concomitant loss (what Bataille calls expenditure) are characteristics of both banking economies and the sumptuary display of the traditional aristocracy, we can see that the distaste for display evinced by Mr Irwine actually evokes an even older – although, according to Bataille, a wholly fantasized – precredit economy. (This is in contrast to Nancy Armstrong's argument, which claims that the rhetoric of moderation and restraint is the sole province of the rising bourgeoisie.) What is important here is not whether the premodern economy was really a credit or a barter economy, but rather the persistent fantasy among nineteenth-century political economists – and George Eliot – that the older economy was characterized by self-regulation, balance, and a lack of surplus. Furthermore, exhortations to moderation, insofar as they attempt to deny the very constitutive feature of the capitalist credit economy, namely surplus, signal anxieties about this economy. As I attempt to show, Eliot invokes these ideals of moderation, and links them to an imagined and fantasized pastoral economic organization of barter, and then banishes/murders the figure rhetorically linked to excess consumption and waste.

5 It is a small step from extravagant desire and consumption (not living within one's means) to the opposite but inseparable vice of miserliness (beating down prices). Both are condemned by the moral world of the

novel as equally immoderate, equally excessive. See the discussion of Mrs Poyser and the old squire, below.

6 I expand upon the problem of sympathy and the interventionist narrator in the article 'Incognito, Intervention, and Dismemberment in *Adam Bede*.'

7 Again, what is at issue here are the lengths to which Eliot goes to portray the economic primitivism of the inhabitants of Hayslope. In this sense, the 'fetishism' of the village denizens is of a different kind than the Marxian fetishism of commodities: it imagines money as having some inherent magical power to effect actual material events. This is different, even, from the fetishism of money that occurs in capitalist societies, which Marx describes in 'The Power of Money in Bourgeois Society.' For a discussion of the relationship between commodity fetishism and anthropological fetishism, see Taussig's *The Devil and Commodity Fetishism in South America*. For a good basic introduction to the anthropological view of fetishism, see Ellen, 'Fetishism,' and Pietz, 'The Problem of the Fetish, I.'

8 In 'Character and Anal Erotism,' Freud summarizes a claim that appears in various forms throughout his work, that 'wherever archaic modes of thought have predominated or persist – in the ancient civilizations, in myths, fairy tales and superstitions, in unconscious thinking, in dreams and in neuroses – money is brought into the most intimate relationship with dirt ... It is possible that the contrast between the most precious substance known to man and the most worthless ... has led to this specific identification of gold with faeces' (174).

9 The importance of the proper funeral recurs, as we shall see, with even greater insistence in *The Mill on the Floss*.

10 The problem of insufficient demand for dairy products will recur, with much greater elaboration, in the final chapter, 'Self-Sacrifice, Skillentons, and Mother's Milk.'

11 For a discussion of the paradox of miserliness, see Michaels, *The Gold Standard and the Logic of Naturalism* 139–44.

12 Mrs Poyser is not the only one to have her problematic gender identity questioned, however. At the end of the scene in the night school that introduces Bartle Massey, the schoolmaster closes his misogynist diatribe with a parting shot at his dog, Vixen: 'But where's the use of talking to a woman with babbies?... She's got no conscience – no conscience – it's all run to milk!' Not three sentences before this, however, he characterizes his own education of Adam and the other labourers in the village as a metaphorical nursing: 'You wouldn't have been what you are if you hadn't had a bit of old lame Bartle inside you. The strongest calf must have something to suck at' (246). The fluid and shifting gender identities of the novel's two most

outspoken characters both enables a certain tenuous power balance and problematizes it, as we shall see later.

13 According to Eve Sedgwick, this checking of Mrs Poyser's strength makes sense within the overall project of the novel; for Sedgwick, 'the basic historical trajectory of *Adam Bede* is to move the novel's normative vision of family from the Poysers' relatively integrated farm to the Bedes' highly specified nuclear household. *As part of this transition*, the normative female role must change from Mrs. Poyser's to one like Mrs. Bede's' (140, emphasis in original). While I obviously agree with her claim that representations of female authority are undermined in the novel, I think the historical argument is rather more complicated than she portrays it. I have attempted to show that nostalgia for an imagined precredit economic organization, and a valorization of that fantasized economy, is the driving force behind Eliot's portrait of Hayslope and the Poyser farm. While it is true that this economic organization is supplanted by the end of the novel, it is not at all clear that this constitutes a 'defense of the status quo' of industrial capitalism (145) on Eliot's part – the question of her political project is much more complicated, her motives much more conflicted, than Sedgwick allows. My disagreement with Sedgwick's argument also holds true for Margaret Homans's in her article 'Dinah's Blush, Maggie's Arm.' Homans's article retraces much of the same ground as Sedgwick's chapter on *Adam Bede*, and reaches much the same conclusion.

14 The moral code of *Adam Bede* is aligned with Spencer's economic description even more closely than this. For Spencer's pure, utopian barter economy is, it will be remembered, a world made up entirely of liars; so too does the novel suggest that the real interpretive problem here is not that everyone is not honest but rather that we cannot assume everyone is a liar. Hetty is upbraided for not understanding what to expect from Arthur, namely that his intentions are not honest, and Adam's mistake is that he does not realize he has been duped by Hetty. The problems in interpretation that the novel foregrounds are problems of naivety; the reader is blamed for misreading almost as much as the 'text' is blamed for dishonesty.

15 Margaret Homans points out the meaning of this trope in *The Mill on the Floss*, where Maggie's large, rounded arms (which are 'beyond everything') are code for a large, womanly bosom ('Dinah's Blush, Maggie's Arm' 175).

16 See Jackson's extremely helpful discussion in *New-Born* 32–4; 142–5.

17 The strong suggestion in this brief childbirth narration is that it is a 'natural,' easy birth, attended only by another woman, and thus aligned with the practices of all-female midwifery that are rapidly passing out of vogue

at the time of the novel's action. In fact, the woman who assists Hetty in the birth is named Sarah Stone – the same name as one of the most prominent publishing midwives of the eighteenth century. See Kreisel, 'Incognito' 563–7. Hetty's 'natural,' prelapsarian childbirth aligns this unnarrated episode with the fantasized preindustrial barter economy Eliot privileges throughout the novel.

3 Superfluity and Suction: The Problem with Saving in *The Mill on the Floss*

1 Contemporary reviews of *The Mill* berated the untimely and tragic ending of the third volume, while modern criticism, from U.C. Knoepflmacher's influential study of the early novels through Gilbert and Gubar's and Nancy K. Miller's treatments, also has tended to focus on the author's 'murder' of Maggie. These critics, with the notable exception of Miller and Mary Jacobus, have emphasized the distortions of plot or character which seem to be required by Eliot's 'punishment' of her heroine. For contemporary criticism, see, for example, the reviews in the *Guardian* (Carroll 129), *Westminster Review* (Carroll 143), and *Dublin University Magazine* (Carroll 151). Knoepflmacher goes so far as to call the ending of *The Mill on the Floss* an 'unquestionable failure' (8), while Barbara Hardy confines herself to some more measured tongue-clucking over Eliot's lack of standard formal elegance (2–12). And while Jacobus and Miller have, in their important and welcome analyses, focused on refuting in fairly narrow terms previous claims about the unnaturalness, clumsiness, or even desperation of the closure of *The Mill on the Floss*, they do so without straying too far from the basic questions of propriety and aesthetics addressed in the work they attack.
2 See Wasserman, 'Narrative Logic and the Form of Tradition in *The Mill on the Floss*'; Mundhenk, 'Patterns of Irresolution in Eliot's *Mill on the Floss*'; Bushnell, 'Maggie Tulliver's "Stored-Up Force"'; and McSweeney, 'The Ending of *The Mill on the Floss*.'
3 One contemporary reviewer of the novel remarks that the 'wrong done to [Stephen] in Maggie's forsaking him was almost as great as the wrong previously done to Philip and Lucy' (Mulock 159); while another declares that 'it is most improbable that if Maggie had strength to break her chain at the last and most difficult moment, she should not have had strength to break it before' (Rev. in *Guardian* 130).
4 I chiefly have in mind Nina Auerbach's greatly influential reading ('The Power of Hunger'). And here is Neil Hertz on this issue: '[Maggie] is al-

legorized as Passion herself, as a figure at once of the natural and of the superfluous, a supplementary force as potentially dangerous as a flood, a messenger from the land of debt, the sort of natural disaster that invariably leaves its mark. That is why she must be destroyed like an IOU ... before the novel can end' (68).

5 The complaint of the irreconcilability of the romantic plot with the rest of the novel is everywhere in both contemporary and recent criticism. See, for example, the critique in the *Saturday Review* ('The third volume seems to belong to quite a new story' [119]); the review in the *Guardian* ('There is a clear dislocation in the story, between Maggie's girlhood and Maggie's great temptation' [129]); and Nancy K. Miller's analysis ('The last two books taken together as they chart the culmination of a heroine's erotic destiny have a plot of their own' [45]).

6 Mary Jacobus, for example, claims that 'the reunion of brother and sister in the floodwaters of the Ripple enacts both reconciliation and revenge, consummation and cataclysm' (212), while F.R. Leavis calls the flood 'the dreamed-of perfect accident that gives us the opportunity for the dreamed-of heroic act ... But the finality of it is not that of great art' (45–6). The 'bifurcation' criticism is one that haunts Eliot throughout her career: it returns, of course, with even greater insistence with the publication of *Daniel Deronda*.

7 See chapter 1, n. 37.

8 The heuristic division of the novel into two separate narratives – one governed by Tom's world view, and one by Maggie's – necessarily becomes complicated when considering the similar traits or attitudes of the other characters in the novel. For the most part, I assume that the narrative of economic striving, and the predilections, assumptions, and attitudes that go along with it, is shared by all the Tullivers and Dodsons except for Maggie. In other words, nearly all the characters in the novel fall on the 'Tom' side of the narrative, and it is Maggie, with her sensitive, dreamy, and complicated world view, who is seen as anomalous (although, of course, privileged by the narrator in many crucial ways). The important exceptions to this rule are those characters who are interested, to a differing degree from Maggie, in things outside the narrow economic viewpoint of industrial St Ogg's: at times this includes Philip, Lucy, and Stephen. However, insofar as all three of these characters explicitly critique Maggie's plan of renunciation and self-deprivation, they do not enter into her threatening challenge to Victorian/Dodsonian economics.

9 This expostulation is, as I have suggested, ironized by the narrator's consistent condemnation of the other Tullivers' inability to use or understand

metaphor; however, it is not entirely an endorsement of Maggie's mode of language, either. It is, after all, the desire to condemn Mr Stelling's single-minded and inefficacious plan for Tom's education that prompts the narrator's outburst on metaphor to begin with: Mr Stelling's problem is that he has got hold of the wrong metaphor for Tom's brain, and he thus has no way into an understanding of how better to teach his reluctant pupil. It seems as though a facility with metaphor is no guarantee against the kind of narrow-minded dogmatism that is the bane of the other Tullivers. The issue of metaphorical language in *The Mill on the Floss* has been much discussed in the critical literature. For Margaret Homans, Maggie is associated with literalness (*Bearing the Word*), while Mary Jacobus argues just the opposite, that Maggie's facility with metaphor poses a challenge to dominant masculine ways of reading ('Question of Language'). For Jules Law, the chiastic figure embedded in the passage on metaphor is part of a larger rhetorical strategy that seeks to critique these ways of reading ('Water Rights'). My own argument sees Maggie's rhetorical association with metaphor as part of that general excessiveness and unstoppability – in language as elsewhere – that constitutes one aspect of her threat to the stability of the Tom plot of economic striving.

10 By 'ethics' I mean simply the question of right behaviour: what should be done and not be done. For Maggie and Tom, as we shall see, the sharpest conflicts can be traced back to profound differences in their ideas of right and wrong – not necessarily to Maggie's supposed inability to control herself.

11 John Kucich's interesting analysis of the novel also insists on Maggie's sense of the multiplicity of both language and the possible human uses of the material world. See 'George Eliot and Objects' 328–30.

12 This passage was originally appended to the end of the third chapter, as a commentary on Riley's recommendation of Stelling as schoolmaster for Tom. It appears on p. 523 of the Oxford UP edition of the novel.

13 For a discussion of Eliot's practice of narratorial commentary, see Warhol, *Gendered Interventions*.

14 Boyd Hilton notices the pervasive use of economic metaphors in Victorian religious rhetoric, and vice-versa (*Age* 127–8). In his brilliant article on *The Mill on the Floss*, Neil Hertz makes the interesting suggestion that Eliot herself thought of her writing as the acquittal of a debt ('George Eliot's Life-in-Debt').

15 In analysing the 'economic narrative' of the novel, I will discuss the Dodsons and Tullivers together, and use their names somewhat interchangeably. For the purposes of my argument, their economic philosophies are

the same – those few instances where a Dodson or a Tulliver attempts to differentiate his family from the other are, I believe, wholly ironic from the point of view of the narrator.

16 In their study of the English middle class in the late eighteenth and early nineteenth centuries, Leonore Davidoff and Catherine Hall discuss the practice of borrowing among family members and friends in a time before commercial credit was widely available. Part of Mrs Glegg's reluctance may have to do with the difficulties, which Davidoff and Hall note, of playing banker to one's kin. Although 'it was kinship and family which provided the most reliable source of finance, both initial capital and credit facilities' (250), and because 'there were few safe outlets for investment, surplus capital could be directed along personal lines at commercial rates of return while at the same time building up reciprocal relationships' (216), such melded relationships could cause problems: 'There were sometimes contradictory pulls on individuals committed to both a business and personal mode. For example, decisions to give financial aid and services could be pressed because of friendship or kinship obligations when it might not be in the best interests of the business' (216).

17 This contradiction is not unusual among the early Victorians; Norman Russell attributes it to 'a new public hypocrisy that speculated with one hand and condemned speculation with the other' (26). Or as Davidoff and Hall put it, 'The growing commitment to new commercial forms among sections of the middling ranks jostled with fears and anxieties of the dangers inherent within them' (20).

18 It is difficult to understand why Eliot would characterize the 1820s as anything other than 'days of rapid money-getting,' but however historically inaccurate her portrait, it is clear that she wishes at this point to emphasize the Tullivers' atavistic fear of speculation.

19 As I have already noted, the more usual view is that Maggie is punished for her inordinate desires; see, for example, Nina Auerbach's analysis in 'The Power of Hunger: Demonism and Maggie Tulliver.' Gilbert and Gubar, on the other hand, suggest that Maggie is 'most monstrous when she tries to turn herself into an angel of renunciation' (491).

20 I am grateful to an anonymous reader of this manuscript for pointing out the parallel to Smith.

21 Smith does seem conflicted on this point: see 4.1.8ff.

22 The zero-sum language takes on an even more startling twist in the *Wealth of Nations*: 'Barrenness, so frequent among women of fashion, is very rare among those of inferior station. Luxury, in the fair sex, while it inflames, perhaps, the passion for enjoyment, seems always to weaken,

and frequently to destroy altogether, the powers of generation' (1.8.37). The literature on the connection between the consumption of commodities and eroticism and sexuality is, of course, vast – stretching from Aristotle to Freud, Lacan, Bataille, Marcuse, and beyond. While a fuller discussion of the history of the connection is beyond the scope of this chapter, I trust that my discussion of femininity and economic management throughout this study will form a small contribution to this wider body of literature.

23 Mary Jacobus suggests such a reading, in the service of a different argument, when she notes that 'Eliot saw in Thomas à Kempis a language of desire' (220).

24 Neil Hertz remarks on this same parallel in his analysis of the novel, 'George Eliot's Life-in-Debt' (67–8).

4 'All Was Over at Last': Epistemological and Domestic Economies in *The Mayor of Casterbridge*

1 Of course, the Œdipus complex is doubly complicated by this novel, since not only does a girl supplant her 'father,' but his paternity turns out to be mistaken. A fuller discussion of fatherhood in the novel is unfortunately beyond the scope of this chapter, which focuses instead on more purely economic relationships, whether familial or exogenous. Marjorie Garson provides a helpful and concise discussion of patriarchy in *The Mayor of Casterbridge* (101–3); as she asserts: 'Though the novel can be read as a critique of patriarchal notions of ownership, I would argue that what it really expresses is the anxiety that such ownership is not possible' (102). Certainly my own reading reinforces the notion that ownership is difficult for Henchard, while it provides a different, complementary etiology of that difficulty.

2 See especially Earl Ingersoll's 'Troping and the Machine in Thomas Hardy's *The Mayor of Casterbridge*' and 'Writing and Memory in *The Mayor of Casterbridge*'; and the chapter 'Wessex and the Border' in Williams, *The Country and the City*.

3 In other words, Henchard is not metonymic enough, or, strictly speaking, not synecdochical enough. In this sense, his actions fit into the metaphor-vs-metonymy schema that Ingersoll proposes – except for the crucial fact that the novel claims that this 'strict correspondence' is an older and more traditional way of doing business, not one of the new-fangled practices associated with young Turks like Farfrae. The image of Henchard as a misrepresenter, as failing to preserve a strict relationship between part and whole, is crucial to my reading of the novel as fundamentally concerned with the epistemological positions of its characters.

4 For an interesting discussion of Henchard's corn-factoring business as a 'fundamental capitalist transaction which places a cash value ... on the primary process of growing food to eat' (146), see Fisher, '*The Mayor of Casterbridge.*' For Fisher, Henchard's alienation in the social sense is directly related to his alienation in the Marxian sense.

5 While the folklore etymology of this phrase has recently been debunked, it was arguably common belief throughout the eighteenth and nineteenth centuries that the expression derived from an English common-law principle that a man is prohibited from beating his wife with a stick broader than his thumb. (A 1782 cartoon by James Gillray that condemns Judge Francis Buller for this putative ruling can be viewed on the Library of Congress website.) While Hardy never explicitly links Henchard's use of the phrase to his other wife-abuse practices, the existence of this folk etymology suggests that the novelist might have had it in mind. For a full discussion of the history of the phrase in the context of Anglo-American jurisprudence, see Kelly, '*Rule of Thumb* and the Folklaw of the Husband's Stick.'

6 Just a few of the many possible examples: we are reminded that had Henchard not opened Susan's testament until Elizabeth-Jane's marriage, 'this pain [of knowing her parentage] would have been spared him for long' (198); the narrator comments that 'much might have resulted' from Henchard and Elizabeth-Jane recognizing each other in the alley behind High-Place Hall (212); when Henchard pays a call on Lucetta after she has fallen in love with Farfrae, we are told that a 'turn of the eye by Henchard, a glance from the window, and the secret of her inaccessibility would have been revealed' (249). This is of course in marked contrast to Eliot, who never stops reminding us why her plots are plausible and why things had to happen the way they did; with Hardy, agency is decentred in an almost ironic way, whereas in Eliot authority flows unmistakably from a central (and overly anxious) narratorial consciousness.

7 Of course, the narrator does go on to claim that 'most probably luck had little to do with it' and that it might very well be an issue of the characters of the two men; however, he cannot state this definitively and backs oddly away from the statement even as he makes it. And of course the novel goes on to undermine this half-hearted assertion with the triumphant entrance of luck writ large during the corn harvest.

8 This is not to suggest that Goode is the only critic to have noted the importance of Elizabeth-Jane's perspective in the second part of the novel; many others – perhaps most notably Julie Grossman in 'Thomas Hardy and the Role of Observer' – have elaborated on this theme. I merely suggest that Goode's analysis takes this observation one step further in making it a central tenet of his argument about Hardy's creation of a new

and particular kind of subjectivity; this is one of the reasons I engage it at such length.

9 See, particularly, Barthes's 'Introduction to the Structural Analysis of Narratives' and *S/Z*; and Frank Kermode's *The Sense of an Ending*.

10 In other words, I am cautioning against reading too paradigmatically – in terms of static binarisms and schematic oppositions – and against reading too syntagmatically – in terms of inexorable chains of causation.

11 For a discussion of the power of labour to mark the objects with which it comes in contact, see Scarry, 'Work and the Body in Hardy and Other Nineteenth-Century Novelists.' For an interesting discussion of textiles and clothing in the novel (which does not, however, cite this particular passage), see Ramel, 'Crevice in the Canvas.'

12 See Shell, *The Economy of Literature*, esp. 84–6.

13 The complicated issue of the epistemological unreliability of figural language has been dealt with at length by Paul de Man in 'The Epistemology of Metaphor.' According to de Man, who reads texts of Locke, Condillac, and Kant as the first to articulate the epistemological problem of metaphor, all tropological language (i.e., all language) is prey to this problem, and thus it would be nonsensical to distinguish metaphor and metonymy in the way I have (and in fact, his reading of Locke claims that metonymy, which describes the 'mere contiguity between words and things in the case of simple ideas' is more epistemologically reliable than metaphor, which enters language at the level of the substance, where there is only a 'metaphorical correspondence of properties and essences' [19]). Since the examples I am working with have to do with the difficulties of reading objects in the world and not with properties of language (the metaphorical properties of metaphor), I would make the small claim that in these cases, a metonymical relationship between objects is a less reliable bearer of readable information about the two objects (where it is, after all, purely accidental and contingent) than a metaphorical one, wherein the two objects bear some necessary relationship to each other.

14 Significantly, one of the points of this exercise in imagining alternative plots is to achieve the process of 'integration' – wherein we piece together elements (and specifically different 'levels') of narrative into a satisfying and plausible whole – that allows us to believe in what *has* happened. For his discussion of 'counter-texts,' see Barthes's 'Introduction to the Structural Analysis of Narratives'; for more on integration and different levels of narrative, see pp. 84–7; and for a fuller and more sophisticated treatment, see his discussion of the hermeneutic and proairetic codes in *S/Z*.

15 As I have suggested before, the way *The Mayor of Casterbridge* strains cre-

dulity at various moments is itself indicative of points of crisis in the text. See Genette's discussion of plausibility in 'Vraisemblance et motivation.'

16 Again, see Genette.

17 This would accord well with our sense of the intensity of Henchard and Farfrae's relationship; as Farfrae himself is aware, their enmity is 'more like old-fashioned rivalry in love than just a bit of rivalry in trade' (315).

18 The reference is to the passage in Ruskin's *Munera Pulveris* that I discuss at length in the introduction: 'The holder of wealth ... may be regarded simply as a mechanical means of collection; or as a money-chest with a slit in it, not only receptant but suctional, set in the public thoroughfare' (*Works* 17:169). We see the same confluence of slits and public spaces elsewhere in the novel; when describing the inn in Mixen Lane, the narrator tells us: 'At first sight the inn was so respectable as to be puzzling. The front door was kept shut, and the step was so clean that evidently but few persons entered over its sanded surface. But at the corner of the public-house was an alley, a mere slit, dividing it from the next building. Half-way up the alley was a narrow door, shiny and paintless from the rub of infinite hands and shoulders. This was the actual entrance to the inn' (330). The process of entering the inn through this portal is rather eccentric, even for Hardyan rustics: 'A pedestrian would be seen abstractedly passing along Mixen Lane; and then, in a moment, he would vanish ... That abstracted pedestrian had edged into the slit by the adroit fillip of his person sideways; from the slit he edged into the tavern by a similar exercise of skill' (330). In both the Ruskin quotation and the passage from the novel, 'slits' are figured as literally suctional, liminal spaces that threaten to purloin what is properly public and respectable (circulating funds, pedestrians) and transform it into a private, and secretive, abomination.

19 See especially Silverman's 'History, Figuration and Female Subjectivity in *Tess of the d'Urbervilles*,' and also, more generally, Grossman's article on the role of the observer in Hardy.

20 Showalter discusses the feminization of Henchard in 'The Unmanning of the Mayor of Casterbridge'; however, it is again John Goode who reminds us that this process is fundamentally a positive one: '"womanliness" is not merely emasculation – it is also bound up with an excluded knowledge' (90).

21 This was a feature of 'wife sales' that contemporary Victorian commentators also failed to note. Chroniclers of English wife sales occasionally noted that a child was included as part of the transaction, without taking particular interest in that fact (see 'Better-Half Barter,' 'The Sale of Wives,' and 'Wife-Selling'). (Of course it bears remembering that the 'sale' of

Elizabeth-Jane was really the sale of an infant now dead – the Elizabeth-Jane who comes to Casterbridge is a different person.) In addition, all three Victorian wife-sale writers were adamant on the point that the wives were just as happy to be 'sold' as the husbands were to sell them, and that all the parties involved were equally ignorant of the illegality of the transaction. This is in marked contrast to the conditions of the sale in *The Mayor of Casterbridge:* Hardy is at pains to make Henchard seem the more guilty party, both by insisting that Susan agreed to the sale only with extreme reluctance, and that she was ignorant of the illegality of the transfer, while Michael knew full well that it was not binding.

22 See J. Hillis Miller's *Thomas Hardy: Distance and Desire* for a discussion of the relationship between detachment and engagement in Hardy; he argues that artistic expression (and the unique stance of the author) are a way for Hardy to combine his paradoxical desires for engagement and self-protective distance. This would fit in well with the claim that Elizabeth-Jane's perspective eventually merges with the authorial voice: it is her very detachment in the face of thwarted desire which aligns her with the perspective of the artist.

23 Garson discusses the strange non-presence of Elizabeth-Jane in some detail (94–9). She attributes this phenomenon partially to the fact that all the women in the novel seem to lack embodiment: 'Casterbridge as an erotic presence displaces and diminishes the individual female characters' (86). This effacement is particularly striking given the erotic and sensual attributes the novelist lavishes on other female protagonists, for example Bathsheba and Tess.

5 Self-Sacrifice, Skillentons, and Mother's Milk: The Internalization of Demand in *Tess*

1 All citations are from the Oxford edition unless otherwise noted.

2 Charlotte Thompson notes that Tess, at the end of the narrative, becomes 'the novel's chosen sacrifice, offered up to vitalize the run-down mechanism of the universe' (760). Thompson, however, makes this point in support of her argument that a new Romantic vision is inaugurated at the end of the novel, an interpretation with which I do not agree.

3 Catherine Gallagher also makes a very convincing case that an even earlier novel, George Eliot's *Daniel Deronda*, is also deeply influenced by marginal utility theory. See her *Body Economic*, chapter 5.

4 See Maas; Mosselmans; Gagnier, *Insatiability*; and Gallagher, *Body* for discussions of this conundrum in Jevons.

5 For a discussion of this debate in Victorian psychological theory, see Ed
   Block and Rylance. I also discuss Huxley and the automaton question in
   my article 'Wolf Children and Automata.'

6 For a fuller discussion of the influence of Quetelet on Jevons, see Mosselmans, especially 28–37.

7 Klaver notes this same paradox (178).

8 For a complex and nuanced reading of the relationship between this opposition and the trope of embodied history in the novel, see Law, 'A Passing Corporeal Blight.' According to Law's argument, the persistent binary
   oppositions of the novel function to 'isolate and de-historicize the body'
   (252). For Law, Tess's interpretations 'tend to distinguish themselves from
   the narratorial ethos precisely by offering social as opposed to ostensibly
   natural or instinctual explanations for her behavior' (252). This argument
   brilliantly explores the tension between narratorial and characterological
   registers of the novel, while I am more concerned here to explore the contradictions between narratorial rhetoric and the logic of plot.

9 I am using this term in the sense described by Brooks in *Reading for the
   Plot*, which I discuss in detail in chapter 4, pp. 166–8.

10 All of these reviews can be found in Lerner and Holmstrom 58–102. I refer
   to, in order (parenthetical page numbers refer to quoted passages above):
   The Speaker and *The Saturday Review*; *The Spectator* and *The Daily Chronicle*;
   The Speaker; *The Spectator* and *The Independent* (81); *The Speaker* and *Punch*;
   The Saturday Review (66).

11 Margaret Higonnet makes a somewhat similar distinction between the
   'repressive' and masculine discourses of biblical orthodoxy and the 'truths
   of the heart' known by women. Adrian Poole also distinguishes between
   the masculine and feminine languages of the novel. However, neither critic
   aligns these two modes with the two strains of heredity – paternal and maternal – within the character of Tess herself.

12 Nunokawa also discusses the process of 'inscription' in this scene, within
   the specific context of nineteenth-century travel books and tourist narratives. See his '*Tess*, Tourism, and the Spectacle of the Woman.'

13 While Angel does make the decision to return to Tess before the murder,
   he leaves again as soon as he learns that Tess and Alec are together at
   Sandbourne, only to return when d'Urberville is dead. Within the logical
   structure of the novel – and the mind of Tess – he will ultimately accept
   her only upon the death of her 'natural husband.' See Goode's insightful
   discussion of this paradoxical imperative: 'Her two decisions – to go with
   Alec and to murder him, which each in their turn trap her into the system
   whose consequences they attempt to subvert – echo Angel's "truth"... We

want to ascribe this to the ideology which her whole development has denied. But in the end it is what is left her' (131).

14 This is the version given by the Clarendon edition, reprinted in paperback by Oxford University Press. The orthography of the Wessex Edition (available in a Penguin Classics edition) makes the similarity between the two moments even more clear: '"O – O – O!" Then a silence, then a heavy sigh, and again – "O – O – O"' (469).

15 F.W. Johnston associates this motion with both general economic activity and the unending circulation of all physical matter: 'Then what a lesson of ceaseless activity does all this circulation teach us! Is all senseless matter to be labouring perpetually – and are we, intelligent beings, made to idle away a precious life?... "Why does this wheel turn? Why its unceasing restlessness? What purpose is effected, or is to be effected, by its endless revolution?" As a whole, the answer is, that the maintenance of life, animal and vegetable, depends upon the perpetual movement of all the wheels at once' (559).

16 This notion of palimpsest is somewhat different from the processes that Silverman and Nancy Miller discuss in their studies of the novel. For Silverman, the inscriptions of history enact a process of 'figuration,' a carving up of the visual field which is indistinguishable from force, while for Miller, the repetitive patterns of history, amoral of themselves, are readable only from the standpoint of the end of the novel. The image of the palimpsest, on the other hand, insists on the coexistence of different historical strata simultaneously: subsequent events overwrite previous ones, but the latter are always still readable within and behind the former. For a discussion of the palimpsestic figure in Hardy more generally, see Law, 'Sleeping Figures: Hardy, History, and the Gendered Body.'

17 Wickens even notes a similar process at work in the language of the novel. Victorian theories of language, he claims, were particularly concerned with the 'geology' of words, or the palimpsestic survival of older meanings alongside new. According to his argument, Hardy deploys this geological understanding to depict Tess as 'caught in the web of changing words' (101).

18 For discussions of the rape/seduction as a form of writing or inscription, see Silverman, Bernstein, and J. Hillis Miller, *Fiction and Repetition*.

19 Johnston has a slightly different take on this process, although he still emphasizes its fundamentally circulatory and excretory character: 'All the parts of the body, even the most solid, are in a constant course of renewal. To this law of change the bones are subject equally with the soft parts, and the phosphoric acid carried in to-day is in a few days carried out again, mixed up with the other refuse and excretions of the body' (557).

20 Ellen Rooney discusses the correspondence between inner and outer in a somewhat different context. For Rooney, this correspondence is essential in order for Hardy to represent Tess without having her tell her own story (which is anathema to the project of the novel), yet according to her argument it tends to break down in the descriptions of Tess's sexuality. See Rooney 107.

21 The narrator claims that his haggard state is due to 'worry and the bad season that Clare had experienced in the climate to which he had so rashly hurried in his first aversion to the mockery of events at home' (356), yet Angel himself says simply, 'I was ill over there, you know' (356). While the narratorial voice insists upon the connection between the moral and the physical malaise, this insight is immediately ironized by Angel's own suggestion that his 'reconversion' is unaccompanied by new powers of self-knowledge or ethical insight that would be equal to the narrator's.

22 This is the metaphorical equivalent to those bodily processes the Victorians conceived of as constantly occurring beneath the threshold of perception; as chemist F.W. Johnston reminds his readers, 'Not only is the living body in constant movement as a whole, but all its parts, even the minutest, are in constant motion. Were our eyes keen enough, we might see every particle which forms the substance of the fingers which hold our pen shaken loose and really separated from each other' (554). This sentiment has a famous echo, of course, in *Middlemarch*, where it also forms a meditation of sorts on authorial insight ('the fingers which hold our pen') and narratorial perception: 'If we had a keen vision and feeling of all ordinary human life, it would be like hearing the grass grow and the squirrel's heart beat, and we should die of that roar which lies on the other side of silence' (182).

23 See chapter 4, '"All Was Over at Last": Epistemological and Domestic Economies in *The Mayor of Casterbridge*' 159–63.

24 Several recent critics have discussed the paradox of Tess's purity. See, in particular, Rooney, Blake, and Bernstein.

25 Rev. of *Tess of the d'Urbervilles* in the *Pall Mall Gazette*, Cox 182.

26 Armstrong's analysis of nineteenth-century attitudes toward domestic economy is again quite helpful here. See especially 59–95.

27 My point here is not that Hardy somehow places the blame for coercive economic relationships on the workers, but rather that the force of his critique is blunted by his recognition of a certain 'failure' on the part of the bodies of the women in this scene. Goode notes that within the logic of the novel, the woman's 'whole economic being is the sale of her body – the violation of the threshing machine is clearly coherent with the occupation of her body' (131). While I agree with this assessment, I feel that the narrator's irony in the passages I have cited does not effect an absolute break

between his moral stance and the 'judgment' of the workers' bodies the machine inaugurates.

28 For a fascinating discussion of the relationship between Tess's history as worker and her seduction by Alec, see Scarry's 'Work and the Body in Hardy' (94–8). Scarry provocatively argues that Tess's pregnancy is 'a hazard of the workplace, an industrial accident' (95).

29 *Tess* certainly does not abandon the issue of true correspondence found in *The Mayor of Casterbridge*, as we have seen in the case of the readings that characters perform of one another's bodies and faces. It also still manifests this concern in the economic realm. In a brief comic vignette toward the end of the novel, Mr Durbeyfield returns home carrying a live hen under his arm: 'The hen had been carried about this morning as it was often carried, to show people that he was in his work, though it had lain, with its legs tied, under the table at Rolliver's for more than an hour' (251). Occurring as it does in the context of Mr Durbeyfield's general, annoying lack of familial economic responsibility (not to mention imminent death), this little *mensonge* demonstrates Hardy's persistent anxiety with misleading bodily signs of occupation and work, an anxiety that certainly has not changed since *The Mayor of Casterbridge* (see, also, Scarry's discussion of signs of work in Hardy). (Just as Durbeyfield lies about drinking instead of working, so Mrs Rolliver often lies about working instead of drinking: she is in the habit of glibly calling out 'Being a few private friends I've asked in to keep up club-walking at my own expense' when she thinks an inspector may be crashing her illegal off-license house [31].)

30 For their general discussions of the growth of the marginal utility school, I am indebted to Dasgupta, esp. 76–98, Landreth 193–233, and Meek, *Smith* 165–75.

31 This new concern with demand is also related to the burgeoning business of advertising, as described by Richards in his *Commodity Culture of Victorian England*. Richards's argument locates the beginning of the great growth in advertising at the Great Exhibition of 1851, thus suggesting, perhaps, that the new economic analysis of demand is as much a result of the growing commodity culture as it is a cause.

32 As we shall see shortly, this quaint idea of a product entirely outside the purview of economic exchange is a bit naive: considered from the perspective of the wet-nursing industry, breast milk does indeed have a price – both literal and metaphorical.

33 Numerous writers discussed this phenomenon. See, for example: 'Our Milk Supplies,' 'The Milk Industry in Cheshire,' and 'Curiosities of Commerce.'

34 As one contemporary commentator noted, 'The relatively small amount of cheese made in England is startling. It has greatly fallen off, especially in the Midlands, since the railways have carried the milk up to town at such low rates [prices]. It has fallen off, too, because you cannot make cheese so cheaply in a dairy as you can in a factory' ('High Dairy-Farming' 35).

35 'Many people imagine that flour, chalk, starch, and the brains of calves or sheep, are intermixed with skimmed milk to imitate the absent cream' ('Milk' 130). See also 'Adulterated Milk.'

36 See, for example, 'Curiosities of Commerce and Trade,' 'Milk,' 'Milk – French and English,' 'Something about Milk,' and Augustus Voelcker, 'On Milk and Its Adulteration.'

37 'A great deal has been said and written about milk-adulteration. Sheep's brains, starch paste, chalk, and other white substances, which are said – on what authority nobody has ever decided – to have been found in milk, only exist in the imagination of credulous or half-informed scientific men … I never met as yet with a chemist who has found any of the clumsy adulterations which popular treatises on food describe as having been detected in London milk' (Voelcker 184.)

38 In her discussion of George Eliot's *Scenes of Clerical Life*, Gallagher glosses another fascinating example of dairying and economic demand:

    'There is no private life which has not been determined by a wider public life, from the time when the primeval milkmaid had to wander with the wanderings of her clan, because the cow she milked was one of a herd which had made the pastures bare' … In the quietly unorthodox way in which the passage briefly plays with the myth of the expulsion from Eden, Eliot's narrator substitutes a purely Malthusian reason for primeval wandering: 'pastures bare.' The primeval milkmaid, symbol of fecundity, has exhausted the food supply. (*Body* 175)

    This reading of course emphasizes the Malthus of the *Essay on Population*, as Gallagher does throughout her study. This is a particularly interesting example of the tension between the 'two Malthuses': while Demand Malthus may worry that milk production will cease due to insufficient consumer demand, Population Malthus worries that milk production will cease due to too-great cow demand.

39 See Fildes, *Wet Nursing* 196–8.

40 Qtd in Fildes, *Wet Nursing* 196–7.

41 Alicia Carroll also notes this likelihood (167, 180).

42 The novel also makes other explicit connections between the labour Tess performs as agricultural worker and her 'labour' as nursing mother. Dur-

ing the last half of the novel, when Tess has been abandoned by Angel and
is looking for work to support herself, we find the following passage:

> Thus she went forward from farm to farm in the direction of the place
> whence Marian had written to her, which she determined to make use
> of as a last shift only, its rumoured stringencies being the reverse of
> tempting. First she inquired for the lighter kinds of employment, and,
> as acceptance in any variety of these grew hopeless, applied next for
> the less light, till, beginning with the dairy and poultry tendance that
> she liked best, she ended with the heavy and coarse pursuits which
> she liked least – work on arable land: work of such roughness, indeed,
> as she would never have deliberately volunteered for.
>
> Towards the second evening she reached the irregular chalk table-
> land or plateau, bosomed with semi-globular tumuli – as if Cybele
> the Many-breasted were supinely extended there – which stretched
> between the valley of her birth and the valley of her love. (273)

43 This tendency was reversed when the working classes started living in
   crowded slums and air pollution cut off their access to sunlight, a source of
   the vitamin D essential to the metabolism of calcium. See Floud et al. 300.

44 See Guggenheim 155–83, 207–24; McCollum 266–87.

45 Goode discusses an analogous phenomenon in his study *Thomas Hardy:
   The Offensive Truth*: 'The cruel law perspective is increasingly located in
   the mind of Tess, who comes more and more to enunciate it in place of the
   author' (114).

Works Cited

'Adulterated Milk.' *Chambers's Edinburgh Journal* 2 ns (1844): 363–5.

Aikman, C.M. 'Milk.' *Good Words* 37 (1896): 763–9.

Armstrong, Nancy. *Desire and Domestic Fiction: A Political History of the Novel*. New York: Oxford UP, 1987.

Auerbach, Nina. 'The Power of Hunger: Demonism and Maggie Tulliver.' *Nineteenth-Century Fiction* 30 (1975): 150–71.

Austin, Linda M. *The Practical Ruskin: Economics and Audience in the Late Work*. Baltimore: Johns Hopkins UP, 1991.

Backhouse, Roger E., and Steven G. Medema. 'Economists and Laissez-Faire.' Durlauf and Blume. 28 March 2009. http://www.dictionaryofeconomics .com/article?id=pde2008_L000232.

Bailey, Samuel. *A Critical Dissertation on the Nature, Measures and Causes of Value*. London: R. Hunter, 1825.

Baird, Henry Carey. 'Recent Popular English Politico-Economic Literature.' *Penn Monthly* 1 (1870): 330–9.

Barker-Benfield, G.J. *The Culture of Sensibility: Sex and Society in Eighteenth-Century Britain*. Chicago: U of Chicago P, 1996.

Barthes, Roland. 'Introduction to the Structural Analysis of Narratives.' *Image, Music, Text*. Trans. and ed. Stephen Heath. New York: Hill and Wang, 1977. 79–124.

– *The Pleasure of the Text*. Trans. Richard Miller. New York: Hill and Wang, 1975.

– *S/Z*. Trans. Richard Miller. New York: Hill and Wang, 1974.

Bataille, Georges. 'The Notion of Expenditure.' *Visions of Excess: Selected Writings, 1927–1939*. Ed. Allan Stoekl. Trans. Allan Stoekl, with Carl R. Lovitt and Donald M. Leslie, Jr. Minneapolis: U of Minnesota P, 1985. 116–29.

Beer, Gillian. *Darwin's Plots: Evolutionary Narrative in Darwin, George Eliot, and Nineteenth-Century Fiction*. London: Routledge and Kegan Paul, 1983.

Beer, M[ax]. *An Inquiry into Physiocracy*. New York: Russell & Russell, 1966.

Benjamin, Walter. 'The Storyteller.' *Illuminations*. Trans. Harry Zohn. New York: Schocken Books, 1968. 83–109.

Berg, Maxine. *The Machinery Question and the Making of Political Economy 1815–1848*. Cambridge: Cambridge UP, 1980.

Bernard, Thomas, et al. *Annual Report of the Society for Bettering the Condition and Increasing the Comforts of the Poor*. Vol. 2. London: W. Bulmer, 1799.

Bernstein, Susan David. 'Confessing and Editing: The Politics of Purity in Hardy's *Tess*.' *Virginal Sexuality and Textuality in Victorian Literature*. Ed. Lloyd Davis. Albany: State U of New York P, 1993. 159–78.

'Better-Half Barter.' *Chambers's Journal* 47 (1870): 126–8.

Bigelow, Gordon. *Fiction, Famine, and the Rise of Economics in Victorian Britain and Ireland*. Cambridge: Cambridge UP, 2003.

Birken, Lawrence. *Consuming Desire: Sexual Science and the Emergence of a Culture of Abundance, 1871–1914*. Ithaca: Cornell UP, 1988.

Blake, Kathleen. 'Pure Tess: Hardy on Knowing a Woman.' *SEL: Studies in English Literature, 1500–1900* 22 (1982): 689–705.

Blaug, Mark. *Economic Theory in Retrospect*. 5th ed. Cambridge: Cambridge UP, 1996.

– *Ricardian Economics: A Historical Study*. New Haven: Yale UP, 1958.

Block, Ed, Jr. 'T.H. Huxley's Rhetoric and the Popularization of Victorian Scientific Ideas: 1854–1874.' *Victorian Studies* 29 (1986): 363–86.

Block, Maurice. 'The Two Schools of Political Economy.' *Penn Monthly* 8 (1877): 96–117.

Bonar, James. *Malthus and His Work*. [1885]. New York: A.M. Kelley, 1966.

Bowlby, Rachel. *Shopping with Freud*. New York: Routledge, 1993.

Brantlinger, Patrick. *Fictions of State: Culture and Credit in Britain, 1694–1994*. Ithaca: Cornell UP, 1996.

Brodrick, George C. *English Land and English Landlords*. London: Cassell, Petter, Galpin & Co., 1881.

Brooks, Peter. *Reading for the Plot: Design and Intention in Narrative*. Cambridge, MA: Harvard UP, 1992.

Bushnell, John P. 'Maggie Tulliver's "Stored-Up Force": A Re-Reading of *The Mill on the Floss*.' *Studies in the Novel* 16 (1984): 378–95.

Caird, Edward. 'Political Economy, Old and New.' *The Quarterly Journal of Economics* 2 (1888): 213–15.

Cairnes, J.E. 'Mr. Ruskin on the Gold Question.' *MacMillan's Magazine* 9 (1863): 67–9.

– 'New Theories in Political Economy.' *Fortnightly Review* 17 (ns 11) (1872): 71–6.

Cameron, Gavin. 'Classical Economics and Economic Growth.' Durlauf
    and Blume. 23 February 2009. http://www.dictionaryofeconomics.com/
    article?id=pde2008_C000603.
Carlyle, Thomas. *Sartor Resartus*. London: Chapman and Hall, 1831.
Carroll, Alicia. 'Human Milk in the Modern World: Breastfeeding and the Cult
    of the Dairy in *Adam Bede* and *Tess of the d'Urbervilles*.' *Women's Studies* 31
    (2002): 165–97.
Carroll, David. *George Eliot: The Critical Heritage*. London: Routledge and
    Kegan Paul, 1971.
Cixous, Hélène. 'The Laugh of the Medusa.' *New French Feminisms: An Anthol-
    ogy*. Ed. Elaine Marks and Isabelle de Courtivron. Amherst: U of Massachu-
    setts P, 1980. 245–64.
Cobbe, Frances Power. 'Wife-Torture in England.' *The Contemporary Review* 32
    (1878): 55–87.
Cowe, James. *Religious and Philanthropic Tracts*. London: J. Robson, 1797.
Cox, R.G. *Thomas Hardy: The Critical Heritage*. New York: Barnes and Noble,
    1970.
Craig, David M. *John Ruskin and the Ethics of Consumption*. Charlottesville: U of
    Virginia P, 2006.
Culler, Jonathan. *Structuralist Poetics*. London: Routledge and Kegan Paul,
    1975.
'Curiosities of Commerce and Trade: The Milk Trade.' *Leisure Hour* 29 (1880):
    651–4.
'Dairy Produce.' *Quarterly Review* 165 (1887): 298–326.
Darwin, George H. 'The Theory of Exchange Value.' *Fortnightly Review* ns 17
    (1875): 243–53.
Dasgupta, A.K. *Epochs of Economic Theory*. Oxford: Basil Blackwell, 1985.
Davidoff, Leonore, and Catherine Hall. *Family Fortunes: Men and Women of the
    English Middle Class, 1780–1850*. Chicago: U of Chicago P, 1987.
Davis, Timothy. 'The Historical Context of the General Glut Controversy.'
    Kates, *Two Hundred Years of Say's Law*. 133–53.
De Man, Paul. 'The Epistemology of Metaphor.' *On Metaphor*. Ed. Sheldon
    Sacks. Chicago: U of Chicago P, 1979. 11–28.
DeQuincey, Thomas. *The Logic of Political Economy*. [1845]. Boston: James Os-
    good, 1872.
Derrida, Jacques. *Positions*. Trans. Alan Bass. Chicago: U of Chicago P, 1981.
Devas, Charles S. 'Lessons from Ruskin.' *The Economic Journal* 8.29 (Mar. 1898):
    28–36.
Dick, Alex J. '"The Ghost of Gold": Forgery Trials and the Standard of Value in
    Shelley's *The Mask of Anarchy*.' *European Romantic Review* 18 (2007): 381–400.

Dickens, Charles. *Dombey and Son*. Ed. Andrew Sanders. New York: Penguin, 2002.

Durlauf, Steven N., and Lawrence E. Blume, eds. *The New Palgrave Dictionary of Economics Online*. 2nd ed. New York: Palgrave Macmillan, 2008. http://www.dictionaryofeconomics.com/dictionary.

Eatwell, John, Murray Milgate, and Peter Newman. *The New Palgrave: Money*. New York: Norton, 1989.

'Elements of Save-all-ism.' *Blackwood's Edinburgh Magazine* 12 (1822): 525–30.

Eliot, George [Marian Evans]. *Adam Bede*. Ed. Stephen Gill. New York: Penguin, 1980.

– *Middlemarch*. Ed. David Carroll. Oxford: Oxford UP, 1996.

– *The Mill on the Floss*. Ed. Gordon S. Haight. New York: Oxford UP, 1980.

Ellen, Roy. 'Fetishism.' *Man* ns 23 (1988): 213–35.

Enock, Arthur Guy. *This Milk Business: A Study from 1895 to 1943*. London: H.K. Lewis, 1943.

Fain, John Tyree. *Ruskin and the Economists*. Nashville: Vanderbilt UP, 1956.

Fawcett, Millicent. *Tales in Political Economy*. London: Macmillan, 1874.

Fetter, Frank W. 'Economic Controversy in the British Reviews, 1802–1850.' *Economica* 32 (1965): 424–37.

– 'The Rise and Decline of Ricardian Economics.' *History of Political Economy* 1 (1969): 67–84.

Fildes, Valerie. *Breasts, Bottles, and Babies: A History of Infant Feeding*. Edinburgh: Edinburgh UP, 1986.

– *Wet Nursing: A History from Antiquity to the Present*. Oxford: Basil Blackwell, 1988.

Fincham, Ernest C. 'Microbes in Milk.' *Chambers's Journal* 1 6th ser. (1898): 548–50.

Finkelstein, Andrea. *Harmony and the Balance: An Intellectual History of Seventeenth-Century English Economic Thought*. Ann Arbor, MI: U of Michigan P, 2000.

Fish, Stanley. 'Comments from Outside Economics.' *The Consequences of Economic Rhetoric*. Ed. Arjo Klamer, Donald McCloskey, and Robert M. Solow. Cambridge: Cambridge UP, 1988. 21–30.

Fisher, Joe. 'The Mayor of Casterbridge: Made of Money.' Wolfreys 132–52.

Floud, Roderick, Kenneth Wachter, and Annabel Gregory. *Height, Health, and History: Nutritional Status in the United Kingdom, 1750–1980*. Cambridge: Cambridge UP, 1990.

Foxwell, H.S. 'The Economic Movement in England.' *The Quarterly Journal of Economics* 2 (1887): 84–103.

– 'Irregularity of Employment and Fluctuations of Prices.' *The Claims of*

Labour: A Course of Lectures Delivered in Scotland in the Summer of 1886, on Various Aspects of the Labour Problem. John Burnett et al. Edinburgh: Co-operative Printing Co., 1886. 186–275.

Frankland, G.C. 'Boiling Milk.' *Nineteenth Century* 40 (1896): 454–60.

– 'Milk Dangers and Remedies.' *Longman's Magazine* 29 (1897): 464–76.

Freedgood, Elaine. 'Banishing Panic: Harriet Martineau and the Popularization of Political Economy.' *Victorian Studies* 39 (1995): 33–53.

Freud, Sigmund. *Beyond the Pleasure Principle*. Trans. James Strachey. New York: Norton, 1961.

– 'Character and Anal Erotism.' *Standard Edition*. Vol. 9. 168–75.

– *The Standard Edition of the Complete Psychological Works of Sigmund Freud*. Trans. James Strachey. 24 vols. London: Hogarth P, 1953–74.

Gagnier, Regenia. *The Insatiability of Human Wants: Economics and Aesthetics in Market Society*. Chicago: U of Chicago P, 2000.

– 'The Law of Progress and the Ironies of Individualism in the Nineteenth Century.' *New Literary History* 31 (2000): 315–36.

– 'Methodology and New Historicism.' *Journal of Victorian Culture* 4 (1999): 116–22.

Galbraith, John Kenneth. 'Professor Galbraith Reluctantly Recommends Wage – Price Controls: The Cure for Runaway Inflation.' *New York Times* 7 June 1970: 25+.

Gallagher, Catherine. *The Body Economic: Life, Death, and Sensation in Political Economy and the Victorian Novel*. Princeton: Princeton UP, 2006.

– *The Industrial Reformation of English Fiction: Social Discourse and Narrative Form, 1832–1867*. Chicago: U of Chicago P, 1985.

Garson, Marjorie. '*The Mayor of Casterbridge*: The Bounds of Propriety.' Wolfreys 80–115.

Geddes, Patrick. *John Ruskin, Economist*. [1884]. N.p.: Folcroft Library Editions, 1973.

Genette, Gérard. 'Vraisemblance et motivation.' *Figures II*. Paris: Éditions du Seuil, 1969. 71–99.

Gilbert, Sandra M., and Susan Gubar. *The Madwoman in the Attic: The Woman Writer and the Nineteenth-Century Literary Imagination*. New Haven: Yale UP, 1979.

Gillray, James. 'Judge Thumb, or – patent sticks for family correction: warranted lawful!' Cartoon. [London]: H. Humphrey. 27 Nov. 1782.

Godkin, E.L. 'The Economic Man.' *The North American Review* 153 (1891): 491–503.

Goode, John. *Thomas Hardy: The Offensive Truth*. Oxford: Basil Blackwell, 1988.

Gordon, Barry. 'Criticism of Ricardian Views on Value and Distribution in the British Periodicals, 1820–1850.' *History of Political Economy* 1 (1969): 370–87.

– 'Say's Law, Effective Demand, and the Contemporary British Periodicals, 1820–1850.' *Economica* 32 (1965): 438–46.

Goux, Jean-Joseph. *The Coiners of Language*. Trans. Jennifer Curtiss Gage. Norman, OK: U of Oklahoma P, 1994.

– *Symbolic Economies: After Marx and Freud*. Trans. Jennifer Curtiss Gage. Ithaca: Cornell UP, 1990.

Greenleaf, W.H. *The Rise of Collectivism*. Vol. 1 of *The British Political Tradition*. London: Methuen, 1983.

Greenspan, Alan. 'Gold and Economic Freedom.' *Capitalism: The Unknown Ideal*. Ayn Rand et al. New York: New American Library, 1967. 101–7.

Griswold, Charles L., Jr. *Adam Smith and the Virtues of Enlightenment*. Cambridge: Cambridge UP, 1998.

Groenewegen, Peter. 'Thomas DeQuincey: "Faithful Disciple of Ricardo"?' *Contributions to Political Economy* 1 (1982): 51–8.

– 'Turgot's Place in the History of Economic Thought: A Bicentenary Estimate.' *History of Political Economy* 15 (1983): 585–616.

Grossman, Julie. 'Thomas Hardy and the Role of Observer.' *ELH* 56 (1989): 619–38.

Guggenheim, Karl Y. *Nutrition and Nutritional Diseases: The Evolution of Concepts*. Lexington, MA: Collamore, 1981.

Hardy, Barbara. *The Novels of George Eliot: A Study in Form*. London: Athlone P, 1959.

Hardy, Thomas. *Collected Letters of Thomas Hardy*. Ed. Richard Little Purdy and Michael Millgate. Vol. 1. Oxford: Clarendon, 1978.

– [Emily Florence Hardy]. *The Early Life of Thomas Hardy, 1840–1891*. New York: Macmillan, 1928.

– *The Mayor of Casterbridge*. Ed. Martin Seymour-Smith. New York: Penguin, 1978.

– 'The Profitable Reading of Fiction.' *Forum* 5 (1888): 57–70. Repr. in *Thomas Hardy's Personal Writings*. Ed. Harold Orel. London: Macmillan, 1966. 110–25.

– *Tess of the d'Urbervilles*. Ed. Juliet Grindle and Simon Gatrell. New York: Oxford UP, 1983.

– *Tess of the d'Urbervilles: A Pure Woman*. Ed. David Skilton. New York: Penguin, 1978.

– 'To Edmund Gosse.' 19 October 1886. *Collected Letters* 154–5.

– 'To Edmund Gosse.' 24 December 1886. *Collected Letters* 159.

– 'To Robert Louis Stevenson.' 7 June 1886. *Collected Letters* 146–7.

Henderson, Willie. *John Ruskin's Political Economy*. New York: Routledge, 2000.

Herbert, Christopher. *Culture and Anomie: Ethnographic Imagination in the Nineteenth Century*. Chicago: U of Chicago P, 1991.

Hertz, Neil. 'George Eliot's Life-in-Debt.' *Diacritics* 25.4 (1995): 59–70.

'High Dairy-Farming.' *All the Year Round* 39 (1886): 33–8.

Higonnet, Margaret R. 'Fictions of Feminine Voice: Antiphony and Silence in Hardy's *Tess of the d'Urbervilles*.' *Out of Bounds: Male Writers and Gender(ed) Criticism*. Ed. Laura Claridge and Elizabeth Langland. Amherst, MA: U of Massachusetts P, 1990. 197–218.

Hilton, Boyd. *The Age of Atonement: The Influence of Evangelicalism on Social and Economic Thought, 1795–1865*. Oxford: Clarendon, 1988.

– *Corn, Cash, Commerce: The Economic Policies of the Tory Governments 1815–1830*. Oxford: Oxford UP, 1977.

Hobsbawm, E.J. *Industry and Empire: From 1750 to the Present Day*. Harmondsworth: Penguin, 1969.

Hobson, J.A. *John Ruskin, Social Reformer*. Boston: Dana Estes & Co., 1898.

– *The Social Problem: Life and Work*. London: Nisbet, 1901.

Hollander, Samuel. *The Economics of David Ricardo*. London: Heineman, 1979.

– 'Ricardo, Torrens and Sraffa: The Untenability of de Vivo's "Summing Up."' *Cambridge Journal of Economics* 22 (1998): 617–22.

Homans, Margaret. *Bearing the Word: Language and Female Experience in Nineteenth-Century Women's Writing*. Chicago: U of Chicago P, 1986.

– 'Dinah's Blush, Maggie's Arm: Class, Gender, and Sexuality in George Eliot's Early Novels.' *Victorian Studies* 36 (1993): 155–78.

Hunter, Ian. *Culture and Government: The Emergence of Literary Education*. Basingstoke: Macmillan, 1988.

Hutchison, T.W. *On Revolutions and Progress in Economic Knowledge*. Cambridge: Cambridge UP, 1978.

Huxley, T.H. 'On the Hypothesis That Animals are Automata, and Its History.' *Science and Culture, and Other Essays*. New York: D. Appleton, 1882. 206–52.

Ingersoll, Earl G. 'Troping and the Machine in Thomas Hardy's *The Mayor of Casterbridge*.' *University of Hartford Studies in Literature* 22.2 (1990): 59–67.

– 'Writing and Memory in *The Mayor of Casterbridge*.' *English Literature in Transition (1880–1920)* 33 (1990): 299–309.

Jackson, Mark. *New-Born Child Murder: Women, Illegitimacy and the Courts in Eighteenth-Century England*. Manchester: Manchester UP, 1996.

– 'Re: Inquiry re New-Born Child Murder.' E-mail to the author. 22 March 2001.

Jacobus, Mary. 'The Question of Language: Men of Maxims and *The Mill on the Floss*.' *Critical Inquiry* 8 (1981): 207–22.

Jessopp, Augustus. 'English Economic History.' *The Nineteenth Century* 25 (1889): 617–21.

Jevons, W. Stanley. 'The Future of Political Economy.' 1876. *The Principles of Economics*. Ed. Henry Higgs. London: Macmillan, 1905. 187–206.

– *The Theory of Political Economy*. 2nd ed. London: Macmillan, 1879.

[Johnston, James F.W.] 'The Circulation of Matter.' *Blackwood's Edinburgh Magazine* 73 (1853): 550–60.

Kates, Steven. '"Supply Creates Its Own Demand": A Discussion of the Origins of the Phrase and of Its Adequacy as an Interpretation of Say's Law of Markets.' *History of Economics Review* 41 (Winter 2005): 49–60.

– ed. *Two Hundred Years of Say's Law: Essays on Economic Theory's Most Controversial Principle*. Northampton, MA: Edward Elgar, 2003.

Kelly, Henry Ansgar. '*Rule of Thumb* and the Folklaw of the Husband's Stick.' *Journal of Legal Education* 44 (1994): 341–65.

Kermode, Frank. *The Sense of an Ending*. New York: Oxford UP, 1967.

Keynes, John Maynard. *The General Theory of Employment Interest and Money*. New York: Harcourt, Brace & World, 1936.

Kincaid, Harold. 'Individualism versus Holism.' Durlauf and Blume. 14 February 2009. http://www.dictionaryofeconomics.com/article?id=pde2008_I000277.

Klaver, Claudia C. *A/Moral Economics: Classical Political Economy and Cultural Authority in Nineteenth-Century England*. Columbus, OH: Ohio State UP, 2003.

Knoepflmacher, U.C. *George Eliot's Early Novels: The Limits of Realism*. Berkeley: U of California P, 1968.

Kramer, Dale, ed. *Critical Approaches to the Fiction of Thomas Hardy*. London: Macmillan, 1979.

Kreisel, Deanna K. 'The Economics of Closure: Political Economy, Gender, and Narrative in Eliot and Hardy.' PhD diss. Northwestern University, 1996.

– 'Incognito, Intervention, and Dismemberment in *Adam Bede*.' *ELH* 70 (2003): 541–74.

– 'Wolf Children and Automata: Bestiality and Boredom at Home and Abroad.' *Representations* 96 (2006): 21–47.

Kucich, John. 'George Eliot and Objects: Meaning as Matter in *The Mill on the Floss*.' *Dickens Studies Annual* 12 (1983): 319–40.

Kurz, Heinz D., and Neri Salvadori. 'Morishima on Ricardo: A Rejoinder.' *Cambridge Journal of Economics* 22 (1998): 227–39.

Laidler, David. 'The Bullionist Controversy.' Eatwell 60–71.

Landes, David S. *The Unbound Prometheus: Technological Change and Industrial Development in Western Europe from 1750 to the Present*. Cambridge: Cambridge UP, 1969.

Landreth, Harry. *History of Economic Theory: Scope, Method, and Content*. Boston: Houghton Mifflin, 1976.

Law, Jules. 'A "Passing Corporeal Blight": Political Bodies in *Tess of the D'Urbervilles*.' *Victorian Studies* 40 (1997): 245–70.

– 'Sleeping Figures: Hardy, History, and the Gendered Body.' *ELH* 65 (1998): 223–57.

– 'Water Rights and the "Crossing o' Breeds": Chiastic Exchange in *The Mill on the Floss*.' *Rewriting the Victorians: Theory, History, and the Politics of Gender*. Ed. Linda M. Shires. New York: Routledge, 1992. 52–69.

Leavis, F.R. *The Great Tradition: George Eliot, Henry James, Joseph Conrad*. New York: New York UP, 1960.

Le Gallienne, Richard. Rev. of *Tess of the d'Urbervilles*, by Thomas Hardy. *Star* [London] 23 Dec. 1891. Repr. in Cox 189–92.

Lerner, Laurence, and John Holmstrom, eds. *Thomas Hardy and His Readers: A Selection of Contemporary Reviews*. London: Bodley Head, 1968.

Leslie, T.E.C. 'The Philosophical Method of Political Economy.' *The Penn Monthly* 8 (1877): 411–35.

Lévi-Strauss, Claude. *Structural Anthropology*. Trans. Claire Jacobson and Brooke Grundfest Schoepf. New York: Basic Books, 1963.

Lowe, Robert. 'Recent Attacks on Political Economy.' *The Nineteenth Century* 4 (1878): 858–68.

Maas, Harro. *William Stanley Jevons and the Making of Modern Economics*. Cambridge: Cambridge UP, 2006.

MacKenzie, Scott R. *Be It Ever So Humble: Poverty, Fiction, and the Invention of the Middle-Class Home, 1742–1834*. Forthcoming, U of Virginia P.

Maclachlan, F. Cameron. 'The Ricardo-Malthus Debate on Underconsumption: A Case Study in Economic Conversation.' *History of Political Economy* 31 (1999): 563–74.

Maloney, J. 'British Historical Economics.' Durlauf and Blume. 6 March 2009. http://www.dictionaryofeconomics.com/article?id=pde2008_H000189.

Malthus, T.R. *An Essay on the Principle of Population*. 6th ed. London: John Murray, 1826.

– *Principles of Political Economy*. Ed. John Pullen. 2 vols. Cambridge: Cambridge UP for the Royal Economic Society, 1989.

Markovits, Stefanie. *The Crisis of Action in Nineteenth-Century English Literature*. Columbus, OH: Ohio State UP, 2006.

Marx, Karl. 'The Power of Money in Bourgeois Society.' *Economic and Philosophic Manuscripts of 1844*. Trans. Martin Milligan. Moscow: Progress Publishers, 1967. 126–31.

– *Theories of Surplus Value*. Trans. G.A. Bonner and Emile Burns. New York: International, 1952.

Martineau, Harriet. *Illustrations of Political Economy*. 9 vols. London: Charles Fox, 1832–4.

McCollum, Elmer. *A History of Nutrition: The Sequence of Ideas in Nutrition Investigations*. Boston: Houghton Mifflin, 1957.

McDonagh, Josephine. 'DeQuincey, Malthus, and the Anachronism-Effect.' *Studies in Romanticism* 44 (2005): 63–80.

– *DeQuincey's Disciplines*. Oxford: Clarendon, 1994.

McSweeney, Kerry. 'The Ending of *The Mill on the Floss*.' *English Studies in Canada* 12 (1986): 55–68.

'A Meditation; on Skeletons – and some other Things.' *Cornhill Magazine* 7 (1863): 622–8.

Meek, Ronald L. 'The Decline in Ricardian Economics in England.' *Economics and Ideology and Other Essays*. London: Chapman & Hall, 1967. 60–7.

– *Smith, Marx, and After: Ten Essays in the Development of Economic Thought*. London: Chapman & Hall, 1977.

Michaels, Walter Benn. *The Gold Standard and the Logic of Naturalism: American Literature at the Turn of the Century*. Berkeley: U of California P, 1987.

'Milk.' *All the Year Round* 13 (1865): 126–31.

'Milk – French and English.' *Leisure Hour* 12 (1863): 733–5.

'The Milk Industry in Cheshire.' *Chambers's Journal* 6 5th ser. (1889): 362–5.

Mill, John Stuart. *Principles of Political Economy*. Ed. J.M. Robson. Toronto: U of Toronto P, 1965. Vols 2–3 of *Collected Works*. F.E.L. Priestley, gen. ed. 33 vols. 1963–91.

Rev. of *The Mill on the Floss*, by George Eliot. *Dublin University Magazine* Feb. 1861: 192–200. Repr. in Carroll 145–53.

Rev. of *The Mill on the Floss*, by George Eliot. *Guardian* 25 April 1860: 377–8. Repr. in Carroll 124–31.

Rev. of *The Mill on the Floss*, by George Eliot. *Saturday Review* 14 April 1860: 470–1. Repr. in Carroll 114–19.

Rev. of *The Mill on the Floss*, by George Eliot. *Westminster Review* July 1860: 24–32. Repr. in Carroll 139–44.

Miller, Andrew. *Novels Behind Glass: Commodity Culture and Victorian Narrative*. Cambridge: Cambridge UP, 1995.

Miller, D.A. *Narrative and Its Discontents: Problems of Closure in the Traditional Novel*. Princeton: Princeton UP, 1981.

Miller, J. Hillis. *Fiction and Repetition: Seven English Novels*. Cambridge, MA: Harvard UP, 1982.

– *Thomas Hardy: Distance and Desire*. Cambridge, MA: Harvard UP, 1970.

Miller, Nancy K. 'Emphasis Added: Plots and Plausibilities in Women's Fiction.' *PMLA* 96 (1981): 36–48.

Moore, George. *Esther Waters*. London: Walter Scott, 1894.

Mosselmans, Bert. *William Stanley Jevons and the Cutting Edge of Economics*. New York: Routledge, 2007.

[Mulock, Dinah.] Unsigned rev. of *The Mill on the Floss*, by George Eliot. *Macmillan's Magazine* April 1861: 441–8. Repr. in Carroll 154–61.

Mundhenk, Rosemary. 'Patterns of Irresolution in Eliot's *Mill on the Floss*.' *Journal of Narrative Technique* 13 (1983): 20–30.

'The New Political Economy.' *Penn Monthly* 10 (1879): 779–88.

Newcomb, Simon. 'The Two Schools of Political Economy.' *The Princeton Review* ns 14 (1884): 291–301.

Nicholson, J. Shield. 'A Plea for Orthodox Political Economy.' *The National Review* 6 (1885): 553–63.

Nunokawa, Jeff. *The Afterlife of Property: Domestic Security and the Victorian Novel*. Princeton: Princeton UP, 1994.

– 'Tess, Tourism, and the Spectacle of the Woman.' *Rewriting the Victorians: Theory, History, and the Politics of Gender*. Ed. Linda M. Shires. New York: Routledge, 1992. 70–86.

'Our Households and Homes.' *The Englishwoman's Domestic Magazine* 15 (1873): 75–6.

'Our Milk Supplies.' *Chambers's Journal* 19 4th ser. (1882): 798–800.

Parry, Jonathan. *The Rise and Fall of Liberal Government in Victorian Britain*. New Haven: Yale UP, 1993.

Peach, Terry. *Interpreting Ricardo*. Cambridge: Cambridge UP, 1993.

– 'On *Interpreting Ricardo*: A Reply to Sraffians.' *Cambridge Journal of Economics* 22 (1998): 597–616.

– 'On the Interpretation of Ricardo: A Response to Professor Morishima.' *Cambridge Journal of Economics* 22 (1998): 221–6.

Pietz, William. 'The Problem of the Fetish, I.' *Res* 9 (1985): 5–17.

'Political Economy in the Clouds.' *Fraser's Magazine* 62 (1860): 651–9.

'Politics, Sociology, and Travels.' *Westminster Review* 78 (1862): 530–43.

Poole, Adrian. '"Men's Words" and Hardy's Women.' *Essays in Criticism* 31 (1981): 328–45.

Poovey, Mary. *Genres of the Credit Economy: Mediating Value in Eighteenth- and Nineteenth-Century Britain*. Chicago: U of Chicago P, 2008.

– *Uneven Developments: The Ideological Work of Gender in Mid-Victorian England*. Chicago: U of Chicago P, 1988.

Pullen, John, ed. Introduction. *Principles of Political Economy*. By T.R. Malthus. Ed. John Pullen. 2 vols. Cambridge: Cambridge UP for the Royal Economic Society, 1989.

– [Pullen, J.M.] 'Malthus, Thomas Robert (1766–1834).' Durlauf and Blume. 23

March 2009. http://www.dictionaryofeconomics.com/article?id=pde2008_M100018.

Ramel, Annie. 'Crevice in the Canvas: A Study of *The Mayor of Casterbridge.*' *Victorian Literature and Culture* 26 (1998): 259–72.

Rauner, Robert M. *Samuel Bailey and the Classical Theory of Value.* Cambridge, MA: Harvard UP, 1961.

Ricardo, David. *The Principles of Political Economy and Taxation.* London: Dent, 1973.

– *Works and Correspondence.* Ed. Piero Sraffa, with the collaboration of M.H. Dobb. 11 vols. Cambridge: Cambridge UP for the Royal Economic Society, 1951–73.

'Ricardo on Political Economy.' *Monthly Review* 93 (1820): 416–30.

Richards, Thomas. *The Commodity Culture of Victorian England: Advertising and Spectacle, 1851–1914.* Stanford: Stanford UP, 1990.

Richardson, Alan. *Literature, Education, and Romanticism: Reading as Social Practice, 1780–1832.* Cambridge: Cambridge UP, 1994.

Rooney, Ellen. '"A Little More than Persuading": Tess and the Subject of Sexual Violence.' *Rape and Representation.* Ed. Lynn A. Higgins and Brenda R. Silver. New York: Columbia UP, 1991. 87–114.

Rosenberg, John D. *The Darkening Glass: A Portrait of Ruskin's Genius.* New York: Columbia UP, 1986.

'Rubbish.' *Chambers's Journal* 56 (1879): 598–600.

Rubin, Gayle. 'The Traffic in Women: Notes on the "Political Economy" of Sex.' *Toward an Anthropology of Women.* Ed. Rayna R. Reiter. New York: Monthly Review, 1975. 157–210.

Ruskin, John. 'Home, and Its Economies.' *The Contemporary Review* 21 (1873): 927–37.

– *The Works of John Ruskin.* Ed. E.T. Cook and Alexander Wedderburn. 39 vols. London: George Allen, 1903–12.

Russell, Norman. *The Novelist and Mammon: Literary Responses to the World of Commerce in the Nineteenth Century.* Oxford: Clarendon, 1986.

Rylance, Rick. *Victorian Psychology and British Culture 1850–1880.* Oxford: Oxford UP, 2000.

'The Sale of Wives.' *Chambers's Journal* 36 (1861): 238–40.

Samuelian, Kristin Flieger. '"A Mine of Pure, Genial Affections": Money and the Construction of Class in *Jane Eyre.*' Wealth, Poverty and the Victorians Conference. Leeds Centre for Victorian Studies. Leeds, England. 14 July 1999.

Sawyer, Paul L. *Ruskin's Poetic Argument: The Design of the Major Works.* Ithaca: Cornell UP, 1985.

Scarry, Elaine. 'Work and the Body in Hardy and Other Nineteenth-Century Novelists.' *Representations* 3 (1983): 90–123.

Schumpeter, Joseph A. *Economic Doctrine and Method: An Historical Sketch.* Trans. R. Aris. London: Allen & Unwin, 1954.

– *History of Economic Analysis.* Ed. from MS by Elizabeth Boody Schumpeter. New York: Oxford UP, 1966.

– 'On the Concept of Social Value.' *Quarterly Journal of Economics* 23 (1909): 213–32.

Schwartz, Anna J. 'Banking School, Currency School, Free Banking School.' Eatwell 41–9.

Sedgwick, Eve Kosofsky. *Between Men: English Literature and Male Homosocial Desire.* New York: Columbia UP, 1985.

Shaw, Albert. 'Recent Economic Works.' *The Dial* 6 (1885): 210–13.

Sheldon, J.P. *Dairy Farming: Being the Theory, Practice, and Methods of Dairying.* London: Cassell & Co., [c. 1880].

Shell, Marc. *The Economy of Literature.* Baltimore: Johns Hopkins UP, 1978.

Sherburne, James Clark. *John Ruskin, or the Ambiguities of Abundance: A Study in Social and Economic Criticism.* Cambridge, MA: Harvard UP, 1972.

Shionoya, Yuichi. 'Rational Reconstruction of the German Historical School.' *The German Historical School: The Historical and Ethical Approach to Economics.* Ed. Yuichi Shionoya. New York: Routledge, 2001. 7–18.

Showalter, Elaine. 'The Unmanning of the Mayor of Casterbridge.' Kramer 99–115.

Silverman, Kaja. 'History, Figuration and Female Subjectivity in *Tess of the d'Urbervilles.' Novel* 18 (1984): 5–28.

Smart, William. 'The Old Economy and the New.' *Fortnightly Review* 56 (1891): 278–92.

Smith, V.E. 'Malthus's Theory of Demand and Its Influence on Value Theory.' *Scottish Journal of Political Economy* 3 (1956): 205–20.

'Something About Milk.' *Littell's Living Age* 144 (1880): 819–22.

Solly, Henry Shaen. 'Political Economy for Questions of the Day.' *The Theological Review* 16 (1879): 468–87.

Sowell, Thomas. *Classical Economics Reconsidered.* Princeton: Princeton UP, 1974.

– 'The General Glut Controversy Reconsidered.' *Oxford Economic Papers* 15 (1963): 193–203.

Spear, Jeffrey L. *Dreams of an English Eden: Ruskin and His Tradition in Social Criticism.* New York: Columbia UP, 1984.

Spencer, Herbert. *Social Statics.* New York: D. Appleton and Co., 1881.

– 'State-Tamperings with Money and Banks.' *Westminster Review* Jan. 1858:

210–32. Repr. in *Essays Scientific, Political, and Speculative.* Vol. 3. New York: D. Appleton, 1907. 326–57.

'Sterilized Milk.' *Saturday Review* 82 (1896): 197–8.

Stimson, F.J. 'Ruskin as a Political Economist.' *Quarterly Journal of Economics* 2 (1888): 414–45.

Talbot, E.S. 'The Verdict of Political Economy upon Luxury.' *Contemporary Review* 8 (1868): 199–207.

Taussig, Michael. *The Devil and Commodity Fetishism in South America.* Chapel Hill: U of North Carolina P, 1980.

Rev. of *Tess of the d'Urbervilles,* by Thomas Hardy. *Athenaeum* 9 Jan. 1892. Repr. in Cox 197–9.

Rev. of *Tess of the d'Urbervilles,* by Thomas Hardy. *Pall Mall Gazette* 31 Dec. 1891: 3. Repr. in Cox 180–3.

Rev. of *Tess of the d'Urbervilles,* by Thomas Hardy. *Saturday Review* 16 Jan. 1892: 73–4. Repr. in Cox 188–91.

Rev. of *The Theory of Political Economy,* by W. Stanley Jevons. *The North American Review* 114 (1872): 435–40.

Thompson, Charlotte. 'Language and the Shape of Reality in *Tess of the d'Urbervilles.*' *ELH* 50 (1983): 729–62.

'Unrecognized Forces in Political Economy.' *The New Englander* 36 (1877): 710–24.

Vaggi, Gianni. *The Economics of François Quesnay.* London: Macmillan, 1987.

Van, Annette. 'Realism, Speculation, and the Gold Standard in Harriet Martineau's *Illustrations of Political Economy.*' *Victorian Literature and Culture* 34 (2006): 115–29.

Voelcker, Augustus. 'On Milk and Its Adulteration.' *Popular Science Review* 5 (1866): 177–87.

Wade, John. 'Harlotry and Concubinage: A Supplementary Chapter to *Women, Past and Present: Exhibiting Their Social Vicissitudes; Single and Matrimonial Relations; Rights, Privileges, and Wrongs.*' London: Charles J. Skeet, 1859.

Wallace, R. Hedger. 'Our Imported Milk and Cream.' *Chambers's Journal* 12 5th ser. (1895): 657–9.

Walsh, Vivian, and Harvey Gram. *Classical and Neoclassical Theories of General Equilibrium: Historical Origins and Mathematical Structure.* New York: Oxford UP, 1980.

Warhol, Robyn R. *Gendered Interventions: Narrative Discourse in the Victorian Novel.* New Brunswick, NJ: Rutgers UP, 1989.

Wasserman, Renata R. Mautner. 'Narrative Logic and the Form of Tradition in *The Mill on the Floss.*' *Studies in the Novel* 14 (1982): 266–79.

Weiss, Barbara. *The Hell of the English: Bankruptcy and the Victorian Novel.* Lewisburg, PA: Bucknell UP, 1986.

Wickens, G. Glen. 'Victorian Theories of Language and *Tess of the d'Urbervilles.*' *Mosaic* 19 (1986): 99–115.

'Wife-Selling.' *All The Year Round* ns 55 (1884): 255–60.

Williams, Raymond. *The Country and the City.* London: Paladin, 1973.

Wilson, D. Munro. 'John Ruskin, Economist.' *The Unitarian Review* 23 (1885): 241–57.

Winch, Donald. *Malthus.* Oxford: Oxford UP, 1987.

– 'Marginalism and the Boundaries of Economic Science.' *History of Political Economy* 4 (1972): 325–43.

Wolfreys, Julian, ed. *The Mayor of Casterbridge.* New Casebooks Series. New York: St Martin's, 2000.

Woodmansee, Martha, and Mark Osteen. *The New Economic Criticism: Studies at the Intersection of Literature and Economics.* New York: Routledge, 1999.

Wormald, Mark. 'Microscopy and Semiotic in *Middlemarch.*' *Nineteenth-Century Literature* 50 (1996): 501–24.

Index

accounting. *See* bookkeeping

accumulation: in *Adam Bede*, 87–8; of capital, 11, 13, 22, 26, 45–6, 217, 235–6n11, 247n47; — in Malthus, 32, 36, 45, 239n3; — in physiocrats, 30; — in Ricardo, 25–7, 45, 245n37; — in Ruskin, 9, 36, 38, 45, 56, 233–4n4, 247n46; — in Spencer, 26, 52–3, 87, 247n46; of currency (*see* currency: accumulation of); excessive, 4, 9, 20–1, 27, 32, 36, 38, 42, 45–6, 139 (*see also* excess; surplus); and female sexuality, 9–10, 22, 38; in *The Mill on the Floss*, 21, 114, 116, 123, 126–8, 139–40. *See also* gluts; profit; surplus

aesthetic judgment, 15, 19, 39, 58, 112–14, 237n21, 258n1

agency, 14, 72, 97–8, 263n6. *See also* free will

agrarianism. *See* agriculture; pastoral

agriculture, 30, 45, 82–3, 85, 150, 211, 219–22, 242n20, 245n36, 245–6n38, 271–2n42. *See also* dairy farming

Aikman, C.M., 220

amends. *See* compensation

ancestry, 189–92, 199–200, 206–7, 227–8. *See also* heredity

anomie, 179, 211. *See also* appetite; consumers: stimulating desire in; desire

aphorisms. *See* maxims

appetite: in *Adam Bede*, 84–7; excessive, 21, 84, 86–7, 118, 124–5, 131, 133–5, 137–9, 145–6; failure of, 85 (*see also* anomie; demand, economic: failure of; underconsumption); in *The Mill on the Floss*, 21, 115, 118, 122–5, 131–9, 145–6; in *Tess of the d'Urbervilles*, 188, 190, 198, 208, 229. *See also* consumers: stimulating desire in; demand, economic; desire; luxury

aristocracy, 20–1, 75, 78, 86, 88, 93, 96, 160, 191–2, 203, 217, 227, 255n4. *See also* luxury

Aristotle, 118, 255n3, 261–2n22

Armstrong, Nancy, 86, 92, 234n8, 255n4, 269n26

Auerbach, Nina, 258–9n4, 261n19

Austin, Linda M., 241n17

avarice. *See* greed

average (mean), 184–5, 231, 247

See also management: household; separate spheres
Dunbar, Charles Franklin, 70

economic demand. See demand, economic
economic growth. See growth, economic
economic intervention (by state). See intervention: economic (by state)
economic man, 60–1, 66–7, 72, 78, 226
economic woman, 14, 91
economics (as professional discipline), 10, 12, 29, 42, 59–66, 68–73, 75–6, 183–5, 211, 217, 242–3nn24–5, 243–4n31, 249–50n67, 251–2n76, 252–3n80. See also political economy
economics, demand-side. See demand-side economics
economics, evangelical. See Christianity: evangelical economists
economics, heterodox. See heterodox economics
economics, historical school. See historical school (economics)
economics, neo-classical school. See neo-classical school (economics)
economics, supply-side. See supply-side economics
economy, self-regulating, 3–4, 11, 13, 26, 28, 36–7, 47–9, 52–3, 240–1n11. See also intervention: economic (by state); laissez-faire; organicism; physiocrats; Say's Law
education, 40, 47, 75, 92, 125, 135, 149, 154, 174, 203, 234–5n9, 241n18, 253n83, 256–7n12, 259–60n9
elimination: of characters, 21, 83, 113, 124, 131, 146, 176, 179, 231 (see also

banishment; death: as closure of novels; infanticide; murder); of excess, 82–3, 99, 101 (see also balance)
Eliot, George (Marianne Evans), 10–11, 14–15, 19, 23–4, 28, 79, 156, 169, 235–6n11, 238n23, 253–4n84, 255n3, 260n13, 263n6; Adam Bede, 14, 20–1, 25, 75, 81–111, 114, 122, 140, 154, 163–4, 176–80, 209, 216 (see also individual concepts in; notes to chapter 2); Daniel Deronda, 259n6, 266n3; Middlemarch, 7, 47, 84, 134, 234n7, 269n22; The Mill on the Floss, 14, 21, 24, 75, 81–4, 89, 94, 99, 112–46, 176, 178–80, 209, 216, 218, 256n9, 257n15 (see also individual concepts in; notes to chapter 3); Scenes of Clerical Life, 83–4, 271n38
emasculation, 74–8, 109–10, 179, 265n20. See also castration; feminization
endings, 10, 21, 82–4, 114–15, 142–5, 152, 167, 231, 254n1. See also capitalism: death/end of; closure; death: as closure of novels
Enock, Arthur Guy, 220
epigrams. See maxims
ethics, 12, 255n3, 260n10; in Adam Bede, 20–1, 84–5, 88, 95–106, 110–11, 179, 209, 216; in economics/political economy, 11, 20, 41, 62, 65, 67–9, 73–4, 76–8; in The Mayor of Casterbridge, 164, 216; in The Mill on the Floss, 114, 116, 118–24, 130–2, 138, 141, 209, 216, 260n10; in Ruskin, 37–41, 62, 65, 67–8, 73, 76–7, 241n17, 241–2nn19–20, 246–7n45; in Tess of the d'Urbervilles, 182–3, 187–8, 201–2, 204, 207–9, 216, 229, 269n21. See also morality